Transformation of Pension Systems in Central and Eastern Europe

Transformation of Pension Systems in Central and Eastern Europe

Edited by

Winfried Schmähl
Professor of Economics and Director, Economics Department, Centre for Social Policy Research, University of Bremen, Germany

and

Sabine Horstmann
Project Manager and Researcher, Association for Social Security Research and Policy, Cologne, Germany

Edward Elgar
Cheltenham, UK • Northampton, MA, USA

Published by
Edward Elgar Publishing Limited
Glensanda House
Montpellier Parade
Cheltenham
Glos GL50 1UA
UK

Edward Elgar Publishing, Inc.
136 West Street
Suite 202
Northampton
Massachusetts 01060
USA

A catalogue record for this book
is available from the British Library

Library of Congress Cataloguing in Publication Data
Transformation of pension systems in Central and Eastern Europe / edited by Winfried Schmähl and Sabine Horstmann.
p. cm.
Includes bibliographical references and index.
1. Old age pensions—Europe, Eastern. 2. Europe, Eastern—Social policy. 3. Europe, Eastern—Economic policy—1989– I. Schmähl, Winfried. II. Horstmann, Sabine, 1965–

HD7105.35.E852 T7 2002
331.25'0947—dc21 2001040762

ISBN 1 85898 769 5

Printed and bound in Great Britain by MPG Books Ltd, Bodmin, Cornwall

Contents

Figures

Tables

Contributors

Inara Bite is adviser to the director general of the State Social Insurance Agency, Riga. From 1990 to 1993 she was deputy minister, Ministry of Social Protection and from 1993 to 1996 she was director of the Social Insurance Department. She has participated in international research projects and has published widely on social security and pension legislation.

Dr Ottó Czúcz is Professor of Law of the University of Széged, Hungary. He is the head of the Social Security Research Centre at the University of Széged and has been a member of the Executive Committee of EISS and the Hungarian Pension Insurance self-government. He has published studies, articles and books on the reform of the Hungarian social security system.

Dr Stanislawa Golinowska, Professor of Economics, was the initiator and co-ordinator of the reform debate in the fields of pensions, health and non-profit organizations. She studied economics at Warsaw University and was appointed professor of economics in 1995. From 1991 to 1997 she was director of the key research institute in the fields of the labour market and social affairs – IPiSS – in Warsaw and adviser for the government of Poland. She is associated with the CASE (Centre for Social and Economic Research) Foundation and has published numerous articles and books on social aspects of economics and social policy reforms.

Dr Sabine Horstmann is project manager and researcher at the Gesellschaft für Versicherungswissenschaft und -gestaltung in Cologne, Germany. She studied economics at the Friedrich-Alexander University Erlangen Nürnberg and was a researcher at the Centre for Social Policy Research, University of Bremen from 1991 to 1998.

Dr Margita Hurcíková is regional director of the supplementary pension insurance company 'Stabilita'. From 1990 to 1997 she was a lawyer at the Ministry of Labour and Social Affairs, pension department, where she was responsible for international treaties on social security and pension legislation.

Jiri Král is Director of the Social Security Department, Ministry of Labour and Social Affairs, Prague and has been responsible for the preparation of key social security laws in the Czech Republic since the beginning of the 1990s. From 1991 to 1998 he was a member of the European Social Security Committee of the Council of Europe. Since 1998, he has been vice chairman of the Permanent Committee of Actuaries and Statisticians of ISSA. Since 2000, he has been a member of the Committee of Actuaries of the UN Joint Staff Pension Board.

Lauri Leppik is an adviser to the Estonian Ministry of Social Affairs. In the past, he has been a lecturer of social policy at the Tallinn Pedagogical University (1991–1995), a deputy director general of the Estonian National Social Insurance Board (1995–1998), and a research fellow at the European University Institute in Florence (1998). Since 1997, he has been a member of the government's Social Security Reform Commission.

Martin Mácha is a sociologist who has been working for many years on transitional issues of social policy in the Czech Republic. He was head of the Research Institute of Labour and Social Affairs and has participated in a number of international comparative projects in the fields of social reform and pension reform.

Dr Georg Männik is a physician and member of the board of BICO Life Insurance Ltd and the Baltic Insurance Co Ltd. From 1992 to 1993 he was first deputy minister at the Ministry of Social Welfare and from 1993 to 1995 he was director general of the Estonian National Social Insurance Board. He has been involved in international consultancy projects and has published widely on social security reform in Central and Eastern Europe.

Dr Teodoras Medaiskis is Social Policy Unit Director and associate Professor at Vilnius University. In 1973 he graduated in mathematics from Vilnius University, and obtained a doctorate in economics in 1978 (System Research Institute of the Academy of Sciences, Moscow). From 1988 onwards he was involved in the development of Lithuanian social security; from 1989 to 1991 he was the chairman of the preparatory team and from 1992 to 1993 he was minister of social security. He has published several research papers and reports on the Lithuanian experience of social security development.

Karol Pekník, PhD, is an economic and social researcher. From 1975 to 1992 he was senior researcher at the Federal Institute of Economic Research, Bratislava and a lecturer in demography and social policy at the Department of Sociology, Comenius University Bratislava. He has had many years of research in the fields of living standards, poverty measurement, demography and statistics and has numerous publications.

Dr Mária Pintér is an economist and was the secretary of the Social Insurance Scientific Committee. She then was the head of the project management unit of the Hungarian 'Pension administration and health insurance project' carried out by the World Bank.

Dr Winfried Schmähl is Professor of Economics and Director of the Economics Department of the Centre for Social Policy Research, University of Bremen. He has been a member of several advisory commissions to governments and parliaments in Germany: the Social Advisory Board of the German Federal Government on Pension Policy (1984–2000, since 1986 chairman); the Pension Reform Commission of the Federal Government (1996–97); and the Commission on Demographic Change of the Federal Parliament (during three election periods). He has published widely on the economics of social security, pensions policy, employment of older workers, income redistribution and income development.

Dr Maciej Zukowski, is a teacher and researcher at the University of Economics in Poznan, Poland. From 1994 to 1996 he held a Fellowship of the Alexander von Humboldt Foundation at the Centre for Social Policy Research in Bremen. His PhD thesis in 1997 was on 'Multitier pension systems in the European Union and Poland between state and market'.

Preface

About ten years ago Central and Eastern Europe underwent a fundamental change in nearly all areas of individual and public life. Social policy has been involved in many ways in this still continuing process. This book is an attempt to describe analytically the transformation process since 1989 in old-age security in seven Central and Eastern European (CEE) countries. It mostly covers the period from the end of the 1980s to the end of 1997. It is based on a close collaboration between the two German editors and researchers and high-ranking administrators in Estonia, Latvia, Lithuania, Poland, Hungary and the Czech and the Slovak republics. This collaboration was made possible by a grant from the German Volkswagen Foundation. This support is gratefully acknowledged.

The concept underlying this research as well as the country reports and the comparative chapters of this book were intensively discussed for two years. Even during this period of joint work on this topic, many changes took place in many countries – often unexpectedly. The process of designing the fundamental future structure of old-age security is far from completed in some countries. Therefore this publication should be viewed as an interim report of a continuing process. The main aim of our work reported here was to give an overview of the reform processes, the main actors involved and a broad spectrum of influencing factors.

The first part of the book outlines the approach used in this research and gives some comparative information based on the country reports in the second part. The chapters focus on framework conditions, the transition process, and the main actors and influencing factors of relevance to this process. The information provided here is of a particularly explorative nature, and we hope it will help in breaking new ground for further and additional comparative work.

We are grateful to our colleagues for their collaboration, not only by their country reports but also by their critical review of the comparative parts, their stimulating discussion and feedback. We would also like to thank Angelika Oelschläger from the Centre for Social Policy Research who has contributed to the project and this book in many ways.

Winfried Schmähl and Sabine Horstmann

Bremen, December 2001

PART I

Transformation of Pension Schemes in Comparative Perspective

1. Introduction: Design of the analysis, its methodological approach and basic decisions in designing pension schemes

Winfried Schmähl

1.1 INTRODUCTION

Just as in industrialized market economies, old-age security was also an important factor in socialist countries, having lifelong effects on the living conditions of the entire population. It was an important part of social policy and had a significant economic impact in many areas. Therefore the fundamental political changes of the late 1980s and the social and economic transformation processes from a 'planned' or 'command' economy towards a 'market' economy affected old-age protection in several ways: living conditions of pensioners and older workers, exit from the labour force, problems in the financing of pensions caused by a drop in revenue and an increase in pension expenditure, and the adaptation of institutions and organizations of old-age security are all indicative of the manifold problems in 'countries in transition'. Reforms in pension schemes are themselves linked to economic policy (for example, financing in some countries is linked to privatization of firms) and influence economic conditions because of their high microeconomic and macroeconomic impacts, while economic conditions are constraints on as well as a cause of pension reforms.

The fall of the 'iron curtain' and the integration process of former socialist countries into the world economy was also accompanied by a stream of proposals flowing in from abroad for changes to old-age security, from governments and social security institutions of many countries with different historical backgrounds and different types of pension arrangements, as well as from consultants from international organizations. Actors in Central and Eastern European (CEE) countries were looking for models of how to cope with urgent present needs as well as future problems. However, the role of the state and the public-private mix in old-age security was debated not only in former socialist countries but also in market economies, where it was given additional impetus concerning the role of the state because of the collapse of state-dominated and centrally planned socialist countries.

Although old-age security is only a section of the complex area of restructuring in the process of transformation, it has always been an important and interesting area, for example, because of its interaction with many other spheres of economic, political and social life.

As can be seen from the following chapters, more fundamental reform in this area often took place much later than economic policy reforms. For example, an analysis carried out in the mid-1990s mainly showed how pension policy was coping with the pressing immediate problems caused by a collapsing economy. We can now see some major trends in the development of old-age protection.

This study focuses on seven countries of Central and Eastern Europe. It seemed useful to restrict the number of countries for the cross-national study because of our complex approach.[1] There are reasons for the assumption that the most economically developed countries in transition have the best preconditions for fundamental reforms in old-age security. Therefore we included the countries whose transformation process is most advanced, namely Poland, the Czech Republic and Hungary. The three Baltic states that were part of the former USSR were also included, for reasons of comparison of the developments in countries which had the same institutional starting conditions as regards their pension schemes. In addition to the Czech Republic, Slovakia is also included in the study because it was part of the former Czechoslovakia. This allows us to examine not only the effects of different institutional starting conditions, but – keeping this variable constant – to look more closely at the influences of, for example, different political actors. On the whole, the countries included in this research present a fundamental variety of political and economic development and different historic traditions in their social security systems and thus present good opportunities for comparison.

This introductory chapter has two main tasks: to outline briefly the approach on which this study is based (1.3), and to give a short overview of the main elements and fundamental decisions in designing formal old-age security schemes (1.4).[2] This is useful for the comparison of different approaches as well as developments in pension policy, not only in the countries in transition of Central and Eastern Europe, but also with other parts of the world, which are partly influential in the decision process in transition countries.[3] We shall start with some brief remarks on the need for pension reform in the process of transformation.

1.2 THE NEED FOR PENSION REFORM – THE STARTING CONDITIONS

The year 1989 was chosen as a starting-point for empirical analysis in this book, because it was in that year that many fundamental political changes and decisions took place in many countries in Central and Eastern Europe. In analysing the process of transformation it will, however, be necessary to go further back and look at decisions, objectives and developments before 1989. The reason is that not only was there a legacy from communist times, but some countries also saw a revival of the ideas and experiences of pre-communist times. We shall investigate whether there is a twofold path dependency to be taken into account, for example from periods of state independence and from the communist period.

The starting conditions for old-age security at the end of the communist period are mainly determined by economic conditions, existing legal regulations and organizations and the behaviour of the actors, shaped by conditions and experiences of the past. The radical political, social and economic changes in Central and Eastern Europe since 1989 have influenced all parts of life. There was broad agreement about the need for the planned economy to be transformed into a market economy and about the basic ingredients for a market economy.

In principle, there was no disagreement about the basic elements on the way towards a market economy and integration into the world market, such as establishing a price system which reflects scarcity. Differences existed concerning the speed and sequence of politically induced changes. Inefficient production became apparent, and enterprises had to be restructured or even closed down; unemployment, shrinking public revenues, and increasing public deficits, financed by an extension of the money supply and resulting in inflation, were some common challenges.

In the beginning of this process of fundamental restructuring the fact that a well-functioning market economy is also based on formal and informal institutions which generally develop only over time was often neglected, for example by many consultants from Western market economies. Many of the elements necessary for the functioning of a market economy and democratic societies were looked upon as more or less self-evident; but they became an issue, because formal institutions can be changed relatively quickly (for example, through legislation), while the intended effects are often apparent only after a period of time, because behavioural changes are required.[4] This fact, along with the differences between the countries, rooted in their histories and traditions, was only gradually acknowledged.[5] Although there were many similarities, especially concerning the economic challenges, we must not forget that the CEE countries did not constitute a homogeneous group.

Another important element of the starting conditions in the late 1980s were existing laws and organizational structures. Until the Second World War, old-age security systems in Central and Eastern Europe had been as varied as in Western Europe. But by 1989, the systems in the socialist countries had become quite similar to one other. Pension schemes at that time were almost always public schemes. Hence, CEE countries were confronted with quite similar problems concerning the restructuring of their social security systems. Some of the typical elements of these systems were the following.[6]

There was no division between the different branches of social security. Social security was integrated into the state budget and was an important part of it. Social security was planned and organized by the state. Benefits were financed from the state budget. The 'contributions' usually had to be paid by the employer, the employee's contribution was merely symbolic.[7]

There was no or only a weak link between the individual income of the working population and individual pension benefits. Most people received only a flat-rate pension or a slightly higher amount because of the importance of minimum elements in benefit formulas. But there was less equity than one would expect, because there were many special rules for specific professions (for example, ballet dancers, teachers), certain types of jobs (for example, those involving hazardous working conditions) or for specific groups of the population (such as war veterans). Social security instruments focused mostly on the 'productive', or working part of the population, as an element of a conception of social policy founded on labour supply and economic growth. The effect was a relatively low income level of pensioners compared to working people. Furthermore, there was no regular adjustment of pension benefits. This was derived from the static concept of social security in planned economies. The lack of regular pension adjustments resulted in a remarkable difference in pensions within the group of pensioners: the longer they had been retired, the lower their pension in relative terms.

Retirement ages were relatively low, not only in general but also because of specific retirement ages for specific groups of workers. In addition, there were generous eligibility rules for disability pensions. As a result, many of the insured persons received pensions before the official retirement age. On top of that, there were lower retirement ages for women, depending, for example, on how many children they had.[8]

Although the conditions for pension entitlement were easy to fulfil, the level of pension benefits was rather low and as mentioned already, not indexed.[9] Even in countries characterized by a high benefit level (that is, *relative* to wages) – such as Hungary and Poland – the purchasing power of pensions was as low as that of wages. Holzmann (1992:6) summarized the situation as 'too little for too many too early'.

Another characteristic of social policy was the important role of firms in the organization and financing of social policy. State firms acted as an instrument of economic policy and also of (public) social policy. They did not provide supplementary (firm-based) pensions. There were hardly any formal arrangements for private provision for old age, such as life insurance. Therefore old-age security provision was generally made only by the state.

The large amount of product subsidies has to be taken into account when considering pensioners' real income. Subsidies were an important instrument of social policy in socialist economies.

In the first phase of the transformation process, there was already a broad consensus that the public old-age security systems of Central and Eastern Europe were too expensive in the long run, especially because of the low retirement ages, the generous eligibility criteria for disability pensions, many redistributive benefits (for example, family allowances included in pension schemes) and the expected growing budget deficit.[10] Additional financial challenges were expected to arise from demographic changes due to decreasing birth rates and increasing life expectancy. This was not an immediate problem, but had to be taken into consideration when planning the future.[11]

Changes in public pensions became necessary not only in the process of adapting conditions to the emerging market economy, but also due to the changing role of enterprises under conditions of a market economy reform of the firm-based social policy. This, as well as the reduction of subsidies had to be considered when building up and developing a new old-age security system. There was a fundamental need for reform and it could be expected that the purely state provision in old age would slowly shift towards some private pension provision – how much, when, and towards what type was a question left unanswered. It was obvious that a very complex and comprehensive process could be expected. How to analyse this process? The approach we used for our research project will be outlined next.

1.3 MAIN ELEMENTS IN ANALYSING THE TRANSFORMATION PROCESS IN OLD-AGE SECURITY

The main task of the research reported here is an analytical description of the transformation process of old-age security in seven CEE countries. We also make an attempt to explain the major objectives and the reasons for planned and realized measures from the point of view of the main actors as well as giving some information on their expected and actual effects.

The analysis therefore explicitly takes the *process* into account. The time dimension is highly important in analysing transformation. Economics, however, were not prepared for this, because often only equilibria are analysed,[12] while in reality – as well as in politics – the transition from one status or situation to another and the time this will require are of great importance.

Analysing such processes requires looking at the three basic elements of economic and social policy:

- the present conditions (situation) in economics, politics and administration, in demography (including household and family structures), in the social security system regarding concepts, organization, financing and benefits, as well as including country-specific traditions ('history') and above this the expected future conditions based on hypotheses about effects and developments;
- the concepts and objectives of social security, especially in pension policy;
- instruments and the expected effects of implemented measures.

Figure 1.1 illustrates the interaction of these elements:

Figure 1.1 Reforming social security as a process

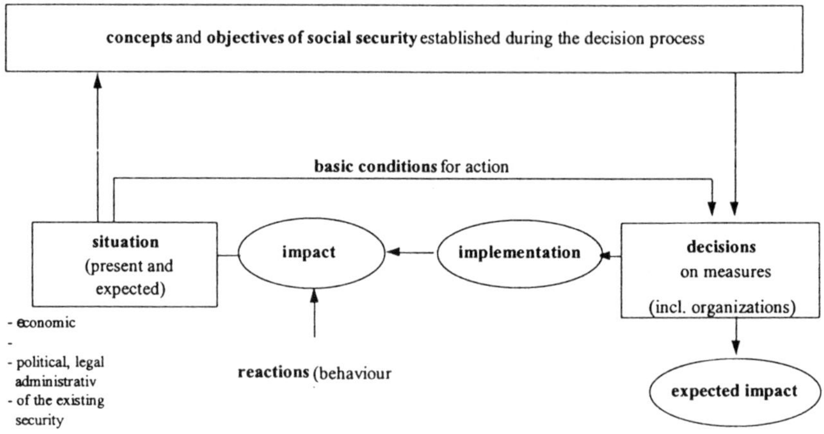

Decision making is of special importance, taking into account framework conditions, constraints, objectives and also the political actors. In Figure 1.1 two different types of decisions in pension policy are mentioned:

- decisions on concepts and objectives,
- decisions on concrete measures, organizations, instruments and so on.

These decisions are made against a background of specific framework conditions, constraints for politicians and other economic agents. This includes constraints in economics and demography, but also in administrative capacity, cultural values and informal institutional rules. These may also influence the 'mental model' they have of the environment and constrain the actors' ideas of what will be aspired to in the country. In Figure 1.1 the dynamic approach is outlined, showing the interaction of the central elements. It is important to notice that there are no linear sequences. The conditions at the different stages have to be considered, conditions that may or will change over time, be it as a result of decisions made or independent of them.

We think it is important to start our analysis with a description of the situation. This, however, needs theoretical considerations, for example, concerning dependencies. Descriptive work needs reliable empirical information which, especially in the beginning of the transformation process, was often rare – a legacy of former socialist times. But difficulties also result from the large informal economic sector in many countries.

Changes in behaviour – especially in these radical transformations – can play a decisive role with respect to reactions to measures implemented and expectations about the effects of political decisions on instruments and so on. What is needed is information on real behaviour, and not reasoning on the basis of the hypothesis of rational maximizing behaviour, which 'has become the religion of economics. The broader perspective, that the function is to explain human behaviour, and that this behaviour may not be consistent with rational maximizing behaviour, or even with an as if version of rationality' (Stiglitz 1983:999) has to be taken into account.

The behaviour of economic actors – firms, households, government and so on – is based on objectives and preferences. In economic analysis, these are normally taken as given and unchanged, even in the long run.[13] The radical changes that take place in the transformation process clearly underline that this conventional assumption is not adequate. As to the restructuring of old-age security, many fundamental decisions on concepts and the design of schemes have to be taken.

There are two different decision processes outlined in Figure 1.1. Assuming a rational political decision making, decisions on instruments should depend on decisions on normative concepts. But they also depend on external and internal framework conditions limiting type and scope of activities. In the following, we shall deal with those framing conditions and with actors looked upon as most important for our topic.

1.3.1 The Framework Conditions

Every transformation of an old-age security system will take place under certain existing conditions, which may change over the years. They must be considered in decision making, but cannot be influenced by the political actors in the short run. There are several relevant framework conditions for the transformation of old-age security, which we will now examine.

Specific traditions in social security
The country-specific traditions in old-age security, and also general traditions in the whole system of social policy will influence the discussion, irrespective of existing institutions at the beginning of transformation in the countries. This includes the developments of social security during the socialist period, but may also be the traditions before 1945. In a larger sense, traditional family relationships and household structures which influence the lives of older people can also be seen as part of traditions in social security, as well as (traditional) economic activities of the elderly.

The political and administrative framework
Every social and economic transformation has to consider existing institutions and rules in the society. This is particularly important for old-age security, which has to be developed in a very long perspective and which also takes a long time developing.

If the risk 'age' is to be covered sensibly, the system needs a long-term stable perspective, so that individuals can rely on the system. Therefore an appropriate transformation should be oriented on long-term objectives. Even though no-one would deny this, reform measures often lack a long-term perspective. Reasons for this might be found in the political restrictions and administrative capacities.

Because the countries under review have representative democratic political systems, politicians with an eye on the next elections are forced to demonstrate short-term political success.

Restrictions that have to be considered in administration are the existing administrative infrastructure, missing data for implementing new concepts (for example the available data on individual working careers), or the technical equipment as well as the necessary knowledge about administration and organization. This is of specific importance in countries belonging to the former Soviet Union because decisions were taken centrally at that time.

Another crucial variable is continuity in time as a precondition for the political actors' long-term objectives. Although all countries under review have seen changes in their political government since the beginning of the transformation process, political stability in terms of the frequency of changes of the leading party or the spectrum of political parties has become quite different in the countries since then. This can result in a discontinuity of reform measures, specifically by a fundamental shift in policy objectives, and a new start in decision preparation and decision making.

Even if there is a long-term perspective for reforming old-age security, conversion will take a long time.[14] In particular, because politicians will not necessarily follow the reforms through over the whole period, political stability and consensus may be a decisive factor for the transformation of old-age security.

Another factor influencing the political framework is the jurisdiction in social policy. A well-organized and stable social jurisdiction could be an important guarantee for the functioning of a social security system and for building up people's trust in the system. In the end, this could also influence the development of old-age security, as can be seen in Western European countries and also in the European Union through decisions of the European Court of Justice.

Economic and demographic framework

A decisive framework for the financing and design of an old-age security system is given by economic and demographic factors. It is obvious that demographic factors cannot be influenced by politics in the short run. Even if family policy has some demographic effects (as has taken place in the past in Central and Eastern Europe)[15] a natural 'time-lag' has to be taken into account. Current population forecasts estimate that all CEE countries included in our sample project will approach the demographic structure of West European countries within the next 30 years – although there is still a more favourable demographic dependency ratio. So the ageing of the population as well as the growing percentage of older people in these countries has to be considered in old-age security reforms. The demographic developments may be even more important if there is East-West migration of younger people. Although migration processes may be influenced by political measures, we take demography here as a framework condition.

Like demographic factors, the economic factors should also be considered as independent factors in the short run. In addition, the economic framework is given also by the 'goals of transformation'. Because there is a broad consensus that the economic and social systems should not be contradictory, the general goals of economic policy, too, will influence the transformation of old-age security. Sometimes there are attempts to use old-age security as an instrument for realizing economic goals. Thus the demand for a capital-funded old-age security system is based on the objective of improving capital markets as well as increasing the capital stock of the country.[16]

1.3.2 Actors

Decisions are made by and depend on the influence of actors, their goals and instruments. In the political arena a great (and over time increasing) number of actors with different interests and objectives have to be taken into account.[17] Figure 1.2 gives an illustrative picture of several of these important

Figure 1.2 Actors in the arena of social policy (persons and organizations)

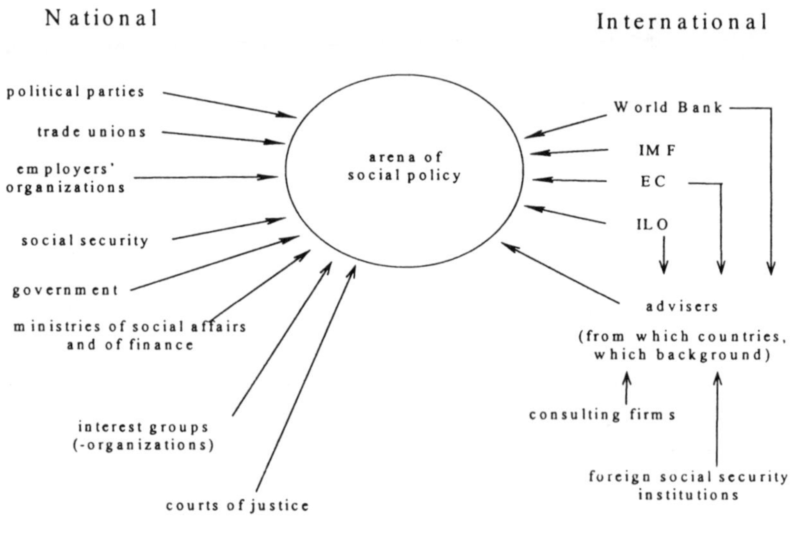

actors, whose influence can be both national and international, for example:

- actors in political and legal spheres;
- actors in the administration on the federal level as well as on the local level (ministries, social insurance agencies);
- international advisers, for example, consultants belonging to international organizations such as the International Monetary Fund (IMF), the World Bank, or the International Labour Organization (ILO) (cf. Deacon and Hulse 1994), representatives of these organizations, free-lance consultants or people from social insurance agencies;

- other socially relevant groups, for example, trade unions and employers' associations, with influence from country to country as well as over time (employers' organizations for example, did not exist at first).

The country chapters in Part II of this book were written not only by scientists but in part also by high-ranking (present or former) officials in the administration. They have a much closer insight into the decision processes compared with researchers, who merely observe from the outside. However, this may shape the perspective.

1.3.3 The Process of Decision Making

The developing structure of old-age security is the result of very complex interactions between the objectives of the political actors involved in the transformation process, their power (influence) and the economic, political and cultural conditions. For example, the socio-cultural framework not only restricts the scope of the political actors, but it also influences their objectives. Furthermore, the structure of old-age security has effects on the economic framework, for example whether savings decisions of households are influenced, the accumulation of capital in the economy, labour supply and/or labour demand, and economic growth. The possibilities of obtaining an insight into the decision processes, the motivation of actors and so on are, however, limited.

It is important to realize that the normative basis of decisions can also change over time. This is often neglected in economics. Objectives and preferences in mainstream economics are treated as constant factors. This assumption would restrict the analysis of developments during transition remarkably.[18]

Political decision processes are analysed in political science using different phases of the 'policy cycle'. A detailed analysis has to take into account the different stages before, say, a draft law is created by a ministry. Will it get government support and be presented to parliament? Will it be supported there? What changes in contents are decided upon during the parliamentary debates? Is a final parliamentary decision taken? If so, is the law really implemented? Taking into account the often low sustainability of governments in the transformation period, this can be a long and interrupted decision process.

All this underlines that 'the course of events is largely determined by the interaction between politics and the economy' (Kornai 1996:3), but 'the interface between economics and politics is still in a primitive state in our theories'.[19]

What we are looking for are changes in the structure and volume of old-age security, public as well as private. This will result from the different decisions taken by political and other actors. New institutions may develop,[20] there will be changes in the amount and type of financing, in benefits and in organization.

The following section deals with the basic decisions to be taken in old-age security as well as major elements for its design. This will also be the basis for the analysis of emerging new tendencies in old-age security in the countries dealt with in this book.

1.4 BASIC OPTIONS FOR DESIGNING OLD-AGE SECURITY

There are a great variety of pension schemes worldwide. Their construction is based on several important elements. Such elements can be used for characterizing schemes as well as for outlining basic options in (re)designing pension schemes and illustrating a country's structure of public and private old-age protection arrangements. In the process of transforming economic and social policy, a great number of options were discussed. Although in reality, country-specific conditions limit the number of relevant alternatives – at least for well-functioning schemes – there is often more than one solution. In particular, the role of the state as provider and regulator of pensions became a central topic.[21] This was especially important in debating fundamental reforms after a period of crisis management.[22] This will be outlined in the following chapters.

After the overwhelming dominance of public pensions, a shift towards private pension arrangements could be expected. This was and is closely linked to the method of financing – pay-as-you-go (PAYG) versus capital funding – because possibilities for PAYG financing outside the public sector are rather limited.

In principle all major topics linked to the design of old-age protection, which had already been discussed during the 'founding period' of public social security at the end of the 19th and the beginning of the 20th centuries, have once more become a topic for political debate.

We shall briefly illustrate the main options for designing old-age protection. This will allow us to characterize and compare the developments in the different countries in later parts of the book more effectively. We shall start with the following elements, which refer mainly to the concept of old-age security in a country:

- the role of the state as provider and/or regulator and the role of the private sector in providing pension benefits;
- mandatory and voluntary pension provision;
- coverage;
- different 'pillars' or 'tiers' of old-age protection;
- distributional objectives for the pension system in general, in particular for different 'tiers' of old-age protection arrangements.

As already pointed out, one of the most important topics in the design of old-age protection in a country is the role of the state and the type of public activities, that is, how and to what extent is the state involved in old-age protection. Public activities that directly affect public budgets can be the financing and provision of pension benefits and the administration of a (public) pension scheme. If pensions are financed by public authorities (for example, by means of social insurance contributions), the provision of pension benefits does not necessarily have to be public as well.

Table 1.1 *Financing and provision of pensions*

Financing / Provision	Public	Private
Public	Social insurance	Voluntary contribution to social insurance
Private	Mandatory contribution to social insurance, but privately managed funds and benefit calculation	Private savings firm-based (occupational) pensions

For example, part of compulsory contributions can be managed by private firms and invested in the capital market as in the late 1990s in Sweden, Poland and Hungary[23] (see Table 1.1). Other public activities are (monetary) incentives to stimulate saving for old age, especially by taxation, or by transfer payments. An important question in general is how, for example, social insurance contributions, interest payments, assets (in funded schemes) and pension benefits are taxed.

These activities affect the public budget. Other activities do not, namely regulating old-age protection which is administered by private actors, above all by (private or public) firms (as firm-based, that is, occupational pension schemes) or by insurance companies and/or banks offering products for old-age protection. It is obvious that using new sources in financing and providing pensions in the emerging market economies will partly shift the public activities from provision to regulation.

This question of responsibility for old-age protection is linked to whether (special types) of old-age provision are mandatory or voluntary and if there is mandating, how much provision (in absolute or relative terms, for example, as a percentage of wages) is required. This is also linked to distributional questions which will be discussed below.

Financing and provision of benefits do not necessarily have to be administered either by public or private organizations only. This is also the case concerning mandatory or voluntary arrangements, as illustrated in Table 1.2. Mandatory schemes – even if they are the major part of pension provision – do not necessarily have to be public, as the examples of Chile and Kazakhstan show. But in most countries, at least the basic mandatory element of pension provision is administered by public authorities.

Table 1.2 Management of pension schemes

	Public	Private
Mandatory	Social insurance	Mandatory private schemes (e.g. Chile)
Voluntary	Voluntary contribution to social insurance	Private life insurance, private savings

Public pension schemes can be

- part of the general state budget,
- part of a unified social insurance budget which also covers, for example, health insurance, or
- a specific separate budget.

During the transformation process a differentiation of tasks took place, resulting mainly in a separation of pension funds from the general state budget. However, the degree of autonomy of the schemes concerning financing and administration can differ.

If we look at industrialized market economies we see that they have different (formal) pension arrangements. This is generally called a 'multi-pillar' structure. It is very common to use the concept of three 'pillars' of old-age security. However, we shall use the term 'tier' rather than 'pillar', because we think it illustrates more adequately that different schemes build upon each other, that is

- a basic first tier,
- a supplementary second tier and
- an additional third tier.

In our opinion, this is not only a question of terminology, but also of substance.[24]

In market economies, this mix of public/private, mandatory/voluntary schemes exists in quite different combinations. As we have already mentioned, socialist economies mostly had mandatory public schemes; sometimes there were voluntary public opportunities for saving, but there were rarely any formal private pension schemes.

There is no doubt that there should be some kind of mandatory scheme as a basis for old-age security, equal for the whole population or for specific population groups. Generally there are such public schemes, with the exceptions being mandatory private basic schemes such as those in Chile and Kazakhstan.

Concerning mandatory (especially) public schemes (first tier), different distributional objectives are relevant for structuring the design of pension financing and pension provision. But this is also highly important for the design of the second tier.

Major aspects concerning income distribution in basic pension schemes are the type of income redistribution aimed at and the dominant distributional objective. The international debate on the appropriate role of the publicly managed first tier is whether it should aim at interpersonal redistribution or intertemporal income transfer over the lifetime, that is, from the working period to the period after retiring from work.[25] For former socialist countries this is quite a new option, because their pension schemes were dominated by the aim to redistribute personal income and only marginally to link pensions to former contributions or former earnings.[26]

Concerning the key distributional objective we can distinguish between

- avoiding poverty in old age (minimum protection), mostly by flat-rate or income- or asset-tested pension schemes, and
- income-related schemes aiming at income and consumption smoothing over the life cycle, that is, linking pensions in some way to former income (mostly earnings).

In transition countries, the difference between these two main objectives will become more obvious over time: the distribution of (labour) income will become more differentiated (unequal) and is reflected in the differentiation of pension benefits in schemes that link pension benefits to former contribution payments or former earnings.

Income(earnings)-related pension schemes can be designed differently. One aspect – which became especially relevant in the debate on reforming old-age security in transition economies, based on World Bank advice – is whether they are defined benefit schemes (defining, for example, a replacement rate) or defined contribution schemes (linking benefits to former absolute amounts of contribution payments and including some additional 'interest').[27] Table 1.3 illustrates these different approaches in designing the first (mandatory and public) tier.

In defined benefit schemes, the contribution-benefit link can be of different strengths, resulting from the mix of different objectives. The link is closest if intertemporal redistribution dominates. In market economies, we can see a trend towards a closer contribution-benefit link in defined benefit schemes (resulting from different types of measures). Another way of achieving this is to establish a defined contribution scheme.

Table 1.3 Design of the first pillar (mandatory public pension schemes)

Goals \ Type of redistribution	Interpersonal redistribution	Intertemporal redistribution
Avoiding poverty	Flat-rate pension means- or income-tested transfer payments	Minimum pension based on contribution payments
Income-related (income and consumption smoothing)	Social insurance based on weak contribution-benefit link	Social insurance with strong contribution-benefit link
	Defined benefit ◄──►	Defined contribution

In schemes aiming mainly at intertemporal redistribution, it becomes especially obvious that the design of the financing instruments and that of benefits – their initial calculation and indexation (pension adjustment) – cannot be decided independently. But the general level of pensions (for example, pension benefits in relation to earnings of employees as an indicator for income distribution between 'generations') can be quite different, just like the so-called 'replacement rate' (mostly defined as individual pension benefit in relation to former income or earnings of the pensioner at time of retirement).

The calculation of the initial benefit in earnings-related defined benefit schemes can consider earnings of different periods of the working life, ranging from the last or best years to all working years. The closer the contribution-benefit link intended, the more it is necessary to take all working years into account for pension calculation. In former socialist countries, such individual insurance records were not used in general and have to be built up step by step if those countries are to introduce schemes that calculate pensions on the basis of individual earnings of longer periods or the whole working life.[28]

Another important aspect for the income situation of pensioners is the adjustment (indexation) of pensions. When life expectancy increases, pension adjustment becomes increasingly important. Different objectives are relevant here: to stabilize the purchasing power of the pension by price indexation of pensions or – as is necessary in a real income-related pension scheme – to adjust pensions according to an income (or earnings) index, which can be defined in different ways (for example, by gross or net average earnings).

The main instruments of financing are social insurance contributions and taxes. Contributions are the instrument for acquiring pension claims, while paying taxes does not create a specific claim. Contributions and taxes can have different assessment bases, different floors and/or ceilings and their tariff scale can have different structures. Contribution financing may be split between employer (firm) and employee. As already mentioned, during the socialist period contributions were paid mostly by the firms. In order to improve contribution collection, many countries try to motivate people to make contribution payments by introducing individual accounts as well as by increasing (although slowly) the employee's part of the contribution payment.

The financing method is of great importance in the debate on redesigning pension schemes in transition countries: PAYG or capital (pre-)funding, which in reality is closely linked to the management of the pension scheme, public or private. PAYG was in principle the only existing financing method for pensions in socialist countries. The debate on financing methods and its effects is as old as social insurance itself. The empirical evidence, for example, concerning its effect on saving, investment, economic growth and development of financial markets, is far from being conclusive.[29] The impact of different financing methods will in reality depend to a great extent on country-specific conditions, a topic elaborated in several chapters of this book. Here it should only be mentioned that (obviously) it is in the interest of actors in financial markets to have a large part of their 'pension money' in capital-funded schemes. PAYG in public schemes can be used in defined benefit as well as in defined contribution schemes, while private pension schemes in general need pre-funding (capital accumulation[30]) and are based on a defined contribution approach.

Concerning supplementary pensions (second tier), an important topic is whether they should be mandatory or voluntary.[31] In general, supplementary schemes are capital funded. The decisions on the design and especially the volume of the first tier will be a decisive factor for the structure and volume of the second and third tiers.[32] Table 1.4 summarizes several important aspects of pension arrangements to be decided in the process of transformation, which are central topics in the following chapters of this book.

Table 1.4 *Design of a three-pillar pension scheme*

Some major choices in designing different tiers of pension schemes	
1st tier	Mandatory, PAYG, public or private major goal: • avoiding poverty in old age • income-related pension (defined benefit–defined contribution) • type of redistribution – interpersonal – intertemporal (close contribution-benefit link)
2nd tier	Mandatory or voluntary Funded or PAYG Public or privately managed Linked to employment or company Defined benefit or defined contribution
3rd tier	Voluntary, privately managed, funded Defined contribution

NOTES

1 Russia is a highly complex exception (cf. Nove 1994:345) and was therefore not included in our country study

2 'Formal' refers here to pension schemes and arrangements for old-age security outside the (extended) family. However, intra-family transfers in a country can be an important factor in the need for formal arrangements.

3 As will be seen from the following comparative as well as the country chapters, the developments in other countries were often an important element in scientific and political debates about the future of pensions, resulting in more or less fundamental reforms. An important example is the developments in Latin America.

4 Alexis de Tocqueville has already outlined the greater importance of moral elements and habits compared to law for democracy in America.

5 This neglect of important facts was recognized less by consultants with a 'European background' than by those from the United States. This becomes obvious when we compare two World Bank publications. The World Bank's mainstream thinking – based on present mainstream economics – is documented in its *Averting the Old-Age Crisis* (1994). Another World Bank publication edited by N. Barr (1994) took into consideration the differences of countries in transition and was based on the experience of researchers with a predominantly European background.

6 We focus here on general dominating aspects, mostly common features. Details concerning the specific conditions in the different countries are outlined in Part II of this book.

7 The situation in the German Democratic Republic was different in that respect: contributions were paid in principle in equal part by the firm and the worker.
8 Widows' pensions were low and usually paid only if there was no own pension claim, which was rarely the case, considering the high female labour force participation in Central and Eastern Europe.
9 There were exceptions. For example, pensions in Hungary were raised by 2 per cent per year until 1988, but the annual inflation rate was between 5 and 9 per cent. However, new pensions were adapted, and the real value of pensions calculated earlier decreased over time. The problem became even more serious in periods of increasing inflation rate (Czúcz 1991:347–8; 1993:746).
10 See, for example, Stangová (1993:733) and Czúcz (1993:747–8).
11 For example, the pensioner ratio in Poland (systemic dependency ratio) was about 0.3 in 1989, but 0.5 in 1992. However, this was not caused by demographic changes but by economic conditions, especially the rise in unemployment. But the ageing process of the population had already been taken into consideration at the beginning of the 1990s (Milewich 1993:12; Ministry of Labour and Social Policy 1993:11).
12 To quote North (1997:14): 'The theory from which we start is static and frictionless – critical limitations to our understanding of the process'.
13 There are not many economists who take into account the variability of preferences over time. See, for example, Dasgupta (1998:4): 'If the period being studied is short, one can simplify by taking some of the emergent features (e.g. cultural values and norms) as given, and thereby, not subject them to analysis. But if the period is long, we are led to study dynamic processes with mutual feedback between millions of micro-decisions and the emergent (macro) features'.
14 The time horizon for radical changes in the financing of pensions is often discussed concerning the shift from pay-as-you-go financing to full pre-funding.
15 See Voirin (1994:196).
16 See, for example, Holzmann (1994a, 1994b), also Johnson (1993) and Schönfelder (1994).
17 These interests can be guided among others by self-interest and the protection of privileges, but also by 'non-self-interest' and the wish for a long-term and 'fair' old-age security system.
18 Richard Easterlin, for example, remarked: 'I think it is unfortunate that there are economists, who arbitrarily define the study of preference change as not "economics" and hence exclude the study of preferences from the field. This has the unfortunate effect of limiting the potential scope of economic analysis, and erecting a barrier between economics, on the one hand, and sociology and psychology, on the other' (Macunovich 1997:125).
19 See North (1997:17).
20 For the transformation and development of institutions, compare Rieger (1992) and Williamson (1993).
21 That this is not only or especially a topic in countries in transition can be illustrated – among many other publications – by the World Development Report 1997 of the World Bank (1997) which addressed the role of the state in a changing world. See also Spulber (1997).
22 This time sequence is quite similar to the experience in Germany after the end of the Second World War: major structural reforms took place about one decade later.
23 For details, see Chapters 3 and 4 in Part I of this book and the country chapters on Poland and Hungary.
24 See, for example, the concept of the 'three-legged stool' (Cutler 1996). The term 'pillar' stimulates the association of a building (old-age security) based on three columns of more or less equal size, that is, of equal 'importance' for old-age security. In reality this is not a realistic picture, because the size of the three elements is usually quite different (a building would look really skewed if based on these pillars). The term 'tier' (or layer) rather than the term 'pillar' is not only more neutral, but illustrates reality more accurately whether, for example, supplementary firm-based (occupational) or additional private life insurance

pensions are built upon the first 'tier' (while a stool or a building needs 'pillars' or legs standing separately and not on top of each other).

25 However, mixed systems are possible as well.

26 There is, for example, a clear answer from the mainstream World Bank proposals: to concentrate interpersonal redistribution within the first tier and leave intertemporal redistribution to the second tier, which should be mandatory, privately managed and capital funded; see World Bank (1994). The World Bank Report uses the 'multi-pillar' concept in a normative sense: the different 'pillars' are connected to specific goals and responsibilities of actors. The World Bank Report (1994:239) clearly points out that the aim of the first pillar is to avoid poverty, while the second and third pillars should contribute to an additional income-related protection. We use the multi-tier approach in its descriptive, positive sense, because – as explained – for example, for the first tier, different objectives can be relevant.

27 For a comparison of real and supposed differences, see Cichon (1999).

28 The link to administrative capacities is obvious. For the initial calculation of the pension, additional information (eligibility criteria such as qualifying periods, retirement age, criteria for disability and so on) is decisive.

29 The debate on this topic is often biased; this is discussed in Schmähl (2000), with further references. See also Aaron and Reischauer (1998). The number of publications on financing methods is high and in economic academic journals this is the most debated aspect of pension reform.

30 This is in the first instance financial capital and should not be looked upon as identical to real capital formation. Whether this results from accumulating financial capital in a capital funded pension scheme is a different question.

31 Looking at the development in market economies there is a tendency that in countries with a low level of mandatory public schemes (first tier) or with schemes mostly aimed at avoiding poverty in old age, the second supplementary tier is also mandatory, while in countries with more elaborate income-related public pension schemes the supplementary schemes are voluntary. For a typology of countries illustrating this, see Schmähl (1991:47–50).

32 In addition, for second- and especially third-tier arrangements, an important element is whether they include risk pooling (insurance schemes) or whether they are purely saving schemes.

REFERENCES

Aaron, H.J. and Reischauer, R.B. (1998), *Countdown to Reform: The Great Social Security Debate*, New York: Century Foundation Press.

Barr, N. (ed.) (1994), *Labor Markets and Social Policy in Central and Eastern Europe: The Transition and Beyond*, Oxford: Oxford University Press.

Cichon, M. (1999), 'Notional defined-contribution schemes. Old wine in new bottles?', *International Social Security Review*, 52, 87–105.

Cutler, D.M. (1996), 'Re-examining the three-legged stool', in P.A. Diamond, D.C. Lindeman and H. Young (eds), *Social Security: What role for the future?*, Washington, DC: National Academy of Social Insurance, pp. 125–49.

Czúcz, O. (1991), 'Ungarn: Die doppelte Krise eines einhundertjährigen Sozialversicherungssystems' (The double crisis of a one-hundred-year-old social insurance system), *Zeitschrift für ausländisches und internationales Arbeits- und Sozialrecht*, 5, 327–51.

Czúcz, O. (1993), 'Das Rentensystem in Ungarn – Leistungsarten. Voraussetzung ihrer Liquidierung und Hauptgründe der notwendigen Umgestaltung des Systems' (Pension scheme in Hungary), *Deutsche Rentenversicherung* 11/93, 737–50.
Dasgupta, P. (1998), 'Modern economics and its critics', 1, Cambridge, UK, mimeo.
Deacon, B. and Hulse, M. (1994), 'The Council of Europe, the European Union, the OECD, the World Bank and the shaping of East-European social policy: a case of varying advice and varying intervention', Paper presented at the third Prague international workshop on social responses to transformation in East-Central Europe, Prague, 6–8 May.
Holzmann, R. (1992), 'Reform der Alterssicherungssysteme in den Mittel- und Osteuropäischen Übergangsländern: Gebot und Chance' (Reforming old-age security systems in Central and Eastern European countries in transition: necessity and chance), Report for the 'Europäische Regionaltagung über die Bildung des Europäischen Sozialraums: Die Folgen der Freizügigkeit für die Organisations- und Strukturprinzipien der Systeme der sozialen Sicherheit', Bonn.
Holzmann, R. (1994a), 'Funded and Private Pensions for Eastern European countries in transition?', Forschungsbericht 9404, Europa Institut, Universität des Saarlandes, Saarbrücken, mimeo.
Holzmann, R. (1994b), 'Kapitalgedeckte und private Renten für Osteuropa?' (Capital-funded and private pensions for Eastern Europe?), Saarbrücken, mimeo.
Johnson, P. (1993), 'A rationale and design for a funded pension system for the low-income transition economies of the CIS', London School of Economics, Centre for Economic Performance, Working Paper 415.
Kornai, J. (1996), 'Economics of transition: present state and future priorities', in *Dispatch from Berlin* (Deutsches Institut für Wirtschaftsforschung, ed.), No. 10, p. 3.
Macunovich, D.J. (1997), 'A conversation with Richard Easterlin', *Journal of Population Economics*, 10, 99–136.
Milewich, L. (1993), 'System of compulsory and optional social insurance: present state and future prospects, Paper for conference on The Reciprocal Connections between Compulsory and Voluntary Social Insurance and Organization of Contributions, Tallin.
Ministry of Labour and Social Policy (Poland) (1993), *Chances and Threats, Construction of a System*, Warsaw.
North, D.C. (1997), 'Understanding economic ehange', in Joan M. Nelson, Charles Tilly and Lee Walker (eds), *Transforming Post-Communist Political Economies*, Washington, DC: National Academy Press, pp. 13–18.
Nove, A. (1994), 'What went wrong with André Gunder Frank', *Review of International Political Economy*, 345–50.
Rieger, E. (1992), 'Strategien der Institutionenbildung' (Strategies of institution building), *Journal für Sozialforschung*, 32, 157–75.
Schmähl, W. (1991), 'On the future development of retirement in Europe especially of supplementary pension schemes', in W. Schmähl (ed.), *The Future of Basic and Supplementary Pension Schemes in the European Community: 1992 and Beyond*, Baden-Baden: Nomos, pp. 31–70.
Schmähl, W. (2000), 'Pay-as-you-go versus capital funding: towards a more balanced view in pension policy', in G. Hughes and J. Stewart (eds), Boston, MA: Kluwer Academic Publishers, pp. 195–208.

Schönfelder, B. (1994), 'Vereinbarkeit von Reformen der sozialen Sicherungssysteme mit der angestrebten Wirtschaftsordnung (unter besonderer Berücksichtigung der Kapitalbildungserfordernisse)(Compatibility of social security reforms with the economic system)', Freiberg, mimeo.

Spulber, N. (1997), 'Redefining the State: Privatization and Welfare Reform in Industrial and Transitional Economies', Cambridge: Cambridge University Press.

Stangová, V. (1993), 'Die Rentenversicherung in der Tschechischen Republik (im Rahmen der Sozialreform)', *Deutsche Rentenversicherung*, 11/93, 732–6.

Stiglitz, J.E. (1983), 'Review of George R. Feiwel (ed.), *Samuelson and Neoclassical Economics*', *Journal of Economic Literature*, 21 (3), 997–9.

Voirin, M. (1994), 'Soziale Sicherheit in Mittel- und Osteuropa: Kontinuität und Wandel' (Social security in Central and Eastern Europe: continuity and change), in *Internationale Vereinigung für Soziale Sicherheit, Umstrukturierung der sozialen Sicherheit in Mittel- und Osteuropa*, Geneva, pp. 103–216.

Williamson, O.E. (1993), 'The economic analysis of institutions and organisations: in general and with respect to Country Studies', OECD, Economics Department Working Papers No. 133.

World Bank (1994), *Averting the Old-age Crisis*, New York: Oxford University Press.

World Bank (1997), *World Development Report 1997*, New York: Oxford University Press.

2. Economic, demographic and institutional background

Sabine Horstmann and Winfried Schmähl

2.1 INTRODUCTION

The economic, demographic and institutional background outlines the framework for social policy transformation. This chapter is an introduction into similarities and differences among the countries under study and an outline of important trends rather than a detailed analysis of the economic and demographic development. The rest of the chapter is subdivided into three sections: the economic transformation and the economic performance since the end of the 1980s in the respective countries is described first; this is followed by a summary of the demographic development as an important background for social security financial development; and, finally, the institutional heritage of the security systems during socialism will be described to outline the starting-point of the transformation of social security.

2.2 SIMILAR PROBLEMS: ECONOMIC TRANSFORMATION RECESSION AND ITS IMPACT ON SOCIAL TRANSFORMATION

Since the end of the 1980s and the beginning of economic transformation in Central and Eastern Europe, several 'hard indicators' have been in use to describe and analyse transformation processes. The gross domestic product (GDP) development has been central in public discussion of success or failure of transition efforts. The comparative 'competitive' view on GDP development was in vogue in the early years of transformation, against a background of ideological battles over which economic transition policy was considered to be the best. In addition, several other indicators such as inflation rates, external balances, foreign direct investments, degree of privatization, unemployment rates, inequality measures such as Gini-coefficients and so on,[1] were used as indicators for describing transition processes from the socialist economy to a market economy. All of these indicators make an important contribution to the evaluation of the Eastern European economies' development. In particular, unemployment and income distribution serve as good indicators of the distribution effects of economic development; others mainly describe the production side. The following selected indicators represent only a section of economic transformation and are chiefly indicators with a direct impact on social transformation as well.

The economic backgrounds in the seven countries under study are highlighted by the study of the economic performance since the beginning of the transformation expressed by the development of GDP compared to 1989/90. We then briefly examine different economic policies in these countries and their macroeconomic development. The latter's impact on social policy is explored in a description of the development of social and pension expenditures as a percentage of GDP. A further important indicator, particularly with respect to pension policy, the development of inflation, and, last but not least, unemployment trends, provides important information for understanding social policy development.

Taking GDP development since 1989 (Visegrad countries) or 1990 (Baltic states) into account, economies are still operating at a low level, even compared to their starting-point.[2]

Figure 2.1 illustrates a typical 'J-curve of transformation' starting with a recession period followed by a step-by-step recovery of the economy. But the picture also reflects clearly that – despite the same general pattern – there are obvious differences in level. The recession has been more serious and deeper in the Baltic states. In 1996, only Poland had regained the 1989 productivity level.

Economic performance and the length and depth of recession in the transition countries is likely to be connected with the economic policy aiming to change the system. This was a main topic in economics, especially in the first years after the fall of the iron curtain.[3] This discourse has been focused on the question whether 'shock therapy' implementing market rules and liberalization instruments all at once is the best economic policy for the transition to a market economy or whether a gradualist strategy liberalizing the economy step by step would promise to be more successful.

Poland, which is the best-known example of a country using a 'big bang' strategy with its 'Balcerowicz plan', shows the first drop in GDP as well as the first recovery and by 1996 its GDP was higher than in 1989. On the other hand, Hungary, as a typical example of a country which implemented a gradualist transformation strategy, shows a slower and more prolonged recession. The economic developments of the Czech and Slovak republics look quite similar to that in Hungary. However, this is again judged in the literature as a 'big bang' approach, at least in the years until the separation, whereas after 1993, economic policy in the Czech Republic is considered to be more market-oriented while the Slovak Republic adopts a more gradualist approach.

Figure 2.1 *GDP development, 1989/90–96 (1989/90=100)*

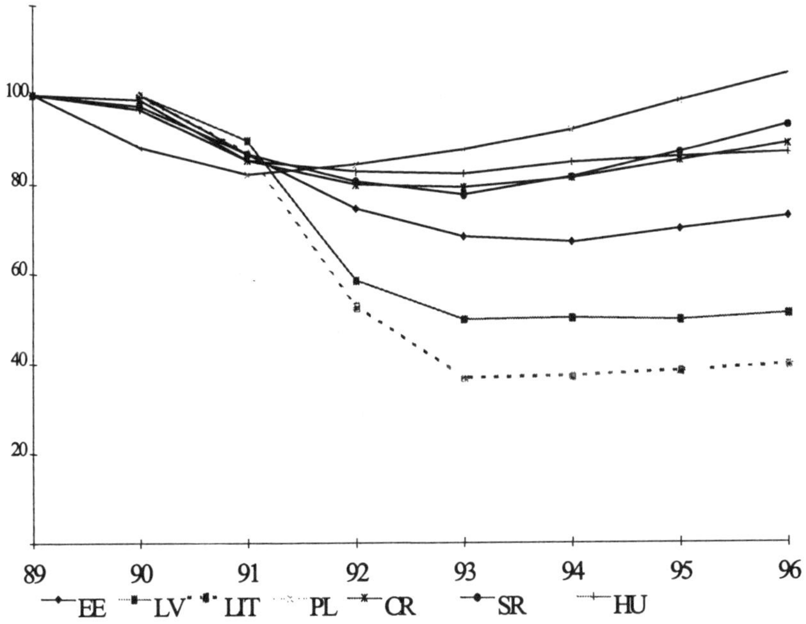

Note: The reference year for GDP=100 is 1989 for Hungary, Poland, and the Czech and Slovak republics, and 1990 for the Baltic states.
Source: Golinowska 1997 (ICDC UNICEF).

Far more obvious is the relatively heavy drop in GDP in the Baltic states compared to the other four countries, caused by different economic conditions at the start. Since the economies of the Baltic states depended very strongly on the Russian economy, the breakdown of their economies was even more serious than in the Visegrad countries.[4]

All in all, if countries are classified by their progress in economic transformation, Poland, the Czech and Slovak republics, and also Hungary and sometimes Estonia are counted as the most successful states, whereas the other two Baltic countries are classified as a second, less effective, group.[5] In our analysis of the transformation processes in pension policy, we shall examine whether and how this different economic performance and economic policy affected the transformation of the pension system. In particular we are interested in the following issues. Do countries with a 'radical change' in the economic system also rapidly reform their social security system?

Does an early recovery of the economy result in a higher level of social security? Did the serious drop in GDP in the Baltic countries lead to different transformation paths in pension policy?

We now turn to state budget development and the concomitant development of social expenditures in the transition economies.[6] Economic transition called for basic changes in the 'socialist' incentive structure, where state budget revenues relied mainly on enterprise (profit) taxes and turnover taxes based on fixed prices while personal income taxes played a minor role (Chand and Lorie 1992). Fiscal reforms were expected to contribute to stabilization programmes in the transition period and to set market-oriented incentives in a new economic surrounding. State budget revenues decreased markedly in the early years of transition, not only due to systemic changes but also because of the bankruptcy of state enterprises (Golinowska 1997:5). Although the share of state revenues in GDP dropped during the first years of transition, this did not affect social expenditures equally. In contrast, the share of social expenditures in relation to GDP rose over the first years of transition – which probably might be explained by some sort of ratchet-effect with regard to social expenditures. In times of economic recession not only additional transfers to the unemployed, but also at least a basic level of social support was politically forced to buffer economic hardship due to the transition process. In addition, a shift from indirect transfers through subsidies to direct transfers influenced the level of social expenditures. Nevertheless, the level of social expenditures in GDP differed across regions between under 20 and up to 30 per cent (Golinowska 1997).

Above all, the development of social expenditures has to be analysed against the background of inflation and a decreasing GDP. In this context, the real value of social protection expenditures dropped in nearly all the countries under study, except Poland (cf. Hagemejer 1998:17).

If one looks at the structure of social expenditures, the most important item among them are pension expenditures, with a share of about 26 per cent (Estonia) up to 50 per cent (Poland) in 1994 (Golinowska 1997:8). In what way did pension expenditures react to a changing budgetary framework? Did they experience a comparable development to other items connected to social expenditures? Figure 2.2 describes the development of pension expenditures in GDP from 1989 to 1996.

The figure reflects a slightly growing trend in pension expenditure share in GDP since 1989 – with a share between 6 and 10 per cent in all of the countries except Poland, which had had an extraordinarily high share of pension expenditures in GDP since 1991 of about 15 per cent. What caused these different levels in pension expenditures? Are these developments reflected in the political discussions, and did they lead to any different decision on future pension policy?

Figure 2.2 Pension expenditures in GDP, 1989–96

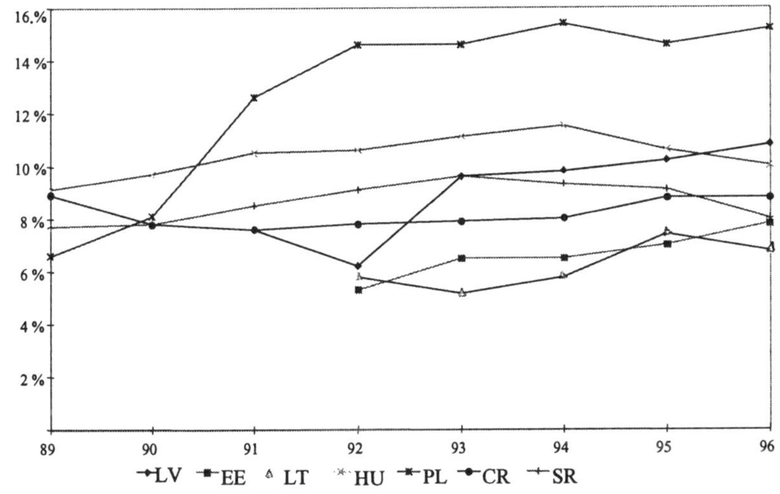

Sources: Country reports, in this volume, and Lodahl and Schrooten (1998).

Another important condition influencing pension reform is the development of inflation. Inflation in these countries had been triggered on the one hand by economic policy as an outcome of different monetary policy approaches, but on the other was decisively influenced by different starting conditions. A high macroeconomic imbalance existed especially in Poland and the Baltic states. This repressed inflation required stronger stabilization efforts than in the Czechoslovak Federation and Hungary, which were characterized by little macroeconomic instability at the beginning of the transformation process (Balcerowicz 1995:156). Table 2.1 gives an overview on the development of average inflation rates.

Table 2.1 Average inflation rate, 1991–97 (%)

	1991	1992	1993	1994	1995	1996	1997
Estonia	211.0	1,076.0	90.0	48.0	29.0	23	11.0
Latvia	124.0	951.0	109.0	36.0	25.0	17	8.4
Lithuania	224.7	1,020.5	410.4	72.1	39.5	25	8.9
Poland	70.3	43.0	35.3	32.2	27.8	20	14.9
Czech R.	56.6	11.1	20.8	10.0	9.1	8.8	8.5
Slovak R.	61.2	10.1	23.2	13.4	9.9	5.8	6.1
Hungary	35.0	23	22.5	18.8	28.2	23.7	18.3

Source: EBRD (1998).

High inflation rates occurred in particular in Poland at the beginning of the 1990s and the high inflation period, and in the Baltic states in 1991–93.

Neither the Czech nor the Slovak republics experienced inflation at comparable levels. Hungary's inflation rates were considerably lower than in Poland or the Baltic states. From 1995 onwards and according to future projections (EBRD 1998), some sort of convergence and monetary stabilization is indicated. Nevertheless, monetary stabilization has not yet been achieved in all countries in transition and is still a serious problem particularly in the new independent states (NIS) (World Bank 1996; EBRD 1998).

Hyperinflation in the first years of transition required adequate measures to secure the value of pensions, but regular adjustments of pensions to inflationary developments were virtually unknown in the existing socialist pension systems. We shall examine in the following, whether and how the transition countries reacted to rising inflation and – again – whether different strategies dependent on different inflationary developments can be observed.

As a last element of economic development, privatization and unemployment will be highlighted. Privatization is obviously a part of transformation policy that cannot be carried out overnight in a 'big bang', at least as far as property rights are concerned. Nevertheless, the speed, methods and success of privatization measures seem to vary widely in these countries.[7] Since the end of the 1980s, these efforts have led to a private production share in GDP varying from 60 per cent (Poland, Latvia) up to 75 per cent (Czech Republic). Hence, the countries in this study are rated as the more advanced privatizers than other transition societies (EBRD 1997:14). Privatization in Lithuania and the Czech Republic took place in the form of 'voucher privatization', while Estonia's and Hungary's economic policy chose to privatize former state enterprises via direct sales (World Bank 1996:65). The first wave of privatization in the Slovak Republic was carried out via vouchers, which was started during the period of the Czechoslovak Republic. After the split of the Republic, privatization in the Slovak Republic was carried out via state obligations and direct sales of enterprises.

Hidden unemployment was characteristic of former socialist economies. With privatization and restructuring of state enterprises the number of unemployed rose significantly in Central and Eastern Europe. Nevertheless, different privatization policies and timing of reforms led to remarkable differences in the level of unemployment, which is tightly connected to social security provisions, especially pension policy, as early retirement was and is a politically feasible way to relieve the labour market.

Table 2.2 shows unemployment rates[8] over the research period. These figures have to be interpreted carefully, because they might reflect hidden unemployment due to a slow privatization process. Rising unemployment

Table 2.2 *Unemployment rates, 1990–96*

	1990	1991	1992	1993	1994	1995	1996
Estonia	–	–	–	5.0	5.1	5.0	5.0
Latvia	–	–	2.3	5.8	6.5	6.6	7.2
Lithuania	–	0.3	1.3	4.4	3.8	6.2	6.4
Poland	6.1	11.8	13.6	15.7	16.0	14.9	–
Czech Republic	0.8	4.1	2.6	3.5	3.2	2.9	3.5
Slovak Republic	1.5	11.8	10.3	14.4	14.8	13.1	12.8
Hungary	1.9	7.5	12.3	12.1	10.4	10.4	10.5

Source: EBRD (1997).

rates can be observed in all of the countries during the 1990–96 period, but to a lesser extent in the Baltic states. Regardless of statistical problems one has to consider that there was a high migration (see below) out of the Baltic states, especially of the Russian population, which might have solved some of the labour market problems, too. Looking at the Visegrad countries, the Czech Republic in the first years of transition had a strikingly low unemployment rate compared to its neighbouring countries. The positive development in the Czech Republic has been interpreted as having resulted from its successful economic policy and – especially compared to the Slovak Republic – to better industrial starting conditions. Furthermore, in the Czech Republic an active labour market policy from the very beginning was seen as a successful means to combat unemployment. However, the recent development of higher jobless rates in the Czech Republic requires a much more cautious interpretation of this development.

Having described many of the developments in economic indicators, many important questions in this assessment remain open. In what way are the labour market development and unemployment rates of importance for the pension system development? Which differences might have caused different developments in the field of old-age security? The labour market development might influence the pension system regarding expenditures as well as financing. Expenditures might rise because of extended eligibility criteria and early retirement, and the financing of pensions (and also other parts of social security) might become difficult because of shrinking tax/contribution revenue due to unemployment. In the analysis of the pension system development in the countries under study, we shall examine in what respect differences in labour market developments have affected the old-age security systems.

2.3 DEMOGRAPHY

The demographic situation and development is an essential explanatory factor for pension insurance finances. The demographic development determines the *old-age dependency ratio* (the number of people of pension age compared to the number of people of working age) and, filtered by the labour market development, the *system dependency ratio* (the number of pensioners compared to the number of insured persons). The latter ratio is – among other factors – a decisive factor for the financial situation in a pay-as-you-go financed pension system.

The demographic development is determined by fertility, mortality and migration. In all three spheres, there have been dramatic changes since 1989 in most of the CEE countries (Ellman 1997). There has been a significant fall in fertility during the transformation in all countries. This fall has been more serious in the Baltic states and least evident in Hungary (Ellman 1997:351). Total fertility rates lay between 1.37 (Estonia) and 1.8 (Poland) in 1994, that is, at the same level or even higher than the Western European average (1.46 in 1993 for the EU, Ellman 1997:351f.).[9] The decline in fertility is explained by a growing uncertainty about economic development, declining real wages and the dismantling of pronatalist socialist family policy (Ellman 1997:352). Nevertheless, we should not ignore the fact that the trend of declining fertility rates had already started in the 1970s in most of the CEE countries (Golinowska 1993:31). However, this was definitely not the case in the Baltic countries. Total fertility rates here improved in the 1980s and reached their peak in the late 1980s. This was followed by a none the less sharp decline after political and economic transformation had taken place.

Life expectancy at birth declined in some of the countries in the first years of transformation but since 1994 has shown a growing trend in most countries (Cerniauskas 1997). Crude death rates in the early years increased, especially in the Baltic states mostly due to a rising male mortality (Goldstein et al. 1996:9).

Finally, in the early 1990s migration, mainly Russian emigrants, influenced demographic development in the Baltic states. During the Soviet regime the Russian population grew for political as well as economic reasons (Sipaviciene 1993).

Decreasing fertility and long-term increasing life expectancy will lead to an ageing population in all of the Eastern European countries. But compared to Western Europe this ageing process is less dramatic and will start to reach the dimensions of the West only later. In addition, significant migration to the Baltic states will cause demographic changes quite soon. There are other differences in the ageing process among the countries which also might affect the old-age security system. Among the Visegrad countries, a significant proportion of Hungary's population will grow older at a faster rate, while within the Baltic states, Latvia already has the largest aged population.

Cross-national studies all over the world have shown that the old-age dependency ratio and the system dependency ratio have been decisive for explaining social expenditure development (Schmidt 1998). With respect to the countries under study, it is evident that there is a general trend of a rise in the old-age dependency ratio in all countries, based on the long-term demographic forecasts. Furthermore, the population in the Baltic states is already older than that in the Visegrad countries. Among the Visegrad countries, Hungary will be confronted with a higher old-age dependency ratio and Poland and the Slovak Republic will be the two 'youngest' societies.

System dependency has been growing in all countries since 1990. The trend – and the level – is essentially the same in the countries under study. System dependency is around or above 50, which means that one pensioner has to be financed by two or less than two insurees. The growing trend of the system dependency ratio could also be observed in several other transition countries (Andrews and Rashid 1996) where there are an increasing number of pensioners and a declining number of contributors.

The difference between system and old-age dependency highlights two different aspects of short- and long-term pension system development. Whereas the growing system dependency ratio is not due to demographic changes but to institutional changes in the eligibility criteria, the countries will be confronted in the future with an ageing population as in Western Europe. When we analyse factors influencing pension reform, we shall look at how the demographic development is perceived in pension reform discussion and in what way demographic changes influence pension system development.

2.4 INSTITUTIONAL LEGACIES: THE SOCIALIST SOCIAL SECURITY SYSTEM

Theoretic approaches of analysing transformation processes emphasize institutional legacies playing a major role with regard to the path-dependency of reforms.[10] In particular, after some unsuccessful attempts with 'blue-print approaches' implementing completely new institutions (for example, in some legal areas and in the area of banking institutions), it was realized that existing 'old' institutions or 'old legacies' are hampering factors. This, for instance, was manifested in old authorities, and in existing attitudes and behaviour, which hindered the successful implementation of new rules. These experiences have made it clear that institutional legacies are of prime importance during transformation into a new economic system and cannot be ignored when choosing appropriate transformation strategies. These old legacies have a significant impact in the field of social security transformation, because new concepts and goals of social policy must contend with existing structures and attitudes. However, analyses of CEE old-age security systems generally consider only their impact as obstacles or as a financial burden in the reform process. Systematic analysis of institutional legacies on reforms and the path of reforms in the field of social security is rare.

This is why in the following section, in addition to economic and demographic conditions, the institutional starting-point is outlined – not only the socialist heritage of social security, but also the origins of social security before the Second World War. So what were the main characteristics of social security under the old 'Soviet satellite system' and before 1945? Some historic elements of social security before 1945 will be outlined, followed by a brief description of the central elements of the 'socialist' social policy and pension systems.

First developments in social security in the Czech Republic and Hungary were mainly influenced by the German and Austrian social insurance systems (Eichenhofer 1995). After the First World War, health, accident and pension insurance regulations were implemented in the former German and Austrian territories in Poland (Zukowski 1995:6). The newly founded Czechoslovak Republic's social security legislation was also based on former Austrian and Hungarian systems. In Hungary, social security drew upon elements implemented during the Austro-Hungarian period as well. Thus this case shows how the roots of social insurance in the Visegrad countries lie in neighbouring influence or transnational learning: large areas of social insurance law can be traced back to the German/Austrian regime. Although in its general philosophy it was strongly based on the German/Austrian model, after the First World War the separate insurance branches developed independently and showed differences.[11]

Social insurance was also introduced at the beginning of the 20th century in the Baltic states. Latvia, for example, had a widespread system of health insurance, and in 1930 old-age and invalidity insurance was introduced. There have always been close relations between the Baltic states, Scandinavia, Germany and Poland; however, because of the political situation, social insurance development was much more directly influenced in the 1940s by the Soviet development.[12]

In the 1950s, the Visegrad countries also started to adopt more and more elements of the Soviet social security system which itself was established 20 years earlier.[13] The main characteristics were a generalization of the schemes, a broadening of the coverage to include the whole working population, a financial merging of the state and the social security budget, no unemployment insurance and a separation of the national health services

(Voirin 1994:174). The main 'socialist' social policy instruments were 'full' employment, that is, giving everyone the opportunity to work, and – to a large extent – price subsidies for goods and services.

Financial autonomy of the social insurance system was abandoned by including social expenditures in the state budget without corresponding revenues. Contribution revenues were just a part of all tax revenues. A separate social insurance budget did not exist. There was no deficit or surplus calculation necessary and the contribution rates remained – independent of the expenditures development – more or less stable over a very long period. Contributions were paid almost exclusively by enterprises or administrations; employee contributions were rare.[14] Contributions were calculated on the basis of the employee's total income without a contribution ceiling. Furthermore, no personal accounts were held but the enterprise had to pay the contribution rate for the whole payroll.

With regard to benefits, the gap between individual contributions and individual benefits continued to grow. Pensions generally were based on the years of service and the income of the last years before retirement. Another overall characteristic of the pension systems was the absence of index-linked pensions, leading to a devaluation of pensions over time especially compared to wage development. In addition, typical elements of the socialist pension system were those providing minimum protection – a minimum pension or flat-rate basic amount. In time, because pensions were not index linked, these flat-rate elements overlaid the income-related factor so that a significant number of pensioners were drawing the same amount of pension. The amount of the pension was determined more by the year when the person became a pensioner than by the former working career. Pensions of the same age cohorts were characterized by low differentiation.

Furthermore, benefit entitlement was characterized by low retirement age, usually lower for women than for men.[15] The official retirement age for men was 60 years, and for women between 53 and 60 years. Average replacement rates of the socialist pension systems were considerably lower than international standards, amounting to approximately 40 per cent of the former income. This is why at the beginning of the transition, pension systems were criticized as 'too low, offered to too many, and are collected too early' (Holzmann 1992). Although social security systems in socialist countries were employment based, restricted to the working population, the communist obligation to work, resulting in high labour force participation, meant that CEE pension systems were characterized by a broad coverage similar to universal schemes.

Institutions in an economic sense are not only social legislation and administrative organizations, but also normative attitudes regarding redistribution by the state, acceptance of inequality and the subjective perception of the current and future economic situations. Therefore, we shall end this chapter with a short overview on attitudes towards social policy in Central and Eastern Europe.

It is often argued that socialist social policy providing security from the cradle to the grave evoked a lack of self-responsibility and private provision for income security. The non-existing opportunities for private insurance of course prevented widespread private 'market' insurance. Nevertheless, additional economic support in old age has obviously taken place in other forms – on the one hand, labour market participation even if people were officially retired was relatively high in most CEE societies; on the other hand, economic support within the family seemed to be more important (Albert and Ferge 1995). This illustrates that self-responsibility was also an important norm and practice during the socialist period, but it was restricted to other forms of private provision than those commonly connected with additional private provision.

Before looking at some survey results on attitudes, we should note that income/earnings inequality also existed under socialism (Atkinson and Micklewright 1992), although this did not fit with official socialist policy goals. Income inequality differed considerably among the countries under study. The Czechoslovak Republic produced the lowest Gini-coefficient and the highest income dispersion was found in the former USSR. The transition to a market economy evoked a rise in inequality in all countries (World Bank 1996:83).

Generally, during the first years of transition, the economic situation was perceived by the population to have deteriorated, although survey findings also showed more optimistic expectations for the near future (see Rose and Seifert 1995; Hayo 1997). This pattern of perception was still evident in a survey carried out in 1995.[16] With regard to social policy and certain target groups, several national studies provide some information about attitudes towards social problems and social policy. An opinion poll in Hungary carried out in 1993 found that the situation of the elderly who live alone is perceived as being much more difficult than that of those who live with family. The economic situation of pensioners is seen as worse than families with several children and single mothers (Nagy 1994:2). In addition, the percentage of people who think that pensioners have a hard time has increased since the beginning of the 1990s: nearly 60 per cent of the interviewees thought that the financial situation during retirement deteriorates considerably. Those surveyed were in full agreement that pensions should keep pace with price increases and that small pensions should be raised. Attitudes concerning the possibility that pensioners should continue working have changed: a deteriorating labour market situation has led to the more frequent belief that pensioners should not participate in the labour market (Nagy 1994:3).

The interpretation of interviews of Polish employees was that these employees did not consider the future to be related to individual activities; they expressed uncertainty about future development, but felt unable to influence future situations themselves (Bielowicki et al. 1996:18). The systemic change in this context obviously evoked uncertainty and risk in comparison with the socialist period. In the Polish interviews, expectations (hopes) of old age are largely determined by the vision of the 'Western pensioner' travelling around the world untroubled by financial problems, on the one hand, and, on the other the fear and anxiety of their own individual economic situation in old age, since existing pensions were regarded as being 'very small'. The current pension system was judged as insufficient, a 'legacy of the past'. More capital-funded pensions were desired; the contribution-benefit link should be stronger; companies' responsibility for pension security (occupational pensions) was seen as rather limited (Bielowicki et al. 1996:21).

Surveys in the Czech Republic found increasing criticism of income inequality. Since 1989, there has been growing support for state intervention and the 'social market' economy rather than a pure liberal market model (Vecernik 1995:19).

NOTES

1 See, for example, World Bank (1996), EBRD (1997), WIWW (1995).
2 Compared to other transformation countries, the countries here reflect the 'more successful' transition countries, compare the data in Golinowksa (1997) or EBRD (1998).
3 See, for example, Hare and Revesz (1992), Coricelli and Milesi-Feretti (1993), Tsang (1996), Balcerowicz (1995); for a review of the early economic debates on tranformation issues, see Silva (1997); for a summary on this issue, see Burda and Wyplosz (1993:449).
4 Cf. Balcerowicz (1995:157) for the differences in the 'socialist output' in the former socialist economies.
5 See, for example, World Bank (1996), Zecchini (1997:1), Quaisser (1997).
6 For different aspects of the 'fiscal' transformation, see Tanzi (1992).
7 For questions of privatization, see Nuti (1994) and Plattner (1996).
8 For statistical problems and various unemployment rates according to national data and ILO standards, see Golinowska (1997). For unemployment issues, especially in the Baltic states, see Cornelius (1995), and in general Boeri (1997), Commander and Tolstopiatenko (1997), OECD (1996), Jackson (1996).
9 The sharpest decline in fertility has been in the former GDR, which had a total net reproduction rate of 0.77 in 1993.
10 Compare, for example, Hauser et al. (eds) (1996), North (1991), Dahlhoff (1996). An overview of the historical context of social security systems in general is given by Köhler (1994).
11 For differences in detail, see Eichenhofer (1995), for the Polish development, see Zukowski (1995).
12 For the pre-Soviet history of social policy, see the Baltic country reports in this book and Leppik (1995).
13 See Voirin (1994:174).
14 There were exceptions to this general trend: an employee's contribution existed in the GDR, in Hungary and – for a restricted period – in Poland, compare Voirin (1994:176).

15 Retirement age for women was in some countries differentiated according to number of children raised, as well: for example, in the former Czechoslovak Republic.
16 See the international report and the country reports of the SOCO project (Social costs of transition), for example, Ferge et al. (1995).

REFERENCES

Albert, F. and Ferge, Z. (1995), 'Social networks in a comparative perspective', Social costs of transition, International Report, Institute for Human Sciences, Working Paper, Vienna.

Andrews, E.S. and Rashid, M. (1996), 'The financing of pension systems in Central and Eastern Europe', World Bank Technical Paper no. 339, Washington.

Atkinson, A.B. and Micklewright, J. (1992), *Economic Transformation in Eastern Europe and the Distribution of Income*, Cambridge: Cambridge University Press.

Balcerowicz, L. (1995), *Socialism, Capitalism, Transformation*, Budapest, London, New York: Central European University Press.

Bielowicki, G., Frankowski, M. and Wiktorow, A. (1996), 'Introduction of occupational pension plans in Poland', SOCO project paper no. 41, Vienna, September.

Boeri, T. (1996), 'Labour-market reforms in transition economies', *Oxford Review of Economic Policy*, 13, 126–39.

Bönker, Frank (1995), 'The dog that did not bark? Politische Restriktionen und ökonomische Reformen in den Visegrad-Ländern' (Political restrictions and economic reforms in the Visegrad countries), in H. Wollmann, H. Wiesenthal and F. Bönker (eds), *Transformation sozialistischer Gesellschaften: Am Ende des Anfangs*, Leviathan, Zeitschrift für Sozialwissenschaft, Sonderheft 15/95, 180–206.

Burda, M. and Wyplosz, C. (1993), *Macroeconomics. A European Text*, Oxford: Oxford University Press.

Cerniauskas, G. (1997), 'Transformation of health care systems in CEE countries', Paper presented at the conference 'Social policy in Central and Eastern Europe', Prague, 24–25 October.

Chand, S. and Lorie, H.R. (1992), 'Fiscal policy', in Vito Tanzi (ed.), *Fiscal Policies in Economies in Transition*, Washington, DC: International Monetary Fund, 11–36.

Commander, S. and Tolstopiatenko, A. (1997), 'Unemployment, restructuring and the pace of transition', in S. Zecchini (ed.), *Lessons from the Economic Transition. Central and Eastern Europe in the 1990s*, Dordrecht, Boston, London: Kluwer Academic Publishers, 331–50.

Coricelli, F. and Milesi-Ferretti, G.M. (1993), 'On the credibility of "big-bang" programs', *European Economic Review*, 37, 287–395.

Cornelius, P.K. (1995), 'Unemployment during transition: the experience in the Baltic countries', *Communist Economics and Economic Transformation*, 7, 445–64.

Dahlhoff, D. (1996), 'Behaviorale Anpassung und institutioneller Wandel in Mittel- und Osteuropa' (Behavioural adaption and institutional change in Central and East Europe), Frankfurt/M.: Peter Lang.

EBRD (European Bank for Reconstruction and Development) (1997), *Transition Report*. London.

EBRD (European Bank for Reconstruction and Development) (1998), *Transition Report Update*. London.

Eichenhofer, E. (1995), 'Deutsche und österreichische Einflüsse auf die Sozialgesetzgebung in Ost- und Südosteuropa' (German and Austrian influences on social legislation in East and South-East Europe), *Sozialer Fortschritt*, 8–9/95, 189–98.

Ellman, M. (1997), 'Transformation as a demographic crisis', in S. Zecchini (ed.), *Lessons from the Economic Transition. Central and Eastern Europe in the 1990s*, Dordrecht, Boston, London: Kluwer, 351–71.

Ferge Z. et al. (1995), 'Social costs of transition', International report by Z. Ferge, E. Sk, P. Robert and F. Albert, Institute for Human Sciences, Working Papers, Vienna.

Goldstein, E. et al. (1996), 'Trends in health status, services, and finance. The transition in Central and Eastern Europe', Vol. 1, World Bank Technical Papers No. 341, Washington.

Golinowska, S. (1993), 'Ageing and the labour market in Poland and Eastern Europe', IPISS Occasional Papers No. 1: Social Policy, Warsaw, 31–51.

Golinowska, S. (ed.) (1996), 'Social Policy Towards Poverty. Comparative Approach', Warsaw: Friedrich Ebert Foundation Warsaw Office.

Golinowska, S. (1997), 'Public social expenditure in Central and Eastern Europe', Unpublished manuscript, Institute of Labour and Social Affairs, Warsaw.

Hagemejer, K. (1998), 'The transformation of social security in Central and Eastern Europe', Paper presented at the conference: 'Transformation of Social Security: Pensions in Central-Eastern Europe', Frankfurt Institute for Transformation Studies (FIT), Frankfurt/Oder, March, mimeo.

Hare, P. and Revesz, T. (1992), 'Hungary's transition to the market: the case against a "big-bang"', *Economic Policy*, 14, 228–63.

Hauser, J., Jessop, B. and Nielsen, K. (eds) (1995), *Strategic Choice and Path-dependency in Post-Socialism: Institutional Dynamics in the Transformation Process*, Aldershot: Edward Elgar.

Hayo, B. (1997), 'How do people perceive their economic situation?', in J.G. Backhaus and G. Krause (eds), *Issues in Transformation Theory*, Marburg: Metropolis.

Holzmann, R. (1992), 'Social policy in transition from plan to market', *Journal of Public Policy*, 12, 1–35.

Jackson, M. (1996), 'Labour markets and income maintenance: a survey of transition', Leuven Institute for Central and Eastern European Studies, Working Paper 58/96, Leuven.

Köhler, P.A. (1994), 'Historical context and origins of social security systems', in B. von Maydell and E.M. Hohnerlein (eds), *The Transformation of Social Security Systems in Central and Eastern Europe*, Leuven: Peeters Press, 19–34.

Leppik, L. (1995), 'Historical roots of social welfare policy in Estonia', in J. Simpura, (ed.), *Social Policy in Transition Societies, Experience from the Baltic Countries and Russia*, Helsinki: Finnish ICSW committee and Finnish Federation for Social Welfare, 23–30.

Nagy, L.G. (1994), 'Public opinion about social policy', Institute for Human Sciences, SOCO (Social Costs of Transition) project paper no. 5, Vienna, April.

North, Douglass C. (1991), *Institutions, Institutional Change and Economic Performance*, Cambridge: Cambridge University Press.
Nuti, D.M. (1994), 'Mass privatisation: costs and benefits of instant capitalism', London Business School, CIS Middle Europe Centre, Discussion Paper No. 9/94, London.
OECD (ed.) (1996), *Lessons from Labour Market Policies in the Transition Countries*, Paris: OECD.
Panther, S.M. (1997), 'Cultural factors in the transition process: Latin center, orthodox periphery?', in J.G. Backhaus and G. Krause (eds), *Issues in Transformation Theory*, Marburg: Metropolis, 95–122.
Plattner, D. (1996), *Privatisierung in der Systemtransformation* (Privatization in system transformation), Berlin: Berlin Verlag.
Quaisser, W. (1997), 'Strategieansätze und Ergebnisse des Übergangs der mittel- und osteuropäischen Länder zur Marktwirtschaft' (Strategic approaches and results of the transition of the Central and East European countries to market economy), *Aus Politik und Zeitgeschichte*, Beilage zur Wochenzeitung Das Parlament, B 44–45/97, 3–15.
Rose, R. and Seifert, W. (1995), 'Materielle Lebensbedingungen und Einstellungen gegenüber Marktwirtschaft und Demokratie im Transformationsprozeß. Ostdeutschland und Osteuropa im Vergleich' (Material living conditions and attitudes towards market economy and democracy in the transformation process. East Germany and Eastern Europe in comparison), in H. Wollmann, H. Wiesenthal and F. Bönker (eds), *Transformation sozialistischer Gesellschaften: Am Ende des Anfangs*, Leviathan, Zeitschrift für Sozialwissenschaft, Sonderheft 15/95, 277–98.
Schmidt, M.G. (1998), *Sozialpolitik in Deutschland. Historische Entwicklung und internationaler Vergleich* (Social policy in Germany. Historical development and international comparison), 2nd edition, Opladen: Leske und Budrich.
Silva, J.R. (1997), 'Five years of reform implementation in the eastern countries', in J.G. Backhaus and G. Krause (eds), *Issues in Transformation Theory*, Marburg: Metropolis, 127–39.
Sipaviciene, A. (1993), 'Migration development and migration policy at the turning point: past influences future', Paper presented for the EAPS/BIB meeting: 'Population-relevant policies in Europe', Wiesbaden (Germany), 25–30 October.
Tanzi, V. (ed.) (1992), *Fiscal Policies in Economies in Transition*, Washington, DC: International Monetary Fund.
Tsang, S. (1996), 'Against "big bang" in economic transition: normative and positive arguments', *Cambridge Journal of Economics*, 183–93.
Vecernik, J. (1995), 'Household incomes and social policies. The Czech Republic in the period 1989–1995', Foundation for Research on Social Transformation, research papers, Prague.
Voirin, M. (1994), 'Soziale Sicherheit in Mittel- und Osteuropa. Kontinuität und Wandel' (Social security in Central and Eastern Europe. Continuity and change), in Internationale Vereinigung für Soziale Sicherheit (ed.), *Umstrukturierung der sozialen Sicherheit in Mittel- und Osteuropa*, Genf, 173–216.
WIWW (Vienna Institute for Comparative Economic Studies) (ed.) (1995), *Countries in Transition 1995*, Vienna: WIWW.
World Bank (1996), *From Plan to Market. World Development Report 1996*, Washington, DC: World Bank.

Zecchini, S. (1997), 'Transition approaches in retrospect', in Salvatore Zecchini (ed.), *Lessons form the economic transition. Central and Eastern Europe in the 1990s*, Dordrecht, Boston, London: Kluwer Academic Publishers, 1–34.
Zukowski, M. (1995), 'Das Alterssicherungssystem in Polen. Geschichte, gegenwärtige Lage, Umgestaltung' (The system of old-age security in Poland. History, present situation, redesigning), ZeS-Arbeitspapier No. 8/95, Bremen.

3. The development of pension systems

Sabine Horstmann and Winfried Schmähl

3.1 THREE PERIODS OF PENSION REFORM IN CENTRAL AND EASTERN EUROPE

In this chapter, pension system development since 1989 will be divided into three phases. The order or sequence of changes and reform of the pension system which have taken place suggests a common pattern of reform. Again, in this chapter we would like to stress the similar developments, not forgetting that there have also been important differences between the countries.

The three phases discussed in the following are: (a) changes triggered by economic transformation; (b) a period characterized by changes representing changing social policy objectives but at the same time hampered by political as well as economic/institutional barriers; and (c) a period in which comprehensive reforms with long-term changing distributional objectives have been accomplished.

A central question is how incremental reforms or 'reform by small steps' can be distinguished from 'comprehensive' reforms. Classification, or judgement, of reform often relies on standards concentrating on certain parts of the pension system arrangements, which are often based on certain normative objectives. This may have led to the result that certain reforms are classified as 'marginal' whereas others are classified as 'comprehensive' or 'central'. To illustrate this with an example, recent international reform debate in the field of pension policy has been concentrated mainly on financing questions, that is, whether to finance pensions by a pay-as-you-go system or by capital funding. Questions of organizational and institutional reform have been rather neglected in the international discourse. But in several transition countries part of the reform programme in the early years included such organizational reforms as the implementation of an independent self-governing institution with extended financial independence. These kinds of changes were given much less attention in the review of reforms in Central and Eastern Europe. Countries which have concentrated on organizational reforms are generally judged as more or less 'unreformed', if the central need of reform is seen in the change of the financing system.

In addition, one can observe in the comparative analysis of pension reform a 'reform package illusion'. While a series of 'reform steps' are not recognized as 'comprehensive reform', bundled reforms implementing changes on several levels have been easier to sell as fundamental reform.[1] This illustrates the problem of classifying reforms, whether they are comprehensive or not. A theoretical approach to scaling reforms has been undertaken by Hall (1993). He proposes a three-level classification: talking of first-order changes, when only the adjustment (of the policy instrument) is changed; second-order changes if the policy instrument itself changes; and finally third-order changes, when not only policy instruments but also the key objectives/goals are changed. He argues that the final 'wholesale changes in policy occur relatively rarely, but when they do occur as a result of reflection on past experience, we can describe them as instances of third order change' (Hall 1993:279). Nevertheless, this classification scheme does not solve the above-mentioned problem of incremental versus comprehensive reforms. Also by making several changes to the setting of an instrument, the underlying goals or objectives can change gradually. An additional problem in this context is that politicians seldom articulate changes in the policy objectives clearly (especially if changes mean retrenchment), so that changing goals usually have to be derived by changing instruments. A clear distinction between first-, second- and third-order changes then becomes even more difficult.

Another important aspect of pension reform – compared to nearly all other policy fields – is long-term distributional effects as a part of social security. Pension policy affects individuals over their whole life, during their working career as well as in old age. Social security in old age, therefore, is always based on lifetime 'contracts'; this makes abrupt changes even more difficult. In fact, even if 'fundamental' or 'comprehensive' reforms are carried out, long-term transition rules for people at the end of their working life are usually implemented. So changing goals might affect generations differently: while in the long run they might be aimed at changes in the distributional objectives, in the short run, relatively small changes will become effective. Nevertheless, the concept of a distinction between adjustment, change of policy instruments and goals is a helpful differentiation when describing pension politics.

In addition to distributional effects in the case of transition countries the time horizon of reforms is also an important aspect when describing and classifying reforms. Even if this has not been a usual approach in comparative analysis of pension system reform – because generally reforms are regarded as long term – in the case of Central and Eastern Europe, it is useful to look at the time perspective, too. Especially in the early years, numerous short-term measures were implemented due to the double function of the pension system in the transition process: that is, on the one hand, changes in the pension system should moderate income distortions triggered by economic transformation; on the other hand, there is a need for pension system reform in the long run.

The following division of different phases of pension reform therefore accounts for aspects of the time horizon and of distributional effects.

3.2 FIRST PHASE: REACTIVE RESPONSES TO TRANSFORMATION PROBLEMS

The first legal changes in pension issues were based on the old socialist system.[2] This first period is marked by the term 'reactive' responses, because changes were not the result of decisions for the future pension system based on new concepts, but for the very first time were necessitated and triggered by economic changes due to the transformation of the economic system. In that sense, first adaptations in the pension legislation were reactive to changing economic circumstances. Against this background, social policy was characterized by a series of ad hoc or 'stop-gap' measures (Cangiano et al. 1998:2) which were implemented between the years 1989 and 1992/93.

These 'reactive' responses were mainly a result of rapidly rising inflation and a changing labour market. In this context, the central measures that we shall summarize in this section are the introduction of indexation mechanisms and the new coverage of self-employed persons. Another very early change, the abolition of (mostly politically motivated) privileges in the pension system, might be interpreted as a reaction to a changing political system. These three issues will be analysed in more detail below.

First of all, why was the introduction of indexation mechanisms considered at all necessary? Pensions in the former socialist systems were not adjusted regularly but were usually increased by discretionary one-off payments. At the beginning of transformation, price liberalization was one of the central measures of economic transformation policy. As pointed out in the previous chapter, price subsidies were central instruments of socialist social policy. Furthermore, centrally planned prices were the main instrument for managing the planned economy. Whereas the latter function was abandoned very quickly after the change to a market economy, some sectoral prices (housing, foodstuff, energy) were liberalized more slowly for a certain period with the consequence that the social policy function of planned prices at least was not abandoned too hastily. In general, transformation policies differ on how fast and how comprehensively prices were liberalized. But the Visegrad states and the Baltic countries adopted a more similar approach of radical liberalization of prices. This led to even more urgent reactions by policy makers with respect to the pension system, because the former pension level was no longer sufficient to maintain the living standard.[3]

But it was not only the inflationary 'shock' triggered by liberalized prices that made it necessary to adapt pensions in the short run. In the long run, in order to adapt to the market economy, an indexation of pensions – mostly by automatic adjustment – was discussed though not implemented during this first period. The introduction of automatic adjustments was postponed until the new monetary policy brought about a more stable economic situation with lower inflation rates.

Two different ways of pension indexation can be distinguished. First indexation by discretion. In the early years, indexation was mostly by discretion, according to the actual state budget resources. In contrast there is automatic indexation, which consists of an automatic adjustment to certain economic indicators. However, such automatic mechanisms entail technical problems, and political ones as well. Automatic indexation affects the *political independence* of the pension system. To the extent that indexation is linked to certain economic indicators or developments, maintaining the value of pensions should be independent of actual state finances. If the decision on whether and how pensions are to be increased is left to parliament or ministers, the required resources compete with those for other purposes and political reliability is thus reduced.

In the context of automatic indexation, crucial questions discussed were whether pensions should be indexed by prices, by wages or both. While price indexation maintains the purchasing power of the pension, wage indexation provides for fair intergenerational distribution and allows pensioners to have a share in the economic growth just as the working population does.

The countries under study chose quite different adaptation paths during the period from 1989 to 1996. The underlying political question which is raised by these different strategies is the level of pensioners' income during times of recession and recovery – since instruments of valorization and indexation directly influence the relative income position of pensioners.

At the beginning of this period, especially in times of hyperinflation, some countries preferred to address this question by adjusting pensions with lump-sum compensation payments rather than increasing pensions by a certain percentage and thus retaining pension differentiation. Lump-sum compensation was often seen as an easier way administratively of coping with hyperinflation, since current pension payments were only topped up and did not have to be individually recalculated each time. But this method was favoured for other reasons as well. It was seen as a means to flatten the pension distribution. Previous pension payments were quite often determined by political motives and privileges. Following changes in the political system, this pension differentiation was no longer desirable, although it was difficult to reduce existing pension claims. Here lump-sum payments, instead of a percentage rise in each pension, served to bring pension payments more into line.[4]

By the end of 1997, Estonia was the only country which had not introduced automatic indexation. In the other countries, regular indexation had been introduced. Over the years the 'reliability' of indexation has increased. While during the early years planned or announced indexations were postponed or reduced, pension indexation became more and more reliable and could not be influenced politically in the short run. It can be argued that with growing democratic habits and experiences in the new democracies and a growing independence of the pension system from everyday political business there has been a change in individual expectations and political culture.

The growing importance of pension increases based on regular rules could also be achieved through the greater influence of the political interests of pensioners. So, for instance, one of the main political demands of the Pensioners' Party in the Czech Republic in the 1998 election campaign was for a regular indexation of pensions twice a year.

At the onset of the transformation, indexation by prices could have been more favourable for pensioners than by wages, if real wages had declined. It was also taken into account that in a period of high inflation yearly adjustment would not be sufficient, and pensions were adjusted as soon as a certain rise in prices of wages had been reached.

Over the years, the experiences with different indexation measures and their financial impact brought nearly all the countries to a combined system of wage/price indexing. However, several examples in the country reports suggest that these rules are still quite vulnerable to short-term political intervention. Pension increases and indexation are used to influence the income position of pensioners. Regular indexation, however, symbolizes a 'fair' participation of old-age pensioners in the intergenerational distribution of income and in a politically 'reliable' pension system.

Exceptional cases of pension reform even prior to a change in the economic system are Poland and Hungary, who had also implemented indexation measures by then. In 1990 in Poland, a quarterly indexation based on average wage growth was introduced. The chief objective was to maintain the real value of pensions, but after subsequent changes Poland reduced the indexation in case wage growth in the previous quarter exceeded 10 per cent. Finally, in 1996 indexation changed completely, aiming at a guaranteed real growth in the pension by 2.5 per cent.

In Hungary, pensions were increased by 2 per cent annually – later by 5 per cent each year – with a maximum and minimum ceiling. This had the effect of flattening pensions. Later on, a newly introduced wage-tied indexation posed problems: pensions should be increased by the expected wage growth, but expectations often exceeded reality. Therefore, in 1995, this system was replaced by a biannual indexation to the average wage growth of the previous year.

In the Slovak Republic pensions were adjusted by a fixed sum to compensate for an increase in the cost of living, and by a certain percentage for an increase in wages. However, since 1993 several indexations had been postponed because of a lack of financial resources. Between 1990 and 1995, in the Czech Republic, where pension indexation is tied to certain wage/price developments but dependent on government decree, pensions were increased ten times.[5]

In the Baltic states, high inflation rates in the early years of transition led to short-term state interventions of lump-sum payments. In 1991, in Latvia, the cost of living adjustments became an essential part of pension payments and consequently led to flat-rate pensions. Two years later an indexation based on changes in salaries and the available social insurance revenues was implemented. Starting in 1997, pensions were increased annually (by prices and wages) until the year 2000 according to the price index, thereafter they are to be based on the trend in wages.

In Lithuania one can observe a similar trend in policy changes. Until 1995, pensions were adjusted by special government decree. Later, in 1995, the basic element of the pension was increased in relation to a price index, the income-related element to a wage index. The latter component is seen as a measure to change the relative weight of the parts according to economic circumstances.

Having discussed the similarities and differences in the policy instruments, particularly indexation, we shall now turn to the relationship between the average old-age pension and the average wage, an essential aspect of policy development. Table 3.1 illustrates the different effects of indexation in these countries.

All in all, in Poland and in Hungary – the first countries to introduce regular indexation mechanisms – pensioners have been better off than in the other countries, at least in the early years of transformation. As a result of valorization and indexation policies, many were able to improve their income position compared to the working population. In contrast the income position of pensioners in the other countries stayed more or less at the same level or even worsened.

Table 3.1 *Average old-age pension to average net wage, 1989–96 (%)*

	1989	1990	1991	1992	1993	1994	1995	1996
Estonia	–	–	–	–	40.0	36.8	40.9	45.7
Latvia	–	–	–	–	36.7	41.7	42.3	48.2
Lithuania	–	44.1	40.7	49.1	43.7	43.2	40.7	40.3
Slovak Republic	54.8	54.7	59.9	55.0	52.7	54.8	52.1	52.2
Czech Republic	63.8	64.9	70.4	67.7	60.1	57.2	56.9	56.2
Hungary	63.1	62.6	64.3	60.9	59.6	56.9	–	–
Poland	55.9	65.0	72.6	74.9	72.8	74.8	75.0	–

Source: Country reports, in this volume; Golinowska (1997).

The effects of indexation are not only illustrated by the relationship of pensions to the average wage. This describes the extent to which pensions and wages are affected by the transformational recession. With respect to the impact on the real value of pensions, pensions have to be deflated by the consumer price index. From this perspective, pensions have lost real value in all transformation countries.

The second very early measure in the pension system which was carried out very quickly after the political change was the abolition of political privileges existing in the former system. This issue was a much more important topic in the Baltic states than in the Visegrad countries.

As we have pointed out, claims based on political criteria were common in socialist social policy. These were various: exceptional retirement criteria, additional insurance records for certain activities or a higher value of insurance years when calculating the pension.

The abolition of political privileges accompanied and corresponded to the changed political setting. With respect to understanding policy development, this raises another important aspect: not all changes in pension legislation, especially in the first stage of transformation, were the result of systematic policy-making decisions depoliticizing eligibility criteria for claims. In fact, one type of politically motivated claim was replaced by another, especially in the Baltic states. Thus, political claims were henceforth granted to persons persecuted under the socialist system.

To conclude, measures taken in the first stage of transformation more or less concentrated on the benefits of existing pensioners. In this period, there were neither changes in the benefit formula, nor important changes in the method of financing, chiefly in the income position of pensioners and the level and distribution of pensions.[6]

3.3 SECOND PHASE: ADAPTATIONS WITHIN THE SYSTEM – FIRST DISTRIBUTIONAL OBJECTIVES

The second period of pension reform from 1992/93 until 1995/96 has been perceived for a long time as the period of delayed reforms in CEE countries. Nevertheless, in this period there were many small changes in the pension systems which symbolized a new direction and new goals. This is referred to here as the second period, in which there were adaptations within the new system and in which the first distributional policy was planned. Moreover, in many countries during this period, further developments were discussed and planned which were later implemented.

At this point in pension policy development, social protection and the need for a minimum standard within the pension system were pressing issues which were considered necessary to smooth the impacts of economic reform. Against this background, the first objectives and directions for reforming the pension system became apparent. There are four developments characterizing this period: changes in the benefit formulas, changes in the organizational structure of the pension system, a growing financial independence and the introduction of a voluntary pension insurance.

The introduction of new pension formulas combined distributive and minimum protection elements with earnings-related elements. These changes in the redistribution in the pension formula, either by elements of minimum protection or by other redistributive elements which took place between the years 1992 and 1995/96 represent the 'double task' with which the pension systems were confronted. While the main task was to protect an important share of the population against poverty in times of dramatic economic changes, pension policy was also expected to become more market-oriented, to implement respective incentives and to adapt to the changing economic and political paradigm.

Following such reforms, the 'solidarity' dimension of the pension system as well as the income relation, for example, strengthening the contribution–benefit link, underwent important changes in CEE countries. At the same time, however, this double task of the pension system hindered rapid transformation into a pure market-oriented old-age security system.

As far as poverty elimination is concerned, this was more or less a new task for the state. Under the socialist system, social security was provided mainly through subsidized prices and planned wages, as well as the right to work. With the turn to market mechanisms, new ways of minimum protection had to be found. This also affected the pension system. In several systems, minimum protection within the pension system was kept or has been introduced since 1989.

What effect can be derived from these elements of minimum protection in the pension system? Figure 3.1 illustrates the replacement rates, that is, the percentage of former income replaced by the pension payment with regard to different levels of income in the year 1996.[7]

Figure 3.1 Theoretical replacement rates, 1996 (40 years of employment, average earner =1)

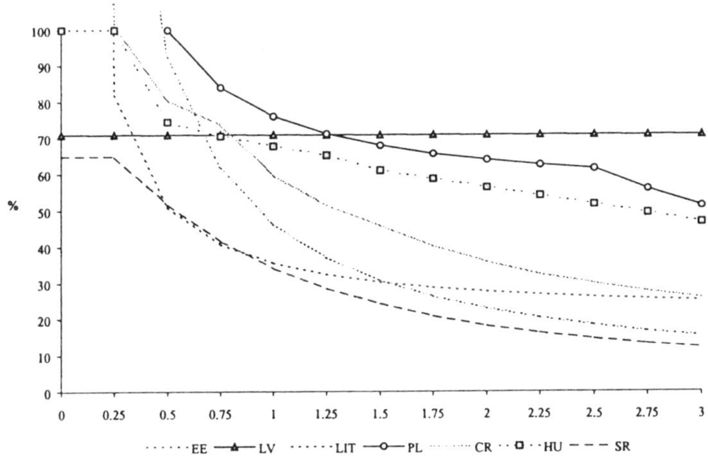

How much of the former individual earnings is replaced by the pension payment? Transition pension formulas provide an almost uniform pattern of high replacement rates in the low-income area and a replacement rate that decreases with increasing income. The exception is the Latvian system, where a defined contribution system was already implemented in 1996. This system provides the same replacement rate for every income level, showing that there is no *ex ante* redistribution in the pension system.

Which legal provisions have triggered the redistribution in the other transition countries? Table 3.2 gives an overview of different instruments in the pension systems.

The elements of redistribution are split into several levels. The first column shows whether there is a minimum pension in the system or not. This means that if there is any entitlement at all to old-age pension, it will be topped up to a certain level. This was the case in 1996 in Poland, the Slovak Republic, Hungary and Estonia. Minimum protection within the pension system could take the form of a minimum pension or, at least, a flat-rate element which redistributes in favour of low-income pensioners. The more important the flat-rate component, the closer the system gets to a minimum pension.

Table 3.2 *Instruments of income redistribution in the CEE pension systems, 1996*

	Minimum pension	Basic part	Degressive income consideration	Upper pension limit	Contribution ceiling
Poland	+	+	–	+	–
Czech Rep.	–	+	+	–	–
Slovak Rep.	+	–	+	+	–
Hungary	+	–	+	–	+
Estonia	+	+	/	+	–
Latvia	–	–	–	–	+
Lithuania	–	+	–	–	–

The second column shows whether there is a basic part in the pension formula. As we can see, in 1996 four of the seven countries had such a basic sum granted to everyone, regardless of their former income or the length of service. This basic sum is then supplemented by an income-related part.

The third element is a degressive tariff with regard to the income considered in the pension calculation. Although part of the pension payment is linked to the former income, not all of the income is taken into account: the full amount is considered only up to a certain level, and above this level only part of the earnings are registered. This way of calculating income-related pensions could be found in 1996 in the Czech and Slovak republics and in Hungary. In Lithuania and Poland, the income is restricted to a certain amount; in addition, there is an absolute upper pension limit in the Slovak Republic.

Redistribution in a contribution-financed system is not only affected by the benefit side: the financing method is of importance, too. In all countries contribution-based financing has replaced the merged budget of social and other public expenditures which was characteristic of social policy under the socialist regime. But on the micro level, a contribution ceiling, which would be an equivalent financing instrument of upper pension limits and degressive pension formulas, had been introduced only in Hungary (and even here, it was only introduced for the employees' share of the contribution payment, which is much lower than that contributed by the employers), and in the case of Latvia.

The above-mentioned protection against poverty and redistributive elements make up one side of the coin when describing the development of pension systems in Central and Eastern Europe. At the same time, the countries aim to strengthen further the so-called 'equivalence principle', that is, a stronger link to the former individual income and broader income differentials even in old age (see Table 3.3). This overview summarizes the reform measures

Table 3.3 *Elements in strengthening the income relation of the pension systems, 1996*

	Extension of years (earnings)	Increase in retirement age	Restriction of redistributive elements	restriction/exclusion of 'external grants'
Poland	X	–	X	X
Czech Rep.	X	X	X	X
Slovak Rep.	–	–	–	X
Hungary	X	X	–	?
Estonia	–	X	X	X
Latvia	X	X	X	X
Lithuania	X	X	X	X

linked to a strengthening of the income relationship, which had taken place in the second phase of transition. First, most countries excluded 'external grants'. Pension claims based on political honours or aimed at promoting labour incentives (which was quite usual under socialism) were excluded from the system. This was an important orientation towards a stronger income relationship.[8]

A second measure taken was to increase the retirement age, which had been remarkably low under the socialist pension system. The retirement age was raised in the Baltic states, Hungary and the Czech Republic.

Another important measure was the extension of the number of years for which earnings are taken into account when calculating the pension. Under the former socialist systems, the pension was based only on the earnings of the last year (or the last few years) before retirement. An extension of the time period considered tends to create a stronger link between paid contributions and the pension. In five countries – Poland, the Czech Republic, Hungary, Latvia and Lithuania – the 1996 reform measures consisted in using a higher number of years of earnings as a basis for pension calculation.

As mentioned above, there are several instruments which limit redistribution (for example, a contribution ceiling adapted to the benefit ceiling). For instance, Lithuania introduced a contribution ceiling in 1995, but very soon abandoned it again because of fiscal problems in the social security institution. Hungary and Latvia also have contribution ceilings. Furthermore, the degressive pension tariff was abandoned in Poland and the Baltic states.

Although an income-related public pension system is being discussed in all of the countries, the transformation described in the reports is characterized by the interactions between objectives and reality. The redistributive elements for fighting poverty often counteract the approach of more income-related benefits and the strengthening of the equivalence principle: high-income-earners, especially, are at a disadvantage. This contradiction between long-term orientation of the system and short-term operating problems seemed to be relevant in all of the countries under study. For example, several countries introduced a contribution ceiling into their legislation in order to strengthen the link between contributions and benefits, but year by year the implementation has been postponed because of financial problems. Latvia, which introduced the most substantial changes by turning to a defined contribution system was forced to set upper pension limits – and therefore redistribute again – because the high differences in the pension payments were not accepted and were judged unfair by the population. Obviously the transition to a more income-related system needs time to be socially accepted as well.

A second important development in the second phase of transition was the beginning of an organizational separation of pension insurance in combination with stronger financial independence. Although these issues were not central to public and scientific discussions, which focused on issues of the benefit formula and – even more importantly – questions of future financing of the pension system, the organizational development is an important issue as well.

A separate organizational structure is often seen as an important condition for an independent social insurance budget. The all-powerful state and the centralized state budget were one aspect of socialism most countries wanted to get rid of. In addition, the self-governance of social insurance is expected to guarantee a long-term consensus policy which includes the state, employers and employees and will therefore help to establish social harmony. Again, transformation strategies differ with regard to their organizational and financial independence. In Hungary, the Slovak Republic and Lithuania, administrative separation was accomplished at quite an early stage. Poland has already had a separate social insurance budget since 1986, whereas in the Czech Republic and Estonia, the social security budget is separate, but still part of the state budget with no organizational division having been carried out.

The final important development in this period was the introduction of a voluntary second pillar in the Czech Republic and Hungary. The necessity for a long-term introduction of additional private insurance was not questioned in any of the CEE countries. A new mix in old-age security and the partial replacement of the former monopolistic state system was seen as a requirement for the transformation of the pension system. Nevertheless, the lack of an institutional and financial infrastructure made rapid introduction of a second pillar difficult or even impossible (which was definitely the case in the Baltic states immediately after they had regained their independence). Therefore, the countries introducing an early second pillar, such as the Czech Republic and Hungary, did so on a voluntary basis. Both countries chose quite different approaches in setting incentives to participate in a voluntary insurance system. In the Czech Republic, the state subsidizes the contribution payment to individual private insurance up to a certain amount for each individual. In Hungary, tax exemptions are provided to encourage private life insurance.

To summarize, this period is often judged as a period of delayed reforms, and – on a second level – reforms already adopted are postponed or revoked: for example, in Hungary, the increase in the retirement age for women was foreseen by the law, but then invalidated by new regulations. A second example might be Slovakia, which decided to abandon the differentiation of working categories (with different pension claims), but continued to maintain the status quo. There are other examples of newly introduced measures which were later changed or adapted, for example, the increase in the retirement age in Estonia. For technical reasons the period in which the retirement age was to be raised has been extended. The trial-and-error period has also been one of extensive political discussion on future pension concepts, social policy goals and the awareness of necessary preconditions for introducing new forms of old-age provision.

3.4 THE THIRD PHASE: A MANDATORY SECOND PILLAR AS A COMMON PATTERN IN CENTRAL AND EASTERN EUROPE?

The third phase of the transformation of the pension system was described in the introductory paragraph as one in which comprehensive reforms have been accomplished. The previous description of changes in the pension system up to 1995–96 has already shown that this was not a static period, but one in which there were many, albeit sometimes small, changes which introduced a changing spirit in the field of old-age security. However, the third phase of reform – from 1995 onwards – has been characterized by different political decisions. In some countries, reforms no longer consisted of changes within the system, but took the form of comprehensive pension reform packages affecting benefits, financing and the structure of public and private provision. In this sense, these reforms could be classified according to Hall (1993) as reforms of a third order, because not only the setting of the instrument and the instrument itself, but also the objectives have been changed explicitly.

Such comprehensive reforms have taken place in Latvia, Hungary and Poland. They are also under discussion in Estonia. We should emphasize that the order of first, second and third phases in the transition of former socialist pension systems is not an inevitable one, and the development in the three countries does not allow us to conclude that development in all countries will be exactly the same. Nevertheless, the pension reforms in Latvia, Hungary and Poland were observed with keen interest in other Eastern European countries. Russia, Slovenia and Croatia recently adopted quite similar pension concepts. In the international scientific discussion, these pension reforms are seen as a possible model for Eastern European pension systems, just as the 'Chilean' model is now a synonym for many Latin American pension systems (Queisser 1998). Therefore we shall take a closer look at the reforms in Latvia, Hungary and Poland.

The first country to introduce a completely new pension system was Latvia. The Latvian country report describes – quite illustratively – several comprehensive pension reforms which had been designed earlier, but were never carried through because of very unstable economic conditions. The pension concept elaborated in 1995 with the assistance of a Swedish World Bank team came into force in 1996. There have been several amendments since its inception, but in general, this new concept, at least the first pillar, has been applied.[9]

The new Latvian pension system is based on the pension reform carried out in Sweden.[10] It consists of a first pillar of designed contribution and a mandatory and capital-funded but privately managed second pillar. Finally, voluntary individual saving is supposed to supplement old-age income. In the long run, the first pillar aims to replace about 40 per cent of the former income, the second pillar about 20 per cent and the voluntary third pillar about 10 per cent, so that the whole system together provides a replacement rate of 70 per cent.

The first pillar is constructed as a defined contribution system. Here the pension benefit is calculated from the individual's accumulated contribution payments during their whole working career divided by the average life expectancy at retirement age. This system (in its pure version) excludes social redistribution as far as possible. The risk of rising life expectancy is completely shifted to the individual insuree and not – as is the case in a defined benefit system – to the current contributors (at least partly). The decision to retire is – after reaching a minimum retirement age – up to the individual. In

Latvia the minimum age for retirement is set at 60. The longer someone works, the higher their individual 'pension capital', the lower the remaining life expectancy and therefore the higher the individual pension.

In Hungary, a new pension system came into force in January 1998. The public–private mix has changed significantly. In contrast to the Latvian and the Polish systems, the first pillar will not become a defined contribution system, but will be a reformed version of the current public system.[11] Central to the reform of the new Hungarian pension system is the replacement of about a quarter of the existing public system by a funded second tier until 2013. People entering the labour market after January 1998 have to be insured in the second pillar, but they are allowed to choose a private insurance fund themselves. Those who entered the labour market before 1998 are free to participate in a so-called mixed system with clear disincentives to join the system for people born before 1957 (Simonovits 1999).

The reformed first pillar in Poland is, as in Latvia, a defined contribution system. Although this is expected to strengthen the link between contributions and benefits significantly, there will still be elements of social redistribution in the first pillar. There will be a minimum pension paid out under the first pillar, amounting to 25 per cent of the current average pay, on the condition that the insuree has a certain number of years of service and is of a certain required age. An additional minimum guarantee is given by the state: if the first and second pillars together do not reach the minimum state pension level, the state government will make up the shortfall.[12] Another element is survivors' and disability pensions, provided by the first pillar.

In Poland, the second pillar is mandatory for people under 30, voluntary for people between 30 and 50 and inaccessible to people over 50. This second pillar will provide old-age pensions only. The insurees will be able to choose the fund where their contributions will be invested, and they will be able to transfer their capital to another fund. The investments of the pension funds will be supervised by the state. In the long run, the replacement rate of both pillars together is estimated at 50 per cent for people retiring at the age of 62 and 76 per cent at the age of 65. The advantage of this is the increased incentives for labour force participation because of a significant increase in the pension amount for prolongation of the working life (Office of the Government Plenipotentiary 1997:5). Contribution indexation paid into the first pillar will be based on the growth of the wage bill (ibid.). Contributions will be accrued on income only up to 250 per cent of the average wage.

A further advantage of this two-pillar system is the shared risk between labour market and capital market development. While the rate of return in PAYG-financed systems depends very much on demography and labour market development, the rate of return of the capital-funded second pillar is the rate of return on investments (see Office of the Plenipotentiary 1997;

Bite, in this volume; World Bank 1996).This leads to a specific transition problem as contribution rates remain constant but part of the contribution revenue is for the new 'mixed' system. This results in a deficit in the PAYG-financed old first pillar. How this deficit will be financed in the future remains to be seen. In Hungary, the initial deficit is counterbalanced by the state budget. In Poland, revenue from the privatization of public enterprises will be used for pension financing. Another possible reaction when the deficit is persistent or even grows could be a cut in pension expenditures.

3.5 SUMMARY

While in general the starting-point for the economic transformation is set at the end of the 1980s, the introduction of new pension laws did not start before the mid-1990s. Indeed, the transformation from a planned to a market economy required substantial changes in the sphere of property rights and liberalization, but in the beginning there was no comparable systemic need for a big bang in social policy. With respect to old-age security, existing and functioning systems were already in place. Although they were generally judged as inappropriate for a market economy, they worked and were able to provide at least a modest level of social security in old age. First adaptations of the pension systems necessitated by the transformation process were generally introduced within the old system. This first phase is called 'reactive' because generally these changes were reactions to the changing economic conditions rather than systematic reform steps. A second period is called the 'reflective' period. Pension reform from 1992 onwards was criticized by many politicians and scientists because it seemed that reforms in this field had been delayed. But in retrospect, it is apparent that, especially during this period, important political processes had taken place which clarified the objectives and consequences of certain reform models and constituted a necessary prerequisite for a broad consensus on pension reform. Moreover, even if during these years no comprehensive reforms were carried out, the incremental measures taken already led in certain directions. On the one hand, elements of minimum protection were still necessary to protect pensioners during the transformation process, but future objectives became evident from the measures taken, which established a closer contribution–benefit link. Finally, a third phase is called the 'reform' period. Especially from 1996 onwards, more comprehensive pension reforms were carried out, changing fundamentally not only the instruments but also the underlying objectives. Table 3.4 illustrates these three phases of reform.

Table 3.4 *Phases of pension reform in CEE countries*

	Reactive 1989–92	Reflective 1992–95/96	Reform 96 onwards
Dominant driving factor	Economy Inflation Labour market	Political discourse Political learning Reaching political consensus	History International advice and assistance

The aim of this ideal-type overview of phases is simply to illustrate how the periods of reform are interlinked and how long pension reform has taken (and still takes), although there was a general consensus that the socialist pension systems had to be reformed. But – in contrast to many other parts of the economy such as liberalized prices and privatized enterprises – there was no general consensus on the one and only 'right' pension system for a market economy. This is why the 'reflective' period from 1992 to 1995/96 was to be witnessed in many countries: a period of political discussion, a period in which there was still no technical infrastructure, and last but not least a period in which every country had to strike a balance between international political advice and internal political objectives.

The dominant factors, the role of internal and external political influencing factors, of economic and demographic constraints as well as institutional legacies and their impact on pension reform will be analysed in the next chapter.

NOTES

1 An example is the Czech pension reform carried out in 1995. Here several measures (raising the retirement age, changes in the pension formula, introduction of a second pillar) were combined. Nevertheless, in its distributional effects the Czech pension formula does not differ that much from the former system, nor does retirement age, for example, differ that much from other transition countries. But generally, the Czech pension system has been classified by many authors as fundamentally reformed, see Götting (1998:168).

2 We should point out here that the Baltic states legally had to implement a completely new pension system directly after their separation from the Soviet Union. In fact the old Soviet system was still applied in the first years of independence in Lithuania, while Estonia, with the introduction of flat-rate allowances, created a clear discontinuity in the preceding (Soviet) path.

3 For the general importance of price subsidies as a form of socialist social policy, see Golinowska (1990).

4 So it is argued, for example, in Chapters 6, 7 and 10, in this volume.

5 In 1996 the following mechanism was introduced. A 5 per cent increase in the price index, (formerly 10 per cent) effected an increase in pensions. In case of wage growth reaching the value of 1 in two successive calendar years, indexation by government decree was foreseen, see Chapter 9 in this volume.

6 Again it has to be noted that this is a very 'general' assessment. The introduction of a uniform payroll-related social insurance contribution paid in to a separate fund, for example, in Lithuania, was already a first measure of institutional financial separation and also indicates a change in the financing system.

7 Calculations are based on the pension formulas used in 1996. The graph represents the theoretical ideas of redistribution within the pension system by minimum provision rules and the pension formula in relation to former income. It does not represent in any sense real pension payment distribution; there is no empirical evidence for this. In addition, it does not consider several special regulations granting pension rights for non-working periods (for example, child-rearing benefits, periods of education and so on). There might be numerous other regulations influencing the distributional effects of the pension system. Nevertheless, the direction of income redistribution within the pension formula can be derived from these typologies of pension systems. For instance, although the 1996 pension formula in Latvia suggests a stable replacement rate of about 70 per cent independently from the individual income position, this represents only the long-term goal of redistribution within the pension system in Latvia. In fact, real pension payment distribution nowadays looks quite different – because today's pension claims are based on the former systems under socialism. Also future pension distribution might look quite different from what is suggested here, because already in the first year after the new Latvian pension system was in place (1996), additional pension claims according to various social circumstances were granted. For details, see Chapter 6, in this volume.

8 However, as mentioned before, at the same time additional grants (for political victims and so on) were newly introduced.

9 For the history and more details of the concept, see Chapter 6, in this volume.

10 Italy is also carrying out a reform in this direction. For more details on the Italian and Swedish pension reform, see Porta and Saraceno (1997), Kruse (1997) and Scherman (1999).

11 Crucial changes in the first pillar are the rise in the retirement age, a change to a combined price–wage indexation and the introduction of means tests in the minimum pension, cf. Chapter 11, in this volume and Simonovits (1999).

12 According to calculations of the Office of the Government Plenipotentiary (1997:5), it is expected that about 10 per cent of pensioners will get this state-guaranteed subsidy.

REFERENCES

Cangiano, M., Cottarelli, C. and Cubeddu, L. (1998), 'Pension developments and reform in transition economies', Paper presented for the conference 'Social Security Reforms: International Comparisons', Rome, 16–17 March. Draft.

Golinowska, S. (1990), *Rola Centrum w kształtowaniu struktury spozycia* (The role of state decisions as to design of consumption structure in Poland), Staatlicher Ökonomischer Verlag (PWE), Warsaw.

Golinowska, S. (1997), 'Public social expenditure in Central and Eastern Europe', Unpublished manuscript, Institute of Labour and Social Affairs, Warsaw.

Götting, U. (1998), *Transformation der Wohlfahrtstaaten in Mittel- und Osteuropa. Eine Zwischenbilanz* (Transformation of welfare states in Central and Eastern Europe. An interim assessment), Opladen: Leske und Budrich.

Hall, P.A. (1993), 'Policy paradigms, social learning, and the state. The case of economic policymaking in Britain', *Comparative Politics*, 4, 275–96.

Kruse, A. (1997), 'The case of Sweden', *Pension Systems and Reforms – Britain, Hungary, Italy, Poland, Sweden*, in European Commission's PHARE ACE Programme 1995, Research Project P95-2139-R, 133–57.

Office of the Government Plenipotentiary for Social Security Reform (1997), 'Security through diversity. Reform of the pension system in Poland', Warsaw.

Porta, P.L. and Saraceno, P. (1997), 'The case of Italy' *Pension Systems and Reforms – Britain, Hungary, Italy, Poland, Sweden*, in European Commission's PHARE ACE Programme 1995, Research Project P95-2139-R, Final report, Budapest, 79–106.

Queisser, M. (1998), *The Second-generation Pension Reforms in Latin America*, OECD Development Study, Paris: OECD.

Scherman, K.G. (1999): 'The Swedish Pension Reform', Discussion paper 7 – Issues in social protection, Geneva, ILO, Social Security Department.

Simonovits, A. (1999), 'The new Hungarian pension system and its problems', in E. Müller, A. Ryll and H.-J. Wagener (eds), *Transformation of Social Security: Pensions in Central-Eastern Europe*, Heidelberg: Physica, 211–30.

World Bank (1994), *Averting the Old-age Crisis*, Washington, DC: World Bank.

4. Explaining reforms

Sabine Horstmann and Winfried Schmähl

4.1 INTRODUCTION

This last of the comparative chapters tries – as far as possible – to explain the reforms in the field of pension policy. Such an analysis of social policy reforms in Central and Eastern Europe can be located at the intersection between welfare state analysis on the one hand and transformation research on the other. Classical welfare state analysis concentrates mainly on Western industrialized countries and focuses (a) (static) on the classification of typologies of welfare states and (b) (dynamic) on developments and determining factors of social expenditure expansion. Less but growing emphasis was given to welfare state retrenchment,[1] which has, especially in the last years, gained more and more in importance.

Typologies of welfare state arrangements have classified 'Three Worlds of Welfare State Capitalism' (Esping-Andersen 1990), that is, the social democratic model (such as is characteristic of the Scandinavian welfare state), a liberal type (Anglo-American) and a conservative welfare state (Continental Europe), which have been completed by an additional category, the Southern European welfare state (Leibfried 1992, Lessenich 1994) and contrasted by a gender-differentiated classification (Lewis and Ostner 1994). There have been attempts to include the socialist welfare state in this category (see, for example, Schmidt 1999b). There is a long history in research of explanations for the development of public expenditure in general as well as for social expenditure.[2] Analysis of welfare state expansion has identified several determining elements on the macrolevel: economic developments, the orientation and constellation of governing coalitions and opposition for example, have statistically proven influence on welfare state expenditures. This has also been exemplified for different fields of social expenditures, for example, health-care expenditure (Schmidt 1999a) or pension expenditure (World Bank 1994).

On the other hand, in the beginning, economic 'transformation research' paid little attention to social policy questions. It focused on macroeconomic performance of the transition countries on the one hand and on optimal transformation strategies (big bang versus gradualism) on the other. Social security was seen mainly as a costly, but necessary accompanying measure to make economic reforms politically viable.

Since the mid-1990s, the burden of social expenditure on young market economies has been emphasized more and more, and structural social policy reforms have attracted more interest in economic research as well. They mostly address normative questions about the optimum social security system for the transition countries. And, lastly, in the years 1997–98, not only have normative questions of optimum social security systems been raised, but the attempt to identify influencing factors for the shape of reforms has been made as well.[3] The most comprehensive analysis of welfare state transformation, touching all areas of social security such as pension policy, health care, the labour market, poverty alleviation and social services, was published by Götting (1998).

Against the background of this short outline of social policy research, we shall draw up some hypotheses for this study. As it does not provide comprehensive empirical and, even more important, comparable data, we will not present statistical evidence, but concentrate on the internal logic and determinants of pension system development. Furthermore, the design of the country reports and the concentration on pension policy is far more suitable for the examination of the internal connections between influencing factors and changes in the pension system than highly aggregated data on pension expenditures. Thus, our approach is to discuss influencing factors as broadly as possible and to consider the institutional legacies and political actors that have shaped the direction of reforms. The results of this 'explorative' study then might enable further research to highlight important influencing factors in more detail.

The 'traditional' welfare state analysis of advanced industrial countries is different from that of transition countries, and some peculiarities of the transition countries must be pointed out. Parallel to the economic transformation, a political transformation took place. Thus, the fragile political setting is not comparable in its impact and influence on social policy reforms. This is why the approach in political sciences focusing on ruling coalitions and opposition and their impact on the shape of social policy reforms and the level of social expenditures does not seem to be an appropriate instrument for reform analysis. Nevertheless, in the country reports it is pointed out that institutional political actors gain more and more importance (for example, social partners). This might lead to a comparable setting of political actors and institutionalized actors in the field of social policy. We shall discuss this in more detail in the section dealing with political actors. Finally, given the international perspective/influence, it is useful to carry out a detailed analysis of the welfare state development in Central and Eastern Europe. This aspect is usually neglected in the analysis of Western European welfare states, although it influences social policy reforms in the West as well, at least on the level of 'international' discourse. An investigation of the interaction between the different levels of influence on the shape of pension systems in the transition countries may shed light on the relationship between global processes and individual events in the transition economies (Blejer and Coricelli 1995:1), and thus strengthen the link between current research on globalization and its impacts on social policy reform on the one hand and case studies analysing the development of the welfare state in a one-country perspective, which usually emphasize the path-dependency of social policy, on the other. A multi-level approach of welfare state development with local or national variables and international developments and influences to explain welfare state adoption is appropriate for the analysis of pension reform in Central and Eastern Europe. The internal – or country-specific – factors have to be analysed together with external international developments in the field of pension reform and the role of international advice and assistance during transformation. On the other hand, international influence must always be analysed together with the country-specific determining factors and internal political developments and restrictions.

What concrete hypotheses can be drawn from these different perspectives on social policy or pension reform, which should be discussed when analysing the development?

First, the economic and demographic situations are seen as important influencing restrictions. With regard to the *economic situation*, the level of economic performance could be expected to influence the level of social expenditures including pension expenditures. Therefore an improving economic situation could relieve distributional conflicts between active and non-active individuals of the society in the sense of 'a good economic policy is the best social policy'. We shall examine whether this could be observed for the transition countries, and whether notable differences in economic performance also led to differences in the expenditures on pensions or the shape of pension reform.

Demography is seen as a second important determinant for pension expenditures. First, it directly influences pension expenditures by means of the old-age dependency ratio, and, moreover, it is seen as the important determinant in a political economy perspective with regard to pension reform. A high proportion of pensioners (representing a high proportion of the electorate) is a significant impediment to cutting pension benefits and especially for introducing changes in financing pensions from a pay-as-you-go (PAYG) to a funded system. In the following section, we shall discuss whether the demographic situation sets 'barriers to change' in the transition countries.

On top of the economic and demographic constraints and as we have already pointed out, the *political setting*, identified as an important determinant in the long-term development of Western European welfare states, is somewhat different in the transition countries. Nevertheless, pension policy is 'expert policy' (Nullmeyer and Rüb 1993) and this seems to be verified by the development of pension systems in the countries under study as well, since the ministries and administrative experts had much influence on changes in the pension system. In the second section, we shall discuss what kind of political actors can be identified, and what influence they have on pension reform.

Third, the *path-dependency* of social security systems will be discussed. To this end, we shall examine the 'institutional legacies' of old-age security systems. There have been hypotheses that the transition countries with their roots in the former German–Austrian social insurance system will revert to this kind of system (Eichenhofer 1995). On the other hand, institutional legacies have been handed down from the 40-year period of socialist social security. These different levels of 'influence of history' will be analysed in the third section.

And, finally, a fourth section is dedicated to the international interaction. This *international dimension* can also be analysed on several levels. The international discussion on pension reform worldwide can play an important role on the level of models or 'spirits': it could exercise influence through conditions for access to international organizations – following their guiding principles (The European Union: EU, the International Labour Organization: ILO; and so on); it could be an influencing factor for the level of conditionality of loans (the International Monetary Fund: IMF; the World Bank); and, finally, it could influence through the level of technical assistance provided.[4]

It has been supposed that Eastern Europe is used as a 'testing ground' for social security innovations and that especially the IMF and the World Bank are trying to implement the Latin American model of pension security in Central and Eastern Europe as well (Deacon and Hulse 1997; Standing 1996). The last section will therefore deal with the shape and impact of international aspects on pension reform.

4.2 ECONOMIC AND DEMOGRAPHIC RESTRICTIONS AS DETERMINING FACTORS?

'The main factors influencing the development of the pension system are of a demographic and economic nature.' (Medaiskis, Chapter 7, in this volume, p. 178). In what way did economic developments constrain the level of pension expenditures in the first years of transformation? The countries under study all experienced a sharp fall in GDP due to the restructuring of the economy.[5]

However, the share of social and pension expenditures did not exactly follow this trend in all countries. Whereas the early years show an increase in the share of pension expenditures in Poland and Hungary, the share in the other countries stayed more or less stable. This was caused by changing indexation measures chosen in the early years of transformation which enabled the countries to respond flexibly to economic performance.

However, if we look at the GDP per capita and average replacement rates, there is a certain correlation between the economic performance and the pension level. The lower GDP per capita in the Baltic states corresponds to a lower average replacement rate – but with a certain minimum limit of about 40 per cent. This basic level of old-age provision is obviously the politically enforced limit of cutbacks in the state's social expenditures. In that sense, developments in pension expenditures compared to general economic indicators illustrate that economic developments influence pension expenditures without restricting them completely. While the absolute figures reflect a certain 'inflexibility' of such expenditures, the development of their relative share in the GDP varies.

A second perspective on economic developments and pension reform looks not only at the level of pension expenditures, but also at institutional 'reactions' within the pension system. Economic transformation in the first period triggered several ad hoc reactions in the pension system. In this respect, economic developments were the decisive influencing factor responsible for changes in the pension system in the short run. It has already been pointed out that the need for social elements in the systems as a first form of 'social assistance' was characteristic of early reform measures. This explains why there is no complete 'flexibility' in pension expenditures as a whole. Implementing a general means-tested social assistance scheme in the first stage of transformation was not an option, because there was no administrative and institutional system to build upon. The existing social assistance schemes provided support for certain specified groups only (for example, the handicapped or drug addicts), because poverty was officially a non-existent problem in socialism. Even now social assistance schemes in CEE countries are often linked to very special situations with no universal coverage. The easiest way to protect pensioners lay within the pension system, by providing minimum pensions or basic elements. Moreover, the necessity for means-tested benefits was not very evident, as in general pensioners did not have any significant assets or other income; a means test would require additional administrative resources (Zukowski 1995).[6]

Different countries have chosen different strategies of protection against poverty and of redistribution. Lithuania provides a minimum income for people of pensionable age who do not have a claim to social insurance but who do fulfil certain criteria, by means of an external tax-financed 'social pension'. Other elderly and disabled are provided for by income-tested social benefits. The amount of the basic part within the pension formula is very close to the amount of the social pension. Other countries opted for a contribution-financed minimum pension (Poland, Hungary, the Slovak Republic and Estonia). Poland, Estonia and the Czech Republic have flat-rate elements with different weightings in the pension formula, while the Czech, Slovak and Hungarian systems additionally redistribute through a so-called 'reduced income' formula, where the former income for pension calculation is considered only degressively. The transformation-caused recession was a main reason for the political decision to keep the existing strong redistributive character of the old-age security scheme. The 'solidarity elements' of redistribution and poverty protection within the pension system seem to have been a 'forced' necessity in all transformation countries, even if there has been one political decision to turn to a less redistributive system: Latvia experienced recession and hyperinflation when the state tried to introduce a more earnings-related formula, which in turn created a situation whereby the state saw itself forced to revert to a flat-rate pension system as a protection against widespread poverty. Similarly, Estonia was forced to apply temporary regulations which led essentially to a flat-rate system.

A second aspect of economic influences on the shape of the pension system is the interaction between labour market developments and early retirement options to reduce the burden on the labour market. Solving at least part of the growing unemployment problem by early retirement meant less political conflict than coping with higher unemployment rates. Nevertheless, not all countries faced the same degree of unemployment – for example, the Czech Republic and the Baltic states had comparably low unemployment rates – nor did they all react in the same way. While Poland faced a high increase in early retirement/disability pensions, in Hungary the burden on the labour market fell less on the pension system. Thus, labour market problems did not necessarily lead to a shift to early retirement, but this option was available.

Another short-term economic constraint for the development of funded forms of old-age security requires well-functioning institutions in the banking sector, a developed capital market and a supervisory system which did not exist at the beginning of transformation.[7] Institutional transformation and restructuring of the banking sector are among the main long-term problems in transition economies. It was soon recognized that implementing the legal framework and legislative control was not the whole story. Capital markets and the banking sector also required fundamental institutional changes on the psychological level, which can be described by, for example, confidence in the banking sector by individuals, the possibilities of domestic investment and so on. These necessary prerequisites for the introduction of the second, funded pillar are still to be developed, especially in the Baltic states, whereas in the Visegrad countries the institutional infrastructure already seems to be in a better shape and additional provision is currently being introduced in the Czech and Slovak Republics (on a voluntary basis) and in Poland and Hungary (on a mandatory basis).

Nevertheless, these economic constraints on the actual pension arrangement do not constrain future objectives; they are seen as inevitable but time-restricted constraints in the early years of transformation.[8] Factors such as GDP or capital markets are expected to improve in the future. This is why long-term goals are oriented towards a less redistributive, multi-pillar system with additional private provision. In the future, with a general improvement in the income situation in growing economies, elements of minimum protection are expected to lose their importance. Their share in pension payments of the first public pillar will diminish, either through the implementation of a new, less redistributive pension formula which is still to be completed by (more redistributive) transition rules, or through adjustments of basic and income-related payments.[9]

To summarize, economic constraints are important for the reconstruction of the pension system, influencing the scope of pension expenditures as a whole and triggering certain institutional rules such as indexation or early retirement schemes. While these aspects were of particular importance in the early years of transformation, the future is characterized by economic influence on a 'paradigmatic level', that is, by a fundamental paradigmatic change towards a stronger responsibility of individuals, changing incentives and, more generally, towards a 'market-oriented' approach shaping the future of old-age provision.

At the moment, economic developments shape the design of pension security; demography is not yet a problem for the transition countries, but will become increasingly important in the coming years. Demographic developments – stimulated also by the international discussion on ageing societies and their impact on old-age security – is one of the main issues in pension reform debates, although the demographic situation in Central and Eastern Europe is still less threatening than in many Western European countries, because the fall in the birth rates started later. However, the CEE countries will also face population ageing.[10]

When looking at the influence of demography and demographic changes, we should distinguish between short-term and long-term aspects. An additional distinction should be made between objective demographic influences and the level of discussion/discourse, dominated by predictions for future developments.

Although the future demographic impact on pension expenditures is a continuing issue everywhere in the region, the actual short-term financial problems are determined by labour market problems rather than demographic developments.[11] While the old-age dependency ratio will start to rise only in 2005, the system dependency ratio has already increased since 1989, as a result of unemployment and early retirement.[12] The current problem for pension finances is the labour market, not demography (see Chapter 5, in this volume).

But future demographic developments have been anticipated in early reform measures, too. As described previously, CEE pension systems were – in international comparison – characterized by a remarkably low retirement age.[13] A low retirement age against the background of an ageing population will lead to growing pension expenditures. Raising the retirement age has been discussed and implemented in all of the countries (with the exception of the Slovak Republic).

Furthermore, these measures are not seen as sufficient to cope with future demographic developments. Demography is – on a level of discourse – the most important influencing factor shaping the long-term development of the pension system. Ferge (1999) has pointed out that the demographic development has been only a relatively recent subject for discussion, even in Western European countries, although the consequences for old-age security systems are plain to see. In that sense, the demographic component of pension reform debate can be seen as an international trend, reaching transition societies as well as many other countries. Nevertheless, the demographic situation is not the only, and – according to some authors[14] – not the essential influencing factor for the future development of pension finances: the development of the labour market, or more precisely the future number of insured employees, is of great importance, too.

Two countries (Latvia and Poland) have already reacted to this 'demographic wave' in the pension reform debate and have introduced the first pillar as a defined contribution system, where the sum of all contributions paid in are converted into an annuity. This means that the average life expectancy at retirement age is a decisive factor for the amount of monthly pension payment. Adaptations to a changing demographic framework are automatically included in the pension formula, so that the additional burden of rising life expectancy will not be carried by the current working population through higher contribution rates – as in a defined benefit system – but will lead directly to lower pension payments, so that the entire burden is carried by the pensioners themselves.[15]

The impact of the demographic setting on pension reform is also discussed with respect to political economy. In several country reports in this volume, aspects of the political economy of pension reform are emphasized. Pensioners are seen as an important and influential group in the electorate,[16] and this should deter political parties from cutting old-age transfers, for fear of losing votes. The political economy of pension reform[17] is debated extensively on a theoretical level (Breyer and Stolte 1999), arguing that PAYG systems in societies with an ageing population will always tend to extend pension payments rather than lower the contribution payments of the active employed generation. This general argument has been modified in different ways. It has been stated that there is no 'ageing-vote' owing to the heterogeneous group of pensioners (Hinrichs 1993:13) in Western countries. The group of pensioners might be more homogeneous in Central and Eastern Europe against the background of socialism. An indicator of more active interest among pensioners might be the existence of 'pensioners' parties' in several CEE countries. On the other hand, the distributional conflicts between older and younger cohorts could in some respect be limited to family responsibility. This aspect might be of even greater importance in Central and Eastern Europe, as family solidarity is cherished much more here.

Finally, intergenerational equity has an unusual dimension in Central and Eastern Europe: pensioners are often judged as the 'losers of transformation', as they had to suffer transformation recession but will not be able to share in the future economic progress. Current pension reforms in Central and Eastern Europe underline that, despite the political and economic reasons against comprehensive reforms, it has been possible to implement comprehensive reforms which will definitely change the way of intergenerational distribution. Why this has been the case, despite a high proportion of pensioners and people of pre-pension age, leads us to the following point: the influence of political actors in pension reform.

4.3 POLITICAL SETTING AND POLITICAL ACTORS OF PENSION REFORM

Analysing the political setting and identifying important actors of the pension reform in Central and Eastern Europe is in many respects different from 'traditional' social policy analysis (Golinowska 1999). The young democracies, especially in the early years of transformation, were confronted with problems of transforming not only the economic system, but also the political system. Political parties and clear-cut political programmes with regard to social policy were still in the making. This 'developing' political arena becomes particularly evident in the Baltic states, which had to build up all political institutions after regaining independence from the Soviet Union. The situation was characterized by a lack of experts in the field of pension policy[18] – because in the Soviet period this was taken care of by the central state in Moscow. As the Baltic states were confronted with this situation in nearly every policy field and as the size of the population did not provide a large potential, pension policy experts in the Baltic states were forced to fulfil a multiple role: they had to be scientists, technical experts and politically responsible persons at the same time:

> The Ministry of Social Security and Labour is the most influential actor in pension reform. ... Ministers and their deputies in the former governments were selected more on the basis of their professional than their political background. Later the ministers were appointed more for political reasons, but this did not have the effect of reducing the level of professional qualifications in the top echelons. (Medaiskis, Ch. 7 in this volume, p. 179)

This led to a situation where a broad political discussion, at least in the first period of transformation, was minimal or non-existent.[19]

> To evaluate the political discussion about pension reform and the factors that have influenced it one has to understand that in Latvia social policy has not yet formally become a separate domain of state policy. Not even a social policy concept has been developed. (Bite, Ch. 6 in this volume, p. 149)

This political setting does not allow a traditional analysis of the impact of ruling parties/coalitions on the shape of social policy in CEE countries.

Over the period under study, political actors became more and more involved in the pension reform debate. Nevertheless, they often dealt with the implementation of concrete, technical measures. For instance, the share of the contribution rate to be paid by employers and employees, respectively, was discussed by employers' organizations and trade unions.[20] Social security administrations fought for a growing institutional independence and the expansion of financial autonomy of the pension system, while the government tried to restrict their independence.[21] Pensioners' associations fought against the rise in the retirement age and higher benefits through higher rates of pension indexation.[22] These examples of intervening political actors are in line with Mancur Olson's theory of collective action which implies that smaller groups with restricted concrete interests are more able to articulate these interests and influence politics than large groups with general interests. It might also be an explanation for the fact that the comprehensive reforms which took place in Latvia, Hungary and Poland did not meet with much resistance, because distributional effects had not yet become visible. It is argued that the new pension model as opposed to the former 'amendments' within the current systems makes it more difficult to identify individual losses and – with the introduction of the new mandatory second pillar – results in a fiscal illusion reducing the resistance against the reform (Müller 1997:11).

It is likely that the complexity of the new pension model hampers the concrete identification of winners and losers of pension reform, or makes the effects less visible or obvious at first glance. Nevertheless, the very early introduction of a new defined contribution pillar in Latvia made actual losses visible and led to direct protest and prompt political amendments in the system.[23] The lack of transparency led to easier political acceptance only to a certain extent. In the long run, people will see through the fiscal illusion, which will in turn necessitate political corrections.

In Hungary and Poland, we can observe a division of interests between the Ministry of Finance, supporting strongly market-oriented pension reforms with a high share of capital-funded provision for old age on the one hand and the ministries of Labour and Social Affairs with reform proposals much more oriented towards a 'reform within the system' on the other. These different positions are supported by both economists (for the radical market-oriented approach) and lawyers (for processual reform). While the economists argue for a systemic reform with an introduction of private pensions, the lawyers generally argue for modest reforms within the current system.[24]

Poland and Hungary are characterized not only by these different positions of the two ministries. In addition, both countries have influential self-governing institutions for social security which play a role in the pension reform debate and take a political stance which is also more oriented towards gradual reforms. In both countries, these institutions were implemented quite early and are therefore a good example of influential institutional actors. The conflict of interests between the Ministry of Finance and the Ministry of Social Affairs does not exist in the Czech and Slovak republics. Generally, the first period of transformation in these two states seems to be marked by a much lower level of critical resistance or opposition; there was a less comprehensive public discussion on pension reform issues. In contrast to Poland and Hungary, the pension systems in the Czech and Slovak republics have so far not produced budget deficits. It is argued that the huge deficit in Poland and Hungary put the Ministry of Finance on the political agenda of pension reform, because it will also be affected by pension policy if the pension fund deficit has to be financed from the state budget (Müller 1999). In fact, this seems questionable, at least in the short run, because the current switch to a partly privatized pension system will increase the pension fund deficit further, as a consequence of the high transition costs.

Compared to Poland and Hungary, the Czech and Slovak republics, the former Czechoslovakian Republic, present a different picture of political actors. Their different political settings might be explained by the fact that Poland and Hungary were reform countries even before 1989 and the political starting conditions therefore were quite different. In some respect the political change in the Czechoslovak Republic was more radical than in the neighbouring countries, which had started to reform their system earlier and already had a (modest) experience in political opposition – reflected for example, in the early introduction of self-governing institutions. This caused a slower start of both public discussion on pension reform issues and political bargaining on social policy objectives than in Poland or Hungary. Moreover, the former political power of the Klaus government in the Czech Republic and its economic performance after the early years of transformation, especially regarding the labour market, may have deterred serious political opposition. Nevertheless, since 1995, the situation has changed significantly, at least in the Czech Republic. In that year, a comprehensive strike, arranged by the trade unions, took place in protest against the rise in the retirement age. In the 1998 election campaign, the pensioners' party's main political goal was a more regular indexation mechanism for pensions; pension issues seem to have become an increasingly public issue.

The situation and developments in the Slovak Republic are again different from those in the Czech Republic. Here, apart from an institutional separation by the introduction of self-government, the public pillar has not yet undergone serious reform. Nevertheless, the introduction of a voluntary second pillar was legally drafted in 1997. But political actors in pension politics in the Slovak Republic are difficult to identify: while economic policy and performance seem to be quite successful, the move towards greater democracy is still under way; political processes are often characterized by a lack of transparency. Nevertheless, there has been pronounced opposition against the introduction of a new pension formula, which also has been criticized in an international forum for its superficial changes.[25]

Analyses of economic transformation stress the role of strong and aggressive trade unions in Poland (Blejer and Coricelli 1995:5). In the early years, the Solidarity movement was an influential actor fighting for the improvement of pensioners' income by advocating indexation and valorization. Nevertheless, their role has changed and they now support the planned, partly privatizing pension reform in Poland (Golinowska 1999). Generally, in all countries the role of employees/trade unions on the one hand and employers' organizations on the other was rather limited in the beginning: while trade unions had a strong political heritage from the former socialist system, private employers simply did not exist and had to build up their networks and interest groups. With continuing transformation, the employees/employers have acquired an increasingly influential role in the pension reform debate.

An important reason for the feasibility of radical economic reforms has been identified as 'the honeymoon effect' in the transition societies. According to Blejer and Coricelli (1995:5), even a short honeymoon period after the break with communism allowed comprehensive economic reforms and marked changes in distribution. Social reforms nevertheless did not belong to these first radical reforms. In the field of pension reform, however, the ability to reform is more protracted – in Poland there was a broad consensus in all parties on the necessity for reform; the socialist government introduced reform and this policy was continued by the following liberal government.

4.4 HISTORY OF SOCIAL SECURITY: PATH-DEPENDENCY OF PENSION REFORM?

To a large extent, welfare state development all over the world is explained by path-dependency, just as the whole field of 'transition economics' emphasizes the importance of path-dependency of economic transition (Crawford and Lijphart 1995:171).

Obviously the change in the economic and political system in Central and Eastern Europe did not require – indeed, did not allow – a blueprint of a completely new social security system to be introduced. The transition of the social security system had to cope with the existing socialist system, with existing claims and acquired rights. This section will outline the influence of the history of social security on the design of current and future old-age security.

Before discussing the impact of the socialist era and the socialist provision of social security, the influence of the pre-war period and the roots of social security systems in Central and Eastern Europe will be examined. In the Visegrad states, German and Austrian influences were the starting-point for their own social security development (Eichenhofer 1995:192). It is often argued that this origin of social security systems in the late 19th century has an important meaning for today's transition of social security systems, too. Central and Eastern Europe are today trying to continue former traditions which were interrupted by the socialist period, including those in the field of social security (Eichenhofer 1995:193).

The influence of pre-socialist social security has to be analysed on a long-term basis. First, the employment-based social insurance, the 'Bismarck model' approach, shaped the developments after the Second World War in Central and Eastern Europe. The socialist transition was not a sudden and comprehensive change to the socialist social security system. It can rather be seen as an evolution from the initially implemented insurance approach to an increasingly provision-oriented model with stronger elements of redistribution (Zukowski 1995). Starting in the 1950s, the countries gradually adopted characteristics of the Soviet social security system. These developments[26] included the abolition of separate branches of social security, a growing financial independence from the state and the introduction of special provision systems mostly due to political incentives.

Nevertheless, social security systems even in the late 1980s were employment based; they were exclusive and did not make general provision based on criteria such as nationality or residence, so in this respect pre-socialist social security was to influence the later shape of social security under socialism. In addition, an important – and often neglected – heritage of the social security system was its extensive coverage. Nearly 90 per cent of the population were included in the insurance scheme. This fact limited the reform options in many ways: it was not possible to introduce a new system without securing the finance for existing claims.

A second aspect of the historical influence is discussed more in the context of social security transformation and emphasizes the link between pre-war history and today's reconstruction of the social security system. This reorientation is often explained by the common values, habits and lifestyles in Western as well as in Central and Eastern Europe. On a psychological level, it is questionable whether these values and habits still prevail in the population, which has experienced more than 40 years of other values and has adapted to other incentives. Indeed, the population has changed and there are few who have personally experienced the pre-war situation with its employment-based, income-related insurance system. In this context, one should also consider that this reorientation on former traditions might be explained more easily by political feasibility. It might be easier to blame massive changes in all parts of the economy and a discontinuation in many parts of everyday life on bygone traditions, than to adapt to 'strange', new institutions.

Nevertheless, the influence of former social security systems is visible. The future 'reorientation' towards a stronger income relation of the pension system is a remarkable trend in all the countries under study. There are doubts whether this is due to former 'traditions', or, more generally, due to the systemic shift from planned to market economy, including a stronger emphasis on the performance-oriented society, more individual self-responsibility, incentives and less redistribution. In addition, this seems to be a general trend which can also be observed in Western European and some Nordic countries. It is clear that this future orientation is a strong tendency in the transition societies and that, even in the first pillar, preferences are not given to flat-rate benefits. In Latvia, in the 1993 election campaign: 'all political parties from the far right to the far left promised to introduce a pension scheme in which benefits would be linked to the previous working life in the best possible way' (Bite, Ch. 6 in this volume, p. 135). Golinowska and Zukowski state: 'income during old age should reflect both the wage level and the length of employment' (Ch. 8 in this volume, p. 211).

All in all, it seems necessary to divide the influence of institutional legacies into 'counter-reactions' and socialist elements that still linger. We pointed out earlier that the need for the current minimum provision is mainly due to economic and political reasons and does not seem to be a long-term social policy goal. If we look at the pension policy concepts for the future in Hungary and Poland, they will have systems similar to the private insurance principle with no substantial redistribution elements. In this (future) perspective, former elements of redistribution and minimum protection will have very little weight. Finally, the orientation on pre-war traditions of social security has only limited influence. Although generally a concept closer to the Bismarckian approach of social insurance – also in the first pillar – is chosen, the construction of future multi-pillar systems does not simply take up past traditions, but is an international, new combination of social insurance in the first pillar with a funded and mandatory second pillar. Therefore, it would be too easy to explain pension reforms in Central and Eastern Europe as a reflection of the social policy tradition of 50 years ago. They seem to reflect an 'international trend' as well as a strategy pushed strongly by the World Bank. These points and the international dimension of pension reform will be discussed in the following section.

4.5 INTERNATIONAL INFLUENCES

This section will concentrate on a final aspect influencing pension reform in Central and Eastern Europe: the role of international advice and assistance. In the introduction to this chapter, we pointed out that the issue of 'international assistance' can be subdivided into several levels, from international paradigms and norms which influence the pension reform debate in Central and Eastern Europe to the conditionality of loans granted by international agencies, which are tied to concrete pension reform measures.[27]

International assistance has taken many different forms, including country-to-country co-operation and international agencies supporting the transformation process, among them the IMF and the World Bank, the ILO, the EU and the Organization for Economic Co-operation and Development (OECD).

Difficult to quantify but surely of importance is the widespread influence of the global social policy discourse. Social policy in OECD countries seems to have undergone a fundamental paradigm change. After the extension of the Western social security systems until the 1970s and the beginning of consolidation in the 1980s, the present years are characterized by the strong promotion of liberalization of social security systems and a targeting of the welfare state primarily on minimum protection. One can clearly connect this development to the 'globalization' discussion in politics and science, emphasizing aspects of international competition and their impact on social policy, as well as the growing activity in the field of social security of the World Bank, which began in Latin America in the 1980s and has now spread to Central and Eastern Europe. The change to a more liberal paradigm of social security is an international trend and – as far as the aspect of financing social security is concerned – especially an international trend in economics. In that respect, it should be questioned whether 'the making of post-communist social policy is a testing ground for the future of social policy elsewhere in the industrialised world' (Deacon and Hulse 1997:43).

It seems to be more appropriate to say that the international discussion on pension reform is reaching CEE countries as well:

> Above all, pension reform cannot be divorced from the relentless external pressure to 'cut back the state', and it is in that context that variants of the 'Chilean model' of pensions have been advocated throughout the region, often through representatives of the World Bank. (Standing 1996:241)

The agenda-setting on demographic problems may be one reason why the necessity for a partly capital-funded system has been emphasized in reform discussions. Although there are many problems connected with the reform of the pension system, foreign experts seem to act in some respect as 'gate-keepers' in the reform discussion – especially during the early years – and to concentrate on the demographic problems to be solved by capital-funded systems:

> When we talk to them, for example, about their social security systems, we try to talk to them about systems which don't just meet the challenges of today but will be ready to meet the challenges of the future as well. So we talk to them about where their demographics are going. (Fox 1996:35)

A second dimension of international co-operation is set by the access to international organizations. All the countries under study are by now members of the Council of Europe and have applied for EU membership. Since 1995, the Czech Republic has been a member state of the OECD. However, access to the Council of Europe does not imply concrete influence on the pension system. The Social Charter of the Council of Europe – not yet ratified by all the countries under study – deals with social policy development, but signing the Charter is not a precondition for access to the Council of Europe. In this institution, much more emphasis is put on the issue of guaranteeing human rights and developing political stability (Deacon and Hulse 1997:50). Even when the Social Charter is ratified, general standards have been set without any concrete means to achieve them.

With regard to EU access, pension system reform does not require a certain system or a certain paradigm. Even now, the current EU member states have quite different pension systems. Nevertheless, there are two important factors: first the Maastricht criteria, including a budget deficit no larger than 3 per cent, which might indirectly influence decisions on social expenditures and, within this, pension expenditures. It is expected that economic developments in the applicant countries will ensure that the Maastricht criteria will soon be met.[28]

On the other hand, European politics and especially the decisions of the European court are likely to influence different aspects of future pension policy. One is the issue of sexual equality, and another is the requirement to ensure full labour mobility and make pension claims transferable. In this context, it is interesting that several countries do not plan to bring the retirement ages for men and women in the public scheme in line, although this will be a definite requirement of European social policy in the long run. The sex-differentiated retirement age seems to be an institutional rule of the socialist period which still rates highly among the population.[29] All these conditions for access do not influence the general shape of the whole system but only certain aspects, as European social policy requires no harmonization of pension schemes, no defined degree of convergence or unification of the schemes, but it does require co-ordination.[30]

The country-specific advice of different agencies is much more directly oriented towards concrete reform measures in the pension system. Country-specific advice was given in a broad span ranging from technical assistance, for example, introducing individual files for the insured, and comprehensive reform packages for the design of a multi-pillar system.

There has been much close co-operation between individual Eastern and Western European countries since the beginning of transition. Much of it can be classified as technical advice (Meierkord 1996), although from the perspective of the advising country, it is interpreted as non-ideological, demand-oriented support (Hagen 1995:198); expertise provided in training and information is often tied to the particular social security system of the supporting country.

On a more comprehensive systemic level, one can identify certain paradigmatic approaches within the different international agencies. But the 'missions' also differ according to the individual background and paradigmatic orientation of the advisers. So, for instance, ILO advice can be divided – referring to the analysis of Deacon and Hulse – into two wings (tightly connected with individuals): on the one hand a group advocating the 'citizens' income idea' and, on the other, a more conservative wing promoting the Bismarckian insurance supplemented by a means-tested social assistance system (Deacon and Hulse 1997:46).

The positions of the agencies have changed over time. The old-age security system proposed in the World Bank's *Averting the Old-age Crisis* (1994) was promoted mainly in the early years. But reforms which are currently being introduced in Latvia, Hungary and Poland with the assistance of the World Bank, do not exactly copy the approach advocated, but are in line with the World Bank's multi-pillar approach and the division of labour between the public and the private sectors. It has been pointed out that a chief adviser in pension reform from the World Bank admitted after a few years of transition that the formerly encouraged 'Chilean model' might not be the appropriate way for Central and Eastern Europe, because of their social insurance tradition. Deacon and Hulse indicated that within World Bank policy, there is substantial disagreement on the pension issue as to whether they should be flat rate or income related: 'In fact, this issue of pensions is by no means settled in the Bank' (Deacon and Hulse 1997:57).[31]

Positions and advice of the agencies differed according to the countries and were adapted to economic circumstances. In the Baltic states, for instance, the World Bank recommended flat-rate living allowances, at least for the early years, and suggested that the introduction of a mandatory second pillar be postponed until there was overall improvement and development in capital markets.

Although the different positions of, for example, the World Bank and the ILO have sometimes been seen as (and obviously are) a 'deputy battle' of paradigms in Central and Eastern Europe, there has also been co-operation between the single agencies. On the one hand, there seems to be a fundamental paradigm discourse between the World Bank and the ILO.[32] On the other, the different agencies co-operate in certain projects on a more technical level in the form of co-financing (see Fox 1996:31).

Finally, a last level of influence is that given by the conditionality of loans – here the assistance of the World Bank/IMF and the European Bank for Reconstruction and Development (EBRD) has to be mentioned. Influence on this level is subject to some criticism – the main perspective is the consolidation of state finances; social goals are less important (Standing 1996:234). There are several examples where certain recommendations of the World Bank were rejected.[33]

It is argued that the radical reforms in Poland and in Hungary are a response to their external debt, plus a higher degree of pressure from the World Bank (Müller 1999), whereas the lower external debt of the Czech Republic allowed them to choose their own approach to pension reform. Nevertheless, the Czech Republic had also discussed the introduction of a mandatory second pillar with increasing seriousness in the years 1997/98.

International influence should be analysed not only in the West–East perspective, but also between CEE countries. Transition societies witness the changes taking place in neighbouring countries, which are faced with the same problems under historically specific conditions. They profit by their neighbours' experience and learn from their mistakes. This 'transnational learning' has been observed during several phases of welfare state development and in different countries.[34] This was also the case in the implementation of social security systems in Western Europe at the beginning of this century. The 'transnational learning' or the 'wait and see' model (Abbott and DeViney 1992:268) describes policy adoption taking place in only a few countries while the others stand by and observe the success or failure of the strategy. There is no evidence that there has been direct transnational influence between the countries under study. However, the reforms and their outcome have been discussed by experts of the CEE countries as well.

4.6 CONCLUDING REMARKS: INFLUENCING FACTORS AND THEIR RELEVANCE TO THE PROCESS OF REFORMING THE SOCIAL SECURITY SYSTEM

Coming back to the competing approaches of 'legacies of the past' versus 'imperatives of liberalization' in the field of pension policy, the results of the project 'Transformation of pension systems in Central and Eastern Europe' show that both aspects have an influence on future pension arrangements. While the current pension system can be interpreted as an important legacy and is the main reason why Eastern European pension systems differ remarkably from the choices made in Latin America in the 1980s, the 'imperative of liberalism' has an important influence on the future pension system, too, and will probably result in CEE pension systems orienting themselves more on insurance principles than the traditional 'Bismarckian' system ever has.

NOTES

1 See Pierson (1995).
2 An overview is given in Schmähl (1981).
3 Cf., for example, Müller (1997) and Cangiano et al. (1998) for pension reform, Blejer and Coricelli (1995) for economic reform in general and focusing on the background individual political actors by interviewing Balcerowicz, Bod and Klaus.
4 This distinction of external political influence follows Hoffer (1998).
5 See Chapter 2, section 2.2.
6 The connection between poverty and old age in Central and Eastern Europe also has historic roots: in the socialist era with social policy mainly targeted on people of working age so that poverty was mainly a pensioners' phenomenon. The poverty discourse in transition therefore also concentrated mainly on the income situation of pensioners (Götting 1998:211).
7 For an early assessment of the possibilities of private funds in Central and Eastern Europe, see Holzmann (1994).
8 See for example Chapter 5, in this volume.
9 On the shape of the pension formula in Lithuania, see Chapter 7, in this volume.
10 Cf. Chapter 2, section 2.3.
11 For empirical evidence, see World Bank (1994).
12 See Chapter 2, section 2.3.
13 See Chapter 2, section 2.4.

14 The international discussion on the interaction between demography and the labour market is summarized in Schmähl (1989), and Beattie and McGillivray (1995).
15 There is a long-lasting discussion of demographic impacts on different ways of financing pensions and so on. For an overview for transition economies, see Schmähl (1994). An ageing population with capital-funded pensions may experience an excess supply of funds in periods when more pensioners will dissave by selling assets than younger cohorts plan to invest. This is why the introduction of partly funded pensions may also lead to lower pension payments when the population is ageing. In this respect, demographic developments (or demographic risks) are not disconnected with risks of the capital markets, although this risk-sharing is often used as an argument for introducing a partly funded pension system. This depends, however, on many internal and external factors, especially the absolute amount of capital-funded pensions and its relative weight in the economy as well as in the capital market. This is discussed in more detail in Schmähl (2000).
16 Cf., for example, Chapters 8 and 10, in this volume.
17 For the political economy of transformation in general, see Rosati (1992), Williamson (ed.) (1994), Rodrik (1996) and Balcerowicz (1996).
18 See Chapter 7, in this volume.
19 Cf Chapters 5, 6 and 7, in this volume.
20 See, for example, Chapter 5, in this volume.
21 See the description of administrative reforms and financing in the Slovak Republic and in Poland in Chapters 10 and 8, in this volume.
22 See the discussion in Chapters 9 and 10, in this volume.
23 In this context, even the new Latvian system which introduced a strong link between benefits and contributions by a so-called contribution defined system had to struggle with its political consequences. When the new law came into force and led to enormous differentiation in the pension payments, the government introduced a new category of 'part of the pension paid out' – in other words, they once more introduced an upper pension limit restricting income differentiation (see Chapter 6, in this volume).
24 Cf. for the Polish situation Golinowska (1999:18), for Hungary, Chapter 11, in this volume and as an example for an influential economist in Hungary, Kornai (1996).
25 See the critical review of pension reform by Wolekova (1996).
26 Cf. for the history of social security in Central and Eastern Europe in detail, Chapter 2, section 2.4.
27 In their research on international agencies and their influence on social policy reform in CEE countries, Deacon and Hulse (1997) distinguish between implicit and explicit social policy advice.
28 Cf. 'Are the acceding countries ready', *Transition*, April 1998, 13–14.
29 An indicator is, for example, the initial resistance against the rise in the retirement age in Estonia, which was, however, adopted later on in 1998, and the reintroduction of exceptional rules for lower retirement ages in Latvia.
30 Cf. Schmähl (1993), Jorens and Schulte (1999).
31 This also becomes obvious when comparing the two World Bank publications *Averting the Old-age Crisis* (1994) and the book edited by Nicholas Barr (1994).
32 See the World Bank publication *Averting the Old-age Crisis* (1994) and the critical review of it by the ILO (Beattie and McGillivray 1995).
33 See, for example, Chapter 7, in this volume.
34 For the Nordic countries, see Kuhnle (1987) and for an even broader perspective on various countries and the introduction of social security systems, see Abbott and DeViney (1992).

REFERENCES

Abbott, A. and DeViney, S. (1992), 'The welfare state as transnational event: evidence from sequences of policy adoption', *Social Science History*, 16 (2), 245–74.

Andrews, E.S. and Rashid, M. (1996), 'The financing of pension systems in Central and Eastern Europe', World Bank Technical Paper No. 339, Washington.

Balcerowicz, L. (1996), 'Socialism, Capitalism, Transformation', Budapest, London, New York: Central European University Press.

Barr, N. (ed.) (1994), *Labour Markets and Social Policy in Central and Eastern Europe. The Transition and Beyond*, Washington, DC: Oxford University Press.

Beattie, R. and McGillivray, W. (1995), 'A risky strategy: reflections on the World Bank report *Averting the Old-age Crisis*', *International Social Security Review*, 3–4, 5–22.

Blejer, M.I. and Coricelli, F. (1995), *The Making of Economic Reform in Eastern Europe*, Aldershot: Edward Elgar.

Breyer, F. and Stolte, K. (1999), 'The political feasibility of pension reform in the light of demographic change', in K. Müller, A. Ryll and H.-J. Wagener (eds), *Transformation of Social Security: Pensions in Central-Eastern Europe*, Heidelberg/New York: Physica, 79–90.

Cangiano, M., Cottarelli, C. and Cubeddu, L. (1998), 'Pension developments and reform in transition economies', Paper prepared for the conference on 'Social security reforms: international comparisons', Rome, 16/17 March, draft.

Crawford, B. and Lijphart, A. (1995), 'Explaining political and economic change in post-communist Eastern Europe', *Comparative Political Studies*, 28 (2), 171–99.

Deacon, B. and Hulse, M. (1994), 'The Council of Europe, the European Union, the OECD, the World Bank and the shaping of East-European social policy: a case of varying advice and varying intervention', Paper presented at the third Prague international workshop on social responses to transformation in East-Central Europe, Prague, 6–8 May.

Deacon, B. and Hulse, M. (1997), 'The making of post-communist social policy: the role of international agencies', *Journal of Social Policy*, 26 (1), 43–62.

Eichenhofer, E. (1995), 'Deutsche und österreichische Einflüsse auf die Sozialgesetzgebung in Ost- und Südosteuropa' (German and Austrian influences on social security legislation in East and South-East Europe), *Sozialer Fortschritt*, 8/9, 189–93.

Esping-Andersen, G. (1990), *The Three Worlds of Welfare Capitalism*, Princeton: Princeton University Press.

Ferge, Z. (1999), 'The politics of the Hungarian pension reform', in K. Müller, A. Ryll and Wagener, H.-J. (eds), *Transformation of Social Security: Pensions in Central-Eastern Europe*, Heidelberg/New York: Physica, 231–46.

Fox, L. (1996), 'Principles and goals of consultancy work in CEE states – the standpoint of the World Bank', in Jürgen Schramm (ed.), *Developing a System oj Social Security within a Market Economy*, Baden-Baden: Nomos, 29–41.

Golinowska, S. (1999), 'Political actors and reform paradigms in old age security in Poland', in K. Müller, A. Ryll and Wagener, H.-J. (eds), *Transformation of Social Security: Pensions in Central-Eastern Europe*, Heidelberg/New York: Physica, pp. 173–99.

Götting, U. (1998), *Transformation von Wohlfahrtsstaaten in Mittel- und Osteuropa. Eine Zwischenbilanz* (Transformation of welfare states in Central and Eastern Europe. An interim assessment), Opladen: Leske und Budrich.

Hagen, E. (1995), 'Beratungstätigkeit des Bundesministeriums für Arbeit und Sozialordnung in mittel- und osteuropäischen Ländern – Erfahrungen und Eindrücke' (Consulting activities of the Federal Ministry of Labour and Social Order in Central and Eastern European countries – experiences and impressions), *Sozialer Fortschritt*, 8–9, 198–200.

Hinrichs, K. (1993)'Public pensions and demographic change: Generational Equity in the United States and Germany', Working Paper 16/1993, Centre for Social Policy Research, University of Bremen, Bremen.

Hoffer, F. (1998), 'Modernisierung sozialer Sicherheit in Rußland – einige methodische Überlegungen' (Modernization of social security in Russia – some methodological reflections), *Zeitschrift für internationales und ausländisches Sozialrecht*, 1, 29–45.

Holzmann, R. (1994), 'Funded and private pensions for Eastern European countries in transition?', *Revista de Analisis Economico*, 9, 183–210.

Jorens, Y. and Schulte, B. (eds) (1999), *Coordination of Social Security Schemes in Connection with the Accession of Central and Eastern European States*, Brussels: Die Keure, La Charte.

Kornai, J. (1996), 'The citizen and the state', Discussion Paper No. 32, Collegium Budapest, Institute for Advanced Studies, Budapest.

Kuhnle, S. (1987), 'The growth of social insurance programs in Scandinavia: outside influences and internal factors', in P. Flora and A.J. Heidenheimer (eds), *The Development of Welfare States in Europe and America*, New Brunswick/London: Transaction Books.

Leibfried, S. (1992), 'Towards a European welfare state?' in Z. Ferge and J.E. Kolberg (eds), *Social Policy in a Changing Europe*, Frankfurt, New York: Campus.

Lessenich, S. (1994) '"Three worlds of welfare capitalism" – oder vier? Strukturwandel arbeits- und sozialpolitischer Regulierungsmuster in Spanien' (- or four? Structural change in labour market and social policy regulation patterns in Spain), *Politische Vierteljahreszeitschrift*, 35, 224–44.

Lewis, J. and Ostner, I. (1994), 'Gender and the evolution of European social policies', ZeS-Working Paper 4, Bremen.

Meierkord, J. (1996), 'Supporting pension insurance institutions through technical assistance', in J. Schramm (ed.), *Developing a System of Social Securtiy within a Market Economy*, Baden-Baden: Nomos.

Müller, K. (1997), 'The "New Pension Orthodoxy" and beyond: transforming old age security in Central-Eastern Europe', Frankfurter Institut für Transformationsstudien, Discussion Paper 16, Frankfurt/Oder.

Müller, K. (1999), 'Changing the public–private mix: Central-Eastern European pension reforms', in K. Müller, A. Ryll and H.J. Wagener (eds), *Transformation of Social Security: Pensions in Central-Eastern Europe*, Heidelberg/New York: Physica, pp. 291–305.

Nullmeyer, F. and Rüb, F.W. (1993), *Die Transformation der Sozialpolitik. Vom Sozialstaat zum Sicherungsstaat* (Transformation of social policy. From social state to security state), Frankfurt, New York: Campus.

Oks, D.F. (1998), 'Accession to the EU – A reform and growth strategy for Poland', *Transition*, April, 9–11.

Pierson, P. (1995) 'The new politics of the welfare state', Working Paper 3/1995, Centre for Social Policy Research, University of Bremen, Bremen.
Rodrik, D. (1996), 'Understanding economic policy reform', *Journal of Economic Literature*, 34, 9–41.
Rosati, D.K. (1992), 'The politics of economic reform in Central and Eastern Europe', CEPR Occasional Paper No. 6, London.
Schmähl, W. (1981), *Sozialausgaben, Handwörterbuch der Wirtschaftswissenschaft* (Social expenditures, Concise Dictionary of Economics), Stuttgart: G. Fischer, pp. 562–603.
Schmähl, W. (1989), 'Labour force participation and social pension systems', in P. Johnson and D. Thomson (eds), *Workers versus Pensioners: Intergenerational Justice in an Ageing World*, Manchester/New York: St. Martin's Press, 137–61.
Schmähl, W. (1993), 'Harmonization of pension schemes in Europe?', in A.B. Atkinson and M. Rein (eds), *Age, Work and Social Security*, New York: St. Martin's Press, 308–40.
Schmähl, W. (1994), 'Fundamental issues of financing of social security with respect to the transformation of former socialist economies', in B. von Maydell and E.M. Hohnerlein (eds), *The Transformation of Social Security Systems in Central and Eastern Europe*, Leuven: Peeters Press, 285–325.
Schmähl, W. (1996), 'Umgestaltung und Ausgliederung von sozialen Einrichtungen und Sozialleistungen der Betriebe' (Transformation and outsourcing of social activities and social expenditure), in B. von Maydell et al., *Die Umwandlung der Arbeits- und Sozialordnung*, Opladen: Leske und Budrich, pp. 383–401.
Schmähl, W. (2000), 'Pay-as-you-go versus capital funding: towards a more balanced view in pension policy', in G. Hughes and J. Stewart (eds), *Pensions in the European Union: Adapting to Economic and Social Change*, Boston/Dordrecht/London: Kluwer Academic Publishers, pp. 195–208.
Schmidt, M.G. (1999a), 'Warum die Gesundheitsausgaben wachsen. Befunde des Vergleichs demokratisch verfasster Länder' (Why health expenditures grow. Results of comparing democratic states), *Politische Vierteljahresschrift* 40, 229–45.
Schmidt, M. (1999b), 'Grundzüge der Sozialpolitik in der DDR' (General issues of social policy in the GDR); in E. Kurth, H.F. Buck and G. Holzweißig (eds), *Die Endzeit der DDR Wirtschaft*, Vol. 4, Opladen: Leske und Budrich, 273–319.
Standing, G. (1996), 'Social protection in Central and Eastern Europe: a tale of slipping anchors and torn safety nets', in G. Esping-Andersen (ed.), *Welfare States in Transition. National Adaptations in Global Economies*, London: Sage, 225–55.
Williamson, J. (ed.) (1994), *The Political Economy of Policy Reform*, Washington, DC: Institute for International Economics.
Wolekova, H. (1996), 'Sozialpolitik in der Slowakei nach 1989' (Social Policy in the Slovak Republic after 1989), *Südosteuropa*, 3, 219–31.
World Bank (1994), *Averting the Old-age Crisis*, Washington, DC: World Bank.
Zukowski, M. (1994), 'Mindestsicherung in Polen' (Minimum protection in Poland), in International Social Security Association (ISSA) (ed.), *Umstrukturierung der sozialen Sicherheit in Mittel- und Osteuropa. Trends – Politiken – Optionen*, Geneva: ISSA.
Zukowski, M. (1995), 'Das Alterssicherungssystem in Polen – Geschichte, gegenwärtige Lage, Umgestaltung' (Old-age security system in Poland – history, present situation, transformation), ZeS-Working Paper 8, Bremen.

PART II
Country Reports

5. Transformation of old-age security in Estonia

Lauri Leppik and Georg Männik

5.1 GENERAL DEVELOPMENT AND FRAMEWORK

5.1.1 General Political Background in 1989

In 1989, Estonia was still de facto a part of the Soviet Union as one of the Soviet republics. Formally, the Estonian Soviet Socialist Republic had its own ruling bodies: a Supreme Council, perfunctorily freely elected, and a government, which made laws and decisions. In reality, all legislation was formulated in Moscow by the strategists of the Communist Party and the officials of central ministries. The republics could make only contextual changes, such as changing the words 'Soviet Union' to 'Soviet Estonia'. Policy issues could not be changed. Among others, fiscal policy, budgeting and banking were directly influenced by the budget and the State Bank of the Soviet Union.

The year 1989 was politically quite critical both in the Soviet Union as well as in Estonia. Changes in international politics, for example, the reunification of Germany, also influenced quite clearly the attitude of the central government of the Soviet Union towards the republics. The strive for independence had started in 1987 with the aim of economic independence and self-sustainability for Estonia. Henceforth the republics could make their own arrangements about internal socioeconomic matters, and the remaining links with Moscow would be mainly political. In 1988, following a congress of creative and liberal arts professionals, the idea of economic and political independence also became widely discussed. Among the main reforms, which had been started by 1989, was the legalization of private enterprises. Small enterprises, especially in the fields of production (so-called 'co-operative units') and services, were even encouraged. As transition variants, economically self-sustainable public or state enterprises were advocated. Furthermore, under the Soviet Law on Economic Autonomy of 1989, the idea of self-sustainable economic areas received growing support.

The area of social policy was more problematical. In the Soviet Union, social policy had always been used as an instrument of (Communist) party policy. Therefore, the bases of social policy decisions had always been political ideas and values, not social or economic realities. It became clear that provision for social areas and problems considered the responsibility of the state far exceeded the available resources. At the same time lifestyles in Estonia started to change visibly. Individualism became more apparent in the population at large. This contrasted sharply with the Communist Party, which was still oriented towards collectivist solutions. This conflict manifested in situations in which publicly many people were still talking about communist collectivist ideals, while privately very few truly believed in the reality of living according to these ideals. By 1989, Moscow realized that the existing system of social protection needed changes, including the pension system. As part of the glasnost campaign announced by Gorbachev, the draft of a new pension law was published.

5.1.2 Starting-point of the Pension System in 1989

The pension system in the Soviet Union had been regulated by two legislative acts. Most people (for example, all employed persons, servants, military personnel, students and so on) were covered by the Soviet Union Law on State Pensions passed in 1956. For the *kolhoz* (collective farm) members there had been a separate scheme regulated since 1964 by the Law on Kolhoz Members' Pensions. The system resembled that of many other countries by having two schemes, one for the workers and one for the farmers. The general pension scheme offered protection against old age, invalidity and loss of the breadwinner. Differential treatment of men and women in the pension system was considered normal and justified. The retirement age for men was 60 and for women 55, and the qualification period 25 and 20 years, respectively. Women who had given birth to five or more children were entitled to retire five years earlier. Pensions were determined according to a fixed scale, indicating the percentage of the final wage (either the average of the last year or of five consecutive years from the last ten years). The percentage (replacement rate) varied with the income ranging from 100 per cent for low-income earners down to 50 per cent for higher-income earners.[1] Thus, the formula for the calculation of pension payments was clearly redistributive from higher-income to lower-income earners. Also, in general, in spite of the link to final income, pensions under the Soviet system were in practice more a kind of award than deferred earnings, as multiple social and political objectives imposed on the pension system made the (re)distribution mechanisms of the system quite complex.

Those, for example, who had uninterrupted length of service, were entitled to a pension supplement of 10 per cent.

According to the law, several categories of persons were entitled to receive an old-age pension on more favourable conditions. These favourable conditions were granted to people who had been employed in difficult or hazardous working conditions. Categories of these jobs were determined by lists approved by the Council of Ministers. In essence, this meant early retirement. Those who had been working under such conditions could retire ten years earlier: women at the age of 45, and men at 50. Another list approved by the Council of Ministers specified categories eligible for super-annuated pensions, such as the militia, aircraft personnel, seamen, artistes (for example, ballet dancers) and so on. Generally, pensions were not taxable.

As to the financing of the pension system, the Preamble of the Pension Law of 1956 stated that 'pension insurance in the Soviet state is implemented fully on account of state and collective revenues'. In practice, this meant that the scheme was financed directly from the state budget. Although all enterprises and organizations paid so-called social tax to the general state budget, there was no clear link between revenues from social tax and expenditures for pensions. Social tax was calculated on the payroll and the rate varied (for example, seven per cent on servants' wages; 18 per cent on workers' wages).

Rules applying to two rather similar categories (that is, agricultural workers and collective farmers) were, however, different. For agricultural workers, the general rules were applied for calculation of pensions, while the rate of social tax on this category was 4.4 per cent of the payroll. However, for collective farmers, a separate law (mentioned above) was in force. According to this law, all collective farmers paid 2.4 per cent of their annual income to a special centralized social welfare fund for *kolhoz* members. In addition, a special payroll tax at the rate of 4.1 per cent of the collective farmers' gross wage was imposed. Their pensions were considerably lower than the state pensions. As of 1989, collective farmers could transfer from the *kolhoz* members' scheme to the general state scheme.

The Law on State Pensions from 1956 took account neither of the possible effect of inflation, nor of the ageing population. According to the official ideology, inflation did not exist in the Soviet Union. In reality, this meant that pensions lost their real value. The Soviet system took pride in extending social rights and, accordingly, there was an increase in the number of categories of persons eligible for early retirement.

5.1.3 General Economic Conditions 1989–98

Expanding economic autonomy in the Soviet Union at the end of 1980s created a situation whereby the existing policy failed because of conflict between needs and possibilities. The Soviet state was practically incapable of steering economic policy: determining the budget was impossible, economic output decreased, and inflation increased rapidly. These conflicts culminated in the coup of August 1991, which gave the Baltic states an opportunity to claim political independence. The economic development in Estonia can be subdivided into three periods: from 1989 to mid-1992, the period of the 'rouble zone'; from 1992 to 1994, the period of radical reforms; and from 1995 onwards, the period of economic stabilization and growth.

During the first period – the last years of the Soviet Union (1989–91) and the first years of newfound independence for Estonia (1991–92) – there were serious economic difficulties. Since the Estonian economy had formed a part of the economy of the Soviet Union, the economic crisis in Russia caused failure of enterprises in Estonia. The liberalization of formerly regulated and largely subsidized prices began in 1990. This, however, further contributed to the process of inflation. High inflation created a situation of a deficit of banknotes. For a certain period, an abnormal situation persisted in which in essence there were two different currencies in use – bank account money and cash, of which cash was considered to be more valuable. As a result, bank transfers were often delayed for more than a month, which caused delays of pension payments, amongst others.

After regaining its independence, Estonia chose a radical approach to economic reconstruction. The cornerstones of economic reform have been a currency principle, a liberal trade policy, a balanced budget with low national indebtedness, and far-reaching privatization.

In June 1992 Estonian currency, the kroon, was introduced, and this marked the end of the 'rouble zone'. The Estonian kroon was fixed to the German mark at a constant rate of eight Estonian kroons to one German mark. The currency reform radically changed the economic situation in the country. Inflation as high as 1,100 per cent in 1992 dropped to 90 per cent in 1993.

Privatization, ownership reform and land reform initiated in 1992 was also taking place at this time. This was the start of a period of dramatic economic reconstruction, which lasted until 1994. Gross domestic product (GDP) declined as the Estonian economy reach its lowest point. On the one side two of the main structural changes in GDP were the rapid decline in the share of industrial and agricultural production and the growing share of the service sector. On the other side, the share of wages and private consumption increased substantially.

Basic macroeconomic indicators for the current period of economic development show optimistic trends. The year 1995 marked the first year of economic growth with annual GDP growth at 4.3 per cent. GDP growth at 4.0 per cent continued in 1996 and reached an exceptionally high level of 10.6 per cent in 1997. Several factors have contributed to the cooling down of the economy. The annual rate of inflation has been steadily declining from 15 per cent in December 1996 compared to December 1995, down to 11 per cent in December 1997 compared to December 1996 and further down to 8.2 per cent in 1998. The unemployment rate, although growing over the last few years, is still relatively low.

Less positive economic developments are the uneven regional development and the growing deficit in the foreign trade balance. The last problem in particular has been stressed by the international monetary organizations, such as the IMF and the World Bank. The government was thereupon called to continue prudent fiscal policy by limiting expenditures to available resources or preferably even to a general surplus in the public budget. The state budget of 1998 was adopted with a surplus. This surplus has been stockpiled into a stabilization fund, which in 1998 exceeded two per cent of GDP. The IMF and the World Bank have also both advocated the introduction of a pension system with funded components with the purpose, among others, of generating national savings.

5.1.4 Demographic and Social Background

The number of pensioners in Estonia had been growing steadily since 1956. This was a result of two main factors: the maturation of the system – more people became eligible by fulfilling the qualification period; and an increase in life expectancy in a situation where the retirement age had not been changed for almost 40 years. The growth in the number of pensioners continued until 1993, when the number of pensioners was at its highest. In 1991, primarily as a result of migration and the number of deaths exceeding the number of births, the population began to decline.

The three-year time lag between the trend changes in the total population and the number of pensioners raised the percentage of pensioners in the total population to a new level in 1993. The decrease in the number of pensioners in 1994–96 has prevented this percentage from increasing further (see Tables 5.1 and 5.2).

When we the developments of the old-age and system dependency ratios we can observe that while the old-age dependency ratio has been relatively stable since 1994 – mainly as a result of an increase in the pension age – the system dependency ratio has increased steadily. Although the number of

Table 5.1 *Total population, the economically active and pensioners, (in thousands), Estonia, 1990–97*

Year	1990	1991	1992	1993	1994	1995	1996	1997
Total population	1,572	1,571	1,562	1,527	1,507	1,492	1,476	1,462
Economically active	823	802	760	708	692	656	646	n.a.
Pensioners	361	368	374	383	383	376	374	371

Source: Estonian Statistical Office.

Table 5.2 *Persons over age 60, old-age pensioners and all pensioners in total population, Estonia, 1990–97 (%)*

Year	1990	1991	1992	1993	1994	1995	1996	1997
Persons 60+	17.0	17.3	17.6	18.1	18.3	18.5	18.8	19.1
Old-age pensioners	18.7	19.2	19.7	20.6	21.0	20.7	20.5	20.3
All pensioners	22.9	23.4	24.0	25.1	25.4	25.2	25.4	25.3

Note: The number of old-age pensioners includes those receiving superannuated pensions and national pensions.
Source: Estonian Statistical Office.

Figure 5.1 *Old-age and system dependency ratios, Estonia, 1992–97*

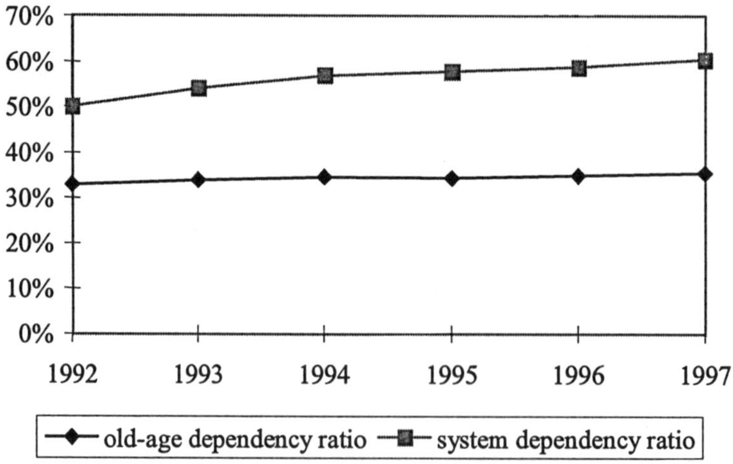

Note: Old-age dependency ratio: (60+/20–59) in per cent; system dependency ratio: (pensioners/contributors) in per cent.
Source: Estonian National Social Insurance Board.

pensioners has declined, the number of insured employees has declined even more rapidly (see Figure 5.1).

Among the general public, the lower life expectancy during the years of transition has been one of the main arguments against the option of raising the pension age. Quite often in newspaper articles it is argued that if pension age is continuously raised, men will not be able to enjoy retirement at all. Indeed, the years of transition witnessed a dramatic drop in life expectancy at birth, especially among men. Also, the difference of 11 years between the life expectancy of men and women at birth is striking.

However, the development of life expectancy at ages 60 and 65 show a different pattern. The average life expectancy at ages 60 and 65 in 1997 was higher than in 1990, and is showing an increasing trend. By the age of 65, the difference between the life expectancy of men and women has fallen to four years (see Table 5.3).

Table 5.3 Life expectancy, Estonia, 1990–97

Year	1990	1991	1992	1993	1994	1995	1996	1997
At birth								
Men	64.6	64.4	63.5	62.5	61.1	61.7	64.5	64.7
Women	74.6	74.8	74.7	73.8	73.1	74.3	75.5	76.0
Total	69.7	69.7	69.1	68.2	67.0	67.9	70.0	70.4
At 60								
Men	14.8	15.0	14.6	14.2	14.1	14.5	14.8	15.2
Women	19.4	19.6	19.8	19.3	19.3	19.9	20.1	20.6
Total	17.6	17.8	17.6	17.3	17.2	17.7	17.8	18.5
At 65								
Men	12.0	12.3	11.9	11.7	11.7	12.0	12.2	12.6
Women	15.6	15.8	16.0	15.6	15.6	16.1	16.2	16.8
Total	14.3	14.5	14.4	14.1	14.1	14.6	14.6	15.2

Source: Estonian Statistical Office.

5.1.5 Labour Market Developments

During the years of transition, the labour market has been one of the most dynamic spheres of the economy. As we know, the socialist economic system was characterized by apparent full employment. Under a market economy, many jobs were deemed both inefficient and unnecessary (Marksoo 1996). The rapid reorientation of the economy required a high degree of labour mobility. Between 1992 and 1994 – the years of most rapid changes – an estimated 300,000 out of the total labour force changed jobs (World Bank

1996). According to the 1989 census of Estonia, over 838,000 (53.5 per cent) of the total population were gainfully employed (Marksoo 1996). By 1994, the number had decreased to 693,000 (that is, a difference of 145,000 persons) or 46 per cent of the total population.

The decline in employment did not, however, translate entirely into unemployment because the size of the labour force also shrank, owing to emigration to Russia, the increased employment of Estonian citizens abroad, and a decline in labour force participation, that is an increase in the number of those who are non-active (World Bank 1996). Even with the significant reduction over recent years, the employment level in Estonia is still quite high compared to many Western European countries, especially with respect to employment of women who are 35–54 years of age. According to the 1989 census, 29.4 per cent of pensioners were working. After the introduction of the economic reforms, these elderly workers were among the first to be dismissed. The number of workers who have passed retirement age continues to decline. However, it is estimated that close to 40 per cent of pensioners work during the first five years after retirement. The strained financial circumstances of the elderly obviously forces them to seek additional sources of income (Marksoo 1996). While the number of employed persons has decreased, the number of employers has steadily increased. This can be illustrated by the growth in the number of employers affiliated to the pension insurance system.[2] This demonstrates the growth of small and medium-sized enterprises to replace the previous big state-owned enterprises. Another new development for the Estonian labour market after regaining its independence was the emergence and subsequent growth of self-employment (Leppik 1997). Self-employment was virtually non-existent during the Soviet period. This was an aspect where the Baltic states differed from the former socialist countries of Eastern Europe, which did have self-employment during the socialist period.[3]

5.1.6 Pension System Development up to 1998

National legislation in the field of social law was started in March 1990 following the decision of the Supreme Council on the status of Estonia, even before formal independence was regained in August 1990. Since legislation had been under Soviet control in Moscow nobody in Estonia had been responsible for social security issues which meant that there was no local expertise. As with other areas of social science, there was no academic training in the field of social security. To exacerbate the situation, lawyers in the field of social security were trained to implement pension law, but not to develop new legislation. This was against the background of a history of political censorship which did not allow for criticism of the system and thus deterred any dialogue regarding an alternative pension system. This led to the bizarre situation in which, given the chance to develop a legal framework for a new pension system, but lacking expertise and know-how, the new Soviet pension law was translated into the Estonian language and the Ministry of Social Welfare took this as a base for its reform. To take this oddity one step further, the prime minister ordered that no paragraph of the new pension law should be a copy of the text of the Soviet pension law. However, when we look at the final result, the ideology behind the new Estonian pension law was still quite close to that of the new Soviet law. Despite doubts of local and foreign experts about the possibilities of implementing the new pension law because there had been no cost estimates, the law was adopted in April 1991, to be implemented on 1 January 1992.

Problems soon arose. Tax collections fell short of expectations. Monetary flows were disrupted as many financial operations by companies were made in cash, avoiding the banks. Subsequently pension payments arrived late because of the irregularity of monetary flows and the low level of computerization. There was also increased dissatisfaction with the system by pensioners. For example, according to the new law, pensioners had to provide additional documents to establish extra claims and therefore long queues formed in social affairs offices.

In December 1992, parliament suspended the new pension law, and introduced temporary flat-rate living allowances, promising to restore the Pension Law three months after the introduction of Estonian national currency. As it turned out this promise was impossible to implement. Flat-rate benefits facilitated administration, the calculations were easier to make and payments easier to arrange. To compensate for the high inflation, benefits were increased three times.

By the end of 1992, the system of payment of flat-rate benefits, which had been struggling with problems for some time, worked quite smoothly. The question was whether the Pension Law of April 1991 should be restored, or whether a new law should be developed. The National Social Insurance Board prepared the draft for a new law which was presented to parliament in February 1993 for consideration. Under public pressure to end the system of flat-rate benefits, parliament adopted the law in March.

Since then, the Law on State Allowances has been the primary legal instrument regulating the state pension system. Several amendments have followed, changing some of the elements but not the basic nature of the scheme. Finally in 1998, a legal framework for a new pension system was enacted.

5.2 LEGAL AND ADMINISTRATIVE CHANGES AND QUANTITATIVE DEVELOPMENTS

5.2.1 Legal Changes, 1989–97

As part of the development of national legislation the area of social law was also established, of which the Pension Law of the Estonian Republic of 15 April 1991 was a component.

This law did not change the retirement age and required qualification periods but it did change the pension formula and the principles of determination of pensionable length of service. Non-contributory periods (that is, the periods equated with employment) were extended: the time spent studying at professional schools and institutions of higher education, military service, periods of raising children and so on, were considered as pensionable service. The basic old-age pension was calculated as 60 per cent of the minimum wage, supplemented by an earnings-related component amounting to 40 per cent of the average personal wage during the reference period. In February 1992 this pension law was superseded by the Resolution of the Estonian Supreme Council on the Establishment of State Living Allowances.

At the beginning of 1992, Estonia witnessed a government crisis, and in April a 'transition government' was formed. Regular elections were scheduled for autumn 1992. The task of the 'transition government' was to stabilize (both politically and economically) the situation and to bring about currency reform.

The Law on State Allowances came into force on 1 April 1993. It regulates four types of pensions: old-age, invalidity, survivors' and national. Some of the older citizens and some politicians argue that the use of the term 'state allowances' indicates that a true 'Pension Law' is still needed.

An essential change made was a decision to raise the retirement age by six months each year until it reached 65 for men and 60 for women in 2003. During discussions it was suggested that the retirement age for men and women be standardized at the age of 65. The draft presented to parliament also included raising the level to 65/65, but put to the vote, female politicians succeeded in changing the scale to 65/60. Old-age pensions were linked to the minimum wage, and the main individual variable depended on the length of service.

The formula used to calculate the amount of old-age pension was the following:

$$P = 0.85\,MW + E * \alpha(E) * MW,$$

where

MW is the minimum wage,
E is the employment period,
α is a coefficient, which is a function of *E* (see Table 5.5).

National pensions were introduced for persons with a length of service less than 15 years and payment levels were set at 85 per cent of the minimum wage. Age criteria for the national pension were established at 65 years for men and 60 for women, that is, the retirement age for a national pension was higher than for a normal old-age pension. However, as the general pension age is being increased, the age criteria for an old-age pension and a national pension will eventually be the same.

Earnings could add up to pensions only if the earnings were below the minimum wage. Since 1 April 1994 pensions have been increased by increasing the coefficients for the length of service. Since 1 July 1994 pensions are no longer calculated based on the minimum wage but according to the national pension payment levels. The main reason for this change was make the system more flexible – that is, to allow an increase in pensions without changing the minimum wage and vice versa. The amount of the national pension was to be fixed by parliament for each fiscal year, while the new amount of a national pension could not be less than that of the previous year. As of 1 July 1994 the basic pension was set at the level of 300 Estonian crowns (EEK) and earnings could add up to pensions only if the monthly earnings were below the level of the national pension.[4]

From 1 September 1995, a new concept of a national pension rate (NPR) was introduced, as a basis for calculating old-age pensions. This meant that old-age pensions were no longer linked to national pensions, but to a fixed sum, the NPR. The national pensions themselves were calculated as 110 per cent of the NPR. Lastly, the coefficients for the length of service were further increased on 1 September 1995, on 1 January 1996 and on 1 April 1996.

In March 1996, the Minister of Social Affairs, representing the liberal Reform Party and supported by parliament, initiated the use of pension capital revenues from the social insurance budget to allow for the amalgamation of pension and earnings of old-age pensioners, and to pay full pensions to working pensioners. This plan was implemented in two steps. As of 1 April 1996 the pensions of men over 65 and women over 60 were fully amalgamated with earnings, but restrictions applied to old-age pensioners, that is, men below the age of 65 and women below the age of 60. Pensions could be amalgamated with earnings only if monthly earnings were less than the NPR (that is,.EEK 410). From 1 September 1996, pensions could be fully amalgamated with earnings without any age restrictions.

Starting on 1 April 1996, the scale determining the retirement age in a given year was modified. This was to remove social injustice caused by the previous scale between those born in the first half of the year and those born in the second half. However, the change in the retirement age of 65 years for men and 60 years for women, respectively, was delayed from 2003 to 2007. Pension payments were further increased on 1 January and 1 November 1997 and 1 March 1998 by increasing the coefficients for the length of service. Table 5.4 summarizes the important legislative acts in the state pension system from 1991 to 1997.

Table 5.4 Main legal changes of the state pension system, Estonia, 1991–96

Legislative acts	Date of adoption	Main features
Pension Law of the Republic of Estonia	15.04.1991	Modification of the new pension law. Universal coverage; pensions linked to minimum wage
Resolution on State Allowances	01.02.1992	Flat-rate benefits
Law on State Allowances (LSA)	01.04.1993	Flat-rate basis, length of service; increasing pension age; politically motivated supplements
Amendment to the LSA	01.07.1994	Pensions no longer linked to minimum wage; balance of resources secured
Amendment to the LSA	01.09.1996	Full amalgamation of pensions with earnings

5.2.2 The Pension System as of 1998

The main legislative act regulating the state pension insurance system is still the Law on State Allowances with its later amendments. It defines a compulsory general scheme covering all categories of economically active persons. However, in essence the scheme has two levels. The 'zero level' of national pensions replaces the normal old-age pension for those with a length of service less than 15 years and provides flat-rate basic protection on the basis of residence.

The retirement age in 1998 was 62 years for men and 57 years for women. The qualification period for an old-age pension is 15 years of pensionable service in Estonia. There is no general provision for early retirement. The old-age pension depends currently on two factors: the NPR and the length of service (employment or equivalent activity). It is calculated according to the following formula:

$$P = B + E * \alpha(E) * B$$

where

B is the basic amount (NPR),
E is the employment period (pensionable length of service) and
α is a coefficient, which is a function of E.

Table 5.5 *Pensionable length of service and respective coefficients, Estonia*

Length of service	α
15–29 years	0.047
30–39 years	0.048
over 40 years	0.049

There is a slight progression in the length of service component of the pension, which makes the longer service record more beneficial. According to the formula, the amount of pension for a person with 42 years of employment (which is the average for men in Estonia) would be

$$P = 410 + (42 * 4.9/100 *410) = \text{EEK } 1{,}254.$$

When defining the pensionable length of service, the following periods are equated with employment:

- working as a family member of a self-employed person,
- military service,
- studying at an institution of higher education or in a professional school,
- caring for a severely disabled adult family member or a disabled child,
- caring for a child during the first two years,
- periods of registered unemployment,
- membership of liberal art associations or professional societies,
- serving a congregation of a registered religious organization,
- periods of unlawful repression count threefold.

All permanent residents of Estonia with a service record of 15 years are entitled to a national pension at the age of 60 for women and 65 for men. National pension payments in 1998 amounted to 160 per cent of NPR. Invalidity pensions are available to all permanent residents of Estonia following the expiry of sickness benefits and medical determination of invalidity. There is no qualification period. Invalidity pensions are paid at three different rates depending on the degree of disability: 245 per cent, 205 per cent or 160 per cent of NPR. Survivors' pensions are also calculated as a percentage of NPR. For a dependent adult (at retirement age or disabled) the survivors' pension is 175 per cent of NPR. For dependent minors, the survivors' pension is 165 per cent of NPR. The NPR is determined by parliament each year. There is no automatic adjustment mechanism or indexation of pensions. Pensions are increased according to the level of pension capital reserves of the social insurance budget. For each increase, amendments by parliament are required (see Table 5.6).

Table 5.6 Number of beneficiaries by type of benefit, Estonia, 1992–97 (in thousands, yearly average)

	1992	1993	1994	1995	1996	1997
Old-age pensions	318.1	308.3	299.9	296.9	291.5	289.7
Superannuation pensions	6.5	5.9	5.0	3.2	3.2	2.7
Invalidity pensions	39.9	50.0	51.7	52.9	56.1	58.1
Survivors' pensions	13.8	20.7	18.0	20.1	21.5	21.8
National pensions	1.7	2.3	1.8	1.6	2.1	2.0
Total	380.0	387.3	376.4	374.8	374.5	374.4

Source: Estonian National Social Insurance Board.

Some categories of workers (particularly those working in hazardous conditions, but also certain professions) are granted more favourable conditions in the general pension scheme concerning retirement age and required length of service. These exceptions are regulated by the Law on Superannuation Pensions and the law on old-age pensions relating to 'favourable conditions'. The payment of national pensions, old-age, invalidity and survivors' pensions, but also superannuation and 'favourable condition' pensions is administered by the Estonian National Social Insurance Board through regional pension offices.

In addition to these major pension schemes, there are three minor schemes, which are meant to be a substitute for benefits of the general scheme and for which certain groups of state employees are entitled: the president and members of parliament; state audit officials; and judges. There is also a special supplementary scheme for civil servants. Eligibility criteria for age, length of service and payment level vary. Members of parliament[5] become eligible for an old-age pension at the age of 60 for men with 25 years of service and 55 for women with 20 years of service, provided that he/she has been a member of parliament for at least two years up to the end of the mandate. The old-age pension amounts to 75 per cent of a parliamentarian's salary. The old-age pension for state audit employees amounts to 60 per cent of the previous salary. According to the Law on Civil Service, effective from

1 January 1996, civil servants are entitled to pension supplements. The amount of supplement depends on the length of service in civil duties and on the amount of old-age pension.[6] Judges are entitled to a pension after 15 years of service as a judge. The amount of old-age pension is 75 per cent of the previous salary. All pensions are financed from the state budget and administered by the Estonian National Social Insurance Board (ENSIB) through its local departments whereas those of the president, the members of parliament, and the judges are administered by the clerical office of parliament. Pensions and other benefits payable by the state constitute a non-taxable income and can be fully amalgamated with earnings.

5.2.3 Changes in Insurance Coverage

One of the earliest general changes in the pension system was the elimination of two separate schemes (for workers and collective farmers) and their replacement by a single general pension scheme. One of the aims of such a design was to avoid obstacles to labour mobility (which during the first years of economic reforms was quite high) that might be created by the pension system.

Table 5.7 *Number of insurers affiliated to the pension insurance and insured employees, Estonia, 1992–97 (in thousands, yearly average)*

	1992	1993	1994	1995	1996	1997
Insurers	23.8	32.5	41.5	48.6	51.3	58.5
Insured employees	760.0	702.7	657.8	650.1	632.6	619.7
Participation rate (%)	100.0	99.9	95.7	99.0	98.0	n.a.

Source: Estonian National Social Insurance Board.

In Table 5.7, insurers are employers and the self-employed. Both pay social tax. The insured are employees on whose behalf the employers have paid social tax. The number of the insurers has increased while the number of the insured has declined. It is to be noted that the number of beneficiaries has declined since 1993, as well. However, the number of the insured has declined more rapidly, resulting in an increasing system dependency ratio as demonstrated above. We can see that the participation rate (the percentage of the insured in the total employed) has been quite high and stable. As this is the head-count participation rate it does not reflect the problem of 'envelope salaries'.

5.2.4 Organizational Changes

During the Soviet era, the payment of pensions was carried out by the regional departments of social welfare, functioning within the administrative system of the Ministry of Social Welfare. The same department also provided social assistance and social services.

In 1990, even before independence, a Social Fund, independent of the budget of the republic, was created. The Social Fund's main revenue was a social tax, calculated and deducted by employers, totalling 20 per cent of the gross payroll. A separate fund was created to reduce the republic's budget, and in this way, to channel resources away from the budget of the Soviet Union, as transfers to the central budget of the Soviet Union constituted a set percentage of the budgets of the republics.

The next organizational reform measures were carried out in August 1992: the Social Fund was abolished and a separate administrative system for state social insurance was created. As a part of these measures, the responsibility for the Social Fund was temporarily given back to the Ministry of Social Welfare. Subsequently, a new Law on State Government sanctioned the creation of the Estonian National Social Insurance Board (ENSIB) within the Ministry of Social Affairs (replacing the three separate ministries of health, labour and social welfare). In February 1993, ENSIB started its work as the main administrative body in the field of social insurance. At the same time, the revenues from the social tax were earmarked solely for social insurance expenditure.

In Estonia there is no Department of Social Security at the Ministry of Social Affairs. The functions which ENSIB have to fulfil are therefore diverse. The main ones are administration of the state social insurance budget and supervision of regional pension offices. The latter are responsible for the collection of pension insurance contributions, part of the social tax, and the payment of benefits (pensions, child benefits, funeral grants). Moreover, ENSIB has the authority to reallocate resources between regional offices to guarantee the payment of benefits. Its participation in policy development in the field of social security, including the drafting of new legislation and bilateral social security agreements, is an important activity and source of influence. Finally it is also responsible for the development and maintenance of the social insurance information system.[7] Thus ENSIB has substantial power: it develops legislation and co-ordinates and supervises the implementation of legislation. Such a system has advantages and disadvantages. It can be considered advantageous that in a small country like Estonia, know-how on social security concentrated in one administrative office has the potential for a highly efficient use of the available limited human resources. Moreover, first-hand knowledge on policy impact and appropriateness of a certain policy by being involved with policy implementation can be beneficial for policy development. On the other hand, this overlapping of responsibilities in policy making carries a serious potential disadvantage – the lack of a clear distinction between the political and expert roles.

5.2.5 Changes in Financing

Under Soviet rule and continuing into 1990 until the Social Fund was introduced, pensions were financed from the state budget.[8] This Social Fund not only served the purpose of decreasing resources to be transferred to the central Soviet budget, but also developed an independent account for social expenditures, separate from other budgetary expenditures, and made the balance of revenues and expenditures more transparent.

Since its introduction, the rate of social tax payable for pension insurance has been 33 per cent of the tax base,[9] for which only employers and individual entrepreneurs (the self-employed) are taxed. The share payable for pension insurance was established at 20 per cent of the tax base, while the 13 per cent share was designated for health insurance, but this division was not based on calculations about any specific target for the average replacement rate and was chosen quite arbitrarily.

At the beginning, some excise taxes were collected by the Social Fund. The use of its revenues was not clearly legislated, but left to the discretion of a Fund Council. At first the revenues from the 20 per cent share were used mainly for the payment of pensions but also for some social benefits and salaries of certain categories of public employees. In addition, the fund had the authority to make economic investments.

When the new Pension Law of the Estonian Republic was implemented, it became apparent that a budget deficit was going to develop. Athough local experts had recommended making revenues and expenditures of the Social Fund more transparent, this was not done in 1990–91. Furthermore, experts had suggested that for the implementation of the new law, the rate of social tax should be raised from 20 per cent to 26 per cent, which was not done either. In the event, the system was unable to pay benefits enacted by the new law. Consequently the pension law was suspended and earnings-related pensions were replaced by flat-rate benefits.

In spring 1992, under the 'transition government', the revenue side of the Social Fund became limited to social tax and expenditures to social security benefits. The payment of social welfare benefits was transferred back to the state budget.

In 1993, the Social Fund was reorganized into the state social security budget, administered by ENSIB. Before the adoption of the Law on State

Allowances, financial calculations were made. In March 1993, parliament amended the law, clearly formulating that the level of benefits should depend directly on revenues. Since then, the social tax has essentially been an earmarked state tax. The social security budget appears as an appendix to the state budget, but still separate, both with respect to the collection and administration of revenues and to the budgetary process.

Certain problems with the collection of the social tax persisted during the early years. Some of the most influential external factors have been the collapse of big state-owned companies, the shadow economy and bankruptcies. But there have also been important internal factors: an inefficient Tax Board in the role of tax administrator, the government's occasional waiving of social tax debts, and sanctioning of tax debts in general, to name a few. The last is a good example of a faulty construction of institutional arrangements. Information on the collection of social tax is sent to ENSIB, while only the tax administration has the right to apply sanctions. In this situation, effective collection of social tax relies on the successful co-operation between these two administrations.

Table 5.8 Total wage bill and social tax base in prices of 1997, Estonia, 1992–97 (EEK m.)

	1992	1993	1994	1995	1996	1997
Total wage bill	4,470	8,223	12,284	16,468	20,068	23,511
Total social tax base	4,551	8,339	12,441	16,717	20,330	23,814
Wage bill from the social tax base (%)	98.2	98.6	98.7	98.5	98.7	98.7

Source: Estonian National Social Insurance Board.

By far the dominant component of the social tax base is the wage bill, constituting more than 98.5 per cent, other components (in-kind benefits recalculated in money, and so on) constitute a minor source (see Table 5.8).

Table 5.9 Reported social tax, revenues from social tax and the collection rate, Estonia, 1992–97 (EEK m.)

	1992	1993	1994	1995	1996	1997
Reported social tax	910	1,667	2,487	3,342	4,065	4,762
Social tax revenues	731	1,514	2,170	2,917	3,844	4,637
Collection rate (%)	80.3	90.8	87.2	87.3	94.6	97.4

Source: Estonian National Social Insurance Board.

Problems with the collection of contributions were quite substantial in the years 1992–95. The collection rate – revenues from social tax divided by social tax calculated from the reported wages – improved and the trend continues (see Table 5.9).

Table 5.10 Revenues of the pension fund, Estonia, 1992–97 (EEK m.)

	1992	1993	1994	1995	1996	1997
Social tax revenues	731	1,514	2,170	2,917	3,844	4,637
State budget allocations	–	–	30	–	26	19
Other revenues	–	49	162	214	73	198
Pension fund total revenues	731	1,563	2,362	3,131	3,943	4,854

Source: Estonian National Social Insurance Board.

Social tax revenues constitute overwhelmingly the dominant part of all revenues of the state pension capital. Other revenues are generated by bank interest, dividends, interest on late payments, and the like (see Table 5.10).[10]

Table 5.11 Pension expenditure by type, Estonia, 1992–97 (EEK m.)

	1992	1993	1994	1995	1996	1997
Old-age pensions	592	1,211	1,619	2,389	3,322	3,860
Superannuation pensions			20	19	24	25
Invalidity pensions	69	158	219	340	467	556
Survivors' pensions	22	50	69	108	138	161
National pensions			6	7	12	13
Other costs	11[a]	21[a]	36	83[b]	104	113
Total pension expenditure	694	1,440	1,970	2,908	4,067	4,728
Cash reserves at year end	67	190	582	769	618	744
Annual change in reserves	+36	+123	+392	+186	−151	+127

Notes: [a] Includes expenditure for superannuation pensions and national pensions. [b] Includes transfer to the state budget of EEK 37 million.
Source: Estonian National Social Insurance Board.

Old-age pensions constitute by far the largest part of expenditures, although the share of old-age pensions from total expenditure has declined from 85.3 per cent in 1992 to 81.6 per cent in 1997. This was partly due to increased expenditures on invalidity pensions because of the higher number of invalidity pensioners. Table 5.11 shows the size and development of cash reserves of the pension capital. The reserves rose in 1992–94, but they have been exhausted. This reflects the increased political pressure to increase pensions as soon as sufficient current reserves are available. However, when calculating reserves at the end of the year, some caution is needed, as the size depends on the month of the last pension increase. In 1996, the decision to increase pensions caused a current deficit, that is, pension expenditures for 1996 exceeded revenues from social tax for the same year.

Table 5.12 Pension expenditure and GDP in current prices (EEK m.), and share of pension expenditure in GDP, Estonia, 1992–97

	1992	1993	1994	1995	1996	1997
Pension expenditure	694	1,440	1,970	2,908	4,067	4,728
GDP	13,054	22,060	30,268	41,279	52,379	65,080
Pensions in GDP (%)	5.3	6.5	6.5	7.0	7.8	7.3

Source: Estonian Statistical Office.

Pension expenditure as a percentage of GDP increased from 1992 on, while the contribution rate for pension insurance was unchanged, and there were no open transfers from general state revenues (see Table 5.12). The growth is explained by a combination of factors. In 1992–94, the growth of pension expenditure as a share of GDP is explained by the fact that the total wage bill in GDP was growing. As expenditures for pensions were based on social tax revenues, the increased wage bill (as a share of GDP) was transferred to cover an increasing pension expenditure (as a share of GDP), though some social tax revenues were used to build up reserves. In 1994–97, the total wage bill (as a share of GDP) decreased, but the pension expenditures continued growing in 1995 and 1996 mainly due to the use of reserves from earlier years. Since 1996 there has been an improvement in the collection of social taxes. In 1997, pension expenditures (as a share of GDP) again shrank as the total wage bill continued declining and some social tax revenues were left in reserve.

Table 5.13 Consumer price index (CPI) growth and pension expenditures, Estonia, 1992–97 (real terms)

	1992	1993	1994	1995	1996	1997
Growth of CPI (%)	1,076.0	89.8	47.7	29.0	23.1	11.2
Cumulative CPI Growth (1992=100)	100.0	189.8	280.2	361.6	444.9	494.7
Pension expenditures (1992=100)	100.0	207.5	283.9	419.0	586.0	681.3

Sources: Estonian Statistical Office and ENSIB.

Table 5.13 demonstrates that compared to 1992 not only has there been a nominal increase in pension expenditures and an increase as a share of GDP, but also real expenditures have been growing. In a context of a declining number of pensioners, transfers went into the growth of the purchasing power of pensions.

When looking at the share of pensions in the total social safety-net expenditures, we also see a growing trend (see Table 5.14). However, it would be incorrect to conclude that this is because of political competition between pensions and other social benefits. Again, we should remember that in Estonia pensions are financed from social contributions (social tax) while other social benefits are financed from general revenues (either from the state budget or local budgets). Therefore, the structural changes are chiefly caused by the fact that the share of general revenues allocated for social benefits has not kept pace with the increasing revenues from social tax.

Table 5.14 Social safety-net expenditures, Estonia, 1992–95 (per cent of total spending and as share of GDP)

	1992	1993	1994	1995
Pensions	56.8	57.3	62.3	67.8
Child benefits	23.2	19.1	19.9	17.7
Other social security cash benefits	2.1	1.5	n.a.	n.a.
Social protection of the unemployed	0.9	1.6	1.2	1.3
Social assistance (state budget)	14.4	16.4	14.7	12.0
income support	0.0	1.0	2.1	1.8
housing support	10.1	9.7	7.8	5.3
institutional care	4.0	4.9	4.5	4.3
other social services	0.3	0.8	0.3	0.6
Social assistance (local budgets)	2.6	4.1	1.9	1.2
Total social safety-net spending	100.0	100.0	100.0	100.0
Total social safety-net expenditure as a share of GDP	9.4	11.5	10.3	10.3

Source: World Bank calculations.

5.2.6 Changes in the Benefit Side

The benefit formula has been changed nine times between 1992 and 1997 (see Table 5.15 for an overview). Changes in the formula have been made mainly for the purpose of increasing pension levels, with the exception of the change effective from 1 July 1994 when pensions were no longer linked to the minimum wage. Two methods have been used to increase pensions: by increasing the basic amount (flat-rate component of the pension) or by increasing the coefficients for the years of service. From 1997, the basic amount has been left unchanged and the coefficients have been increased. This has diminished the relative importance of the flat-rate component and increased the length-of-service-related component; the system has also become more advantageous for people with long periods of service, particularly those who have suffered periods of persecution.

Table 5.15 Changes in the pension formula, Estonia, 1993–98

	4/93	4/94	7/94	9/95	1/96
Minimum wage (MW)	EEK 300	EEK 300	EEK 300	EEK 450	EEK 680
National pension rate (NPR)	–	–	-	–	EEK 410
National pension (NP)	85% MW	85% MW	EEK 300	EEK 410	110% NPR
Old age pension = basic amount B	85% MW	85% MW	NP	NP	NPR
+ length of service component $y * \alpha(y)$ A:					
15–19 years	0.5%MW	1.0%MW	1.0%NP	1.7%NP	2.3%NPR
20–24 years	0.6%MW	1.1%MW	1.1%NP	1.8%NP	2.4%NPR
25–29 years	0.7%MW	1.2%MW	1.2%NP	1.9%NP	2.5%NPR
30–34 years	0.8%MW	1.5%MW	1.5%NP	2.2%NP	2.8%NPR
35–40 years	0.9%MW	1.6%MW	1.6%NP	2.3%NP	2.9%NPR
Over 40 years	1.0%MW	1.7%MW	1.7%NP	2.5%NP	3.1%NPR

	4/96	1/97	11/97	3/98
Minimum wage (MW)	EEK 680	EEK 680	EEK 680	EEK 1100
National pension rate (NPR)	EEK 410	EEK 410	EEK 410	EEK 410
National pension (NP)	120%NPR	135%NPR	145%NPR	160%NPR
Old age pension = basic amount B	NPR	NPR	NPR	NPR
+ length of service component $y * \alpha(y)$ A:				
15–19 years	2.6%NPR	3.2%NPR	3.9%NPR	4.7%NPR
20–24 years	2.7%NPR	3.3%NPR	3.9%NPR	4.7%NPR
25–29 years	2.8%NPR	3.4%NPR	3.9%NPR	4.7%NPR
30–34 years	3.1%NPR	3.7%NPR	3.9%NPR	4.8%NPR
35–40 years	3.2%NPR	3.8%NPR	4.1%NPR	4.8%NPR
Over 40 years	3.4%NPR	4.0%NPR	4.3%NPR	4.9%NPR

However, the degree of progression in the length-of-service component has been reduced. In 1998, the pension formula was non-earnings related. The individual replacement rates chart reflected a strong vertical redistribution inherent in the pension formula. Also, some adverse effects could be observed: for example, people who were earning a minimum wage, received a replacement rate of 140 per cent of their former income.

Table 5.16 presents the development of the average wage and the average pension. We can observe that from 1994 to 1997 the average net replacement rate of old-age pensions has improved from 37 per cent to 45 per cent, in spite of the fact that the system dependency ratio was declining and the contribution rate did not change. The improvement in the replacement rate resulted from the improved collection of contributions and use of reserves created from 1992 to 1994.

Table 5.16 Development of the average wage of contributors and average pension, Estonia, 1993-97

	1993	1994	1995	1996	1997
Average gross contribution wage (EEK)	975	1,556	2,111	2,644	3,162
Average net contribution wage (EEK)	800	1,230	1,640	2,086	2,479
Average pension (EEK)	311	431	637	889	1,027
Average old-age pension (EEK)	320	453	671	953	1,110
Average pension/average gross wage (%)	31.8	27.7	30.2	33.6	32.5
Average pension/average net wage (%)	38.8	35.1	38.8	42.6	41.6
Average old-age pension/average net wage (%)	40.0	36.8	40.9	45.7	44.9

Source: Estonian National Social Insurance Board.

The increase in pensions has correlated highly with the increase in wages and the cost of living. From 1993 to 1997, the growth of the average gross wage of contributors has exceeded the increase in the consumer price index (CPI), that is, real wages. During the same period, the growth of the average old-age pension exceeded the growth of the average gross wage, except in 1994. At the same time, however, with the slowing of inflation, the annual nominal growth of wages and pensions also slowed down.

Table 5.17 shows that the average old-age pension grew faster than the average pension. This demonstrates that there is some competition inside the pension insurance scheme. As old-age pensioners constituted a larger proportion of the electorate, politicians were tempted to increase old-age pensions more than invalidity and survivors' pensions.

Table 5.17 Gross wage, average pension and average old-age pension in real terms, Estonia, 1992–97 (1992=100)

	1992	1993	1994	1995	1996	1997
Gross contribution wage	100	105	113	119	121	130
Average pension	100	107	101	116	131	136
Average old-age pension	100	111	106	122	141	148

Source: Estonian National Social Insurance Board.

The real value of the average old-age pension increased 48 per cent by 1997 compared to 1992. During the same period, the average contribution wage increased by only 30 per cent. Note that compared to 1993, in 1994, the real value of pensions declined. This was the result of increased cash reserves of pension capital, in connection with preparations to form a quasi-fund for the payment of earnings-related pensions. However, after the change of government, the idea of a quasi-fund was abandoned.

5.2.7 Pension Reform in the Pipeline

In 1998, several acts were adopted, which established the cornerstones of a new pension system. These acts were based on the 'Concept Paper of the Pension Reform' elaborated by the Social Security Reform Commission and approved by the government in June 1997. The concept paper suggested the introduction of a three-pillar system, where the pillars have the following meaning:

- I – state-managed compulsory pay-as-you-go pension scheme,
- II – privately-managed compulsory funded pension scheme,
- III – privately-managed voluntary funded scheme.

The reform of the first pillar was initiated with the adoption of the new Law on Social Tax, followed by the Law on State Pension Insurance. The new Law on Social Tax was passed on 15 April 1998 and was due to enter into force from 1 January 1999, replacing the current version of the law.

The Law on State Pension Insurance was passed on 26 June 1998. The main body of the law will enter into force from 1 April 2000. The law will overrule the existing Law on State Allowances Act and change some of the key principles of the present state pension system. Among the most crucial changes, the Law on State Pension Insurance will equalize the retirement age of men and women, and make the pension formula earnings-related for new retirees.

To guarantee the equal treatment of men and women, the retirement age will be equalized at the level of 63 years. Compared with the previous scale of retirement age increase, that for men was halted in 2001 when it reached 63, while that for women will be further increased until it reaches 63 in 2016. At the same time, the law provides for the option of early retirement up to three years before the normal retirement age. In this case, the amount of pension will be reduced by 0.4 per cent per month.

According to the new law, the pensionable length of service is counted up to 31 December 1998. From 1 January 1999 pension insurance periods will be registered on the basis of social tax paid by or on behalf of the insured person. The old-age pension will consist of three components:

- basic: fixed by the parliament for each fiscal year,
- length of service: calculated as the pensionable length of service multiplied by the value of one service year,
- pension insurance: calculated as the sum of annual pension insurance coefficients multiplied by the value of an annual coefficient.

In the pension formula, the length of service component will take into account periods up to 31 December 1998, while the pension insurance component will be calculated on the basis of annual pension insurance coefficients, taking into account registered social tax paid after 1 January 1999, thus anticipating a gradual transition from the old rules to the new rules. To calculate the pension insurance coefficients for insured persons, the amounts of social tax registered on the account of the insured person in the pension insurance register will be summed up and divided by the average amount of social tax paid in the given calendar year.

The concept paper had suggested the introduction of pension indexation, but this was not implemented. The payment levels and any increase thereof depend upon the values of a service year and of a pension insurance coefficient, determined annually on the basis of financial constraints. Besides the changes relating to pension entitlements, the two new laws also brought some changes to the financing and administration principles of the state pension system.

While the total rate of social tax remains unchanged, employers and the self-employed will pay the total rate of social tax to the Tax Office, declaring the amount of social tax paid on behalf of each insured person separately. The Tax Office will then transfer the 20 per cent part of the tax into the state pension insurance budget. Under the new Law on State Pension Insurance, a State Pension Insurance Register was established as a new structural unit of the National Social Insurance Board. The register keeps data on the insured, including the amounts of social tax paid on their behalf. Concerning budgeting, the current pension capital of the state social insurance budget will be transformed into a pension insurance budget.

As to financing, the expenditures not related to the insurance principle will be financed out of the state budget. In particular, this concerns national pensions, pension supplements (including the periods of political persecution), and the administrative costs of the pension offices. The previously long list of equivalent service periods has been abolished. Instead, the state will pay social tax on the minimum wage on behalf of the following persons:

- a parent on leave caring for a child or a non-working parent raising a child under three years,
- the non-working spouse of a diplomat working abroad,
- a conscript of the armed forces,
- a disabled person working in a special production establishment for the disabled,
- persons registered as unemployed.

The two main underlying features behind these changes are the introduction of an insurance principle, and increasing transparency of the financial system.

The legal framework for a voluntary third pillar was established by the Law on Pension Funds, which was adopted by parliament on 10 June 1998 and entered into force on 1 July 1998. In its implementation the law also makes substantial amendments to the Insurance Law (from 5 November 1992, with later amendments) and the Law on Income Tax (from 8 December 1993, with later amendments). Participation in supplementary voluntary pension schemes can take two forms: pension insurance policies offered by licensed private insurance companies or units of pension funds managed by private fund managers. To encourage participation in voluntary schemes, strong tax incentives have been introduced. Contributions (premiums paid in accordance with the insurance policy or units purchased from the pension funds) are tax deductible up to a ceiling of 15 per cent of annual taxable income. Benefits of the schemes are taxed at the rate of 10 per cent, compared to the regular income tax rate of 26 per cent. In the case of the defined-benefit type of insurance policy, where benefits are paid for life in equal or increasing amounts, the benefits are fully tax exempt. The minimum contractual age, in which case tax deductions are applicable, is 55 years. In 1998, eight private life insurance companies operated in Estonia. Four of them are licensed to sell pension insurance policies, which give entitlement to tax deductions. The pension funds to be set up in accordance with the Law on Pension Funds are open-ended contractual investment funds. Government policy concerning the supplementary pension arrangements has been in favour of individual-centred solutions to the occupational schemes to avoid obstacles to labour mobility.

5.3 FACTORS INFLUENCING PENSION POLICY

5.3.1 Factors Influencing the Changes

When analysing retrospectively the development of the pension system from 1989 onwards, it would be useful to divide this time span into five periods:

- up to April 1991 or before the Pension Law of the Estonian Republic was adopted,
- from April 1991 to February 1992, the period in which the Pension Law of the Estonian Republic was effective,
- from February 1992 to April 1993, the period in which flat-rate benefits were paid out,
- from April 1993 to 1998, the period in which the Law on State Allowances was effective, and
- from 1998 onwards, the period in which the Law on State Pension Insurance is effective.

In each period a different constellation of factors have played a major role in policy development. From 1987 to 1988, in Moscow, a draft of a new pension law was elaborated to replace the law of 1956. Under the Gorbachev principle of glasnost, this draft was sent to the republics for public discussion. It is hard to evaluate whether any proposals from the public were taken into account or not. But the Supreme Council of the Soviet Union did adopt the law in May 1990. The attempt to draft a genuinely Estonian pension law failed and the new pension law bore a strong resemblance to the Soviet one.[11]

The following period was intended to be the implementation stage of the new law, but problems ensued, one after the other. The main ones were related to insufficient financing, as the first more precise calculations showed that expenditures exceeded the expected social fund revenues. Another problem was the large number of debtors. The national tax administration was only in the process of formation and essential registers were missing.

In August 1991, although Estonia had regained its political independence, it still remained a 'rouble zone' for a short time. The collapse of the Soviet Union also resulted in the collapse of its economy, which subsequently caused hyperinflation and a scarcity of banknotes. With respect to the pension system, this caused severe problems with the prompt payment of pensions. In addition, the organizational and administrative division of responsibilities was unclear, particularly between the Ministry of Social Welfare and the Social Fund. Therefore the same coalition which adopted the new pension law took the necessary actions to rescind it.

In February 1992, considered here as the start of the third period, the Supreme Council of Estonia adopted flat-rate living allowances. The decision included a provision calling for the implementation of the rescinded Pension Law three months after the introduction of the Estonian national currency. In January 1992, the government no longer functioned and a 'transition government', consisting of lay people, was given power until regular elections were held, scheduled for autumn 1992. This government was entrusted with implementing the currency reform as well as reimplementing the pension law. Currency reform was successfully achieved in June 1992, and after elections in September, a new coalition, led by the Pro Patria Union, came into power.

The new government established a new Ministry of Social Affairs and began to investigate the feasibility of reimplementing the pension law. This, however, could not be realized for financial reasons. But no clear political alternatives were on the agenda. The Centre Party argued for a reimplementation of the pension law, but these arguments were primarily to discomfit the new government, rather than a serious attempt to implement the failed law.

Confronted with diverse practical problems such as prompt payment of flat-rate living allowances, pensioners protested strongly against the government. In the course of currency reform, savings as well as cash were converted to Estonian kroons at the rate of 10:1. Many pensioners felt that the currency reform had made them instantly poor. They especially protested against the decision to convert their savings at the same rate as cash. There was a widespread feeling of insecurity that had not been anticipated, since the new pension law had promised high pensions. Pensioners therefore demanded what had been promised. The focus of these claims was not the rationale of the law so much as the level of pensions. Many of the protesters could simply not understand that in contrast to the Soviet period, the amount of available resources was limited, and banknotes would not be printed without legal reserves.

Under these circumstances, ENSIB took the initiative and even without political demands or directives began to formulate a new pension scheme. The goal was to develop a financially sustainable pension system to be implemented in stages. In the first stage, the pension level would be determined by two amounts: a flat-rate basic amount and a supplementary amount depending on the length of service. An earnings-related amount was planned for the future. It was clearly stipulated that pension expenditures were not to exceed social tax revenues and that there would be no subsidies from the state budget.

By spring 1993, there was widespread public rejection of flat-rate benefits, and a demand for reform. ENSIB responded with a scheme which was simple in its principles and easy to understand. When put to the vote in parliament, the law unexpectedly received full approval and was immediately implemented. The opposition insisted that the new law was called the 'Law on Living Allowances', the main argument being that it was not a pension law since pensions are dependent on former wages.[12]

During the implementation of the Law on Living Allowances, practical administrative tasks were to improve the financial management of pension revenues, to establish a proper system of accounting and to improve organization. ENSIB also started to develop ideas on implementation of the earnings-related component of the pension payment. This consisted of a quasi-fund for payment of the earnings-related component. To establish a short-term surplus funded from a fraction of the social tax would allow for the introduction of an earnings-related component of the pension. Funds would be accumulated over the period of one year, after which payments could start. A legal draft received support from both employers and employees, and by the end of 1994 was ready to be presented to the government and parliament.

However, as a consequence of a government crisis in autumn 1994, this was not done. With regular elections in spring 1995, the second transition government was not prepared to make important decisions. In autumn 1994, financial specialists had presented an alternative draft pension law based on the idea of compulsory private insurance. As the draft described only the 'steady state', and ignored issues like transition costs from one to another system and the need to finance current pensions, the draft did not receive much attention.

Since 1995, every minister of social affairs has promised to present a new pension law draft and has done so. Altogether four different drafts have been presented, each by a different minister. These have all, however, been different variations of the model elaborated by ENSIB in 1994. The later versions abandoned the idea of a quasi fund, and presented a pure pay-as-you-go (PAYG) system. The main reason why none of the laws received broader consideration was the short life of the governments – no government has had sufficient time and sufficient support to work through all the details of the suggested pension reform.

A further complication since 1995 has been the existence of competing proposals at the state level. Besides the government's proposal, the parliamentary Social Commission put forward its own draft. The Social Commission tends to represent the interests of the Union of Pensioners and Families, which is one of the coalition parties, and had two distinguishing features in its proposal: raising social tax and taking into consideration wages earned under Soviet rule. This put the government in a delicate situation, as the coalition partners had difficulties finding a common language for the underlying principles of pension security.

To solve the controversy, which had persisted for three years, a minority government, which came into power in March 1997, established a Social Security Reform Commission in April 1997. This non-political commission, consisting of experts, elaborated a reform proposal by the end of May 1997. The proposal was strongly backed by the prime minister and the leading Coalition Party, and as a result, the government approved the concept paper in June 1997. However, no clear political consensus on the reform proposal was achieved. The proposal received severe criticism from the other coalition partners, while the opposition parties indicated their support. Working groups of ENSIB and the Ministry of Finance were further entrusted to formulate the necessary legislation to implement the reform measures described in the concept paper.

In July 1997, the European Commission delivered its opinion 'Agenda 2000' concerning the Estonian application for EU membership. The Commission, among other things, also noted that the reform of the pension system had not yet started. In December 1997, at the Luxembourg summit of the European Council, Estonia was invited to the EU accession negotiations. The Accession Partnership of Estonia, adopted by the European Council in March 1998, stressed among the short-term priorities for 1998 the introduction of key legislation linked to pension reform.

Some domestic political controversies persisted, in particular over the issue of 'rouble salaries'; nevertheless, parliament adopted the new Law on Social Tax on 15 April, the Law on Pension Funds on 10 June, and the Law on State Pension Insurance on 26 June 1998. The first and the third laws laid down the cornerstones for the new first pillar, while the second established the legal framework for the third pillar.

5.3.2 Important Actors and Debated Issues

In principle, the most influential actors in pension policy development have been the experts, the politicians, public opinion and representatives of financial markets. The development of a pension system in Estonia has been based primarily on the ideas of experts working in public administration.

When Estonia first became independent there was little available expertise in social policy within the country. Policy development was thus considerably hindered with respect to goals and tasks. This left administrators with extensive discretion in problem-solving and to some extent innovation.

Regaining independence generated much enthusiasm which was the source of motivation and hope for a new start in the years from 1992 to 1994. The present concept is a compromise between the different ideas: such as PAYG versus funded concepts for financing the pension system and universality and solidarity versus individual contributions as underlying principles behind pension security.

Against the background of a situation which has persisted since 1995, in which different drafts were prepared, none of which received support, the attitude of administrators changed somewhat. It became clear that without political consensus as a starting-point, much work would be wasted. Nevertheless, there has been no agreement about general goals. Debate concentrated particularly on four questions:

1. With respect to the organizational management of the pension system, the question is whether to establish a separate autonomous public legal body with a tripartite council or to continue with the government institution. The social partners have been advocates of an autonomous institution, while the government has been in favour of a governmental institution.
2. Concerning the distribution of the burden of the social tax at issue is whether to divide the social tax between the employer and employee and, if yes, what is the employee share. This has primarily been a debate between the social partners. Employers' organizations have been suggesting taxing both employers and employees, while trade unions have questioned the feasibility of such a proposal. The government has also supported the latter approach.
3. A problem for current pensioners is in connection with earnings-related pensions. A major point is whether to recalculate the pensions of current pensioners on the basis of their former rouble salaries. The organizations representing pensioners have been strongly in favour of taking the former rouble salaries into account and recalculating the pensions accordingly.
4. The replacement rate is addressed in relation to the level of protection the state pension system has to provide, that is, what is the target replacement rate for the statutory system? During the parliamentary elections in March 1995, several political parties promised to raise the average replacement rate to the level of 50 per cent of the average wage. The organizations representing pensioner interests have used the same political slogan when advocating higher pensions.

At the beginning of 1996, a working group was established including experts from ENSIB, the Ministry of Finance, Insurance Inspection, trade unions and employers' organizations, in order to develop a conceptual framework for pension reform. The working group concentrated on determining goals and basic principles of the reform proposals rather than drafting laws as was the practice earlier. The group suggested moving towards a two-pillar system: a state-provided compulsory pension insurance supplemented by privately provided voluntary pensions.[13] It should continue to operate on a PAYG principle, but be modified to include an earnings-related component. The level of protection should guarantee the European minimum standard prescribed by the European Code of Social Security, i.e. 40 per cent of the previous wage of the beneficiary with an employment record of 30 years, but also be limited to this standard. The working group also suggested equalizing the retirement age of men and women at 63 and introducing a ceiling on compulsory contributions at the level of 15 times the minimum wage, which would limit the scope of solidarity.

Supplementary voluntary systems were recommended in two forms: as insurance policies provided by private insurance companies and as units of the pension investment funds. To encourage participation in supplementary pension arrangements, the working group suggested introducing tax incentives.

In 1997, a new wave of discussions started among experts and politicians. In April, a new working group was formed by the Minister of Social Affairs to make proposals on how to proceed in the given situation. In its final report, it noted that one of the reasons why attempts to reform the pension system have been unsuccessful was perhaps because the wrong political procedure was applied. Pension reform, affecting the whole population, has to be based on a broad consensus. Therefore it was suggested that a two-level (with political and expert levels) pension reform commission should be set up to achieve political consensus on the basic features of the new pension system. Suggestions were made for the improvement of financial stability, political stability and securing stable rules for a reformed pension system. This working group proposed a three-pillar system: in addition to the state PAYG scheme and the voluntary funded scheme, a compulsory funded scheme could be gradually phased in. As a result of their analysis, they concluded that the average replacement rate of 50 per cent could not be achieved, especially as the system dependency ratio had been declining and even the current replacement rate could not be maintained without further restrictions in eligibility criteria. It further recommended non-recalculation of earlier awarded pensions on the basis of rouble salaries and elimination of superannuated pensions and special categories for entitlement, a legacy of the old Soviet pension system. The group also suggested that the social tax burden for the PAYG system should not be shared, but to keep it as an obligation of employers.

In the end, the government established a Social Security Reform Commission, an expert commission with the task of elaborating a more detailed concept paper on the elements of pension reform. The concept paper presented relied largely on the proposals of the earlier working group, and also suggested the introduction of a three-pillar pension system. It described the basics of the possible reform and offered some key solutions to debated issues. Much attention was devoted to economic and demographic factors to provide motivation as to why major reform is needed.

5.4 CONCLUSIONS

The collapse of the communist system and the subsequent change in the basic societal order provided unique opportunities for major social and economic change. In the area of economic policy these opportunities were taken and a path of radical and rapid reform was chosen. In the field of social security, including the pension system, a more gradual way of reforms has been chosen.

Objectively, the starting-point of the reforms was not a favourable one. Estonia inherited the benefit side of the pension system from the Soviet past, while the financial side had to be organized from scratch. Public expectations of higher social security benefits conflicted with reduced prospects, reflected in the rapidly declining system dependency ratio which resulted from an ageing population and a decline in formal employment. The age structure of the Estonian population led to the decision to raise the pension age. Also, the decision to separate the financing of pensions from the general state budget and to finance pensions solely through an earmarked payroll tax was considered to be a rational solution. The financing base and the limits of benefits were thereby clearly defined. Left as an item of the general state budget, expenditures on social security, like expenditures on consumption, would have caused unnecessary competition with the need to finance public investments to facilitate the general economic development.

In the early years of independence, in the absence of any sound analysis of the existing system together with demographic and economic factors, many policy decisions were based on common sense. The main driving forces were the enthusiasm of those involved, sometimes combined with a denial of the past. There was also a common view that pensions are a 'social', not an economic issue. Social sciences have been unable to contribute to the understanding of how such systems function or to provide knowledge for policy development. This left administrators with a key role in policy making. There has been a gradual acquisition of and access to know-how, particularly through international co-operation.

Estonian macroeconomic policy, namely the currency policy which has secured the stability of the national currency and the balanced budget approach limiting the expenditure to resources available, has had an impact on the pension system. The scheme which has been set up can be characterized as a defined-benefit one on the micro (individual) level, with benefits being differentiated on the basis of length of pensionable service, while on the macro level operating on a defined-contribution system, with the level of benefits being dependent on revenues from contributions (that is, social tax).

In the second phase of reforms, the optimism and unanimous support of the early years was replaced by a prolonged debate about the possible future reform measures together with conflicting views over the ultimate goals of reform. First, the generally higher level of information has contributed to the elaboration of alternatives. Contacts with the world as a source of information have been important. However, the more direct impact from foreign consultants has been less fruitful. Proponents of different systems usually advocate a particular aim or argue on the basis of a stable economy model. However, any steady state can be fully implemented only after a long transition period, and instruments for transition, as a rule, are not readily available.

Second, an increasing importance of the political dimension is evident. In general, social policy issues have received rather superficial consideration in the party programmes. However, in the search for their political identity, political parties are increasingly elaborating their views on social policy, as well. The continuing ideological debate on a liberal market economy ('Economic development is the best social policy') versus a social market economy ('Economics are just a means to facilitate social development') has also had its impact on the reform proposals. More concretely, as the experience of consensus-building has been modest, the continuity of social security reform has been dependent on the strength of the government coalition. Frequent changes in the government have had a clearly negative impact on the reform progress.

The absence of a clear political agenda on the issue has resulted in numerous incremental changes over several years, while any broader scale reform proposal was blocked. In 1997, Estonia took a path towards a three-pillar system. In 1998 the crucial reform measures concerning the reform of the first pillar and the introduction of the third pillar were finally legislated. Part of the implementation of the reform still lies ahead. Also, a number of key decisions, among them concerning the controversial issue of the second pillar, still have to be made.

NOTES

1 In the case of a final wage of up to 35 roubles, the pension amounted to 100 per cent of the final wage. Further, for a wage between 35 and 50 roubles there was an 85 per cent replacement rate; 50 and 60 roubles, 75 per cent; 60 and 80 roubles, 65 per cent; 80 and 100 roubles, 55 per cent; and over 100 roubles, 50 per cent. Minimum and maximum pensions were 30 and 120 roubles, respectively.

2 The number of employers and the self-employed affiliated to the pension insurance system increased from 1992 to 1996: the number of employers fell from 22,038 to 39,770 and the number of self-employed increased from 1,782 to 11,544. (Data from the Estonian National Social Insurance Board).

3 The main areas where self-employment has developed in Estonia are: agriculture, hunting, fishing; wholesale and retail trade and related services. Although the agricultural and fishing sectors in Estonia are relatively small, self-employment has become a dominant form of entrepreneurship in these fields.

4 However, as the resources of the social insurance budget grew, parliament increased the national pension to EEK 360 in October 1994, and also decided to authorize the government to raise the national pension (being also the base for calculating old-age pensions) twice a year (from 1 April and 1 September). During this time, the coefficients remained unchanged. From 1 April 1995 the government increased the national pension to EEK 410, although parliament decided not to raise the national pension at the same rate as old-age pensions.

5 The pension rights of the president and members of parliament are regulated by the Law on Salaries, Pensions and Social Guarantees of the President and the Members of Parliament, the pension rights of the State Audit staff are regulated by the Law on State Audit. The pension rights of judges are regulated by the Law on the Status of Judges.

6 Between 10 and 15 years of civil service should increase the normal old-age pension by 10 per cent, 16 and 20 years by 20 per cent, 21 and 25 years by 25 per cent, 26 and 30 years by 40 per cent, and over 30 years by 50 per cent. These supplements are financed from the state budget.

7 A particular technical problem has been the development of a register of insured persons. As employees are not social tax payers and the pension is not currently dependent upon earnings, there has not been an administrative need to register individual employees and their wages. So the development of a register is one of the priorities for future development.

8 See above, section 5.1.2. The Social Fund was set up under the 1990 Law on Social Tax.

9 The law defines the tax base as all sums paid to individuals, and payments in kind as recalculated in money and drafts made on behalf of individuals.

10 In 1994 and 1996, the state budget allocated resources to cover part of the administrative costs of regional pension offices.

11 See above, section 5.1.6.

12 Those who were in a less advantageous position under the new law were those who had high earnings or those who had connections with party or trade union structures under Soviet rule.

13 Other possible forms such as state-provided voluntary supplementary pensions, or privately operated mandatory pension schemes were also discussed by the working group, but were abandoned.

REFERENCES

Leppik, L. (1995), 'Historical roots of social welfare policy in Estonia', in J. Simpura (ed.), *Social Policy in Transition Societies: Experience from the Baltic Countries and Russia.* Sosaaliturvan Keskusliitto, Helsinki.

Leppik, L. (1997), 'Social security for self-employed in Estonia', Paper for the 6th Baltic conference on Social Security, mimeo, Stockholm.

Marksoo, Ü. (1995), 'Labour market situation', in J. Groegaard (ed.), *Estonia in the Grip of Change*. NORBALT Living Conditions Project, Fafo, Oslo.

World Bank (1996), 'Estonia: Living standards during the transition', Report No: 15647 EE, Washington, DC.

World Bank (1997), 'Estonia: Public expenditure review update', Washington, DC.

6. Transformation of old-age security in Latvia

Inara Bite

6.1 ECONOMIC AND DEMOGRAPHIC FRAMEWORK

6.1.1 Economic Background

In 1991, when the independence of Latvia was internationally recognized, first attempts were made towards a market economy. Latvia, along with many other countries in transition encountered the classic problems (weak capital markets, hyperinflation, supply and demand crisis and so on).

The initial stage of economic reform in Latvia between 1991 and 1992 witnessed an enormous drop in manufacturing, instability in the financial system, rapid price rises and the threat of hyperinflation. As reforms continued, the strict fiscal and monetary policy of the government and the Bank of Latvia from 1993–94 contributed to the stabilization of the economic situation. Gross domestic product (GDP) calculations show that production volume in 1991 decreased by 8 per cent, but in 1992 and 1993 it decreased by 34 per cent and 15 per cent, respectively. The cumulative GDP fall from 1991 to 1993 was approximately 50 per cent, which is one of the greatest and fastest decreases of any post-communist state. This decrease varied across branches for the economy: the production volume in agriculture decreased by 40 per cent, the production volume in industry by 65 per cent and the volume of services by 33 per cent. The most important factors causing the decrease in production volume were:

- interruption of economic relations with former USSR republics, which had been largely in the raw material and product markets;
- attempts by local manufacturers to attain monopoly profits by exploiting the goods deficit;
- an increase in the cost of raw materials; mutual enterprise debts, that is, the destruction of the payment system.

In accordance with the statements of many experts, the presence of the 'shadow' economy ensured that the decline of GDP has been less than published in the statistical reports (see Table 6.1). The rapid fall in GDP reflected an increase in unemployment. At the end of 1991, in contrast to the chronic lack of labour in the centralized economy, unemployment reached 0.2 per cent of the total economically active population. In 1992 and 1993 the percentage of registered unemployed people increased accordingly to 2.3 per cent and 5.8 per cent, respectively. In 1995 the average unemployment rate was 6.6 per cent and in 1996 7.2 per cent. There is also 'hidden' unemployment in Latvia, which takes the form of forced stoppages, compulsory unpaid leave and job downgrading to part-time. The 'black' labour market partly buffers the effects of unemployment.

Table 6.1 *Gross domestic product, Latvia, 1990–96*

Period	Million lats at 1993 prices	In relation to previous year	At constant prices (1990=100)
1990	2,952.9	102.9	100.0
1991	2,645.4	89.6	89.6
1992	1,723.2	65.1	58.4
1993	1,467.0	85.1	49.7
1994	1,476.5	100.6	50.0
1995	1,453.2	98.4	49.2
1996	1,493.1	102.8	50.6

Source: Central Statistical Bureau of Latvia.

In 1994, for the first time since the restoration of independence, GDP rose by 0.6 per cent instead of falling. In 1995, GDP in Latvia declined by 2 per cent (in 1993 constant prices), primarily because of the banking crisis and the growing budget deficit. The Central Statistical Bureau (CSB) of Latvia calculated that industrial production in 1995 totalled 1.025 billion lats in current prices, which was less than the 1994 total of 1.076 billion lats. Thus, production fell by 6.3 per cent from 1994 to 1995.

However, not all economic news was bad in 1995 and 1996. Inflation continued to fall, unemployment remained relatively low, and the national currency, the lat, remained stable.

Important factors for increasing the prospects for growth are privatization and investments to promote more efficient production. While 1995 has certainly been the most active year for privatization, the privatization process has lagged and still lags behind the rest of the reform process and structural reform of enterprises is very slow. The process of privatizing state property in Latvia started two years later than in Estonia, and unfortunately owners were first found for arguably the worst enterprises. In 1995, a total of 240 enterprises were privatized, representing 12 per cent of all state-owned enterprises. The international tender programme has not been as successful as had been hoped. Since privatization began, Latvia has offered 125 enterprises to foreign bidders in three rounds of international tenders. Initially there were over 2000 responses, but in the end there were only 40 realistic offers to buy these enterprises.

According to the legislation in effect, 5 per cent of the privatized enterprise shares is handed over to the state Social Insurance Fund (SIF). Initially it was envisaged that means obtained in the privatization process would be used for financing the transitory (fourth) tier foreseen in the Pension Reform Concept in order to provide additional income support for retired and elderly workers not participating in the new funded scheme (second pillar). But there is nothing to indicate that there will be a transitory tier. On the other hand, the shares transferred to SIF did not have any real value.

Inflation (based on the consumer price index) in Latvia has continued to decrease over the past several years. According to the annual consumer price index there was a decrease from 34.9 per cent in 1993, to 26.3 per cent in 1994, to 23.1 per cent in 1995, to 13.5 per cent in 1996.[1] Although inflation continues the downward trend of the past few years, co-ordination between macroeconomic stabilization and economic reform measures has been insufficient to reduce adequately the consequences of the transition.

6.1.2 State Budget Development

The government tax revenue collection difficulties have contributed to the large budget deficit which, in turn, has restricted the ability of the government to raise state sector wages and provide means of social support. As a result, the Law on the State Budget for 1995 was amended in the latter part of the year to allow for a basic budget deficit of 92.4 million lats. The main sources of deficit financing for 1995 were short-term government treasury bills sold in the domestic market, and securities sold abroad. Credit extended by the Bank of Latvia was also used to cover the 1995 budget deficit. The state's internal debt for 1995 was approximately 162 million lats, a sum composed of government bonds, treasury bills and bank credit. Internal debt derives largely from the need to service the sizeable budget deficit. The Sixth Saeima (parliament) approved a state budget for 1996 that includes expenditures of 460 million lats and a deficit of 59.39 million lats.

After the elections in October 1995 there was no leading party in the Saeima. There were two attempts to form a government but both of them failed. Finally a coalition government was formed by representatives of many different parties. The president asked Andris Skele, who was a successful entrepreneur and did not belong to any party, to take over as prime minister.

Being independent from any parties the prime minister worked out a Government Action Programme for 1996. This programme contains strong measures in order to increase economic growth and productivity, to free privatization from the stranglehold of bureaucracy and accelerate the pace of privatization and foreign investment and thereby re-establish order within the banking system. The prime minister promised a balanced budget for 1997.

Having weathered the storm of the 1995 banking crisis, the government's top economic priority was to reduce the size of the budget deficit. As noted earlier, the 1996 state budget anticipated reducing the budget deficit, which stood at 92 million lats in 1995, to approximately 59 million lats in 1996. The State Revenue Service and SIF were obliged to report weekly to the prime minister about revenue collection and measures taken to improve it. As a result of these efforts the budget deficit in 1996 was brought down to 39.9 million lats. In spite of the resistance from various parties, including those represented in the Saeima, the latter approved a balanced budget for 1997.

6.1.3 Demographic Background

The demographic prognoses have been taken into consideration in working out a model of pension reform. Since 1991, the population in Latvia has decreased. The total decrease over the five-year period from 1991 to 1995 was 143,000 individuals, or 5.3 per cent of the population. This figure also reflects natural migration of 112,000 persons. The social economic development during the post-war decades has substantially influenced the age structure of Latvia's population. In 1970, 17.4 per cent of the population was

Table 6.2 Resident population, Latvia, 1980–96

Year	Total (1000)	0–14 years (%)	Working age[a] (%)	Above working age (%)	Demographic burden[b]
1980	2,508.8	20.4	59.7	19.9	675
1985	2,570.0	21.2	58.6	20.0	707
1990	2,673.5	21.5	57.7	20.8	733
1991	2,667.9	21.5	57.7	21.0	739
1992	2,657.0	21.4	57.3	21.3	746
1993	2,606.2	21.3	56.9	21.8	757
1994	2,565.9	21.0	56.8	22.2	761
1995	2,529.5	20.7	56.8	22.5	761
1996	2,501.7	20.3	56.9	22.8	758

Notes: [a] Males: 15–59; females: 15–54. [b] Persons under the age of 15 and above working age in relation to working-age population (*1000).
Source: Central Statistical Bureau of Latvia.

older than 60 years of age, but now the percentage has risen to 19 per cent and it is higher in the rural regions.

Resident population composition by age and demographic burden is shown in Table 6.2. The decrease in the size of the population recently has been caused by several factors: by changes in the natural growth of population, with a decrease in the birth rate and an increase in the death rate and migration. Much of this change has to do with the loss of confidence in the economic and social spheres. The maximum levels of migration from Latvia and of repatriation were reached in 1992. In 1992, 47.2 thousand people left Latvia. In 1995 this figure was just 10.6 thousand. These emigrants are mostly the young and early middle-aged.

A significant social and demographic problem has been the extremely low birth rate. With few exceptions the generations have not achieved replacement levels since the Second World War. In the latter half of the 1980s, the average birth coefficient for each woman was at its highest since the war: between 2.0 and 2.1. In the 1990s the birth rate fell steeply again.

The sustained low birth rate has fostered the ageing of the population. The average age of a Latvian – 36 years – is one of the highest in Europe. Only Hungary's population is ageing at a faster rate than that of Latvia.

Until recently the death rate had increased sharply, which was also a result of a decrease in the average life expectancy. In 1995, the median life expectancy for both sexes – 66.5 years – was one of the lowest in Europe; moreover, it was much lower for men (60.3 years) than for women (73.1 years.) During the following five years, the average male life expectancy decreased by five years, primarily because of the high death rate by unnatural causes for age groups from 20 to 50. In particular, the erosion of medical care, a direct result of limited financial resources, also had a negative impact on life expectancy (see Table 6.3). The situation analysis and calculations show that the demographic processes will not change substantially in the near future.

Table 6.3 *Life expectancy, Latvia, 1990–96*

	1990	1991	1992	1993	1994	1995	1996
at birth							
Female	74.6	74.8	72.6	72.7	72.9	73.1	75.7
Male	64.2	63.8	60.9	60.6	60.7	60.3	63.3
Total	69.5	69.5	68.7	67.2	66.4	66.5	69.2
at retirement age							
Female	–	24.0	24.5	23.9	23.4	23.1	25.2
Male	–	14.8	14.8	14.5	14.2	14.2	14.1

Source: Central Statistical Bureau of Latvia.

6.2 REFORM MEASURES SINCE 1990 AND DEVELOPMENT OF THE PENSION SYSTEM UP TO 1997

This section deals with the transformation process of the pension system, starting with an overview of the pension reform development. A description of detailed changes in legislation then follows, especially the new pension law which came into force in 1996. Finally, problems of implementation problems of the new system as well as financing issues will be discussed.

6.2.1 Starting Point and Outline of the Reform Process

Until the restoration of independence in 1991, the Latvian social security system was part of the social programme operated in the Soviet Union. From 1990 to 1991, the Latvian government started to prepare, and partly to implement, changes in the structure and administration of the inherited social programme. The aim was to redesign the system according to national preferences and to introduce a clear accounting of social expenditure and earmarked revenue. The government was keen to get social security 'off budget', that is, to make the system financially autonomous from the state budget. Thus the new system applied social insurance principles.

During 1990, new legislation was formulated: the Law on State Pensions was passed on 29 November, followed by the Law on Social Tax on 14 December.[2] Both came into force on 1 January 1991. The regulations were a response to the existing political situation, without economic and demographic estimates as to possible long-term costs. At the end of the 1980s a new pension law in the USSR was under discussion, and the aim of new legislation in Latvia was to create better conditions for retirement pensions and other benefits as was foreseen in a draft law (but which was never passed), worked out in the former USSR. On the other hand, the generous entitlement criteria for pensions and other benefits expressed the belief that the renewal of independence would ensure the elimination of all injustice under which the people suffered under the former Soviet regime.

There were other political reasons for creating a new system, too. During the Soviet period some social insurance functions were carried out by the trade unions, which collected contributions – 6 per cent from the payroll for sickness insurance. This was a considerable amount of money to be used for sickness benefits, prevention and rehabilitation. Controlling the social insurance budget ensured that the old Soviet trade unions had extensive resources for financing their political activities and influencing the workers in 1990, when the political situation was uncertain and the acquisition of independence was problematical. Under the influence of the People's Front, the government decided to hand over social insurance means to the newly established State Social Insurance Administration, supervised by the Ministry of Social Affairs. In society there was a growing belief in social insurance principles and that the statutory social insurance system offered the possibility of linking social insurance benefits with working life.

With the continued fall in output and the rising liquidity squeeze of enterprises, the financial situation of SIF deteriorated slowly during 1992. There was a general tendency on the part of the government (Ministry of Finance) to overload the system with expenditures that had nothing to do with social insurance. Thus, for example, family benefits introduced in 1991 and financed from the general state budget were transferred to the social insurance budget in 1992. Pensions were no longer earnings-related but only flat-rate adjusted to the minimum standard of living. This caused a serious loss of belief in social insurance principles among the population and created space for many new ideas and theories.

Firstly, there were many objections from economists concerning the contribution rate (38 per cent). This rate was characterized as very high and a deterrent to foreign investment because the response from foreign investors had not been as enthusiastic as initially anticipated. The CSB calculated that by September 1995, direct foreign investment in Latvia only totalled 260 million lats. The ministries of Finance and Economy explained this situation as a result of the high payroll taxes which made Latvian enterprises not competitive internationally. In the author's opinion this was not the main reason for foreign investors' hesitation. International circles were aware of the uncertainties in the Latvian political and economic situation, especially in 1995 after the insolvency and bankruptcy of Banka Baltija. Besides, Latvia had not created a hospitable environment for direct foreign investment. Current restrictions on land ownership by foreigners, conditions of sale regarding investments and (until recently) discriminatory treatment of foreign investors *vis-à-vis* local investors were all factors which discouraged foreign investors from pursuing investment opportunities in Latvia.

Nevertheless, ideas for the implementation of a cost-saving social security system developed and gained support in political circles. Social programmes of different political parties did not differ much in 1993: they were all influenced by the old Soviet notions on social security. The only alternative offered was the implementation of funded pension and other benefit schemes.

The 1993 elections were won by the Latvijas cels ('Latvian way') party, a party characterized as being 'right of centre'. Many representatives were from financial and business circles. The position of minister of welfare was taken by Jânis Ritenis (Latvian Peasants Union coalition party), a Latvian who had been living in exile and had worked for private insurance companies in Australia. He developed a pension reform concept fully based on notions about private insurance. His ideas were met with strong resistance in the society at large, for example, by the Latvian Association of Free Trade Unions, the Pensioners' Federation and left-oriented parties. The pension reform concept was also criticized by German pension specialists and the World Bank delegation. Nevertheless the ideas of funding gained weight in political circles. In 1994, Minister Ritenis redesigned a new pension reform concept in co-operation with the World Bank team. This concept corresponded fully to the World Bank's recommended '3-Pillar System' consisting of:

- Pillar 1, the public pillar, which is a very modest state insurance scheme financed by contributions, with an average replacement rate of initially 30–35 per cent of the average wage, falling to 20 per cent over time as other pillars phase in;
- Pillar 2, the mandatory savings pillar, which is financed by contributions to a privately managed fund from all those employed; and
- Pillar 3, the voluntary pensions insurance.

This concept suited well the government's and leading political parties' goals, by not only helping to reduce the public sector but also by providing some of the required savings to finance the huge investment needs of the Latvian economy, bearing in mind the underdeveloped banking system and financial market. The economists were certain that against this background, the implementation of private and funded pensions could make an important contribution to the rapid development of the financial sector and would thus stimulate economic growth. It was also meant to link public pension reform and the introduction of funded schemes with the privatization process.

At this stage it is clear that pension reform was designed to be the main contributor to the continuing overall reform process, targeted only towards economic goals while ignoring social concerns. It was thought that once the economic goals were reached it would become possible to strengthen the social safety net and increase the benefits paid. Elections for the following Saeima were held in 1995, leading to the formation of a coalition government, comprising many political parties. The new government announced that the social protection reform would be continued and the Pension Reform Concept would be left intact. But after adoption in 1995, some significant changes in the legislative process were made.

The first pillar, the state insurance scheme, differs from the scheme described in the Pension Reform Concept and is designed in the same way as the defined-contribution Swedish reform model. The expected effects of the pension reform on expenditures of the first pillar and its development are illustrated in Figure 6.1.

Figure 6.1 Effects of pension reform, Latvia

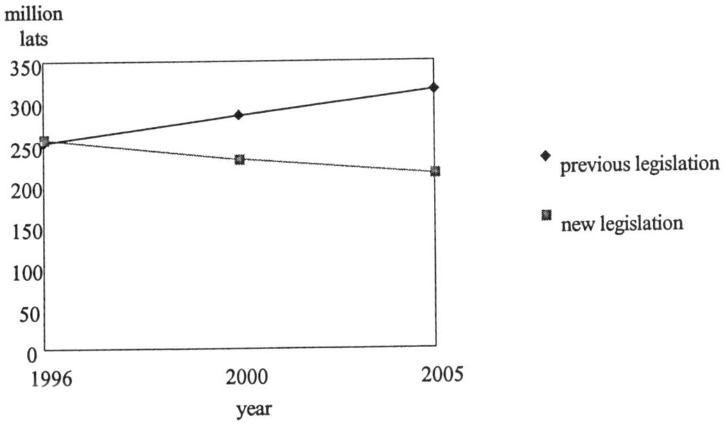

Furthermore, the original concept stated that the second pillar would be privately managed. But it was decided that the funds would be transferred back to public management within the basic retirement system (the Social Insurance Fund). The third pillar is also linked to a public managed scheme. At the request of the individual, pension benefit assets which had accrued in the private pension fund, at the option of the individual, can be transferred to the SIF, where they are credited to the individual account of the socially insured person and combined with the pension benefit assets (according to the Law on State Pensions). The draft Law on Private Pension Funds was adopted by the government in November 1996 and passed to the Saeima. The Pension Reform Concept development is testimony to the fact that the government will have to have some responsibility beyond the establishment of a strong regulatory agency to ensure that the funds collected do not simply disappear. Such regulations were worked out after the banking crisis in 1995 in order to improve the safety of funds in the new system.

6.2.2 The Development of Legislation from 1990 to 1997

The first pension law was passed in 1990 and became effective on 1 January 1991. It was designed as an earnings-related, defined-benefit pension scheme financed by contributions (social tax) on a pay-as-you-go (PAYG) basis. Coverage was universal: the scheme included wage and salary earners, entrepreneurs and agricultural workers. People without social insurance (service) records were covered by social assistance pensions, which belong to the same scheme.

Entitlement to old-age pension was based on age and service record. Men were required to have reached the age of 60, women 55. Men were required to have contributed 25 years of service, women 20 years. More favourable terms applied for those working in hazardous or arduous working conditions as well as for permanently disabled people, mothers with many children or with children who were disabled from childhood, and the blind and those suffering from dwarfism.

Pensions were fully earnings related. The pension was granted at the rate of 55 per cent of average monthly earnings, calculated on the basis of:

- any consecutive five-year period (selected by the pensioner) during the last 15 years of work before pension application, including interruptions of employment, or
- any 10 consecutive years during the person's working life.

For each full year of work in excess of the qualifying period for an old-age pension, the pension was increased by 2 per cent of earnings. The pension was not permitted to exceed 80 per cent of earnings, with the exception of pensions for those who were disabled or had suffered unjustifiable repression during the Soviet totalitarian period.

The disability pension was calculated on a similar basis according to disability. Such pensions included substantial supplements for dependants, to provide for constant attendance, care and treatment; benefit levels for disability were therefore higher than for retirement pensions. This was deliberate policy, aiming at improving the poor situation of the disabled: people with extensive functional impairment would be confined to their homes unless they were provided with the means to obtain technical aids. Thus financial support was justified as necessary to improve the living conditions of disabled people.

In 1991 all pensions were calculated according to the new law. But at the same time, price liberalization took place. As a result, inflation in 1991 reached 262 per cent (in 1992 it was 958 per cent). As a response, cost of living adjustments were made which became an essential part of the pension system, fundamentally changing the original scheme as foreseen in the legislation.

As of January 1992, the price compensation payment was replaced by the basic pension, which was linked to the minimum wage (80 per cent of the minimum standard of living – but this principle was not strictly applied). So all three pension benefits (old-age, disability and survivors') became of the two-tier kind, consisting of a flat-rate (basic) pension and an earnings-related pension (calculated according to the Law on State Pensions). During 1992, due to the rapid rate of inflation, the earnings aspect lost its meaning and the flat-rate element dominated. In this sense, the pension law ceased to operate. The main reasons for this were the general decline in the economic situation, lack of liquidity at the enterprise level, high inflation, rising unemployment, and last but not least the 'over-generous' pension formula and pension entitlement criteria.

When the budget for 1993 was drawn up, the separate social insurance budget was abolished and social expenditures were again included in the state budget. Meanwhile, dissatisfaction grew in society. The pensioners, who had expected to receive earnings-related pensions throughout their working lives – and had actually been receiving such pensions – were, of course, bitterly disillusioned. In addition, workers and officials currently in employment were also losing faith in the principle of insurance – and that, from the social standpoint, was a serious loss.

In summer 1993 new Saeima elections were held. During the pre-election campaign, in the light of the pension scheme problems, all political parties from the far right to the far left promised to introduce a pension scheme in which benefits would be linked to the previous working life in the best possible way.

In an attempt to meet these promises, new regulations were worked out and in November 1993 the Law on State Pensions was revised and succeeded by the 'Temporary Regulations for the Calculation of Pensions'. The crucial aspect of these regulations was that the pension level was linked to the length of service (but not to individual earnings).

Old-age pensions were calculated according to the following formula:

$$P = (0.3 * W) + (W * 0.004 * L),$$

where

P = pension,
W = national average wage for previous quarter and
L = total length of service.

Indexation of benefits was granted by changes in salaries and according to available social insurance revenues. Disability and survivors' pensions were calculated similarly. There were three categories for the disabled: those in the first category received an additional 40 per cent of the basic pension and those in the second category 20 per cent. As a result the average disability pension was considerably higher than the average old-age pension. According to the 'Temporary Regulations' the replacement rate was 43 per cent of the (gross) national average wage.

The dissatisfaction in society remained. This was because of the low level of pension benefits, which was partially due to calculations based on service records, rather than earnings. In 1995 a new pension law was drafted. The last version was worked out in co-operation with a Swedish team, commissioned by the World Bank, which explains why the new law which came into force on 1 January 1996 bears the hallmarks of the Swedish pension model.

6.2.3 The New Law on State Pensions[3]

The new Law on State Pensions changes the existing pension system significantly. It is designed as an earnings-related, defined-contribution pension scheme which is financed on a PAYG basis, but is similar with respect to construction to a funded pension insurance scheme. The norms included in the law apply to those insured persons who will retire or whose pensions were recalculated after the law took effect. The law stipulates three types of pension: retirement, disability and survivors'. The main traits and their underlying considerations are expounded upon below.

Retirement age

Any reform of the pension system involves an examination of the much disputed topic, the interaction between the labour market and retirement age, which gives rise to the following fundamental questions:

- How can an ageing population influence the financing of social security?
- Can pensions be used as weapons to combat unemployment?

Looking for an answer to the first question, a prevalent response has been to address the input side of financing. This raises the issue of increasing the retirement age in order to improve the ratio between contribution payers and benefit receivers, thus furnishing better conditions for the financing of the system.

On the other hand, growing unemployment forces us to look for other alternatives. The predictable changes in the structure of the population will also effect changes in the structure of the employed in the long run. All over the world employees themselves are seeking early retirement, and consider a raising of the retirement age to be a retrograde step. Such a view has been repeatedly emphasized by employee delegates through trade union organizations. Employee representatives loudly calling for the right of older people to continue working are rare. On the contrary most proposals have put forth plans for a wide-scale release programme for employees over the age of 50. Whether or not this is a sensible strategy has been discussed in most of the countries in transition in Central and Eastern Europe. Latvia, too, is faced with the question whether it is more sensible to keep the elderly working in spite of them adapting less readily to the new market conditions, or should they be let go to accommodate the younger workforce which is far more flexible? Another important point to consider is that if the young people cannot find a job when they have finished their education, will they ever learn to work?

Turning to the process of reforms in Latvia, the following questions are of importance. What is the socio-historical development of the concepts of 'employment' and 'retirement age'? Under Soviet rule in Latvia, as in other states under communist rule, unemployment did not exist. Through work distribution, unemployment was avoided. The consequences of this centrally planned labour market policy are well known: in particular, the so-called phenomenon of 'hidden unemployment' in which several persons were employed to do the work that could be done by one. Since the beginning of the 1990s the situation has changed substantially. The forced employment of superfluous labour ended and unemployment was stimulated by processes described above.

In the planned Soviet economy the pension system had its role in masking unemployment. The pension system in the former USSR had a lower retirement age than in Western Europe. By law it was 60 years for men and 55 years for women. Sometimes earlier retirement was permitted: for example: age requirements were reduced for those in hard and hazardous work. Benefits for these people were, so to speak, postponed reimbursement for unhealthy work. What was neither a priority in state policy nor an issue for trade unions was the creation of better working conditions.

Even if low life expectancy (at birth) is disregarded, demographic trends show a remarkable ageing of the Latvian population and a diminishing proportion of the working-age population in jobs. To what extent changing the retirement age will influence the labour market situation is unclear. Early retirement proposals have often been met with opposition, even though the highest rate of unemployment is among the age group from 30 to 49, among which 23 per cent are men, and 29.6 per cent are women. At the age close to retirement, unemployment is less marked.

Considering the demographic situation and avoiding a politically less feasible rise in the retirement age, the pension law has introduced a new component into the pension formula: an average post-retirement life expectancy. Thus, the amount of the pension depends directly on the contributions credited to individual accounts at the time a pension is requested. The longer contributions are paid and the later the pension is paid out, the higher the annual pension will be.

The insured are eligible for the retirement pension at the age of 60. The increased age required (of women) to be eligible for a pension is 60 years, to be implemented gradually: in 1996 the age requirement was increased by one year, and in each subsequent year it was to be increased by six months. For women early retirement (from 55 years of age) is also possible. Psychologically this has been a success. The 1996 statistical data show that only very few women at the age of 55 make use of this regulation. Yet, the knowledge of existing rights gives a feeling of security and reduces the social tension provoked by the rise in the retirement age. The flexible retirement conditions thus take human aspects at retirement into consideration. One may conclude that the pension age set by law is still flexible. In addtion, for men there is a financial incentive to postpone retirement. In comparison with West European countries the retirement age in Latvia was uncommonly low. A rapid rise would none the less not only be unpopular but would also increase social tension. Flexible retirement conditions can go hand in hand with the labour market and supply a balance between the working population and those who retire.

Insurance record and contributory basis

The insurance record consists of periods of contribution paid by the employer and the insured person. The Law on Social Tax does not envisage any non-contributory periods, but there are certain times when contribution payments can be made by other institutions.[4] In order to achieve a balanced state budget for 1997 (under other measures taken to balance the state budget), the period of higher education was excluded and payments for the period of child-care leave were reduced (until the child reaches the age of 18 months). A minimum insurance record requirement to be eligible for receipt of old-age payments has been set at ten years.

Social tax (social contributions) is calculated according to the taxable income, that is 'any cash payment and material values given to a paid employee to satisfy personal, family or household needs'. Minimum and maximum taxable income will be determined by the Council of Ministers.[5]

Pension formula and indexation

The pension level is determined by the individual's lifetime earnings (or by the total amount of the social insurance contributions paid in). The aggregate pension (the sum of the contributions paid in and the amount by which this sum of pension credits has been increased) is divided by the so-called divisor. The divisor is based primarily on the average remaining life expectancy at the time of retirement. This totals the annual pension in the reformed system.

The retirement pension is calculated according to the following formula:

$$P = K / G$$

where

P = annual pension,

K = the pension capital and
G = life expectancy.

The pension capital of the insured is composed of the amount of the individual social insurance contributions registered and the annual capital growth, and is dependent on the social insurance contributions earnings index determined by the Cabinet. G is the time period (in years) counted on the basis of the life expectancy of the years during receipt of the pension; this period is to be determined by the Cabinet based on data from the CSB and calculations done by the Ministry of Welfare. G depends on the age at which the individual wishes to retire and also on the life expectancy forecast in that period. Therefore it is possible that G is different from the life expectancy predicted by the official government statistics for the particular year. As the same life expectancy figure is used for men and women (for retirement at the age of 60), there will be some redistribution of resources within the system due to the differences in the average age of men and women.

The method for the calculation of the pensions allows for a change in life expectancy, but it does not compensate for the fluctuations in the demographic burden of pensioners for society. They will be compensated by a buffer fund which consists of the surplus of the contributions over the costs. The buffer fund is needed, for example, in years when the relatively large share of the generation of working people (those born in the 1960s) becomes a relatively large share of retired people.

Eventually, the pension will be increased annually, taking into consideration both inflation and the development of real wages, by way of so-called economic adjustment indexing. This means that pensions will be linked to real wages, but until the year 2000, pensions were recalculated half yearly, based only on the price index. From January 1997 the part of the pension exceeding 100 lats is taxed as income (25 per cent).

Transition regulations

Transition regulations provided by law stipulated the procedure for calculating a pension for an insured person in the transition period. The law provides transition provisions for those who will retire during the first ten years after the law comes into force. For these people the insurance period until the year 1995 (inclusive) is credited with an initial capital K, which is increased with further contributions.

$$K = V * A * 0.2$$

where

A = insurance record until 1995
V = average earnings.

The average social security contributions earnings are adjusted to the 1996 level of wages. In order to compensate for the special rights that were provided by the previous Law on State Pensions, there is a coefficient determined for the pensions of insured persons for whom the previous pension legislation had provided better conditions with respect to pension age.

The amount of pension for those retiring at the age of 60 or later would not be smaller than the amount of the state social maintenance benefit. Those who retired in 1996 received an additional payment if the pension calculated in accordance with the new law was less than the pension calculated in accordance with the previous law.

During the transition period, those who need to retire earlier due to the nature of their work, have the right to receive a service pension. The categories of those who are entitled to the service pension are provided by governmental regulations.[6] It is foreseen that the service pensions will be replaced by special pension schemes, such as occupational pensions, for example, for railroad employees, seamen and port workers, pilots, the armed forces and some other occupations.

Pensions that were allotted before 1995 are not be recalculated. Recalculation of these old-age pensions is made only in the case of an increase in the insurance record which has accumulated by the time the new law takes effect. Here the pensions are recalculated according to the pension formula under the 1993 temporary regulations.

In the Pension Reform Concept the transitory tier (4th tier) was seen as providing additional income support for those who had retired before the new law took effect, although this idea was not realized.

Administration

The social security system in Latvia is supervised by the Ministry of Welfare, headed by the minister and state minister, who are politically responsible. The administrative work of the ministry is supervised by a state secretary who is a civil servant. There are nine separate departments: Social Insurance, Social Assistance, Labour, Health, Environmental Health, Pharmacy, Strategy, Drug Control, and the Administration Head.

The Department of Social Insurance is responsible for the organization of the statutory insurance, which ensures a uniform application of the social insurance legislation, the elaboration of targeted social insurance programmes and the co-ordination of international relations and agreements related to social insurance. The Department of Social Assistance supervises and controls the activities of social assistance and social care institutions financed by the state. The Labour Department is responsible for implementing government policy in the field of employment and work protection.

The Social Insurance Fund, which comes under the direct supervision of the Ministry of Welfare, is responsible for the collection of the state social insurance contributions and for the payment of pensions and other benefits. The fund operates through 37 local offices, both rural and urban, which have their own legal identity. They are responsible for collecting the applications and all necessary documents, the calculation of benefits and the payment of all different kinds of social insurance benefits such as pensions, unemployment benefits, family benefits, sickness and maternity benefits. The information is passed on to the computer centre of the Social Insurance Fund in Riga where the calculations are reviewed and computerized.

In 1994, a tripartite Social Insurance Council was founded which consisted of nine representatives: three governmental representatives, three representatives of employers and three representatives of employees. The three government delegates to the Social Insurance Council are representatives of the Ministry of Welfare, Economics and Finance. The employers are represented by the Latvian Employers' Confederation and the employees by the Latvian Free Trade Union Association. All delegates are treated on an equal footing. The deliberations of the council are led by an elected chairman. The main functions of this council are: to define current and prospective objectives in the field of state social insurance; to submit proposals to the Ministry of Welfare concerning the rates of state social insurance contributions and their division between employers and employees; to analyse the revenues and expenditures of the SIF as well as the effectiveness of the fund's activities in general; to prepare proposals for investing the free resources of the state social insurance system; and to prepare proposals for the necessary modifications.

The new laws entail new requirements for the administration. Administrative reform was supported by a number of international donors. There are many donors involved in the project (World Bank, PHARE, the Swedish government). Since January 1995, the social insurance budget has been separated from the general state budget and has its own special budget status.

6.2.4 Implementation Problems of the First Pillar

The law came into force on 1 January 1996. Since individual earnings were not registered in 1995, pensions were calculated according to the average contribution earnings (85 lats) for the years prior to 1995. Additional payments were granted, which were supposed to offset differences due to the new law. From January 1997 pensions were calculated according to the individual's earnings in 1996, as registered in the personal account. The outcome caused an outcry. The variation between the lowest and highest pension payment was enormous. Some of the lowest pension levels were between 5 and 8 lats, whereas the highest were more than 1000 lats. The lower pensions were generally allotted to women taking early retirement (at age 55). With respect to high pension levels, those with high earnings who had claimed their pensions in 1996 were incensed. They were only entitled to pensions which were calculated according to nationwide average earnings. Meanwhile the people who claimed pensions in 1997 with the same career record and earnings received a considerably higher pension.

The law stipulated that the Cabinet will determine the limit of the annual income on which the social insurance contributions are to be based. This was done only in March 1997 and the 'ceiling' for the current year was set at 12,000 lats. Thus pensions could not exceed approximately 400 lats a month. In order to minimize the number of small pensions the law was amended twice during 1997. Other amendments came into force on 1 June 1997. They stipulated that the minimum pension for women choosing early retirement (at age 55) should not be smaller than 80 per cent of the state social maintenance benefit (for example, in 1997, 80 per cent of 25 lats was 20 lats). Furthermore, the retirement conditions were improved for those with a 30-year work record in Latvia.[7]

The first pillar forms the basis of the future system, but its functional role can no longer be seen as providing basic security for all during old age. Coverage is not universal and the scheme contains no guarantee of a subsistence pension for everybody. Social security for those who never manage to build up a sufficient contribution according to the first pillar system will be provided through the Law on Social Assistance, which allows for state-guaranteed social maintenance benefits. Social assistance is therefore likely to grow in significance and become a major source of income for a larger proportion of the elderly.

People who are not eligible for the state social insurance retirement pension may be entitled to social maintenance benefits if they have attained an age which exceeds the age for retirement pension by more than five years. In 1996 it was 61 years for women and 65 for men. The amount of state social security allowance was 25 lats.

6.2.5 Financing and Problems of Social Tax Collection

The financing of the pension system is one of the main topics in the pension reform debate. To illustrate the financial situation of the pension system, the development of social insurance revenues and expenditures from 1991 to 1997 is given in Table 6.4. In 1995, the revenues of social insurance contributions amounted to 272.7 million lats and the year ended with a surplus (16.5 million lats). In 1996, social insurance budget revenues were expected to be 346.5 million lats.

Under the present system contributors are wage or salary earners who pay their social taxes and for whom employers pay social taxes. A possible point of departure for determining the number of contributors would be to begin with official participation rates. Participation rates were very high when the

Table 6.4 *Social insurance budget, Latvia, 1991–97 (lats m.)*

	1991	1992	1993	1994	1995	1996	1997[a]
Revenues	15.2	101.3	168.3	235.3	290.8	327.9	390.4
State subsidies	–	–	–	–	–	–	1.8
Expenditures	13.2	96.1	201.4	265.9	274.3	337.2	390.4
Pensions	10.9	62.1	141.1	199.6	239.1	299.3	351.4
Short-term benefits	1.9	26.0	47.9	51.9	19.7	18.5	11.7
Unemployment	–	1.2	7.8	9.5	9.7	12.0	16.7
Others	0.4	6.8	4.6	4.9	5.8	7.4	10.6
Balance	2.0	5.2	–33.1	–30.6	16.5	9.3	0

Note: [a] Estimated
Source: State Social Insurance Fund.

last survey was conducted in 1990, suggesting that almost everyone of working age who was not on total disability must have been classified as participating in the workforce.

In 1990 there were 1416.3 thousand economically active people of whom 1408.7 thousand were employed. In the first half of the 1990s, the number of

Table 6.5 *Number of insured, Latvia, 1991–96 (1000)*

	1991	1992	1993	1994	1995	1996
1. Working-age population	1,534	1,522	1,484	1,457	1,437	1,432
2. Not in the labour force[a]	–	132	138	138	138	139
3. Unemployed	3	31	76	84	83	91
4. Potential contribution payers (= 1–2–3)	–	1,359	1,270	1,235	1,216	1,202
5. Average number of insured persons	1,439	1,344	1,303	1,043	983	973
6. System dependency ratio[b]	2.2	2.1	2.0	1.6	1.5	1.5
7. Coverage rate (%)[c]	93.8	88.3	87.8	71.6	68.4	68.4

Notes: [a] Students, secondary schools enrolment, non-working disabled. [b] Number of insured to number of pensioners. [c] Number of insured to working-age population.
Sources: State Social Insurance Fund; Central Statistical Bureau.

contributors in Latvia displayed a marked downward trend (see Table 6.5). In 1995 there were 1,437 thousand people of working age. Even when we reduce the size of the working-age population by the number of unemployed, students, non-working disabled, and so on, 232 thousand people are not paying contributions. Naturally, it is a serious problem that only three quarters of those employed, who are obliged to pay social tax, actually contribute to the costs.

Since many of those contributing apparently attempt to minimize their tax liability by deliberately underestimating and concealing the real value of their income, Latvian authorities are faced with a serious problem of dwindling revenues. The main reasons for this situation seem to be a well-developed 'shadow' economy, a low-level but still intact hidden unemployment and the failure of employers to register with SIF.

The 'shadow' economy, defined as unregulated or illegal economic activity, plays a significant role in Latvia. The difficulties posed by the transition period leave many opportunities for economic activity to go unchecked by the authorities. On the other hand, such 'activity' allows many to survive the harsh realities of transition (for example, the unemployed factory worker undertaking car repair services for cash).

The unemployment rate in the country has stabilized at 7 per cent. Latvia also has hidden unemployment, which is estimated to involve another 8 per cent of the economically active population. Many social tax arrears are caused by hidden unemployment and lack of income (that is, people remaining on the payroll without pay and regular work in the hope of being fully reinstated in the event of economic upturn).

It is impossible to establish just how many taxpayers have not been registered, but there is at present a very big discrepancy between the number of companies registered by the Business Enterprise Register and the number registered by the SIF: in 1998 twice as many companies were registered with the Business Enterprise Register than with SIF. Some companies and self-employed taxpayers deliberately register a false address with the authorities. Their reason for registering with the Business Enterprise Register is solely to be able to open a bank account. Another way to reduce their contributions is to underreport and conceal the real value of employees' incomes.[8]

Many problems of social tax collection can be explained by the privatization process. In order to aid the privatization of enterprises by alleviating social tax debts, the Law on Social Tax was amended. Now the law determines that when an enterprise is privatized, social tax debts can be capitalized. This means that the debt is replaced by shares handed over to the SIF. Thus those enterprises that are anticipating privatization are no longer motivated to pay social tax debts.

With regard to employees, at first there was no resistance to paying contributions because of the low contribution rate (one per cent). When the contribution rate was raised to 5 per cent (from 1 July 1996) all employers were obliged by Cabinet regulation to pay compensation to their employees in 1996 (equal to 4 per cent of the payroll).

There have been various attempts to improve and control contribution collection procedures. If the taxpayer does not pay in time, a late fee of 0.1 per cent of the taxes is charged for each day the payment is overdue; and SIF can initiate collection proceedings against the taxpayer (though these proceedings are generally not very successful). Furthermore there are technical problems of contribution collection, which need to be dealt with. Information on registration and its changes given to the Business Enterprise Register is not passed on directly and automatically to SIF, neither electronically nor on paper. For this kind of information the fund is instead dependent on the co-operation of the State Revenue Service, which gets some information from the Business Enterprise Register. Also the resources, including the number of well-trained specialists and the standard of technical equipment, are not sufficient to handle all the documents, to calculate benefits, and for instance to monitor each social taxpayer at least every second year.

Overall, the control and auditing procedures in the social insurance district offices are at present inefficient. Formal procedures for imposing penalties are in place, but there are problems in implementing them.

The introduction of pension reform with individualized social insurance accounts will probably improve the tax collection rate, because in addition to control by the authorities, there will now be a kind of control by the employees. Employees will be kept updated on the payments made by their employer; they will be motivated to oversee payments since non-payment affects their retirement pension negatively. It is expected that this factor will be sufficient motivation for an employee to take action against his/her employer if necessary. For the year 1996, SIF ended with a deficit of 9.3 million lats. None the less, revenue collection stabilized in the first quarter of 1997.

In addition, under the influence of the World Bank and other foreign experts, the government (in December 1996) decided to merge the State Revenue Service and the part of SIF that handled collection and audit, in order to improve the interchange of information and control. In the long term, a merging of these two offices could foster greater efficiency.

Under political pressure the Saeima also made some other amendments to the Law on Social Tax. The law stipulated equal contribution rates across sectors. Under the influence of peasant parties, the Sixth Saeima amended the law so that for persons working in agriculture, 22 per cent of the social tax rate would be paid by the employer, 5 per cent by the employee, and 15 per cent by the state budget as of 1 January 1996. The law also stipulated a partial shifting of the contribution burden to employees. This has been done twice. From 1 July 1996 the employer contributed 33 per cent and the employee 5 per cent; from 1 January 1997, 28 per cent has been paid by the employer and 9 per cent by the employee. Subsequently the redistribution of social tax has been suspended to alleviate the tax burden of low-waged income earners and households with low living standards.

There has been no real competition between social expenditures, because social insurance benefits are financed by social insurance revenues and other social benefits and services are carried by the general state budget. There has been some competition between types of insurance. For example, between pension and unemployment insurance. Very often the resources initially planned for unemployment insurance were redistributed to cover pension insurance payments. It was not difficult to transfer them because there was a single contribution rate for all types of social insurance. New legislation has been amended and stipulates that the distribution of the rate of compulsory insurance contributions should vary by type of social insurance. Each of the funds is supposed to have a reserve fund, which consists of the surplus of collected compulsory social insurance payments.

6.3 MULTI-PILLAR PHILOSOPHY AND CONSTRUCTION OF THE SECOND PILLAR

The general philosophy of the multi-pillar pension system in Latvia is briefly elaborated in the following. If the mandatory state PAYG financed pension system, operating according to the solidarity principle, is the only scheme, then before long, because of both demographic and economic factors, there is a strong likelihood that the system will become overburdened. This will necessitate an increase in the contribution rate for old-age pensions and subsequently a budget increase for old-age pensions.

In order to reinforce the state mandatory pension insurance system, an additional pillar is required: the state-funded pension scheme is dependent on both individual contributions and investment profitability. Ideally the state-funded pillar should reduce the burden of the state PAYG financed pension insurance, facilitating the involvement of individuals in the state pension insurance scheme, optimizing utilization of money facilities and promoting financial market and economic development in general. This second pillar has yet to be implemented.

If the first-pillar scheme provides approximately 40 per cent of the labour income replacement, then it is envisaged that the first and second pillars together, under generally developed finance market conditions, will be able to provide 60 per cent of the income replacement for those retiring at 65 with an insurance period of 40 years. Figure 6.2 illustrates the future goals of a consolidated old-age pension scheme.

Figure 6.2 Consolidated scheme for old-age insurance, Latvia

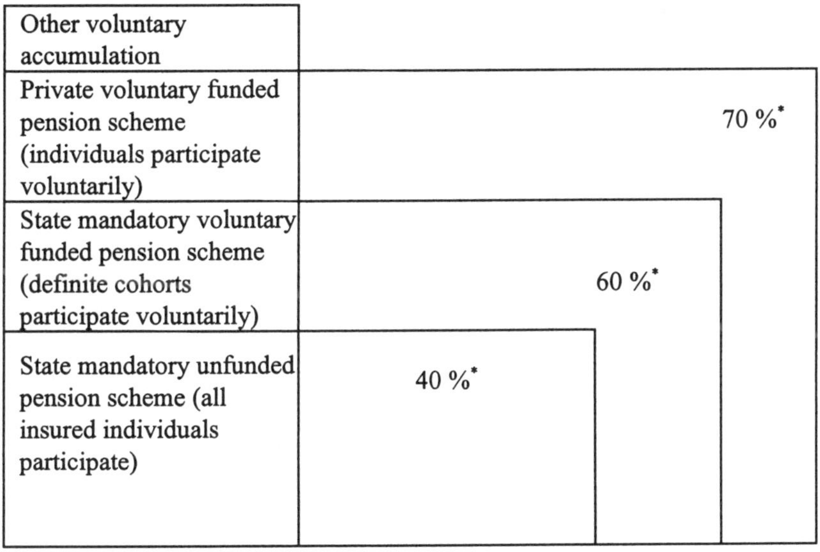

Note: * Labour income replacement level.

The main advantages of the second mandatory pillar are seen to have a positive impact on financial markets and economic growth, to ease the future demographic problems with a higher proportion of funded old-age security, to redefine individual responsibility and to improve flexibility and transparency. On the other hand, there are risks in the development of the capital market and through state influence in investment.

The goal of the three-level pension system in Latvia is the following:

- the first-pillar state mandatory unfunded pension scheme will provide a stable, medium/low income replacement at retirement age;
- the second-pillar state mandatory/voluntary funded pension scheme will provide a stable supplement to income replacement without requiring an increase in contributions. Simultaneously, the scheme of the first pillar is reinforced and the development of the finance market is facilitated;
- the third-pillar privately funded pension scheme will provide for additional social security, generating additional contributions.

Implementation of the second pillar is feasible however only in the event that certain conditions exist.

There are several economic prerequisites. The contributions which are being generated under the first-pillar scheme have to cover all the liabilities of existing pensioners and feed the reserves created for long-term investments. It will then be possible to redistribute the contribution rate in favour of the second pillar, reducing the revenues in the first pillar without decreasing the income of the current pensioners. Additionally, the financial market has to be developed and legally regulated. Private pension funds will also need operational regulations to provide a legal basis for the second-tier operation.

Finally, the state guarantees for the funded pension scheme will have to be calibrated. It is estimated that the working age to retirement age ratio will be at its lowest about the year 2010, to be followed soon after by an increase due to demographic factors. It may be assumed that by about the year 2050 the ratio will be approximately 1.5 times larger than it currently is. Consequently, the time span for commencement and development of the second pillar is limited. With an increase in the demographic load of working-age residents, the second pillar will create a stable component for the state social insurance system and will act as a support for the first pillar. The second pillar may provide relief to the first-pillar scheme through a reduction in the contributions and also a decrease in the respective benefit payments in the solidarity scheme. The labour income replacement level in the solidarity scheme will gradually fall as a result of an increase in replacement transfers from the second pillar, in aggregate maintaining the envisaged labour income replacement in the state social insurance scheme (60 per cent).

If pension reform does not increase the retirement age, then in order to commence implementation of the second pillar it will be necessary to increase the contribution rate to above 20 per cent. However, the increase in the retirement age to 60 would not provide a short-term solution capable of building up reserves to include all those insured. In such an event the reduced contributions in the first-pillar scheme would not be able to cover liabilities to the existing pensioners as well as to those planning to retire in the near future. Therefore, at the initial stage it would be necessary to organize the second pillar as a mandatory/voluntary scheme, that is, with mandatory participation for younger insured cohorts but for optional participation for the older ones. It will also be necessary to set additional criteria, for example, stipulating the level of labour income at which the insured individual will be required to participate in the second pillar and fixing the level of labour income required for affiliating with the scheme.

With the actual increase in GDP, a cash reserve is created for the first pillar: the difference between the increase in the contribution wage (depending both on inflation and on actual economic growth), and the increase in the pension payment (which in the transition period depends only on inflation). However, this financial source is also available only for a limited period, pursuant to the Law on State Pensions as of the year 2000, pensions will be indexed, taking both inflation and the increase in the contributions wage into consideration.

Since the second pillar consists of the state mandatory/voluntary pension scheme, this imposes a certain responsibility on the scheme. While regulations for the private pension funds are incomplete and in view of the fact that experience on operation and supervision of the funds and creation of the finance market is lacking, implementation of the second pillar of the system has been delayed. It is projected that the privately funded third level will be implemented first, which will serve as the basis for the complementary state-funded scheme. Only the future will show how the financial market will develop, how stable and competent insurance companies will be, and which variant of the second pillar will be more reliable and advantageous both for the pensioners and the state social insurance system. During the period of transition, the second-pillar scheme will function similarly to that of the third pillar. This period of time will be decisive for which variant within the second pillar scheme will be chosen and to accumulate information on developments as each trial scheme is implemented. The role of private institutions in the area of social protection has so far been very limited in Latvia. There are nine private insurance companies licensed for health insurance operations but they are mainly oriented towards people temporarily visiting other countries and foreigners, rather than to the domestic insurance market. The first private National Pension Fund was established in 1994 but ceased to operate after the 1995 banking crisis.

6.4 PENSION REFORM DEBATE

To evaluate the political discussion about pension reform and the factors that have influenced it one has to understand that in Latvia social policy has not yet formally become a separate domain of state policy. Not even a social policy concept has been developed.

In summary, one can say that during the early period just after the restoration of independence, the idea of creating a new sovereign system prevailed. Such a system was introduced, however the new system was greatly influenced by Soviet notions of social protection. With this as a problem in 1992, a co-operation agreement was signed with the German

Ministry of Labour and Social Affairs. As a result of successful collaboration, a social insurance concept was worked out according to the guiding principles of social security, international law and the development of social security systems found in Western European welfare states.

As this was taking place, characteristic economic problems of transition were emerging (for example, the breakdown of economic structures, hyperinflation, pauperization of a significant part of the population) leading to a situation in which social security and social needs were neglected and a one-dimensional approach, from a purely economic standpoint, predominated.

By 1994, the influence of the International Monetary Fund and the World Bank grew in Latvia. Their proposals corresponded fully to the position of the ruling coalition: promoting an individualistic approach and the formation of provident funds to encourage savings and growth. For the latter years this has been the only concept to be backed and promoted by political parties. There is still little or no difference at all among different parties' programmes with respect to social matters. The only exceptions are the programmes put forth by the social democrats and other left-wing parties, whose political influence rose significantly between 1996 and 1997. These programmes do not, however, contain any concrete suggestions for reforming the social security system. They only stress the necessity of improving living standards and alleviating poverty. There was no politically viable force in Latvia which can substantially influence decision making on social issues. The general population, especially the workers and their organizations, is disoriented and on the defensive. A feeling of impotence is common among those who are not among the market's leading players. People were unable to understand the ideas inherent in the continuing reform process. This might explain many of the reactions of those who are cognizant only of the consequences of an unfamiliar system, as in the case of the implementation of the pension law.

In an effort to promote understanding among its citizenry, the Ministry of Welfare and SIF have introduced public relations units which aim to provide better information about social security reform. A series of television programmes on social insurance issues has been prepared by SIF. Every programme was broadcast twice a week (in Latvian and Russian). Thus different media are being used to introduce to the general population, step by step, the various kinds of social insurance in the reformed system. Sociological research shows that people have started to understand how important it is to pay social insurance contributions and the way they are linked to benefits.

In recent years the growth of non-governmental organizations (NGOs) has intensified in Latvia. Government efforts to stimulate active participation by social organizations in decision-making processes have brought some positive results. For example, a tripartite council with representatives from trade unions, employers' organizations and the state, is active in co-ordinating decisions on wages, benefits and other matters. It remains an open question as to whether the involvement of government representatives in the leadership of these organizations will bring them under government control or whether such involvement will enable the relevant NGOs to present their aims more effectively to state institutions.

The next stage in pension reform will be the creation of the second pillar. A task force was convened in 1997 to begin preparing the legislation and the implementation plan. Until then there had been discussions about some key issues of the concept, but the only protagonists were the specialists from the Ministry of Welfare, the Ministry of Finance and the World Bank. There have been no discussions in political circles or society at large, so the implementation of the second pillar will also require a massive public relations campaign. If the supposed goals of reform are to be achieved then there will be a pension system providing protection against two main risks inherent to each of the pillars. The first-pillar PAYG benefits are subject to labour market risks while the second-pillar pension benefits are subject to capital market risks. Because capital market and labour market risks tend to be unrelated, a retirement income subject to both risks receives better protection from a diversified system than one offering protection against only one risk.

NOTES

1 In 1997 it was supposed to be 18 per cent. The Law on the State Budget for 1995 initially provided for the deficit of the basic state budget to be no greater than 40 million lats. However, the banking crisis affected government revenues and the budget deficit increased. The tax base shrank and public distrust of the commercial banking system led to greater reliance on cash transactions, which made tax administration and control even more difficult. State revenues were less than planned and it was difficult to fully fund social and other programmes.

2 The Law on Social Tax, passed on 2.11.95, publ. Latvijas Vestnesis (23.11.95), No. 182. Amendments 8.2.96, publ. L.V., No. 31/32 (20.2.96); 5.6.96, publ. L.V., No. 108 (21.6.96).

3 The Law on State Pensions passed on 2.11.95, publ. Latvijas Vestnesis, Likums 'Par valsts pensijam', No. 182 (23.11.95). Amendments 6.11.96, publ. L.V., No. 201/202 (26.11.96); 27.12.96, publ. L.V., No. 3/4 (7.1.97); 22.5.97, publ. L.V., No. 133 (3.6.97).

4 For example, a period of contributions during which the insured person has been considered disabled, does not work and social insurance contributions from SIF or the Work Injuries and Professional Disease Insurance Fund have been made; periods of unemployment during which the insured person receives benefits and if social insurance contributions have been made by the Unemployment Insurance Fund for this person; a period of contributions during which the person has not been working due to sickness or receiving a sickness or maternity benefit, and if social insurance contributions have been made by SIF; and the following periods of state contributions: compulsory military service, higher education but only for persons below the age of 24 (until 7 January 1997); and lastly

in the case of child-care leave until the child reaches the age of three (until 7 January 1997).

5 Nontaxable income includes state pensions, grants and allowances, sickness and maternity benefits, payments to adoptive guardians, compensation for expenses (maximum determined by the Saeima or Cabinet), dismissal allowances, compensation for damage to health resulting in loss of ability to work, grants to students, compensation for royalties, aid in case of natural disasters, remuneration to blood donors, funeral benefit paid by employer up to 150 lats, and income over the maximum threshold.

6 This pension is granted for several categories: for men at the age of 50 if their work record is not less than 20 years; for women at the age of 45 if their work record is not less than 15 years; for men at the age of 55 if their work record is not less than 25 years; and lastly for women at the age of 50 if their work record is not less than 20 years.

7 When their contribution earnings in 1996 were less then the average contribution earnings of employed persons, the pension will be calculated not from individual earnings, but from the average social insurance earnings in 1996. The same applies to persons who were registered as unemployed in 1996 and have a 30-year work record in Latvia. Some other modifications have been made in the transition regulations of the Law on State Pensions, too.

8 Curiously, according to official statistics, the average wage of employees in state and municipal enterprises is higher than the average wage in the economy as a whole. Some firms report that all employees receive the same (minimum) wage: from the president to the cleaning personnel.

REFERENCES

Bite, I. (1993a), 'A perspective from Central and Eastern Europe', *ISSA Studies and Research*, No. 34.

Bite, I. (1993b), 'The financing of social insurance in Latvia', *ISSA Social Security Documentation: European Series*, No. 20.

Bite, I., (1996), 'Wechselwirkungen des Arbeitsmarktes und des Ruhestandsalters in dem reformierten System der Sozialen Sicherheit Lettlands' (Interrelations between labour market development and retirement age in the reformed social security system in Latvia), *Dokumentation der BfA*, Berlin.

Central Statistical Bureau (CSB) (1993), 'Latvijas statistikas gadagrâmata 1992', Rìga.

Central Statistical Bureau (CSB) (1994), 'Latvijas statistikas gadagrâmata 1993', Rìga.

Central Statistical Bureau (CSB) (1995), 'Latvijas statistikas gadagrâmata 1995', Rìga.

Central Statistical Bureau (CSB) (1996), 'Latvijas statistikas gadagrâmata 1996', Rìga.

European Union (EU) (1996), Social Report, No. 1–2, Brussels.

Greber, P.-Y. (1997), *The Guiding Principles of Social Security*, ILO, Geneva.

United Nations Development Programme (UNDP) (1995), *Latvia – Human Development Report 1995*, Riga.

United Nations Development Programme (UNDP) (1996), *Latvia – Human Development Report 1996*, Riga.

World Bank (1994), *Averting the Old-age Crisis*, Washington, DC.

7. Transformation of old-age security in Lithuania

Teodoras Medaiskis

7.1 INTRODUCTION

The reform of Lithuanian social security started in 1990 when the country regained its independence; the aim was to build a new social security system appropriate for a market economy. Before examining the reform measures and their development, we shall begin with a short description of the history of social security in Lithuania prior to 1990 and sketch the economic and demographic background.

7.1.1 Brief Description of the Social Security System before 1990

Lithuania created its own social security system in the years of independence from 1918 to 1940. At that time Lithuania was an agricultural country with only a small part of the population residing in towns. Social security was mainly designed to support workers and civil servants, that is, the minority of the population. After the Second World War, the Lithuanian social security system was replaced by one of Soviet design. All workers and collective farmers (from 1965 on) were covered by this system. It was partially financed by the transfers from the central budget of the former Soviet Union. The responsibility for social security was distributed among different funds and institutions. Social funds (a combination of state trade union funds as well as various budgets of the Lithuanian Soviet Republic and those of the Soviet Union) were managed by trade unions (for working people) and the state social security administration (for non-working people). A clear distinction between social insurance and social assistance did not exist. A considerable part of social protection was supplied by keeping prices of food and other consumer goods artificially low. The whole system was built upon a system of totalitarian protection with only nominal insurance elements.

The *Social Insurance Fund* was subordinated to the central trade union organization. This fund was a collection of payroll-based contributions from Lithuanian enterprises and paid sickness, maternity and other benefits for workers (almost all of whom were trade union members), as well as pensions for working pensioners. The administration of benefit payments was delegated to the employers. Contribution rates were relatively low and differentiated by the branches of trade unions (branches of industry): from 4.4 per cent to 14 per cent (in the last years up to 18 per cent of the payroll). Employees were not aware of the existence of contributions because these contributions had been paid from one state fund to another. The expenditures for non-working pensioners' pensions were also included in the Social Insurance Fund outlays, but payment of these pensions was administered by local authorities. Because of a low contribution rate, about 50 per cent of outlays were covered by the central Soviet Union budget.

The pensions for collective farmers were financed by the *Centralized Collective Farmers' Fund of Social Protection*. This agency collected the taxes levied on the income of collective farms and paid benefits. More than 50 per cent of the fund expenditures were also covered by the central Soviet Union budget. Some special pensions, such as 'personal' and 'war veterans' were also paid by the central Soviet Union budget. The pension level was not high, though sufficient to cover modest needs. The pensions for agricultural workers as a rule were lower than average. The pensions were calculated according to the retiring person's wages of the few last years before retirement.

7.1.2 Economic and Demographic Setting

The first years of reform were very difficult because of considerable economic decline and high inflation (see Table 7.1). The living standards of all people were affected, including pensioners.

Table 7.1 GDP (m. litas) and consumer price index (CPI), Lithuania, 1992–96

	1992	1993	1994	1995	1996
GDP at current prices	3,386.7	11,107.9	16,980.7	23,829.0	31,115.0
GDP at constant prices 1993	15,948.4	11,107.9	11,217.2	11,551.1	11,963.4
CPI (December to December previous year)	12.63	2.89	1.45	1.36	1.13
CPI (average to average previous year)	11.21	5.10	1.72	1.40	1.25

Source: Lithuanian Department of Statistics.

Economic development is undoubtedly the most important factor for the level of social security benefits, pensions included. The situation in the economy also has a certain influence on the design of the social security system.

The decline of the Lithuanian economy, bankruptcy of large enterprises, which could survive only in the former Soviet market, the disappearance of collective farms as a result of the reform of agriculture and the emergence of many new small business activities considerably influenced the entire social security system. The decline of the economy resulted in a financial shortfall in areas such as education, culture, health and social security. The levels of benefit decreased considerably and have remained very low until recently.

The demographic situation of Lithuania is not very different from other European countries. Despite the problems of transition and economic decline, the ageing of the population is the first and most important long-run problem for the pension system (see Table 7.2).

Table 7.2 Population and age dependency ratio, Lithuania, 1985–96

Year	1985	1990	1991	1992	1993	1994	1995	1996
Total population (1000)	3,528.7	3,708.2	3,736.5	3,746.9	3,736.5	3,724.0	3,717.9	3,711.9
Age 0–19	1,090.0	1,114.6	1,113.8	1,118.4	1,103.6	1,087.8	1,075.3	1,062.7
Age 20–59	1,920.0	2,001.8	2,015.3	2,021.2	2,016.0	2,009.9	2,007.9	2,008.2
Age 60+	518.7	591.8	607.4	607.3	616.9	626.3	634.7	641.0
Age dependency ratio	0.270	0.296	0.301	0.300	0.306	0.312	0.316	0.319

Note: Age dependency ratio is the number of people aged over 60 divided by those aged 20–59.
Source: Lithuanian Department of Statistics.

According to the World Bank, if the retirement age is not increased, the ratio of the number of people at working age to those at retirement age would fall from 3.0 in 1990 to 1.8 in 2030. In the last few years there has also been a considerable decline in life expectancy in Lithuania (see Table 7.3).

Table 7.3 Life expectancy, Lithuania, 1989–96

	1989	1990	1991	1992	1993	1994	1995	1996
At birth	71.8	71.5	70.7	70.5	69.1	68.7	69.3	70.5
At age 50								
women	29.6	29.4	29.6	29.6	28.6	28.8	28.8	29.5
men	23.5	23.0	22.8	22.4	21.3	21.1	21.4	22.1
At age 60								
women	21.1	20.8	21.2	21.2	20.4	20.6	20.7	21.1
men	16.7	16.3	16.2	15.9	15.2	15.3	15.6	15.9

Source: Lithuanian Department of Statistics.

From the point of view of the pension system, this decrease in life expectancy is very inauspicious: the country loses people of working age (mainly due to accidents, suicides and other non-medical reasons) faster than those of retirement age. This fact intensifies the effects of an ageing population.

7.2 PENSION REFORM: MEASURES AND DEVELOPMENT FROM 1990 TO 1997

7.2.1 The Main Reform Measures since 1990

When the reform started in 1990, it was clear that the old Soviet-influenced social security legislation was no longer appropriate: it had provided external financing from Soviet sources for more than half of the social security expenditures. This feature distinguished Lithuania, like other Baltic states, from other post-communist countries, which were more independent. The second very important reason for the reform was the transition to a market economy. The existing pension system did not suit a market economy. The previous system accommodated totalitarian state control and could function only within it: it did not have private elements; participation of employers and employees was formal; personal insurance records did not exist; there was no mechanism to adjust pensions to inflation; the system was overburdened by different privileges for many professional and other groups; and so on. Moreover, the practice of calculating the pension according to each individual's last few years of wages only works when the state controls all wages, but not in the market economy with free agreements on wages. The first steps of the reform were significant and created the foundation of today's system. The most important steps taken were the following:

- the social insurance scheme was separated from social assistance and other branches of the social security system,
- the main branches of social insurance were determined,
- the scope of compulsory insured persons was defined,
- the independent State Social Insurance Fund (SSIF) and its administration was created; supervision of the SSIF was delegated to a tripartite council,
- social assistance implementation was decentralized and local (municipal) administration agencies were set up,
- a compulsory social insurance contribution rate for all employers and employees was determined and collections were started by the new administration,

- sickness and maternity benefits as well as some compensation for health expenses were made available by new laws and payments were begun, and
- the local assistance administration began benefit payments of the newly defined income-tested benefits.

However simple these points may seem, some of them were very new for Lithuania and fundamentally important. The main features of the structure of the social security system were adopted at the end of 1990 / beginning of 1991, when the nation's budgetary system was designed and the SSIF created. Decisions were made by teams of experts working on budgetary and social security reforms. Parliament approved this approach without discussions on any fundamental issues.

The idea of a separate, independent and self-financing social insurance fund was influenced by German and Polish models. Using such a design was also a measure contrary to the frequent practice of treating social security needs as least important, to be financed only after satisfying all other public needs. It is also significant that the principles of *insurance* were much more popular than those of *assistance* or *protection* as a main way of implementing social security. This was part of an attempt to change the mentality of a society of people protected by a paternalistic state into a society of independent individuals each responsible for him- or herself. In this sense the SSIF was rather seen as the fund of social solidarity, a fund of the people, and not the state. It was important to ensure that social benefits were the *rights* of contributors, not the *favours* performed by the state.

After the separation of the SSIF, the national budget (state budget and local budgets) remained financially responsible for some universal and means-tested benefits which were not awarded according to principles of insurance. The main benefits, paid by the state budget, were merit pensions, special pensions for officials and servicemen and -women and social pensions. The state budget was also responsible for full financing of large nursing homes for the aged, disabled adults and children. Local budgets financed family benefits and income-tested special social benefits. In the main, this is also the current division of responsibilities.

7.2.2 General Development of the Pension System

The old-age pension (as well as other types of pensions) reform was not included in the first package of social reforms. It was too difficult to prepare the whole concept and legislation in the first years of reform. Besides, the situation in the country was too uncertain for long-term decisions. Mainly for these reasons, Soviet pension legislation from 1956 was used until 1995 when the reformed pension system came into force.

Despite these obstacles to pension reform in the first year of independence, one special Law on Pension Improvement was, however, passed. This law largely copied Soviet regulations. Its main objective was very simple: 'Lithuanian pension benefits should not be lower than Soviet ones'. In other words, this law did not reform the pension system, it only increased the level of pensions for old-age pensioners as well as for so-called persecuted persons (victims of resistance, war, repression, and so on). The law introduced some Soviet-style regulations that were difficult to rescind later. For example, it was decided to triple the insurance period of the victims of illegal imprisonment and other persecuted persons, with the consequence that almost 100 years of insurance were granted. Also, some non-contributory periods without justification were included in the insurance records; retirement-age privileges for certain groups were created, and so on. The law increased the confusion concerning the division of responsibility between social insurance and social assistance concepts, and continued a system of privileges. Positive features of this law are that pension values increased and that the concept of a social pension was introduced.

The later development of the pension system may be divided into two periods: before 1995 and after. During the first period (1990–94) the values of pensions were calculated according to the rules of the Soviet law of 1956 and of the Law on Pension Improvement of 1990, and then adjusted by special government decisions in order to compensate losses of high inflation. Unfortunately, the desperate attempts of the government to increase pensions by adjusting their values could usually solve the problem only for one or two months, and it was necessary to adjust pensions more and more. Nevertheless, from December 1990 to August 1992 the average pension was adjusted more or less at the same rate as the consumer price index (CPI).

Until the middle of 1992, the government deliberately proceeded with the policy of high inflation. It claimed that since Lithuania was using a common currency (rouble) with the Soviet Union there were certain advantages to having higher inflation by which 'more' money than other common currency users can be generated. When the new temporary national currency (talonas) was ready to be introduced, and it was promised that all inflationary roubles would be changed into talonas, the government started the policy of 'freezing" wages and public expenditures, social expenditures included. This measure was taken to stop the inflationary issue of paper money, to achieve low rates of inflation, and then to introduce a permanent national currency (litas). The last quarter of 1992 and the beginning of 1993, when this policy was realized, was the period of the highest decline in the purchasing power of wages and pensions. The CPI showed that the cost of living remained very high (prices increased by 477 per cent from August 1992 to August 1993), though pensions were adjusted at a much lower rate (increased by 160 per cent at the same time).

The opinion of experts differs on whether the policy of 'freezing' was successful or not. But in mid-1993, the decline in the real value of pensions and wages stopped. Of course, other measures of monetary policy also influenced this development. Pensions and wages became much more stable, at a relatively low level, fluctuating not more than 10 per cent from that level (in real terms). The CPI that time was not much different from the index of the average old-age pension. Nevertheless, in the years 1991–94, the purchasing power of pensions dropped considerably due to a recession, a sharp rise in the cost of energy and a high rate of inflation. At the end of 1994, the pension purchasing power was only 40 per cent of its December 1990 level. However, the purchasing power of the average wage dropped more or less at the same rate as that of pensions, meaning that the average old-age pension usually fluctuated close to 35–45 per cent of the average wage. A similar relationship was also noticeable in Soviet times (see Table 7.4).

Table 7.4 Average pension to average wage, Lithuania, 1990–96 (%)

	1990	1991	1992	1993	1994	1995	1996
Relationship of gross figures	*38.6*	*35.3*	*39.3*	33.5	33.3	30.7	30.4
Relationship of net figures	*44.1*	*40.7*	*49.1*	43.7	43.2	40.7	40.3

Source: Department of Statistics; figures in italics are the evaluation according to SSIF Data.

The package of laws reforming the pension system was adopted in 1994 and came into force in 1995 heralding a new era. There was no formal declaration concerning the main principles and objectives of the reform. A working group of experts prepared the new legislation in dialogue with government and parliament as well as the World Bank and other experts of foreign institutions. Nevertheless, it is possible to see significant efforts being made to reach the following goals in the new pension system design:

- *Universality:* The pension system aimed to cover all residents of Lithuania. This old-age security system was to be achieved by a combination of different pension schemes. However, part of the population was not covered by any of the pension schemes.[1]
- *Solidarity:* One of the main aims was to create a system of solidarity. Working people support those who are not able to work, higher-wage earners contribute more and support low-wage earners. However, the

system was designed mainly as one of worker (wage-earner) solidarity with only the partial participation of self-employed persons.

- *Equity:* Equally important is the principle of equity – equal social insurance contributions result in equal claims to social insurance benefits; privileges for any professional or other groups do not exist. The pension reform increased the separation of state and SSIF responsibilities by shifting payment of pensions for persecuted persons from the SSIF to the state budget.
- *Poverty elimination and income security:* In designing the pension system, there was a choice between two extreme approaches – a flat-rate means-tested pension for everybody or an earnings-related differentiated pension which aims to replace a considerable part of the previous income lost because of old age or disability. The first approach is less expensive and better targeted for protection against poverty; the second is much more expensive, but fairer from the point of view of a contributor. A redistributive quality of the pension system was designed by combining the respective aims associated with the two approaches. Redistribution

Table 7.5 *Theoretical replacement rates, Lithuania*

Rate of insured income	Social insurance period (years) 15	20	25	30	35
0.3	72%	75%	77%	80%	82%
0.4	56%	58%	61%	63%	66%
0.5	46%	49%	51%	54%	56%
0.6	40%	42%	45%	47%	50%
0.7	35%	38%	40%	43%	45%
0.8	32%	34%	37%	39%	42%
0.9	29%	32%	34%	37%	39%
1.0	27%	29%	32%	34%	37%
1.5	20%	23%	25%	28%	30%
2.0	17%	20%	22%	25%	27%
2.5	15%	18%	20%	23%	25%
3.0	14%	16%	19%	21%	24%
3.5	13%	16%	18%	21%	23%
4.0	12%	15%	17%	20%	22%
4.5	12%	14%	17%	19%	22%
5.0	11%	14%	16%	19%	21%

Note: To be read in the following way: a person with 35 years of insurance and a rate of insured income equal to 1.5 (150 per cent of the average wage during the lifetime) may expect a pension equal to 30 per cent of 150 per cent of actual insured income. Based on own calculations.

from the working to the retired, the disabled and orphans is essential for 'pay-as-you-go' (PAYG) schemes which collect money from the working part of the population and distribute it among those not able to work. Redistribution in favour of low-wage earners was implemented by a two-part scheme: a flat rate minimum pension for everybody and an earnings-related supplementary part. High-wage earners contribute more, and their pensions are higher, but not proportionally higher. Pensions are differentiated, but with a reasonable redistributive effect. The replacement rates are thus much more favourable for low-wage earners (see Table 7.5).

Financial sustainability was one of the main goals of the whole system. Among other proposals of the initial draft of pension laws, it was suggested that there should be no recalculation of pensions awarded before reform but they should rather be adjusted at the same time period and rate as the new pensions awarded according to the new law. It was also suggested that new adjusted values of the basic pension and insured income (the main multiplier for the earnings-related part of pension) should be approved according to the financial situation of the fund, rather than automatically according to the price or wage indexes. It was also proposed that the whole value of pensions should be kept relatively low and flat by a fairly small percentage (0.5 per cent) of every year wage contribution into the earnings-related part of pensions. The initial draft also proposed increasing the retirement age and obligatory insurance period needed for full pensions.Not all of these proposals were approved by government and parliament. The pensions awarded before the reform were recalculated according to the new rules (if the new pension was lower, then the old amount of pension was paid and adjusted). Data existing in the pensioners' files could be supplemented with new data on previous wages.[2] The insured income is recalculated automatically according to quarterly data of average wages.

These have all been mainly political decisions. Implementation of these policy decisions has resulted in increased expenditures of the fund and has endangered its financial sustainability. Nevertheless, the main financial worry now comes from another source: the insolvency of employers and contribution evasion.

There were many discussions on the pension system, the pension levels, entitlement and other important details, but the main concepts of the pension system approved in the second period of reform in 1995 have remained unchanged. With the 1995 legislation, the following were introduced:

- social insurance pensions,
- state pensions and

- social pensions.

This system of pensions advanced the separation of social insurance and state responsibilities in social security. *Social insurance pensions* are contribution based, and nobody has special claims or privileges. *State pensions* are financed from general state revenues and are awarded to special merited or professional groups who are resident in the country. *Social pensions* are awarded to those who are not entitled to any other kind of pension because they were not able to enter the labour market and build up the required insurance record due to disability. In the following, more detailed regulations for social insurance pensions and state and social pensions are described.

7.2.3 Institutional Regulations: Social Insurance Pensions

Insurance coverage

State social insurance pensions are awarded for insured residents of Lithuania in cases of old age, disability, widowhood and orphanhood. Insurance for these pensions is compulsory for permanent residents employed under a labour or any other contract and receiving income from work, as well as military personnel and officials receiving remuneration for service, the self-employed and farmers. National defence conscripts and mothers (fathers) on three-year maternity (paternity) leave (as of 1996) are insured by the state in the same way as self-employed persons. The development of the number of insured by state social insurance is presented in Table 7.6.

Table 7.6 Number of insured by state social insurance, Lithuania, 1991–96 (in 1000)

Year	1991	1992	1993	1994	1995	1996
Population of working age	2,114.6	2,126.4	2,113.0	2,103.6	2,100.3	2,110.6
Number of insured:	1,768.0	1,572.8	1,373.8	1,286.8	1,332.4	1,325.2
Employees	1,753.7	1,555.1	1,357.4	1,263.1	1,258.6	1,220.1
Military personnel					30.8	32.3
Self-employed	13.3	17.0	14.9	21.0	41.5	36.9
Farmers[a]	0.6	–	–	–	1.6	1.6
National defence conscripts	–	–	–	–	5.3	5.2
Maternity leave	–	–	–	–	–	28.6
Voluntary insured	0.4	0.7	1.4	2.8	0.8	0.4

Notes: [a] Number of insured farmers in 1992 – 94 is included in the total number of self-employed.

Source: Data of the Lithuanian Department of Statistics and SSIF database.

There were no self-employed people in former times. Therefore the social security system has had no experience of how to treat them. The main obstacle to including them within the scope of compulsory insurance like all employees, was that the self-employed have no wages, so there is no base for calculating social insurance contributions. It is difficult to distinguish 'income from work' (which is the base for contributions) from other types of income. The self-employed are insured through the basic pension scheme only; there are compulsory contributions calculated to cover the cost of their basic pension.[3] However, the question of pension insurance for the self-employed is still open.

Eligibility

A person is entitled to a social insurance old-age pension if he/she meets all of the following requirements:

- retirement age: before 1995 the retirement age was 55 years for women and 60 years for men. In 1995 it was raised annually: by four months for women and by two months for men; the goal is for the retirement age to be 62 years and 6 months for men and 60 years for women,
- minimum contribution period 15 years,[4]
- insured status by state social pension insurance: at least three years within the last five years[5] or the whole of the last year before retirement or not less than 35 years in all.

The social insurance system also provides disability and survivors' pensions. Table 7.7 shows the number of beneficiaries of the different kinds of pensions. Almost all old-aged or disabled persons can claim a social insurance pension based on their former working record. The coverage rate of the pension system is therefore high. However, the situation may worsen as a result of social insurance contribution evasion.

Table 7.7 *Social insurance pension beneficiaries, Lithuania, 1992–96*

Year	1992	1993	1994	1995	1996
Old-age	690,537	656,817	658,427	656,794	655,305
Disability	122,630	129,141	131,296	139,152	147,023
Widow(er)s'	–	–	–	3,406	19,039
Orphans'	–	–	–	2,169	8,287
Survivors' (awarded before 1995)	41,754	40,224	42,102	49,726	47,772
Others (awarded before 1995)	1,233	1,318	1,764	2,548	2,364

Source: SSIF database.

Benefits

The old-age pension consists of two parts: basic and supplementary. The basic part equals the basic pension and is a flat-rate payment to all those who have fulfilled the obligatory period of contributions (for those who do not it is prorated). The supplementary part is calculated earnings related to former income. The pension P is calculated according to the formula:

$$P = B + 0.005 * S * K * D + 0.005 * s * k * D,$$

where

> B is the basic pension, the level of which is approved by the government;
> S is the person's state social insurance period acquired while under employment contract up to 1994, whereas s is the period after 1994;
> K is the insured income rate which is calculated by dividing the annual wage of the insured by the annual average Lithuanian wage up to 1994, whereas k represents the period after 1994;
> D is the average monthly insured income.

Taking into account the fact that there are no reliable data about the wage of the insured person throughout his or her life up to 1994, a pensioner can choose the five most favourable consecutive years from the 1984–93 period, and calculate this average value as K; k is calculated according to SSIF data on contribution payments starting from 1994. As of the year 2004, the data prior to 1994 will gradually be disregarded, and the middle part of the formula will disappear. Pursuant to the law, K and k cannot be higher than 5. A coefficient 0.005 means that 0.5 per cent of the monthly wage is added annually to the supplementary part of the person's future pension.

The reformed pension system began with a relatively low level of pensions. In general, pensions were not increased much. Later improvements in the benefit level increased its purchasing power slightly. The value of pensions, as before the reform, fluctuated at about 40 per cent of the net average wage. Traditionally, pensions are not taxable.

Before the pension reform, in the years of very high inflation (1992–94), faced with rapid price increases and lacking the funds to meet pension payments, the government was compelled to raise large and small pensions at different rates. Small pensions were increased at a higher rate, in order to guarantee at least a minimum income to recipients. The result was a flattening of the pension level.

In this situation the simplest solution would have been to legalize the flat-rate pension system for everyone. In this case the supplementary earnings-related part of the pension would have to be established anew and based on a PAYG or funding principle. This solution was considered as the best way to guarantee all pensioners a reasonable (in existing economic conditions) standard of living, and to develop step by step an earnings-related component of the pension for younger generations. The alternative – the immediate differentiation of pensions – would have implied higher pensions for some pensioners at the cost of lower pensions for the others. Given the low average level of pensions, the group of pensioners receiving lower-level benefits in this case could barely have survived at all.

Nevertheless both parliament and government supported the earnings-related approach to setting pension levels. The main argument was that people who worked longer and earned higher wages should get higher pensions. The earnings-related formula was also to serve as an important incentive for workers not to evade contribution payments to the SSIF. The compromise was found by establishing a two-part pension formula: a basic flat-rate part and a supplementary earnings-related part. Some degree of pension differentiation is therefore being restored, but only in the supplementary part, which for an average pensioner makes up approximately 45–50 per cent of the whole pension. The basic pension[6] is adjusted according to a price index, and the supplementary social insurance according to the insured income (which reflects the average wage in the country). For this reason, if the real income of the working population rises, the supplementary part of the pension should start to dominate, and the differences between high and low pensions will increase. If the real income does not rise, the basic pension dominates and the high and low pensions will differ slightly, a situation that seems unavoidable during recession.

The increase in insured income follows the increase in net average wage.[7] When the ratio of workers to pensioners decreases, there may be financial problems for the SSIF. In order to avoid getting into such a situation, World Bank experts have insisted on amending the law so that the average monthly insured income will be recalculated taking the changes in this ratio into account. Differentiation of old-age social insurance pensions of non-working pensioners at the end of the first year of reform shows that most pensioners received 130–230 litas per month. About 70 per cent of pensioners received below average pensions (180 litas in December 1995).

Early retirement and working pensioners

The first drafts of the pension law provided for the possibility of early retirement with a correspondingly reduced pension. But this idea was not included in the final draft. Calculations showed that one year of early retirement 'costs' about 7 per cent of the pension value. Bearing in mind that even full pensions were very low, early retirement with reduced pensions was not accepted. Instead of early retirement, the concept of deferred retirement was introduced. By law it is possible to collect up to five years of deferred retirement, and accordingly increase the pension by 20 per cent.

According to the initial version of the pension law, the 'working' pensioner was entitled only to a basic pension. Parliament amended this regulation, stating that a pensioner would receive a full pension if his/her earnings do not exceed the threshold of 150 per cent of the minimum wage. The argument was that people could not survive on such low pensions. When the minimum wage was increased, this regulation resulted in a too high threshold (600 litas in the first half of 1997). Today a considerable proportion of pension expenditures (around 14 per cent) is paid out to working pensioners and many of them get wages at a level about 75 per cent of the Lithuanian average. The high threshold creates the incentive for pensioners to work and a relatively low level of average pensions practically forces them to seek work. It is mainly under these circumstances that the number of working pensioners increased in 1996 and by 1997 was officially around 15 per cent. In fact, there are probably even more working pensioners than are officially reported.

7.2.4 Institutional Regulations: State Pensions and Social Pensions

State pensions are awarded and paid irrespective of receipt of state social insurance pensions. However, the limit of 150 per cent of the average Lithuanian wage is applied to the sum of both pensions. If a person has reached retirement age, become disabled or widowed he/she is eligible for a 'state pension'.

The largest group of beneficiaries of state pensions are the so-called 'persecuted persons'. These are persons who under the Soviet regime participated in the Second World War, and were imprisoned in ghettos and concentration camps. In the first years of independence many categories of persecuted persons were added to this privileged system: those who participated in the resistance against the Soviet regime, those who were illegally imprisoned, and so on. The number of recipients reached 60 to 70 thousand. The privileges for these people were created according to the old Soviet rules; hence the social insurance system became responsible for recovering any losses. The pension reform changed the situation by establishing a special State Pension for Persecuted Persons. All special rights of persecuted persons for social insurance pensions were abolished and pensions were recalculated. Instead of social insurance privileges, special additional state pensions were awarded to persecuted persons. As a result none of them (adding both pensions) received less income than before. Nevertheless, it was very difficult to defend the new law against attempts to restore former privileges. Table 7.8 shows the number of all beneficiaries of state pensions.

Table 7.8 *Total number of beneficiaries of state pensions, Lithuania, 1995 and 1996 (end of the year)*

Scheme	1995	1996
Persecuted persons	66,302	72,351
Merited pensions	2,050	2,101
Officials and service personnel	6,350	6,178
Scientists	1,467	1,560

Source: SSIF and MSSL data.

State pensions are also awarded to officials and service personnel[8] who in Soviet times were entitled to special pensions. The reform of 1995 changed this situation. The officials and service personnel now have general social insurance like other public employees. The insurance contributions are paid by the state. The aim is to develop a universal social insurance system. State pensions are also awarded as a kind of 'merited pension' for those whose services to the state in establishing and developing its statehood, economy, culture, science, art and sport are considered of great value.

Merit pensions have their roots in Soviet times. A part of the Soviet pension system consisted in so-called 'personal' pensions. These were awarded according to merit to individuals who added much to the strengthening of the Soviet regime as well as for famous artists, scientists, and so on. People who were awarded personal pensions could not at the same time get any other kind of pension. After Lithuania regained its independence, the list of personal pension recipients was revised; some people lost their right to receive a pension. At the same time, applying former legal guidelines, some personal pensions were awarded (by decision of a special committee appointed by the government) again based on criteria concerning service to the country. In this case pension reform faced two alternatives: to completely abolish these kinds of pension as a Soviet inherited system of privileges, or to legalize them and limit their worth and number. Merit pensions are paid independently of social insurance pensions.

'State pensions for scientists' are awarded to scientists who have reached retirement age or are recognized as disabled. Eligibility is dependent on ten years' minimum service as a Doctor of Science. Moreover, recipients may not be under employment contract. The separate system of scientists' pensions, which did not exist in Soviet times, was introduced by the government in 1992. Its main purpose was to ensure elderly professors a 'decent' pension and to encourage them to retire, so that places for younger scholars would be made available. The plan failed totally. Young scholars did not apply for research jobs because of the low salaries, and especially because of competition from job offers in much more attractive fields like banking and business. Instead of encouraging scientific research, the scientists' pension scheme shifted funds from the research branch to a more privileged pension system. For these reasons it was proposed that the special scientists' pension system should be abolished in the coming reform. Unfortunately, parliament did not dare to do so. On the contrary, the scope of beneficiaries and the amount of special pensions was even increased, although the legislation has stipulated that these amendments should be 'temporary'. For the future it is foreseen that the state will fulfil its obligations by paying into a special fund, and future generations of scientists will be obliged to contribute to this fund in order to acquire rights to additional pensions.

State pensions are calculated according to the actual amount of basic pension (pensions for officials and service personnel are excluded); a merit pension is equal to two or four times the amount of the basic pension. State pension payments for persecuted persons are equivalent to the basic pension, although some groups of persecuted persons are eligible for higher pensions.[9] State pensions for officials and service personnel are calculated according to the remuneration of the last year of service. For every year of service 1 per cent (1.8 per cent for service years before 1995) of this income is considered.[10] State pensions for scientists are calculated according to the length of service: for every year of service for the holder of a doctoral degree, the scientist is paid 10 per cent of the basic state social insurance pension, and if the scientist has completed his/her qualifying *habilitation* 5 per cent of the basic pension is added. State pension levels are set by law. However, the government determines the amount of basic pension (to which almost all other state pensions are related). Every increase in the amount of basic pension results in an increase of both state and SSIF expenditures, which is why the government cannot extend the latter using basic pension adjustment rights without its own expenditures increasing.

Social pensions are based on a categorical approach: those who could not enter the labour market due to disability, child rearing and so on, are entitled to these pensions with no means-testing. Social pensions equal the amount of the basic pension, and are often the only source of income. The amount of social pension today falls below the poverty level, but an increase in social pensions is not politically viable without an increase in the social insurance benefit, because it is strongly believed that insured people have the right to better protection than those who have never contributed. The lowest level of insurance pensions therefore also creates the upper limits for social pensions.

Most elderly and disabled people are protected by the pension system. If this system fails, that is, if someone has no right to a pension or the pension is not sufficient, then it is possible to apply for a means-tested social assistance benefit.

7.2.5 Financing and Problems of Contribution Collection

The Lithuanian *social insurance* pension system is financed on a PAYG basis; *state* and *social* pensions are financed from the state budget. Expenditures for pensions as a part of the social security budget make up an important component of public social expenditures (see Figure 7.1).

Figure 7.1 Financing social security, Lithuania

National budget (state and local budgets)		SSIF
Non-social expenditures	*Social expenditures*	
	Education, health, culture, social security (*state and social pensions, family and social assistance benefits*)	Social insurance pensions; sickness, maternity, unemployment benefits
Consolidated budget		

Social insurance contributions of employers, employees and self-employed persons are collected into the independent SSIF, which is included in neither the state budget nor local budgets. The fund is under the supervision of the State Social Insurance Council, and administered by the State Social Insurance Board (SoDra). The SSIF may have other revenues: those acquired from board activities, use of temporary free funds, those from state subsidies foreseen to cover deficits of the fund (the state budget is a solvency guarantee for the SSIF). The main source of SSIF income is contributions (98.8 per cent in 1996), while only about 1.2 per cent of revenue is acquired from other activities; very small state subsidies (0.8 per cent) were used.

The SSIF has worked on a strictly PAYG basis: all contributions are immediately spent on pensions and other benefits. A small reserve fund which existed a few years ago no longer exists. The law requires that there be reserve funds of not less than 15 per cent of annual revenue, but because of the difficult financial situation the SSIF has not been able to comply with this regulation. Since 1991, the SSIF has been the largest source of social expenditures. According to the figures presented in Table 7.9, the SSIF expenditures amount to almost a third of the national budget, and this proportion continues to increase.

Table 7.10 shows that the SSIF expends almost four times more money for social security than the national budget, so it bears the costs for about 80 per cent of the country's total social security expenditures. Pensions make up about 65 per cent of all social security expenditures paid out by the SSIF, and this percentage is increasing.

Table 7.9 *Expenditures of national budget and State Social Insurance Fund, Lithuania, 1991–96 (in m. litas)*

Expenditures	1991	1992	1993	1994	1995	1996
National budget total	149.3	811.3	2,645.9	4,355.4	6,196.8	7,510.2
Social expenditures of national budget	65.5	378.6	1234.9	2,071.2	2,983.4	3,822.0
State Social Insurance Fund	35.2	249.8	761.2	1,454.8	1,972.4	2,643.3
SSIF compared with national budget in %	24	31	29	33	32	35

Source: Lithuanian Department of Statistics.

Table 7.10 *Public expenditures for social security, Lithuania, 1991–96 (in m. litas)*

Expenditures	1991	1992	1993	1994	1995	1996
National budget[a]	9.5	63.5	229.4	328.3	512.1	746.3
State pensions		3.2	7.9	19.4	71.9	119.8
Social pension		6.4	21.3	43.8	53.9	63.8
Family/other benefits			100.1	135.5	170.2	316.3
Care homes			36.9	72.1	95.3	96.7
Other			63.2	57.4	120.8	149.7
SSIF	35.2	249.8	761.2	1,454.8	1,935.7	2,643.3
Pensions	24.6	187.0	541.9	1,072.3	1,492.1	1,919.0
Sickness, maternity and other benefits	6.8	41.7	100.0	158.9	150,0	237.9
Health	0.8	6.2	50.2	121.7	185.1	252.4
Employment Fund	1.9	4.6	38.3	31.7	53.4	100.7
Other	1.1	10.4	30.8	70.2	91.8	133.3
SSIF/social security expenditures in %	79	80	77	82	79	78
Pensions/social security expenditures in %			58	64	66	62

Note: [a] National budget expenditures are approximate because of contradictory and unclear data from different sources.
Source: Lithuanian Department of Statistics and SSIF database.

The SSIF budget is submitted every year by the SSIF Council and must be approved by the government. According to the approved budget, the government sets a general rate of compulsory insurance contributions and rates for each branch.

Social insurance contributions are calculated on a payroll basis and covered by employers and employees. According to the law, the employee's share is defined by parliament. The rate of contribution for the basic pension (self-employed persons, farmers and so forth) is also approved by government. For the year 1997, contribution levels were as follows: a contribution amounting to 30 per cent calculated from the wage is paid by the employer (for pension insurance 22.5 per cent, sickness and maternity insurance 2.8 per cent, health insurance 3 per cent, unemployment insurance 1.7 per cent), 1 per cent contribution for pension insurance is paid by the employee. Contributions are calculated with respect to the gross wage. The self-employed, farmers and others who are insured only for a basic pension scheme, pay a contribution amounting to 50 per cent of the basic pension.

The contribution rate is relatively low in Lithuania, much lower than in many other post-communist countries. So from this point of view employers in the country have certain advantages. At the same time, it is highly probable none the less that this scheme is considered disadvantageous to employers since almost all of the contribution is paid by the employer. The SSIF's current deficit, however, makes the possibility of a decrease in the contribution rate highly unlikely. At the same time, an increase in the rate is not expected since none of the political parties or trade unions are advocating it.

Different governments have declared their willingness to increase the employee's contribution and decrease that of the employer, but have done so only on one occassion, and that was unsuccessful. The decision in 1991 to split social insurance contributions was not well explained to the general population, and people took it to be an attempt to increase the tax burden in a situation in which their real income was decreasing. As a result of strong resistance the decision was retracted, and contribution rates remained unchanged.

This situation may change soon. The government has submitted to the World Bank requirements to 'enact the legislation to reallocate the SSIF contribution rate so half is paid by the employer and half by the worker'. This requirement is one of the conditions for a Structural Adjustment Loan. World Bank experts argue that increasing the employee contribution would 'increase the public's understanding of the actual burden of public social insurance'.

In accordance with the amendment to the Law on State Social Insurance in the first half of 1995, contributions could not exceed the amount of three average wages in Lithuania. Later this amendment was abolished, allowing contributions to be calculated on the basis of an employee's total gross wages. Tax collection and inspection are separate from those of social insurance systems. This approach ensures financial sufficiency of the SSIF, as well as the independence of its activities.

Expenditures for pensions are presented in Tables 7.11 and 7.12. The tables show that expenditures for pensions as a percentage of GDP and of the consolidated budget generally increase. The fast growth of expenditures for pensions in nominal terms can be explained by high inflation rates (see Table 7.13). The real value of pensions almost halved in 1993 and then began to increase slightly in 1994 and 1995. Initially, increases have not posed any problems, but in the longer term this may develop into a serious problem.

Table 7.11 Expenditures for pensions, Lithuania, 1992–96 (in m. litas)

	1992	1993	1994	1995	1996
Social Insurance pensions	187.0	542.0	1,072.3	1,455.4	1,919.0
Old age	152.9	435.2	856.8	1,144.5	1,494.3
Disability	25.7	82.6	163.6	235.9	314.6
Survivors'	8.2	23.3	49.8	71.1	104.2
Others	0.2	0.9	2.1	3.9	6.0
State pensions	*3.2*	*7.9*	*19.4*	71.9	119.9
State supplement	–	–	–	65.8	–
Social pension	*6.4*	*21.3*	*43.9*	53.9	63.8
Total	196.6	571.1	1,135.6	1,647.0	2,102.7

Note: Figures in italics are approximate.
Sources: MSSL, SSIF database.

Table 7.12 Expenditures for pensions (in m. litas) in relation to GDP and consolidated budget, Lithuania, 1992–96

	1992	1993	1994	1995	1996
GDP	3,386.7	11,107.9	19,680.7	22,230.3	31,115.0
Consolidated budget	1,061.1	3,407.1	5,810.2	8,132.2	10,153.5
Expenditures for pensions	196.6	571.1	1,135.6	1,647.0	2,102.7
as % of GDP	5.80	5.14	5.77	7.41	6.76
as % of consolidated budget	18.52	16.76	19.54	20.25	20.71

Note: Consolidated budget consists of national (state and local) budget and SSIF.
Sources: Lithuanian Department of Statistics, SSIF database.

Table 7.13 *Growth rate (compared to previous year) of expenditures for pensions and CPI, Lithuania, 1993–96*

	1993	1994	1995	1996
Growth rate of expenditures for pensions	2.91	1.99	1.45	1.28
CPI	5.10	1.72	1.40	1.25

Source: SSIF database.

Until 1996, contributions collected by the SSIF were sufficient to pay all social insurance benefits; however, since then there has been a gradually increasing deficit. According to the World Bank, the SSIF experienced a 35 million litas cash flow deficit in 1996. The 1996 experience, however, would have been worse but for an 87 million litas deferral into 1997 of various payments: 36 million in sickness and other allowances, and 51 million in payments to pharmacists and other vendors. It produced a deficit of 122 million litas, or 4.5 per cent of expenditures (including the arrears).

In the long run the main danger for SSIF solvency is the threat of an ageing population. This has been predicted by a long-term evaluation of pension expenditures for an ageing population, prepared with the help of World Bank experts, which shows that this will result in an SSIF deficit (even if all other problems, such as collecting contributions, are solved). This is why the World Bank insists on a faster rate (six months per year) of raising of the retirement age, one of the conditions for the Structural Adjustment Loan (see Tables 7.14 and 7.15).

Table 7.14 *System dependency ratio, Lithuania, 1991–96*

	1991	1992	1993	1994	1995	1996
System dependency ratio	0.476	0.532	0.595	0.649	0.641	0.664

Note: System dependency ratio is the number of pensioners divided by the number of contributors.

Table 7.15 *Ratio of number of people of working age and retirement age, Lithuania, 1990–2030*

	1990	1995	2000	2010	2020	2030
Old law	3.0	2.9	2.8	2.5	2.0	1.8
Actual law		2.9	3.1	3.3	2.7	2.3

Source: World Bank estimations in MSSL (1996).

From a *short-term perspective* the SSIF deficit increases for different reasons. Table 7.16 presents the amount of contributions to be paid and collected. The figures show that the collection of contributions in the 'open'

Table 7.16 Collection of contributions, Lithuania, 1992–96

	1992	1993	1994	1995	1996
Actually collected (litas m.)	260.5	747.1	1,334.6	1,930.4	2,577.6
Should be collected (litas m.)	283.1	881.3	1,548.7	2,080.9	2,660.3
Rate of collection %	92.0	84.8	86.2	92.8	96.9

Source: SSIF database.

and prosperous economy is improving. Unfortunately these figures cannot show the 'hidden' part of the economy and the large share of contributions lost due to the insolvency of enterprises.

According to data of the end of 1996, there are about 196 thousand employers (insurers) registered in the SSIF as contributors. Many of the enterprises cannot make social insurance contributions and find themselves more and more indebted. The debt of employers is increasing steadily. About 8 per cent of them failed to pay contributions for a period of more than three months. Most of these enterprises (65 per cent) are joint-stock companies.

The desperate situation of many employers is so widespread that the SSIF Council, in accordance with a special amendment to the law, is authorized to exempt the employers from paying the fine calculated for delayed payment of contributions if the employer is not directly responsible for delayed payment. In addition, those employees who usually pay contributions regularly are also exempt. The total debt of insurers is approximately equal to two or three months' SSIF income from contribution (see Table 7.17 and Figure 7.2).

Table 7.17 Debt of insurers, Lithuania, 1991–96 (at end of year)

	1991	1992	1993	1994	1995	1996
Debt (m. litas)	0.9	27.3	161.5	375.3	612.9	731.6
As % of SSIF budget	2.6	10.9	21.2	25.8	30.1	26.5

Source: SSIF.

Many enterprises declare only the minimum wages of their employees and calculate contributions on this basis. This is done with the informal agreement of the employees, who prefer cash and thereby avoid every kind of tax. Small enterprises tend not to declare any employees and claim that only relatives and friends of the owner work there free without labour contracts.

Figure 7.2 *Structure of debt, Lithuania, end of 1996 (m. litas)*

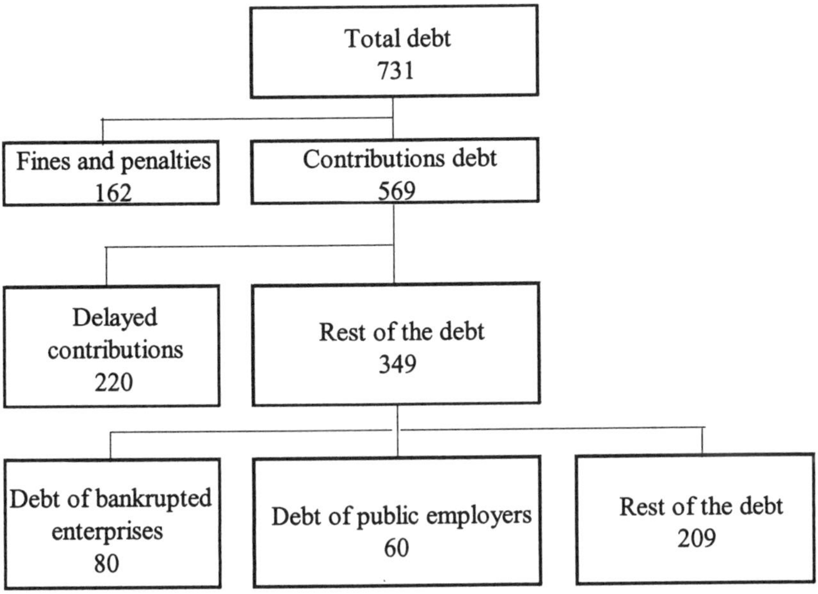

According to the Department of Statistics, the wages declared to the SSIF are about 47 per cent lower than the actual wages. According to an evaluation by fund experts, SSIF loses about 69 million litas every month due to tax evasion or false claims. There have also been preliminary evaluations which estimate that approximately 250 to 300 thousand people (15–18 per cent of all those employed) are working in the 'black' labour market. If this is the case then the SSIF loss is nearly 50 million litas every month. If these figures are reliable, collection of 'lost' contributions would result in a considerable increase in pensions (100 million per month would allow the pension to be increased by a third).

Probably one of the main reasons for the unwillingness to pay social insurance contributions is the low level of pensions and other social benefits. People believe that they are paying a third of their wages for something that is not worth buying. However, all taxes, not only the social security contribution, are avoided. Another important factor is the weakness of employee organizations. Employers usually take advantage of their economically and politically stronger position and abuse the rights of employees who have no real means of defending themselves.

There are also some repayment problems since the SSIF Board is also responsible for carrying out some payments financed from the state budget: sometimes state budget transfers as well as social insurance contributions for state employees are delayed. In such cases the SSIF meets government commitments by making up the shortfall. The situation was extremely difficult in the period from late autumn 1995 to spring 1996 following the government's decision to provide supplements to small pensions without first establishing the source for such payments (such supplements are not foreseen by law). This supplement was to compensate for the inadequate pensions at the lower end of the scale, especially in rural areas, set according to a scheme developed by the government. At first supplements were paid by the SSIF, but the bank crises aggravated the SSIF's financial instability. Then, pursuant to the SSIF Council decision, payments of supplements were suspended. The state budget was indebted to the SSIF to the amount of approximately 60 million litas. As a result, the SSIF was subsequently in debt to the Employment Fund, drug stores, sanatoria, and so forth.

Privatization was not used in Lithuania as a means of solving financing problems of the pension system. Most of the population, including the pensioners, used their privatization vouchers for purchasing flats. The profits received by the state in the privatization process were used for different purposes, with no special attention being paid to social security needs. However, the problem of privatization and pension funds is not a closed book. There are plans for further privatization of larger state enterprises such as the airlines or telecommunications, but the government has not stated whether such revenue could or will be used for pension funds.

As a result of the increase in enterprises in debt and the SSIF deficit, some benefits have fallen in value or been discontinued. Pensions are adjusted at a lower rate, there are delays in medicine cost reimbursement and some Employment Fund programmes have been ended or curtailed. During this period, top priority has been given to the needs of pension payments.[11]

Despite the priority given to the pensions, the most rapid growth in social insurance expenditures occurred in health insurance. In particular, the growth in the cost of medicine and the frequent extensions to the list of those medicines whose costs can be recovered has resulted in an enormous growth in health insurance expenditures.

7.2.6 Administration of the Pension System

The main administrative institution responsible for the pension system is the SSIF Board (SoDra) which is supervised by the Council. Some branches of social insurance are managed outside SoDra, such as the Employment Fund which is managed by the Labour Exchange. All social insurance pensions are managed by the SSIF Board. Some state pensions (for persecuted persons and scientists) and social pensions are administered (awarded and paid, but not financed) by SoDra. Merit pensions are administered by a special division of the Ministry of Social Security and Labour. The SSIF Council supervises the SSIF. The council is organized according to a tripartite principle: five members representing trade unions, five members of employer organizations and five members representing governmental institutions (the ministries of Social Security and Labour, Health and Finance). Personnel are proposed by the corresponding parties and approved by the government; the Minister of Social Security and Labour or his representative is the chairman of the council. The council has a small board of advisers (three experts), but they have no voting rights. The council bears significant responsibility: it presents the SSIF's budget and annual report, and submits them for approval to the government; it fixes the 'insured income' quarterly and appoints the director of the SSIF Board; it oversees SSIF activities, including auditing; it endorses decisions relating to important SSIF management issues and finally, it determines the number of SSIF Board employees, and the regulations concerning personnel and salaries. Decisions of the council are taken by a simple majority of votes. The SSIF Board is responsible for the current administration of the SSIF. The board comprises 56 local offices employing approximately 3000 employees, about 100 of them in the central office. Through its local offices the board registers the insurers (employers), collects social insurance contributions and maintains personal records on the insured and the contributions paid by them. Additionally, it carries out basic social insurance payments: for example, state social insurance pensions, maternity benefits and compensation. The board is also responsible for the payment of some state pensions.

As a first step of the reform the social insurance institution was designed to be independent. The main reason for this was to get and manage social insurance funds independently from other government commitments. It was well known from the past that the government liked to use budget funds for many purposes, treating social security obligations as a low priority. Hence, the SSIF was separated from the state budget, and the government thereafter had no access to it, except when provided by law. Politicians have complained that the SSIF is 'uncontrolled', but this is only partially true. SSIF revenues and expenditures are defined by law, which can be amended by parliament or by government. The government is also empowered to increase the basic pension and in this way increase SSIF expenditures. If the government abuses its powers and creates an SSIF deficit, it is obliged by law to make up the shortfall from the state budget. The government also approves (or disapproves) the annual SSIF budget and holds a third of the seats in the SSIF Council. On the other hand, the government is obliged to obtain a tripartite approval for some important decisions or to use its own funds for additional expenditures, such as supplements for pensions that are not compatible with the existing pension legislation.

7.3 INFLUENCING FACTORS AND FUTURE PLANS

7.3.1 Influencing Factors

The main factors influencing the development of the pension system are of a demographic and economic nature, and last but not least the legal framework of the social security system. Some of these factors were described above. In the following, we shall concentrate on the description of the main *actors* of old age-security reform.

The old-age security system was designed mainly by the team of Lithuanian professionals who remained in permanent consultation with parliament, the Committee for Health, Labour and Social Affairs, the government, the Ministry of Social Security and Labour as well as with the World Bank missions visiting the country. Experts hired for this mission by the International Labour Organization (ILO) were also invited for a short visit. Political parties did not take a particularly active part in shaping the legal system framework. The Lithuanian Labour Party's strong majority in parliament in 1994 made it possible for all pension laws to be passed largely unopposed; the opposition voted against only one law in the package concerning the privileges of officials and service personnel.

At first, the decision to raise the retirement age was not met with much resistance in parliament. Later, however, when the law was passed, some political parties tried to have it revoked. At the end a compromise was reached: the rate at which the retirement age was to increase was not changed but the whole issue was subject to reconsideration in the year 2009 (in the initial law retirement age was to increase until the year 2024, reaching 65 years for men and women). Some other amendments to the law were also authored by political parties or individual members of parliament. The regulations on pension payments for working pensioners were liberalized. The initial version of the law provided only a basic pension payment for working pensioners (and a full pension as of age 65). Members of parliament insisted on amending the rules of special compensation for entitlements to early retirement due to unhealthy work conditions or in connection with certain professions (such as ballet dancing, some performing arts, and so on). The original law provided lump-sum compensation, which was replaced by periodical compensation.

The President of Lithuania also has the right to propose a draft law to parliament, and he has exercised this prerogative for social security legislation on several occasions: one proposal was passed; another one (on increasing the lowest pensions) has been 'frozen' because of budgetary restraints. The next proposal came from the president's office at the beginning of 1997. It sought to renew Soviet-type pension privileges of early retirement for performing artistes (ballet dancers, musicians, and so on) who leave their career before the standard retirement age. As of July 1997, the fate of this proposal is unclear; it has been neither adopted nor rejected by parliament. The Ministry of Social Security and Labour is the most influential actor in pension reform. It is responsible for drafting laws and, in some cases, amendments for parliament. This does not, however, mean that parliament automatically approves plans prepared by the ministry or the government. Parliament has also opposed or ignored ministry or government proposals.

Ministers and their deputies in the former governments were selected more on the basis of their professional than their political background. Later the ministers were appointed more for political reasons, but this did not have the effect of reducing the level of professional qualifications in the top echelons.

The number of civil servants working on pension policy issues in the ministry is very small – not more than ten people (almost all of whom also have other responsibilities). They are supported by SSIF Board researchers and experts, who have a university education as economists or lawyers. Politically as well as academically isolated under the Soviet regime, these experts had lacked knowledge and international experience in the area of social security and pensions. But recently with international support through special intensive training courses in different countries and international organizations, they have been able to improve their skills and subsequently prepare proposals for pension reform development.

The Constitutional Court became involved in pension regulation for the first time at the beginning of 1997. The Court ruled on the problem of insurance records of employees when an employer fails to fulfil the obligation to pay social insurance contributions. The decision favoured employees: they do not lose their pension rights even if employer contributions are not paid.

Other national influential actors on the pension scene are the Tripartite Council (the main body used for government, employer and employee high-level representative consultation), the SSIF Council and non-governmental organizations (some of whom are closely affiliated with strong political pressure groups representing pensioners).

The main international influence on Lithuanian pension reform came from World Bank teams, who visited the country two or three times per year during the preparatory period. There has also been some indirect influence from the Scandinavian and especially German pension systems, because Lithuanian experts involved in the reform preparation studied these countries' systems in particular.

World Bank experts proposed or supported some essential decisions, such as the separation of social insurance pensions from state ones, the raising of the retirement age and the dichotomizing of the pension scheme into basic and supplementary parts. The World Bank also advised 'freezing' all pensions awarded before the reform and to apply the new system only to people retiring after 1 January 1995. This advice was rejected.[12]

Later (1994/95) the World Bank changed its team and advice on pension policy. The experts started to insist on excluding the earnings-related part of pensions and turning to a flat-rate system. This proposal was not approved by the government, and the World Bank experts also stopped insisting on it. The main activity of the World Bank in the social sector has now changed to the preparation of the 'Social Policy and Community Social Services Development Project' financed by a World Bank loan and other sources. Part of this project was (and still is) the establishment of a Policy Evaluation Fund designed to finance research in the social policy field. This fund may serve the World Bank as a means of influencing social policy indirectly.

Another way to influence social policy is through the so-called Structural Adjustment Loan (SAL). This is done by including conditions in social policy-related aspects for this loan. The most important requirement is for example, to prepare legislation for the establishment of capital-funded private pensions. The work in this direction is at an advanced stage, and the law has already been drafted taking this requirement into account (see the details below). Other SAL requirements are to increase the retirement age at a faster rate, to consider the whole working career in the pension formula (not only the 25 best years) and to de-link the supplementary part of the pension (the upper earnings-related tier) from automatic wage indexing. The latter proposal aims at better financial sustainability of the SSIF. In the initial version of the World Bank proposal it was intended to adjust both parts (basic and supplementary) of the pension according to the respective lower index (prices or wages). This point was renegotiated because this would have frozen the awarded pensions at a very low rate, leaving pensioners unable to share the expected future recovery of the economy. The government approved amendments to the law which allow the decrease in 'insured income' if the ratio of beneficiaries and insured persons goes down.

The World Bank's proposal to de-link the basic part of the pension from the minimum standard of living (MSL) aims officially to set the real value of the MSL. Because of the connection between the basic pension and the financial constraints of the SSIF, the value of the MSL was always set much below its real value. Finally, the World Bank required that there be state budget transfers for all non-contributory periods (which has been realized) and that employees be responsible for an increasing proportion of social insurance contributions. This last proposal aims to increase the public understanding of the burden of public social insurance. The current government, like all governments before, agrees with this proposal. Nevertheless, it has yet to be realized because its implementation is not easy politically and technically (that is, it also implies a personal income tax reform).

Other prominent international institutions such as the UNDP, the ILO and the EC PHARE were also involved in pension reform in Lithuania. The UNDP provides essential support for socioeconomic analysis and policy making.[13] The ILO concentrates mainly on labour sector issues, but recently expressed its willingness to be more active in social security issues, that is, pension reform, poverty studies and social policy budgeting. EC PHARE runs a project that aims to improve social insurance administration. Special attention in this project is paid to contribution collection matters.

7.3.2 Further Reform Plans

The main topic of the further reform plans is privately funded pension funds. There are some obstacles to the creation and establishment of these. First of all, people are not well off and cannot contribute twice: that is, for both compulsory and supplementary pension insurance. It is also politically difficult to shift a part of the contribution from a compulsory system to a private one because this would decrease the income of the compulsory system and actual pensions would thus be reduced. Another important problem is the necessary financial infrastructure. Financial management of pension funds requires the existence of a strong and well-developed financial infrastructure. Unfortunately these institutions are not yet sufficiently developed. Moreover there is the problem of financial security of pension funds. Many people lost their savings as a result of irresponsible and criminal behaviour on the part of the firms in which they had invested their money. The bankruptcy of two big Lithuanian banks in December 1995 exacerbated the financial situation and increased the general distrust of all banks, savings and funds. Under such circumstances it is difficult to persuade people to invest anywhere, including pension funds.

Nevertheless, now the main task of the reform is to prepare the non-state-funded pension system. Preliminary work was started in 1995, and two legislative proposals were drafted. The first proposal was presented by the Confederation of Lithuanian Industrialists and the second by the Lithuanian Institute of Free Market. At the beginning of 1997, the government appointed a commission to be responsible for the preparation of the joint final draft. The commission presented the joint concept of pension funds and in June 1997 it was approved by the government. The final draft is being formulated; however, opposing opinions among employers (presented by the Confederation of Industrialists) and independent experts are causing a delay in its completion.

The social aim of private pension funds is to supplement the current state social insurance pension system. A state social insurance pension scheme would implement the first tier of pension protection. This tier (with basic and earning-related components) would not exceed 35–40 per cent of the previous wage of the retired average wage earner. The second funded tier would be a supplement and augment the total pension to a level about 60–70 per cent of the previous wage.

The economic aim of a private pension fund system is to encourage economic growth. Pension funds are considered an important element of a capital market capable of making a considerable contribution to economic growth. Participation in such a scheme would be voluntary, but the contribution to the non-funded (SSIF) tier still needs to be revised. Contribution to the mandatory social insurance might be changed by establishing a ceiling for the contribution base. This would encourage earners of higher wages and the self-employed to join pension funds. The earlier draft by the Institute of Free Market provided the possibility of directing a part of the compulsory contribution to the pension funds. Another possible method to encourage participation in pension funds is through tax incentives. Pension fund contributions and any profits gained through the pension funds will to a certain extent be tax free. This does not, however, exclude taxes being imposed on benefits. The level to which tax exemption should be applied is under discussion.

The current concept of pension funds prohibits the distribution of profits from investments among the founders. Founders of the fund may be employers, associations, insurance companies, banks and other persons or organizations licensed to establish a pension fund. Whether pension funds should be profit or non-profit institutions is one of the most controversial issues. In addition, regardless of this issue the legal status, for example, non-profit public institution, joint-stock company or co-operative organization, which should be applied to pension funds is also controversial. This controversy is largely between the two groups of actors who prepared the initial drafts. The Confederation of Industrialists' proposal foresaw as a precondition for the establishment of a pension fund that at least half a million litas and not less than 100 potential members are required. Statutory capital, *inter alia*, was to ensure fund security. The Lithuanian Institute of Free Market opposed this provision. They argued that only large-scale enterprises would then be able to set up pension funds, thus leaving a major part of the population without additional pension insurance. According to the draft developed by the Institute, not less than 15 individuals may establish a pension fund without any additional conditions. Moreover, employers' representatives disagreed with the proposal that some pension funds could be established by state or local governments, or their institutions. Many experts do not see this to be an insurmountable obstacle to the establishment of, for example, a 'teachers' pension fund' by the Ministry of Education. According to this concept, fund security would be assured by strict financial supervision.[14] The mandatory diversification of investment portfolio and restrictions in the case of high risk investments would serve as a measure to achieve higher security of the funds. In connection with this, employers' representatives are trying to push through the idea of allotting a higher proportion of the investments to the enterprises which establish pension funds and contribute to them.

Reform proposals for the first compulsory pillar are being worked on by the government. In particular this concerns some important amendments to the existing pension legislation. One of them is the idea of increasing the smallest social insurance pensions. Many pensioners complain that their pensions are too small despite the fact that they have worked all their life. They therefore advocated increasing the influence of the number of insurance years and decreasing that of wages in the pension calculation formula, especially for the years before the reform. The same proposal by experts was rejected by parliament in 1994. The new government, however, has increased the basic pension twice in 1997 and the real value has increased by 10.7 per cent. The government also intends to implement a new contribution ceiling. For financial reasons the introduction of a fourfold average wage ceiling in 1998 and threefold average wage ceiling starting in 1999 has been proposed.

NOTES

1 For example, graduate students, who had not entered the labour market within a year of graduation (and are not insured), have no right to receive either social insurance or a social pension in the event of disability. They are only entitled to a low income-tested special social benefit. Those who are working in the shadow economy and avoid paying into social insurance schemes are also left outside the pension system. Year by year they lose their pension claims, acquired earlier, and are eligible only for special social benefits. Lastly, the so-called small land users who are not registered as farmers are also not covered in the legislation.

2 Difficult to impossible to check these new data; this regulation is often abused.

3 There were proposals to treat the self-employed as employees with a minimum wage (they could voluntarily declare a higher wage). Their contributions would be collected on this declared (minimum) wage. This approach was criticized as creating advantages for the self-employed, at the cost of insured employees because of the redistributive nature of the social insurance system. Paying contributions on a minimum wage basis, the self-employed would receive on the benefit side relatively more than average and high-wage earners. Redistribution in favour of low-wage employees seemed acceptable as part of employee solidarity, but redistribution in favour of the self-employed was rejected.

4 To draw the whole pension it is necessary to be credited with the so-called obligatory state social insurance period for an old-age pension, that is, 25 years (since 1995 this requirement has been increased by one year per year, until it reaches 30 years). Minimal period (15 years) is the necessary condition to be eligible for a pension; obligatory period (25–30 years) specifies the condition for a full basic pension.
5 These additional conditions mean that people may lose their right to a pension if they stop contributing for a longer time. These conditions were discussed intensively in parliament before the law was adopted. At the end it was decided that they are necessary to encourage contributions, but would first be made effective in five years.
6 The amount of the basic pension was 90 litas at the end of 1995, 110 litas at the end of 1996 and 132 at the end of 1997.
7 The insured income was adjusted from 431 litas at the end of 1995 to 557 litas at the end of 1996 and to 716 litas at the end 1997.
8 The requirement is 20 or more years of service in Internal Affairs, State Security or National Defence.
9 Pensions to those who became disabled as a consequence of the hostilities of 11–13 January 1991 are paid 150 per cent of the basic pension; there are other exceptions for disabled persons.
10 An increased percentage for the years before 1995 was introduced as a means of ensuring a smooth transition from very high levels of pensions (which existed before) to lower ones. For retired officials and service personnel who have no other income, the basic pension is paid as a supplement until they have no right to a social insurance pension. This supplement will be paid until the year 2005 when the system of officials' vocational retraining is expected to be developed.
11 From this point of view the division of contributions by insurance branches is superfluous, because it is not forbidden by law to use money from one branch to cover the deficit of another.
12 Government and parliament decided to recalculate all pensions awarded before the reform. The proposal to take into account only periods of insurance before 1995 but not wages, was also rejected. It resulted in the recalculation of all pensions.
13 For instance, the UNDP made important contributions to the poverty study which has had a significant impact on pension policy.
14 Supervision of the pension funds will be conducted by the Ministry of Finance, the Ministry of Social Security and Labour, the State Securities Commission, and the Council of Insurance.

REFERENCES

Lazutka, R. (1994), 'Organization of social security in Lithuania', in ISSA, *Restructuring Social Security in Central and Eastern Europe*, Geneva.

'Lithuania: Country Policy Paper', Paper prepared by PHARE Consensus programme 1996.

Medaiskis, T. (1995), 'The reform of pensions in Lithuania', in J. Simpura (ed.), *Social Policy in Transition Societies: Experience from the Baltic Countries and Russia* Sosaaliturvan Keskusliitto, Helsinki.

Ministry of Social Security and Labour and Health Economic Centre (MSSL) (1996), 'Social insurance in Lithuania' (White Paper), Vilnius.

United Nations Development Programme (UNDP) (1995) 'Lithuanian Human Development Report 1995', UNDP,Vilnius.

8. Transformation of old-age security in Poland

Stanislawa Golinowska and Maciej Zukowski

8.1 INTRODUCTION: HISTORIC, ECONOMIC AND DEMOGRAPHIC FRAMEWORK

The notion of a pension system is understood in this chapter as all the institutions of systematic financial security provided for the period of old-age. In the case of Poland, the pension system was and – as regards the majority of people – still is confined to one institution of pension insurance (provision) within the social insurance system. Therefore attention in the present analysis is focused on the social insurance system, while development of other levels of pension security is considered in connection with the problems of reconstruction of the existing system. Attention is focused on old-age pensions and the issue of disability and survivors' pensions is not expanded upon. Before proceeding to legal regulations of the pension system, how it functions and the direction its reconstruction is taking in the subsequent sections, the environment in which the system operates needs to be characterized.

8.1.1 Development of the Pension System in Poland prior to 1989

Historical development of social insurance, including old-age pensions, in Poland has in general shown a large degree of continuity in its institutional arrangements despite numerous changes especially after the Second World War.[1]

The Polish state that was restored in 1918 after the partition era inherited varied conditions, including those in the pension system. On the territory of the former German sector, pension insurance for manual and white-collar workers and benefits for clerks, which at this time was the most developed in the world, were operational – also, to a limited extent, company schemes and life assurances. On the territory of the Austrian sector, pension insurance covered white-collar workers only. On the territory of the Russian sector, the pension system had in fact not developed into a national system. Only some of the big employers offered occupational pensions (Landau 1991). In all three sectors different pension systems covered coal miners. Thus one main goal was to consolidate the institutional arrangements of social insurance. It was assumed that the existing situation of the insured would not deteriorate, but because of economic and political difficulties this task was not accomplished until the end of the interwar period. Nevertheless, significant development in the field of social pension security was achieved (Piatkowski 1991).

Insurance for white-collar workers, introduced in 1927, and old-age pensions for manual workers, initiated after several years of discussion in 1933, were based on rules similar to those of German and Austrian pension insurance: contributions shared between employees and employers, a required period of insurance and income-related pensions. Pensions of white-collar workers were at the same time more advantageous than the invalidity pensions of manual workers, the latter also being granted at retirement age. The organization of both insurance systems, initially separate, had been unified by the Uniting Act of 1933.

However, old-age pension insurance did not include the self-employed and farm workers, which in the latter case accounted for approximately one-third of the working class (Piatkowski 1991). Yet, on the whole, the coverage in the interwar period was broadened as a result of the replacement of restricted regulations originating in the partition period by Polish institutions.[2] Coal miners were also included in a specific occupation insurance category. Neither the clerks working in the public sector nor the military were granted social insurance, but they had access to separate systems of state provision.[3]

After the Second World War the main aim was the reconstruction of the social insurance system. At first the system was based on the law established before the Second World War. Yet, in the ten years following the war (1945–54) some far-reaching modifications were soon introduced. First, insurance coverage was extended to include farm workers, clerks and public sector workers (except those in the armed forces). The rights of blue- and white-collar workers thereafter gradually became equal. Second, several structural changes were introduced into the system. Similar to other countries of the region, these resulted largely from the new, communist system.[4] The changes generally consisted in the weakening or rejection of some insurance features in favour of the introduction of certain state-provided elements (Plawucka 1995). Consequently, specific insurance for coal miners was abolished; company schemes were not allowed to develop; life assurance was taken over by the state, leaving PZU (National Institution of Insurance) a marginal role in this market segment. Post-war history of pension security in Poland therefore pertains to social insurance exclusively.

Social insurance was gradually expanded to include the self-employed. The laws which followed guaranteed insurance protection for the members of farm co-operatives, craftsmen, and finally (in 1977) independent farmers. The construction of the old-age pension system within social insurance, formed in the first years after the Second World War, continued throughout the immediate post-war period. The resulting organization and financing has been maintained to the present day.

Contributions collected in the workplace became the exclusive source of financing the entire social insurance of employees.[5] Also a social insurance fund was standardized and included in the state budget. It was not until 1968 that a Pension Fund was set up and until 1986 that the whole Social Insurance Fund was separated from the state budget. The organization of social insurance was also standardized, centralized and taken over by the state. ZUS (Social Insurance Institution) as an organ of state administration, had been managing all social insurance programmes during the post-war period except between 1955 and 1960. This kind of organizational and financing framework of the insurance system enabled the state to use a surplus of contributions over expenses for other state objectives not connected with insurance.[6] Pension law was standardized. On the other hand, within one system several regulations existed: this affected eligibility criteria and benefit levels of individual groups of the insured (categories of employment).

The right to a pension was connected with the period of employment. There were many exceptions in the law with respect to retirement age (for men it was 65 and for women 60). For a short period following the Second World War, the level of an old-age pension varied according to the wage from the last year of employment. The calculation formula had a highly redistributional character and a minimum pension was also a fixed element of the system. Old-age and disability pensions were increased at the discretion of the government. Since 1986, however, an indexation mechanism has been operational. Consequently pensions granted earlier were lower than those granted more recently. In this context the year of retirement had a greater significance for pension levels than the previously earned wage. The problem of 'old pensions' was an important one in the entire post-war period. Most changes of the pension law after the Second World War did not concern the rudiments of the system. Rather, they were aimed at the increase in the level of benefits or the liberalization of eligibility criteria. The level of pensions was increased, but it was not stable because of the initial absence of an indexation mechanism.[7]

To recapitulate, during the socialist era an evolution of the pension system and the whole social insurance took place during which it was transformed from an insurance to a mixed system. Several features of the insurance system were maintained (mostly and more significantly, in regulations concerning benefits) while several new features of state provision were introduced (Zukowski 1994a). An unquestionable achievement was the extension of insurance coverage. Similar to other socialist countries, Poland developed a comprehensive social security system. However, this system as an element of 'socialistic social utopia' (Hrynkiewicz 1995) was excessively liberal and therefore ran into financial difficulties. Moreover it created expectations towards the state regarding social security and considerably decreased individual providence.

8.1.2 Demographic Situation

The demographic situation in Poland is more advantageous for a pension system than in West European countries (Table 8.1). In particular, its population is younger. According to the latest CSO (Central Statistical Office) research (Microcensus 1995) the share of the population below 20 years of age in relation to the total population accounts for approximately 30 per cent, while in other West European countries it is some 5 to 10 percentage points lower (Golinowska 1996c). However, population ageing is also taking place in Poland. This process had been slowed down by the wars, but demographic transformation has been accelerating significantly since the early 1990s and is likely to continue into the twenty-first century.

Table 8.1 Breakdown of the population by age, Poland, 1990–2030

Population breakdown (%)	1990	1995	2000	2005	2010	2015	2020	2030
0–14 years	25.1	22.5	19.6	18.9	20.0	20.4	19.5	19.4
15–59/64 (women/men)	62.2	64.3	65.8	66.3	65.4	63.9	62.9	61.5
60/65 +	12.7	13.2	14.6	14.8	14.6	15.7	17.6	19.1

Source: CSO forecasts, own computations and 1995 data of Microcensus. Data for the years 2000 and beyond based on CSO forecast 1995.

The demographic forecast of the CSO (autumn 1995), with predictions until the year 2020, indicates that by the end of the next decade the trend in the number and share of the elderly in the total population will change. This is the result of the cohorts born after the Second World War reaching the age of 60 and over. The post-war baby boom will become a pensioners' boom, starting in 2008 to 2020. This has never happened in Poland before. It is an important reason why fundamental reforms of the pension eligibility criteria should aim to end early retirement privileges. Retaining such privileges along with the natural increase in the pensioner population may otherwise lead to a dramatic decrease in the ratio between the gainfully employed and economically inactive groups. The seriousness of the problem is demonstrated by the difference between the old-age dependency ratio (Figure 8.1) and the so-called system dependency ratio (see section 8.2.7). At present it is a difference amounting to approximately 30 percentage points, illustrating Poland's 'paradox proportions' in the pension system (Augustinovics 1996).

*Figure 8.1 Old-age dependency ratio, Poland, 1994–2020**

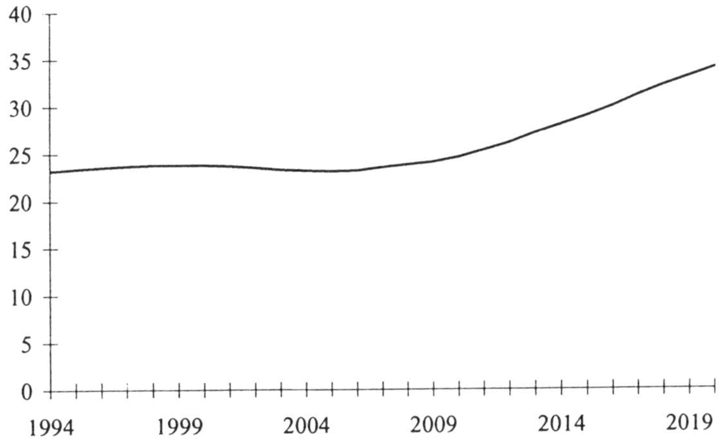

Note: * ratio between 60+ (female)/65+ (male) and 18–59 (female)/18-65 (male) age groups.
Source: Own computations on the basis of CSO data, 1995.

Demographic forecasts also show a change in the elderly population structure. Around the year 2020 Poland will have to deal with a more than 65 per cent increase in the 80-plus age group (see Table 8.2). At the moment this group enjoys additional (nursing) allowances. Such an age structure will mean a considerable increase in the costs of the system. There may also be pressure for provision of additional old-age security (for example, long-term care insurance, expanded benefits in health-care insurance). All these trends

Table 8.2 Growth rate (%) of the elderly population (1995=100), Poland, 1995–2020

Age	1995	2000	2005	2010	2015	2020
60–69	100	96	87	106	139	148
70–79	100	123	127	124	114	144
80+	100	93	120	144	158	165
60+	100	104	104	117	134	149

Sources: CSO (1996) and Holzer (1996).

should not be overlooked while designing a new system.

Considerable differences still appear between the ageing of men and women. The death rate of men in working age increased in Poland as early as the 1960s (Okólski 1988) and is also characteristic of other Central and East European countries (UNICEF 1994). In contrast, in the second decade of the twenty-first century life expectancy for women will reach a level close to the one that nowadays appears in many West European countries (CSO Demographic Yearbook 1995).

The average life span for men and women varies as well (see Table 8.3). The difference is almost nine years. After reaching the age of 60 women live almost five years longer than men. This statistic has often been used to argue in favour of raising the official retirement age for women, which is now five years lower than that of men. Together, the earlier retirement age and the longer average life span have led to higher expenditures in old-age pensions to women: they collect more from the pension system because they draw benefits for an extra 10 years. In addition, women who have worked for at least 30 years can take early retirement at the age of 55, extending the potential period of pension payments.

Table 8.3 Average life expectancy, Poland, 1990–2020 (in years)

Year	At birth		At age 60		At age 65	
	Men	Women	Men	Women	Men	Women
1990	66.5	75.5	15.3	20.0	–	–
1995	67.6	76.4	15.8	20.5	12.8	16.4
2000	68.4	76.7	–	–	–	–
2010	70.4	77.7	–	–	–	–
2020	72.4	78.7	–	–	–	–

Source: CSO data, for 2000, 2010, 2020 – assumptions underlying CSO demographic forecasts.

In contrast to most West European countries, demographic factors will remain advantageous for at least another ten years. The ageing of the population will become more significant in the second decade of the twenty-first century. The large difference in the lifespan between men and women is, however, problematic. Moreover, women are privileged under the Polish system as a result of state family policy. In contrast to other socialist countries, family policy in Poland created incentives for women to retire early in order to take care of their grandchildren and aged parents. It was considered a cheaper solution than alternative ones which would consist in the expansion of state care and educational services for children and homes for the elderly. The consequences of such a policy, namely a relatively poor social infrastructure for children and the elderly, has led to a situation in which social protest against an increase in women's retirement age is exceptionally strong.

8.1.3 Economic Factors

The transition of the Polish economy was dominated by two types of reform. The first type comprises institutional reforms launched in 1988–1989, or even earlier. If we take into account the 1981 Enterprise Act, under which one of the privatization paths has been pursued, or the 1982 Price Act, when the first stage of price liberalization took place, then we can say that the market reforms started at the turn of the 1970s. The next stage of reforms followed at the end of the 1980s. The turning-point in this area was the enactment of the Business Freedom Act (1988/89) and almost complete price liberalization paralleled by the opening of borders for goods and services.

The second type of reform was the stabilization programme known as the Balcerowicz plan. The stabilization programme implemented on 1 January 1990 comprised the following measures (Dabrowski 1995):

- in the monetary policy area there was a reduction in the nominal growth of the money supply (at a lower rate than inflation) and an increase in the nominal interest rate,
- in the fiscal policy area the main goal was to balance the state budget; the budget deficit in 1989 was more than 8 per cent of GDP, while in 1990 it dropped below one per cent of GDP (see Table 8.4),
- in trade the convertibility of the zloty was introduced in so-called current transactions, the home currency rate was made uniform and foreign trade policy was liberalized to a large extent,
- in the income policy area strict wage growth control was introduced (the Popiwek tax), and lastly
- the price liberalization process was brought to an end.

The stabilization programme being implemented in the first phase of the transition period was perceived to be exceptionally restrictive, but the macroeconomic crisis in Poland in the 1980s was exceptionally acute. In the terminal phase of the socialistic economy, the situation in Poland was more difficult than that in the southern countries neighbouring Poland. Therefore, the therapy to be applied had to be stronger. Parallel to the stabilization programme, many institutional reforms were being implemented, including but not limited to:

- setting in motion the process of so-called small privatization and starting the processes of large and mass privatization,
- the organization of a stock market,
- the elimination of central planning and initiating the policy of de-monopolization and deconcentration,

- the commercialization of banking and insurance sectors, and
- laying the legal foundations for the activities of foreign investors.

Table 8.4 Selected economic indicators, Poland, 1989–1996 (growth compared with the previous year, in per cent)

	1989	1990	1991	1992	1993	1994	1995	1996
GDP	0.2	–11.6	–7.0	2.6	3.8	5.2	7.0	6.0
Inflation rate	251.1	585.8	70.3	43.0	35.3	32.2	27.8	19.9
Average real wage	9.0	–24.4	–0.3	–2.7	–2.9	0.5	4.0	5.7
State budget deficit[a]	8.0	0.2	3.8	6.0	2.8	2.8	2.8	2.8
Unemployment rate[b]	0.0	6.5	12.2	14.3	16.4	16.0	14.9	13.6

Notes:[a] As percentage of GDP; [b] At end of the year.
Source: CSO data for selected years.

Despite the fact that the supply-driven economy soon became one driven by a limited demand, and the acute shortage of goods (mostly imported) turned into an abundance of supply, the stabilization programme was perceived in Poland as exceptionally burdensome and restrictive. Indeed, some were of the opinion that it need not have been so radical, that the programme was 'overdone' (Kolodko 1992).

The programme was also perceived as particularly burdensome because in 1991 the output of many enterprises fell dramatically as a result of the loss of Eastern markets (disintegration of the CMEA: Council for Mutual Economic Assistance), and reorientation towards Western markets was impossible in the short term; and in many cases the latter was due to the low competitiveness of state enterprises requiring extensive restructuring.

A consequence of the fall in output was a drastic drop in the state budget income in 1991 – by more than 30 per cent in real terms, which was even more than the GDP. The main source of income, the corporate income tax, was reduced systematically, while new taxes were still not in place. There were also difficulties in collecting taxes from the private sector. Budgetary expenditures were cut in many social areas. State care focused mainly on two areas, protection of the jobless and pensioners, whereas the social measures on the labour market pertained mostly to granting pension benefits to those threatened with unemployment.

The public finance crisis necessitated austerity measures in the budget sector, where in 1993 the real wages of employees were still on average about 20 per cent lower than in the enterprise sector. A wave of strikes by teachers and doctors, which flooded the country at that time, in addition to strikes by manual workers and farmers (more than 7,000 strikes in 1993), was the reason why the Solidarity-led governments lost power.

Tax reform, prepared along with the overall package of economic reforms and stabilization programme, was implemented in 1992, that is three to four years after fundamental reform measures. Accepting 1992 as the year of tax reform implementation, we are referring primarily to a personal income tax system. Prior to 1992 no universal personal income tax had existed and its introduction was a major breakthrough which increased society's awareness of public financing. In 1993, universal indirect taxes were implemented: value added taxes (VAT) and excise taxes. The implementation of these taxes was preceded by a relatively long preparation period, since a high inflation rate in Poland was a source of concern that consumption taxes might trigger an additional inflationary surge (Bolkowiak 1995).

With regard to corporate income tax, no major breakthroughs were recorded here as in the case of personal income and consumption taxes. The turning-point was the reduction of the corporate income tax rate from 65 per cent to 40 per cent, which occurred in 1989. On the other hand new types of taxes were levied upon the companies, but largely on state-owned enterprises (SOEs). These primarily included tax on excessive earnings commonly dubbed 'Popiwek tax', and 'dividends', which in fact were not dividends but rather a mandatory interest paid by the companies on their funds, regardless of the profit level they generated. In the corporate tax system the changes were twofold and divided into two phases. In 1990, within the framework of the radical stabilization programme, numerous forms of tax relief and deduction were abolished, including investment relief.

In 1993 investment relief was first reintroduced in areas of high structural unemployment and in 1994 it was made universal. In December 1994 the 'Popiwek tax' was abolished and a negotiable mechanism for determining wage growth was introduced by the Tripartite Committee.

Pursuant to the changes made in the corporate tax system and the subsequent introduction of a personal income tax system, in the first phase of transition, when a large slump in national income and output was recorded, public finances collapsed. The main source of budgetary income in the previous period – heavily taxed enterprises – was drastically reduced, but it was not paralleled by the growth in budgetary income from personal income and consumption taxes. This situation was termed a 'transformational trap' (Hausner and Owsiak 1992). Fortunately, it lasted only for a short time. Positive fiscal effects pursuant to the changes in the tax system in 1992 and 1993 were recorded together with an economic revival. This allowed public finances to recover from the slump. At present the breakdown of budgetary income is entirely different from that at the onset of systemic changes. The share of corporate income tax dropped drastically by almost 30 percentage points. The growth of the personal income tax share, directly felt by households, was the reason why this tax has become an extremely sensitive and touchy political topic over the last few years.

A new government that came to power in mid-1993 (a ruling coalition comprising social democrats and peasants), with roots in the 'real socialism', eased social transition costs considerably by making an attempt to carry on the stabilization measures with a major focus on the effective anti-inflation policy. The programme of institutional reforms known as 'Poland 2000' and proposed by Minister of Finance G. Kolodko (Kolodko 1994), did not bring the desirable changes in many expected areas, particularly in social insurance. However, the economic growth, already recorded in mid-1992, brought about many advantageous social changes which eased social conflicts. Wages started to grow in real terms; average wage growth was recorded for the first time in 1994; unemployment has been gradually shrinking. The number of strikes has diminished dramatically: while from 1994 to 1995 'only' less than a hundred strikes were recorded, from 1992 to 1993 the number of registered strikes had been a few thousand. Phenomena accompanying the system transformation, especially unemployment, decline of GDP and wages, on the one hand decreased available social security resources, but, on the other hand, increased the need for benefits (Zukowski 1994b).

In the transition period the need for old-age and disability pensions increased significantly: the number of old-age and invalidity pensioners increased. The situation of old-age pensioners improved relatively in comparison with the working population. Therefore redistribution of income took place on a larger scale than previously. This was also expressed by social insurance contribution increases from 38 per cent in 1988 to 45 per cent in 1991. At the same time, state subsidies for social insurance increased four times. The cause of the redistribution was a massive shift of people to social benefits and illegal employment sectors.

In 1995, Poland faced a bigger inflow than outflow of the population into the working sector due to the developing economy. None the less the unemployment rate is still high. Unemployment levels are kept high by strong and persistent structural unemployment in rural regions (including former state-owned farms) and traditional monocultural industry. Outflow for retirement and disability pensions is still very high. Therefore the country is still dealing with a process of exchanging unemployment benefits for retirement or disability pensions. At the political level, labour market policy and the reduction in unemployment have thus gained priority while the anti-inflationary policy spearheaded from 1993 to 1995 is of less importance.

8.1.4 Social and Political Conditions

Social and political conditions are, by definition, more difficult to quantify. Here we pay attention primarily to factors crucial for the reconstruction of the Polish pension system. Generally public expectations of state responsibility for social security cannot be ignored when designing new schemes in the area of social security.

In politics and economic affairs there is a widespread, legitimate desire to safeguard the present status of rights 'legally acquired (granted)' (Hrynkiewicz 1995). This can be observed, for example, among present (old-age and disability pensioners) or future (workers, their union and political representatives) beneficiaries or administrative staff and the related group of specialists. In each country the limiting of social services faces resistance (Pierson 1995). In the period of political transition from a totalitarian to a democratic system, pensions became a political issue leading to heated debates. The intensity of these debates has not subsided but instead has increased with the number of pensioners (see 8.2.7, first subsection).[8]

Also, other elements of the socialist heritage have exerted influence on the pension system.[9] Attitudes towards the state are characterized by a lack of trust. Therefore there is a tendency to believe that funded pensions would be better than those secured through a system of state redistribution. On the other hand, there are those who expect the state to do exactly that. Social research has pointed to the continuity of egalitarian ideologies in Polish society. Moreover, legal measures have yet to be put in place which can be used to curb black market employment, tax evasion and negligence in making social insurance contribution payments. The situation is made even more difficult by the lack of experience in the implementation of reforms. Political instability manifest in the governing coalitions or parties since the beginning of transformation remains a problem as well, since reform of the pension system has to be based on a political consensus and a long-term vision.

8.2 THE LEGAL FRAMEWORK OF THE PENSION SYSTEM

8.2.1 General Background

The collapse of socialism has not yet been followed by the fundamental rebuilding of the pension system. The social insurance system still has a monopolistic character. Company schemes do not exist. Personal pension plans, which started to develop recently, still play a marginal role. The fact that social insurance is the sole component of old-age security hampers the performance of its various functions.[10] Second, the situation of being the sole security system with a centralized state administration is vulnerable to direct political intervention.

With regard to organization and financing of the general system, not much has changed. However, the social insurance system for independent farmers was organized separately. Eligibility criteria were changed by law in 1990 and 1991. The change in the pension formula and new indexation mechanism undoubtedly strengthened the insurance feature of the system. Controversial revaluation of all old-age and disability pensions ironed out the problem of 'old pension purses'. All in all the 'Revaluation' Act of 1991 rationalized considerably the law governing the granting of pension benefits. On the other hand the pension system came under pressure because of drastically mounting unemployment. In response the opportunity of earlier retirement was used increasingly and this contributed to a large extent to the 'explosion' of a number of benefits and financial difficulties experienced by the system. Subsequently an attempt was made to iron out the emerging problems by means of indexation curtailment. Thus the pension system was still used to serve temporary political goals.

8.2.2 Insurance Coverage and List of Benefits

The regulations on social insurance coverage did not undergo any essential changes in the period under discussion. The social insurance system covers almost the entire population of Poland, including attached eligibility rights, for example, to survivors' ('family') pensions. Old-age pension claims can, however, only be made by the given insured person. Participation in social insurance is obligatory for all employed persons. There are separate laws regulating respective occupational categories.[11] Although separately regulated, the subsystems are uniform in organizational terms (with the exception of the system for farmers); financing follows similar principles; eligibility criteria are based on the principles of the employee insurance system.

Pension schemes for state officers such as military personnel, the police, persons providing border services, prison guards as well as war and military invalids are regulated separately. In these schemes no social contribution is applied. They are partially separated in organizational and financial terms, while benefit payment is the same as in the employee insurance system. No limit for insurance obligation exists in the Polish pension system. The insurance obligation has to be met by employees (and other employment categories, respectively) regardless of the working hours or income level of a job position.

8.2.3 Organization

The organization of social insurance – except those for farmers – is standardized and was changed insignificantly. It is regulated by the Act on Organization and Financing of Social Insurance.[12]

The entire social insurance system is administered by ZUS with a head office, 55 branch offices covering its operations (as a rule, of the territory of one voivodship), and local offices. ZUS is a central organ of the state administration. It reports to the Minister of Labour and Social Policy. The chairman of ZUS is appointed by the prime minister, subject to prior consultation with the Chief Supervisory Board. The head office and each ZUS branch office have supervisory boards. Following an amendment that came into force on 1 January 1996, 50 per cent of the board are representatives of the insured as well as of old-age and disability pensioners, 25 per cent are employers' representatives, and 25 per cent are state administration representatives. The members of the supervisory boards are appointed by the prime minister (for the head office) or head of the voivodship (for a branch office) from among the candidates presented by the trade unions, old-age and disability pensioners' organizations and employers' unions. The supervisory boards have reviewing and control powers, whereas their supervisory powers are still strongly limited. In the case of objections to ZUS's decisions, the supervisory boards represent the first level of appeal.

Until recently, ZUS also administered all provision schemes for state services employees and staff: for example, the armed forces, police and prison guards. Gradually these functions are being taken over by the bodies of relevant ministries. During the period of the Polish People's Republic, the organizational independence of the miners' insurance scheme was abolished, although an independent scheme was kept in force for rail workers. In the latter case, old-age and disability pensions are paid by the railways administration. Since 1991, a separate institution administering social insurance for farmers has been operating (KRUS: Agricultural Social Insurance Institution) and reports to the Minister of Agriculture.

8.2.4 Financing

The only group of insured to have paid a separate pension contribution since 1991 is that of farmers (there is an additional contribution-based scheme for 'short-term benefits' in the case of accident, sickness and maternity leave) whose pension contribution amounts to 10 per cent of the lowest old-age pension monthly. The second and main source of financing farmers' pensions are state subsidies. Pensions for all remaining groups are financed in the same way as all other social insurance, so that there are no separate contributions or subsidies. Financing principles have not been changed fundamentally since 1989.

ZUS administers the Social Insurance Fund. The primary source of revenues is from contributions. Wage earners' contributions are paid exclusively by employers. The rate of contribution has been 45 per cent of the wage fund since 1991. For workers working directly in agricultural production their contribution amounts to 35 per cent of the wage fund, while the remaining part (10 per cent) is refunded by the state. Individual contribution accounts for individual workers do not exist. The contribution calculation base includes practically all wage components, except those determined by the Council of Ministers. It is not limited – the contribution is assessed according to the full wage.

A self-employed person outside the farming sector makes a social insurance contribution in full based on declared income; the contribution rate amounts to 40 per cent of the calculation base. Declared income may not, however, be lower than 60 per cent of the average national wage in the previous quarter, nor may it exceed the declared income for the previous month by more than 50 per cent. The contribution for those working under agency or mandate contracts amounts to 40 per cent of the calculation base as well and is paid on a fifty–fifty basis, respectively, by the insured and the employer who is a party to the contract. The lowest contribution is paid by writers and artists: 29 per cent of the calculation base, since under their social insurance plan they are only eligible for pensions.

After contributions, state subsidies are the most important source of social insurance provision. There are two types of subsidies. An earmarked subsidy is allocated to cover expenses of groups for whom social insurance contributions are not paid. However, benefits for such groups have been gradually separated from the Social Insurance Fund.[13] At present, an earmarked subsidy covers expenses for benefits paid to war and military invalids and veterans and for 'other non-insurance benefits' (ZUS 1996:7). The latter category includes some small benefit categories such as exceptional old-age and disability pensions granted by the chairman of ZUS in place of a minimum pension. A second, the make-up subsidy, is allocated when insurance fund revenues and earmarked subsidies do not meet expenses. In 1994 and 1995 an additional state subsidy was granted to companies in the public sector for the purpose of 'restructuring' their social insurance contribution debt. As a whole, the Social Insurance Fund operates on a PAYG basis.

8.2.5 Benefits

Many more significant changes affected benefits.

Eligibility criteria

In Poland employees are eligible for a pension at the age of 65 for men or 60 for women provided that men have had 25 and women 20 years of contributory and non-contributory periods. The so-called contributory and non-contributory periods were terms and categories applied first in 1991: they replaced earlier categories of employment periods and periods equal to or recognized as employment. The 1991 act also introduced the rule that non-contributory periods may not be proportionately larger than one-third of contributory periods. Contributory periods are periods in which insurance contributions were paid and also periods of military service, of service in the police force or State Protection Office, of employment in border and prison services and periods in which maternity benefits are claimed. Prior to 15 November 1991 all contributory periods are regarded as employment periods. Non-contributory periods include, among others, periods of claiming sickness allowance, bringing up children (three years per child, but not more than six years altogether), taking care of persons requiring permanent care and university study. There are numerous exceptions to statutory pension eligibility criteria. Women who reached the age of 60 (men 65) during an employment period are eligible for an old-age pension if they can prove a total minimum 15 (men 20) years of contributory and non-contributory periods. There are also early retirement schemes for numerous groups, that is, opportunities to retire before reaching the statutory retirement age.[14] Some employee groups are entitled to earlier retirement regardless of age.[15] Combining pension benefits with income from work is possible only under certain conditions.[16]

Pension calculation formula

In 1991, the pension calculation formula was fundamentally changed. Previously the pension level had been determined on the basis of income of the insured in nominal terms in the last two calendar years prior to retirement. The present old-age pension calculation formula consists of two components:

$$P = 0.24 * BA + (0.013 * C + 0.007 * NC) * IE$$

where

BA = base amount,
C = contributory years,
NC = non-contributory years and
IE = individual earnings.

The first 'social' component is the same for everybody and accounts for 24 per cent of the base amount. Initially the base amount level corresponded to 100 per cent of the average national wage in the quarter preceding the date of the last indexation. In 1993, in order to cut the fund's expenses, the base amount was lowered to 91 per cent. In 1994 it was increased to 93 per cent and since 1 September 1996 to 94 per cent, with further increases to follow – by 1 percentage point at each subsequent indexation.

The second 'individual' component depends on the individual insurance record. The calculation basis is the wage (income) earned by the insured (in 1997) in the subsequent eight years selected by the insured from the last 17 years prior to retirement. The periods have been lengthened each year, for example, in the year 2000 the old-age pension will be calculated taking into account earnings for ten years out of the last 20 years. For each of the years selected by the insured, the ratio of his/her income to the average national wage is calculated and then the ratio is multiplied by the base amount. The individual calculation basis may not be higher than 250 per cent of the base amount. For each contributory year 1.3 per cent, and for each non-contributory year 0.7 per cent of the calculation basis is given. The old-age pension calculated according to the above formula may not be lower than the minimum old-age pension, which itself was linked in 1990 to the level of the average national wage – minimum wage (and minimum pension) were 35 per cent of the national average wage and 39 per cent as of 1 January 1994.[17] According to the 1995 act this linkage was abandoned and since 1996 the lowest old-age and disability pensions have been indexed pursuant to the principles applied to other benefits. The calculation formula continues to ensure a relatively favourable relationship between old-age pension level and the former income of the insured.[18]

The old-age pension under the farmers' scheme is made up of contributory and supplementary components. The contributory component level depends on the length of the insurance period. The minimum old-age pension equals the lowest employee old-age pension; the maximum old-age pension may not exceed 135 per cent of the minimum old-age pension.

In the period under study the number of allowances attached to the old-age pension declined considerably.[19] The 1991 act abolished numerous sectoral allowances to the old-age pension for which many groups of the insured were eligible.[20] All allowances accounted for 10 per cent of the average wage in the quarter preceding the indexation date. Since 1996 the allowance levels have no longer been combined with the average wage. They are raised at normal indexation dates pursuant to the principles applied to all old-age and disability pensions. Parallel to the 1995 conversion of family benefits, financed from within the social insurance system to income-tested state social benefits financed from the budget, the character of family allowances supplementing old-age pensions was changed along the same lines.

Indexation and taxation

The principles of indexation in the period under study were changed fundamentally a few times. Initially changes were aimed at the protection of the real value of old-age pensions under conditions of very high inflation. Later, however, indexation was curtailed and no longer automatic in order to reduce the escalating cost of pension benefits.

Indexation for pensions had functioned in Poland since 1986. The mechanism, however, was insufficient to protect the value of old-age pensions against the negative effects of inflation during the first stage of transformation. In 1990, quarterly indexation was introduced, fully equivalent to the growth of the average wage. After subsequent changes, indexation was applied (at most on a quarterly basis) when the growth of the average wage compared to the quarter when the previous indexation took place, exceeded 10 per cent. This regulation allowed the maintenance of the old-age pension level in relation to wages, but at the same time became one of the major sources of escalating pension system costs. In 1993 the base amount, used as the indexation basis, was reduced to 91 per cent of the average national wage; thereafter, adjustments were made accordingly. In 1995 a lengthy debate took place on replacing the wage-linked with a price-linked indexation. Finally, completely new indexation principles were adopted for 1996 and the previous system was suspended; a one-off indexation was planned for September. It was assumed that it would ensure real growth (in relation to prices) of old-age and disability pensions by 2.5 per cent. In the budget bill an indexation rate was adopted that was supposed to ensure that real growth (15.2 per cent). The full amount of the pension is indexed. As the real growth of the average pension was lower than 2.5 per cent, a one-off compensatory payment was made in March 1997. Since 1 January 1992, when personal income tax was introduced, pensions became subject to taxation pursuant to the same principles as other income.

8.2.6 Legal Regulations on other Forms of Old-age Security

People who have reached the retirement age may not be eligible for an old-age pension paid from the social insurance system, for example, if they have not fulfilled the required insurance period and do not have any private means of subsistence, or income per capita in the family is lower than the lowest old-age pension level. These groups are then eligible for a so-called permanent social assistance allowance.

There is no legal framework for occupational pension schemes in Poland. Additional old-age security has thus been limited to life assurance policies

(Doan 1995). They are regulated and this is chiefly determined by the Act on Insurance Activity.[21] An insurance company may run insurance activities even if it is a joint-stock company or mutual assurance company. Life assurance operations may not be combined with other types of insurance. Permission to conduct insurance activities is given by the Minister of Finance who also supervises the insurance sector. To date, foreign insurers have been allowed to operate in Poland in the form of companies with foreign participation; as independent insurance companies they have been allowed to operate since 1 January 1999. Under the amendment to the 1995 act a 'Insured' Spokesperson office was created with the primary aim of representing and protecting the consumer interests of the insured and right holders under the insurance contracts.

8.2.7 The Insured, Old-age Pensioners, Pensions and Pension Finances

Number and breakdown of the insured and beneficiaries

The pension system inherited liberal eligibility criteria from the socialist era (see 8.2.5, first subsection).[22] As a consequence of numerous early retirement opportunities the actual average age of new old-age pensioners in 1989 was 61 years for men and 57 years for women and in 1996 it fell to 59 years for men and 55 years for women.[23]

The pension system was used in the transition period to absorb a large number of the unemployed. On the one hand, special opportunities for earlier retirement were created; on the other, a tense situation on the labour market led many employees to take advantage of liberal regulations allowing them to retire earlier. As a result, the number of old-age and disability pensioners increased dramatically. Since the number of insured declined, the number of

Table 8.5 Insured, old-age and disability pensioners,[a] Poland, 1989–96 (in m.)

	1989	1990	1991	1992	1993	1994	1995	1996
Insured	14.7	14.1	13.6	13.3	12.7	12.6	12.9	13.2
Old-age, disability and family pensioners	5.5	5.6	6.2	6.5	6.7	6.9	7.0	7.2
of which old-age pensioners	2.3	2.4	2.8	3.0	3.1	3.2	3.2	3.3
Number of pensioners for 100 insured	37.2	39.6	45.2	49.1	52.6	54.4	54.4	54.4

Note: [a] except farmers.
Source: GUS (1997); ZUS (1992; 1997).

the beneficiaries to the number of the insured increased considerably (see Table 8.5). However, this growth trend continued only until 1995, when increased employment led to an increase in the number of insured. Within the farmers' scheme, a considerable rise in the number of pensioners[24] was also recorded from 1989 to 1996. As a result, the total number of pensioners in Poland increased within that period from 2.1 million to 9.2 million in 1996 (GUS 1997). As a consequence of structural economic changes the breakdown of the insured also changes. The number of self-employed in the total number of insured increased from 6.8 per cent in 1989 to 9.9 per cent in 1996 (own computations based on ZUS 1992).

Old-age pension level and old-age pensioners' income

Old-age pensions have low purchasing power, similar to the income level in Poland in general. In 1994 the average net non-agricultural pension corresponded to 133.2 per cent of the social minimum of single pensioners' household (own computations based on GUS 1995; Sajkiewicz 1995). This implies that the average pension does not meet much more than the rudimentary needs of a socially accepted minimum standard of living. Compared to wages, however, old-age pensions are high. Between 1989 and 1997 the average old-age pension level has increased considerably compared to average wages (see Table 8.6), this was mainly a consequence of changes in the old-age pension calculation formula in 1991 and consistent indexation. The gap between old-age and disability pensions also increased following the stronger dependence of benefits on the length of insurance coverage and income level.

Thus old-age pensioners' income was relatively well protected in the transition period. This is also evident in the rise in real value of the average non-agricultural old-age pension by 12.7 per cent between 1990 and 1996, whereas in the same period the average wage increased by only 3.0 per cent[25] in real terms (GUS 1997). All statistics on poverty in Poland show that poverty among pensioners decreased considerably during the transition period. It was mainly children, the unemployed and young families who faced increasing poverty at that time (Golinowska 1996b).

Table 8.6 Average monthly old-age pension (except farmers), Poland, 1989–96, (expressed as percentage of the average wage)

	1989	1990	1991	1992	1993	1994	1995	1996
Relation								
of gross figures	55.9	65.0	72.6	72.6	71.9	73.8	73.6[a]	70.9
of net figures	55.9	65.0	72.6	74.9	72.8	74.8	75.0	71.9

Note: [a] Comparable to the data from 1996.
Source: Own computations on the basis of GUS (1989–97), Statistical Yearbooks.

At the same time, as a result of the lengthening of the period used for determining the calculation basis, the average pension calculation basis has been gradually decreasing. Thus benefits that have been granted over the past few years, in relation to the average wage, are relatively lower than the total number of old-age pensions.[26] This trend can be expected to continue and in the long term should reduce the financial problems of the social insurance system (Wiktorow 1996). The pension system is still highly redistributive. Although the relationship of old-age pensions to former earned income was considerably reinforced in 1991 it is still limited by the first social component of each benefit[27] and by the minimum old-age pension.[28]

Pension insurance finances

The financial situation of the system has deteriorated dramatically during the transformation period (see Table 8.7). The gap between decreasing contribution payments and increasing pension payments had to be filled by a growing state subsidy. Revenues have decreased in real terms as a result of growing unemployment and as a result of companies' financial difficulties

Table 8.7 Balance of social insurance funds (ZUS and KRUS), Poland, 1989–96

	1989	1990	1991	1992	1993	1994	1995	1996
Contribution revenues								
(bn. zloty)[a]	0.82	5.07	9.43	14.73	18.68	25.98	36.27	45.85
ZUS (%)	98.8	98.1	98.4	99.1	98.6	98.8	98.8	99.0
KRUS (%)	1.2	1.9	1.6	0.9	1.4	1.2	1.2	1.0
State subsidies								
(bn. zloty)[a]	0.23	1.63	3.57	7.20	9.69	13.02	12.10	13.58
ZUS (%)	54.9	54.0	61.8	68.8	68.2	63.7	49.6	44.4
KRUS (%)	45.1	46.0	38.2	31.2	31.8	36.3	50.4	55.6
Total expenditures								
(bn. zloty)	1.12	6.17	13.07	21.11	27.99	38.93	47.67	59.24
ZUS (%)	90.6	87.5	88.1	88.7	88.2	87.1	86.4	86.5
KRUS (%)	9.4	12.5	11.9	11.3	11.8	12.9	13.6	13.5
Pension expenditures[b]								
(bn. zloty)	0.79	4.80	10.20	16.80	22.76	32.34	41.72	51.67
ZUS (%)	87.6	85.2	86.6	87.7	86.8	85.6	85.2	85.3
KRUS (%)	12.4	14.8	13.4	12.3	13.2	14.4	14.8	14.7
Contribution revenue / pension expenditures								
ZUS (%)	118.0	121.5	105.0	99.0	99.5	93.8	99.1	102.9
KRUS (%)	9.8	13.6	11.2	6.7	8.9	6.8	7.0	6.3

Notes: [a] Apart from contributions and state subsidies there are some other minor revenues. [b] Farmers may combine rights to employee and farmers' benefits and then the payments quoted as payments made by KRUS are in fact higher than payments related to farmers' pensions.
Source: ZUS (1992; 1995); GUS (1997); own estimates.

which have led to an increasing contribution debt to ZUS. The shrunken contribution revenues could not meet the pension liabilities, and even less so after the current indexation was introduced, earlier retirement was made possible, a new pension formula was introduced and lastly almost all pensions were revalued. The share of state subsidies in pension payments from ZUS doubled between 1989 and 1993 (from 18.5 per cent to 33.4 per cent). Whereas in 1989 revenues from social insurance contributions were sufficient, and state subsidies financed 'non-insurance' benefits, in 1995 the contributions covered only about 84 per cent of pension payments that should have been financed by contributions (Wiktorow 1996).In 1996, state subsidies accounted for 93.2 per cent of the Pension Fund revenues within the farmers' scheme. In fact, the pension scheme for this group is thus a tax-financed one rather than a contribution-based insurance system. As a result of the finance structure, the farmers' scheme, whose share of the total expenditure on pensions was only 14.7 per cent in 1996, accounted for 50.6 per cent of total state subsidies to social insurance funds. State subsidies of pensions were at their highest level in 1992–93. Since then they have decreased relative to the revenues from contributions. The absolute and relative increase in contributions was partly due to the positive economic development: that is, growth in GDP and in employment.

The 'improvement' in the Social Insurance Fund's financial situation was, however, also a result of shifting the financing of 'non-insurance benefits': since 1993 financing of benefits paid to soldiers and their families has been taken over by the Ministry of Defence; since 1995 pensions for other 'armed groups' have been financed from the budget of the Ministry of the Interior or the Ministry of Justice. Also since 1995, family benefits have been financed from the state budget, while employers have been obliged to finance the first 35 days of employees' absence due to illness. Another measure adopted in 1995 in order to increase the contribution base was the extension of the obligation to pay social insurance contributions to persons working under mandate contracts. Eventually, an additional subsidy from the state budget to companies in the public sector was granted for the 'restructuring' of the social insurance contributions debt.

All these measures improved the financial situation of the Social Insurance Fund (ZUS) by 1995 – the ratio of subsidies to contributions almost halved in 1995 and approached its 1989 level (see Table 8.7). Again, this 'improvement' reflected simply a shift of the financial burden to other sources: general taxation or company finance. The actual financial cost of social insurance to the state budget has remained very high, and for employers it has even increased, because the contribution rate has stayed at the same high level of 45 per cent of the corporate wage fund. The high burden has led to such consequences as:

- growing outstanding liabilities to ZUS (contribution debt) and increasing restructuring costs for companies,
- decreasing competitiveness due to high labour cost,
- unemployment, and
- illegal employment (shadow economy).

A drop in contribution revenues was to a large extent due to employers' liabilities to ZUS (see Table 8.8).

At the end of December 1995 it accounted for 11.7 per cent of total contribution revenues in that year, or 70.1 per cent of state subsidies to ZUS in that year. Developments concerning the amount of liabilities have thus been attributed mainly to changes in financing social insurance. Two-thirds of total liabilities was owed by public sector companies in December 1996. Large companies (such as mines, steel mills or shipyards) tend to have the highest level of liabilities (cf. Malaka 1994). The faster decrease in (relative) debt of the public sector compared to that of the private sector is mainly due to state subsidies granted for 'restructuring' of the social insurance contribution debt. High social insurance contributions paid by employers contribute to labour costs. Although labour costs in Poland are still much lower than in the countries of the European Union – the nominal cost of one hour worked in industry in the EU between two (in Portugal) and ten

Table 8.8 Outstanding contribution liabilities to ZUS,[a] Poland, 1989–96

	1989	1990	1991	1992	1993	1994	1995	1996
Outstanding contribution (m. zloty)	12	31	416	1.468	3.026	3.861	4.207	4.759
public sector	9	17	348	1.082	2.479	3.108	3.150	3.399
private sector	2	14	68	386	547	754	1.057	1.360
Total liabilities = 100								
public sector %	79.5	55.5	83.7	73.7	81.9	80.5	74.9	71.4
private sector %	20.5	44.5	16.3	26.3	18.1	19.5	25.1	28.6
Liabilities/contributions (%)								
Total	1.4	0.6	4.5	10.6	16.4	15.0	11.7	10.4
Public sector	1.2	0.4	4.4	11.2	20.4	18.4	13.8	11.9
Private sector	5.6	3.7	5.1	9.6	9.2	8.9	8.5	7.8

Note: [a] At end of year.
Sources: Malaka (1994); ZUS (1992; 1996); own estimates.

(Germany) times higher than in Poland (Wiktorow and Grabowski 1996) – they are growing in dollar terms[29] and will continue to do so along with economic growth. This issue will certainly gain in importance, especially because Poland will soon face more competition from other countries where labour costs are even lower. The issue of the connection between high social insurance contributions and the high unemployment rate is often raised in Poland. For some it is obvious that the first is an important causal factor of the second (Topinski and Wisniewski 1995). The issue is controversial and difficult to quantify. It is particularly obscured by the effect of illegal employment. High social insurance contributions are also considered one of the main determinants of illegal labour which, at a level of more than 2 million persons, is almost as high as the official unemployment level (Kalaska et al. 1996). Undocumented labour seems to be growing in response to the difficulties of finding legal work in many regions and local areas. Employers who are hiring illegally often offer higher wages without social benefits; these higher wages are supposedly generated through non-payment of social insurance contributions. Thus a higher wage works as a strong incentive to pursue illegal employment. Such an arrangement is preferred to unemployment and the attendant low income, especially if the earnings have to support a family. As a consequence of growing state subsidies, social insurance expenditure exceeded other items of the state budget, including other social spending. Within social expenditures there has been a clear shift towards transfers mainly for old-age and disability pensioners at the cost of investment in human capital.

In the transition period Poland experienced a growth in social expenditures both in absolute terms and in relation to GDP (see Table 8.9). The trend in expenditures has been weakening, however. The growth of expenditures was caused by rising cash transfers, which was a result of the change in instruments applied by the welfare state. Characteristic features of social policy during the era of 'real' socialism no longer held. For example, price subsidies for many goods and services essential for households, social employment, broadly-based social activities at the company level, such as services free-of-charge or those offered for a symbolic charge in such areas as child care, education, health care, culture and recreation, were either abolished or their scope was limited.

Instead cash benefits were introduced to serve such newly common problems as unemployment and poverty. Moreover, the lowest level of the existing benefits started to grow dramatically (for example, the lowest disability and old-age pensions and the lowest allowances). With regard to family benefits, eligibility criteria were changed: the once universal benefits became means-tested. The highest growth of social expenditures was recorded in 1991–92. Their share of the declining GDP almost doubled.

Table 8.9 Cash benefits, Poland, 1990–95

Type of benefit	1990	1991	1992	1993	1994	1995
Total cash benefits:						
as % of GDP	11.2	16.8	19.2	19.3	20.0	19.4
as % of net GDP	–	–	17.1	16.9	16.4	16.8
real growth rate, previous year = 100		128.9	112.6	103.4	106.1	102.5
Pension benefits:						
as % of GDP	8.6	12.6	14.6	14.2	15.8	15.6
as % of net GDP[a]	–	–	12.5	12.6	13.2	13.0
as % of cash benefits	76.5	75.0	75.0	77.2	78.8	80.5
real growth rate, previous year = 100	–	126.4	114.1	105.0	108.4	104.6
Social insurance allowances one-off and short-term:[b]						
as % of cash benefits	2.4	2.9	3.1	3.9	4.5	4.3
real growth rate, previous year = 100	–	185.5	120.6	128.8	122.2	98.0
Family benefits:						
as % of GDP	1.8	2.5	2.4	2.0	1.7	1.3
as % of cash benefits	15.5	14.7	12.5	10.3	8.6	6.5
real growth rate, previous year = 100	–	183.1	95.6	84.9	88.4	77.6
Unemployment benefits:						
as % of GDP	0.2	1.0	1.3	1.2	1.2	1.3
as % of cash benefits	2.1	5.9	6.8	6.1	6.1	6.6
real growth rate, previous year = 100	–	361.6	130.7	92.2	105.7	111.2
Social assistance allowances:						
as % of GDP	0.1	0.2	0.3	0.5	0.4	0.4
as % of cash benefits	1.3	1.4	1.5	2.5	2.0	2.1
real growth rate, previous year = 100	–	135.2	120.7	176.6	84.0	107.9
Scholarships as % of cash benefits	1.3	0.1	0.06	0.05	0.05	0.05

Notes: [a] Net format applies only to benefits taxed with personal income tax, that is, pension benefits. [b] Social insurance benefits/allowances include: sickness, funeral, accident allowances and so on.

Source: Own estimates and computations on the basis of CSO and ZUS data.

Essential to that growth was the increase in pension benefits, which accounted for 75 per cent of total cash benefits in 1990; in 1995 they exceeded 80 per cent.

Pension expenditures went up twice until 1998. For the first time, at the beginning of 1990, expenditures for pensions rose by as much as four percentage points with regard to their share in GDP. The second increase, which was much lower, was in 1994, when the level of the minimum old-age pension was raised from 35 per cent of the average wage to 39 per cent, and the minimum disability pension from 24 per cent of the average wage to 29 per cent. Sickness allowances were also raised, but the impact of the total costs of these benefits was not as high as that of pension expenditures. Thus, in relation to other budgetary problems in the period from 1992 to 1993, expenditures here were not considered to be a major problem. The benefits that declined both in relative and absolute terms since 1992 include family benefits and scholarships. The share of the family benefits together with child support and allowances paid to pregnant women as a proportion of total social benefits almost halved; scholarships almost vanished. Cash benefits paid by the state are oriented at the elderly and the weaker at the expense of assistance to the family and the young. A generation gap in the distribution process as shown in Table 8.9 – pension expenditures increased from 8.6 per cent to 15.6 per cent of total GDP – is also evident in the analysis of overall social expenditures, which include benefits in kind and price subsidies.

Other forms of old-age security

In the transition period the number of long-term social assistance recipients doubled. A significant portion was made up of pensioners who had no claims to a social insurance pension: 88,000 in 1990 compared to 189,000 in 1996 (GUS 1997). Only a small percentage of the population has additional income in old age in the form of life assurance, although this type of insurance sector has developed quite dynamically during the transition period: in 1992 the collection rate of life assurance contributions accounted for 0.44 per cent of GDP; in 1995 this was 0.65 per cent (own computations based on figures in GUS 1995, 1996).

8.3 RESTRUCTURING THE POLISH PENSION SYSTEM

8.3.1 Reasons for Restructuring

In Poland it is more difficult than in other countries to convince decision makers and society of the need for fundamental reform of the pension system. It is indeed a highly complicated problem to 'sell' the reform politically, since the current system is not going bankrupt and will probably operate with continuous adjustments for another 20 years. Countries that have radically reformed their pension systems, such as Chile and Argentina, installed new ones on the ruins of the old. There was little resistance on the part of old institutions and their beneficiaries.

Despite the likelihood that the system will continue to function there are important reasons to go ahead with reform. First, the current system may have a destructive impact on the economy by hampering its development. Second, such a system may prove to be totally inefficient around the year 2010 when significant demographic changes are expected. The aged as a percentage of the total population are expected to increase to such an extent that there will be a high rate of dependence between the retired and the working population and the system will not be capable of financing pensions to the required extent and level. Nevertheless, we have to account for the fact that the system dependency rate without a reform precluding the entry into the system of those no longer applicable (abolition of all privileges and deviations from a universal rule) will be much higher than the demographic dependency rate. Today it is threefold higher. Measures to reduce high expenditures on current pensions will be through indexation restrictions. As a consequence, the real value of the benefits will decline, pensioners will protest and politicians will defend them. A lot of energy will be wasted with no tangible results for the pension system. So the question arises, what does radical yet responsible pension system reform mean? Which target model should be adopted? We would argue that full responsibility must imply reducing the burden of the pension system on the working population. The whole problem boils down to the fact that it should be done with social understanding and acceptance, which means respecting principles that have to be clear and just. These principles, which have been formulated more and more frequently both by experts and by politicians, have common characteristics:

- income during old age should reflect both the wage level and the length of employment of recipients. Consequently both occupational and social privileges should be eliminated;
- only part of the elderly person's income should be guaranteed by the state;
- PAYG financing should be restricted systematically in favour of a funded component;
- funded financing should raise confidence in newly established financial institutions providing old-age income security.

8.3.2 State of Reform in Mid-1997

Since the onset of systemic transition, several proposals on pension system reform have been made.[30] Below, only the state of the reform in mid-1997 is presented.

After several years of debate and postponed reforms, by 1997 the issue of transformation of the pension system in Poland had reached the stage of legal regulations. In July 1997, legislation in parliament was still in process. The parliamentary elections in September 1997 may explain the 'acceleration' of the reforming process by ruling political forces.

The responsibility for the reform was granted to the Plenipotentiary for Social Security Reform. The post was created in 1996 and the Minister of Labour and Social Policy at that time, Andrzej Baczkowski, became the first plenipotentiary. After his death, Jerzy Hausner took the post. Reform plans were presented at the end of 1996, with a second version following in February 1997. The project was entitled 'Security through Diversity' and it was carried through by a team of the Office of the Plenipotentiary for Social Security Reform, directed by Michael Rutkowski, who had worked for the World Bank in several countries. The team worked out a concept which later became the basis for the first laws enacted by the Polish parliament (Sejm). It is based on the idea of a three-pillar pension system. The first pillar of this pension scheme is the reformed social insurance system (ZUS). Eligibility criteria was tightened and a completely new pension formula (a defined contribution PAYG pension scheme) was introduced, with no legal but only a minimum retirement age of 62 for both sexes. The new second pillar constitutes an obligatory pension fund, chosen by the insured and privately managed (similar to the pension system in Chile). The third pillar is made up of additional voluntary insurance and saving schemes, including mainly life insurance and occupational pension schemes.

As of July 1997 three acts passed successfully through the lower chamber of the Sejm: on pension funds (second pillar), on employee pension programmes (occupational schemes within the third pillar) and on financing the reform from privatization. The acts form only a legal framework for reform.

The new system addresses in full those born after 31 December 1968. Persons between 30 and 50 will be able to choose whether to participate in the new system or stay entirely in the old one. Persons over 50 as well as existing pensioners are to remain in the old system. For those participating in the new system, the contribution would be split: 80 per cent would go to the first pillar and 20 per cent (thus in the case of 45 per cent contribution for employees: nine per cent of the contribution base) going to a pension fund chosen by the insured. The contribution is divided equally between employees and employers. In the whole social insurance system both lower and upper limits of the contribution base would be introduced. The lower limit would be the official minimum wage (in mid-1997, approximately 40 per cent of the average wage); the upper is equivalent to 250 per cent of the average wage. Both the contribution for the second pillar (pension funds) as well as the income from their investment is free from tax and future funded pensions are taxed. In the third pillar, however, the contributions are taxed and only employers offering their employees pension schemes could include contributions at company cost.

The level of the new old-age pension from the first pillar depends only on two factors: the sum of contributions collected throughout the insurance career divided by further life expectancy at the time of retirement (equal for men and women). In contrast to the former scheme, no non-contributory periods exist. The minimum pension, or rather the minimum pension guarantee, is to be financed from general taxation. The eligibility criteria for a minimum pension (some 28 per cent of the average wage) would be 25 insurance years and 65 years of age. Financing the transition from the present to the new system is to be supported by proceeds from the privatization of some of the best-performing major state companies.

In the discussion on the new pension reform concept in Poland pension experts have criticized two issues in particular (see Golinowska, CASE 1997). First, it is argued that the obligatory character of the second pillar means maintaining the high level of state involvement and state responsibility for pension finances as well as high obligatory contributions with all the known consequences. The second point of criticism is the equity issue between generations and the problem of age discrimination. Only younger people benefit from the new system. Older persons not obliged to be included in the new schemes have access only to the third pillar as an additional source of income in old age. However, life insurance or occupational pension schemes are rather unlikely sources of real old-age security for people entering the scheme at an advanced age. Thus the people who will benefit most from the new system of 'state (paternalistic) capitalism' with large state involvement and extended obligation are mainly those who are younger and the more affluent.

8.3.3 Driving Forces and Factors Hampering Pension Reform

The main difficulties in launching effective pension reform are of a political nature. These difficulties were already present at the beginning of the 1980s. Between 1980 and 1982 against the background of the Solidarity-led revolution, reforms rationalizing the Polish economic system were implemented within the framework of a centrally planned economy. Central to these reforms was organizing the area of social insurance, aiming at uniting various benefit systems for various employee groups.[31] However, after the introduction of martial law, measures to organize the social insurance system were held back and in 1983 plans were withdrawn. At that time, three acts were adopted that contained favourable exceptions from general rules: for miners, railway workers and employee groups working under specific conditions or in unusual jobs. Such measures aimed at legitimizing political power in order to compensate for ground being lost because of opposition to martial law. In subsequent years in the 1980s, along with growing political opposition and persistent economic recession, more and more employee groups were assigned privileges.

Poland entered the transition period with a social insurance system that had a larger number of privileged cases than those subject to general rules. Therefore a new act systematizing the system was prepared, with the main aim, however, of introducing a benefit indexation system, which in an environment of predominating hyperinflation was a social necessity.

Solutions adopted between 1990 and 1991 were extremely favourable for pensioners. These regulations were also undermined by political considerations. The political interest of anti-communist parties that took over power in 1989 worked primarily towards winning the support of pensioners to strengthen their political position, while systemic changes were less important. The proposed new economic system was creating opportunities mainly for the young and the enterprising. Gaining the approval of pensioners (who also represented a strong electorate, well organized and influential in opinion-forming circles)[32] and a thriving nostalgia for the previous system created conditions which promoted these extremely favourable regulations within the social insurance system, while playing a legitimizing role for new political groups as well. Indexation principles, for example, gave preferential treatment to old-age and disability pensioners. Indexation pertained, first, to the pension calculation basis, second, to the benefit itself and, third, to components of the pension formula related to the average wage (the so-called 'social' component accounting for 24 per cent of the average wage). The surge in the number of beneficiaries between 1990 and 1992, along with the increased level of benefits, triggered a rise in state subsidies to the social insurance fund and this consequently moved the government to revise the adopted indexation principles. Even Solidarity trade unions were against the government, led by the former Solidarity opposition. In mid-1993 the government collapsed and the Constitutional Tribunal not only protested against restrictions in the indexation of the pension benefits but also opposed the elimination of privileges in the social insurance system by virtue of the principle of acquired rights.

Political forces with roots in real socialism came back to power using a slogan calling for a return to wage-linked 100 per cent indexation of benefits. In the environment of economic revival and wage growth this immediately influenced the level of benefits and led to increased subsidies to social insurance once more. In order to stay in power the social democrats spread the same propaganda of harm being done to pensioners (Majcherek 1996) despite available statistics on the relatively better income standing of pensioners than of wage earners. Tension in public finance caused by the growth in spending on social insurance triggered the undertaking of extensive fiscal measures, directed, primarily, at contributions, subsidy levels and the collection rate of contributions (for example the instituting of a social insurance watchdog). These austerity measures implemented by the social democratic government were criticized by the opposition, although their demands for a radical reform of the pension system did not mention specific measures, for example, a decreasing replacement rate, for fear of losing the support of the pensioners. Certainly there are varying degrees of opposition. Right-wing populist extremists still spread the propaganda of harm being done to pensioners, while the more liberal faction of centrist movements (for example, the Union of Liberty) seeks radical reform (but without decreasing benefits, for example, through using privatization proceeds).

No political party can afford to treat lightly a population of 9 million pensioners which accounts for almost 40 per cent of all voters – and, moreover, of regularly active voters. Although politicians might also expect to attract voters from among those paying social contributions and taxes, there is still a conviction in Poland that an old-age pension is a personal saving from wages, and therefore one on which there is a rightful claim. Information on the PAYG system and the need for a new intergenerational contract are noted but seem to arouse little support. Part of the responsibility for the lack of public support lies with the politicians failing to promote any understanding of these problems. Even highly respected politicians will talk with conviction about government funds that have been taken away from pensioners and have to be given back (such was the case, for example, following the announcement of the decision of the Constitutional Tribunal on the indexation for the 4th quarter of 1995).

The largest supportive faction curbing the expansion of the pension system and radical reform mainly comprises employers, especially those in the small business sector. High social insurance contributions (45 per cent of the wage fund) pose an almost unbearable burden, particularly for small companies. Support for such reform should increase along with the privatization of the economy and the integration of employers' interests into party politics.

A catalytic role in the process of reforming social insurance can be played by experts with an economic background supported by the world-wide discussion on the crisis of state pension systems. In Poland, however, a group of politically active lawyers has been defending the interests of current beneficiaries and they tend to overlook long-term economic implications for the social insurance system.

8.3.4 Closing Remarks: Pension System versus Transformation

Systemic transition and the introduction of a market economy system in Poland have brought about a definite improvement in pensioners' income position. These improved economic circumstances are, on the one hand, due to the failure to abandon old privileges and, on the other to the introduction of new principles for benefit assessment (partly included in a new pension formula, that is, the so-called social average wage-linked component) and indexation. It thus became advantageous for pensioners to retire earlier, particularly under threatening labour market conditions.[33] Full job security that existed under real socialism has been replaced by the security provided by guaranteed pension benefits. Employees benefit from this even more because pensioners in Poland are allowed to work while drawing a pension benefit. A direct result of the early retirement policy on a mass scale is the decrease in the average age of those who are granted benefits for the first time. In 1995 this was 57 for old-age pensioners, and 46 in the case of disability pensioners, whereas in 1989 the respective ages had been 59 and 49.

Direct and indirect incentives to early retirement led to a situation where between 1990 and 1995 the number of pension beneficiaries increased by 33 per cent and by the end of 1995 amounted to 9.15 million persons, which accounted for 23.7 per cent of the total population. This rate of growth in the number of old-age and disability pensioners, given the relatively high level of benefits, has created serious and difficult problems, not only economic (the share of national income being spent on pension benefits in 1995 reached almost 16 per cent of GDP), but also social. The latter problem refers to the just proportion of social spending between generations, which has been destroyed: in effect the younger generation has been victimized, including children, among which poverty is on a larger scale than among the elderly (Golinowska 1996b).

The transition period with its economic and political problems led to a situation in which reform of the pension system became necessary. Reducing costs to employers (lower contributions) and to the state budget (in terms of lower state subsidies) are considered a main aim of reform in Poland along-side a proper level of old-age income security. Similar to many other countries, the issue of the structure of old-age security with a 'division of responsibilities' between public (PAYG) and private (funded) schemes plays a central role in pension reform debate in Poland. How well Poland will be able to cope with these problems is not yet clear.

NOTES

1 See Florek (1994).
2 The number of pension insurance holders among white-collar workers increased from 80,000 in 1925 to 343,000 in 1938 and manual workers from 534,000 in 1924 to 2,064,000 in 1938. See ZUS (1987).
3 In 1937 under these separate systems of state provision, pensions were collected by 208,000 people (121,000 pensioners, 57,000 widows and 30,000 orphans). In the same year pensions (of all kinds) from social insurance had been collected by 30,000 white-collar workers and 232,000 blue-collar workers. Expenditures on state-financed pensions (PLZ 271.4 million in 1937) were at the same time significantly higher than expenses for pensions from social insurance (PLZ 161 million). See ZUS (1987).
4 On the 'common heritage' of social security systems in countries of Central and Eastern Europe see Voirin (1994).
5 The social insurance contribution for the employed in the public sector, apart from agriculture, amounted to 15.5 per cent between 1951 and 1972, to 25 per cent from 1981, to 33 per cent from 1982, to 43 per cent from 1983, to 38 per cent from 1987, to 43 per cent from 1990 and to 45 per cent from 1991. See ZUS (1987; 1992).
6 Between 1946 and 1987 the income from social insurance contributions (excluding farmers) was always – with the exception of 1980 and 1982 – bigger than joint expenses for social insurance. See ZUS (1987; 1992).
7 Average old-age pension (excluding farmers) in relation to average salary amounted to 27.5 per cent in 1955, 48.5 per cent in 1960, 64.5 per cent in 1970, 54.4 per cent in 1980 and 56.1 per cent in 1985. See ZUS (1987) (partly own calculations).
8 See section 8.3.3 on driving forces of the pension policy in Poland during transition.
9 For a broader context of social policy in the countries undergoing systemic transition, see Barr (1994a), ch. 3 in particular.
10 In the theoretical analysis of the pension security system, Zacher (1991) states: 'Only institutional linking of various values and objectives with appropriate solutions can guarantee the realisation of the values and objectives rooted in the society that do not always match, sometimes they compete with one another or are contradictory'.
11 The following subcategories can be mentioned: employees (covering some other occupations such as lawyers, cottage industry workers and persons hired under a work contract to learn a trade), self-employed persons (outside agriculture), members of farmers' productive co-operatives and agricultural co-operatives, artistes, priests and farmers.
12 Act on the Organization and Financing of Social Insurance of 25 November 1986 (*Journal of Laws* No. 42, item 202, as amended).

13 Since 1 January 1993, benefits paid to soldiers and their families are funded by the budget of the Ministry of Defence. Since 1 January 1995, pensions for former police officers, employees of the State Protection Office, border guards, state firemen and their families are financed by the budget of the Ministry of the Interior. Benefits for former prison officers and their families are paid by the budget of the Ministry of Justice. The benefits of these groups are thus not classified under social insurance.

14 The following groups have the right to earlier retirement: women aged 55 with 30 years of contributory and non-contributory periods, women aged 55 with 30 years of contributory and non-contributory periods qualifying for the 1st or 2nd disability category, men aged 60 with 25 years of contributory and non-contributory periods and qualifying for the 1st and 2nd disability category, war veterans aged 60 (male) and 55 (female), war and military invalids can retire 5 years earlier if they qualify for the 3rd disability category and 10 years earlier if they qualify for the 1st or 2nd disability category, invalids pursuant to accidents at work can retire at the age of 60 (male) and 55 (female), numerous employee groups working in specific conditions or in certain job positions can retire 5-20 years earlier depending on occupational group provided that the required minimum of contributory and non-contributory periods is met, including at least 15 years of work in specific conditions or in a certain job position.

15 Regardless of age the following employee groups have the right to earlier retirement: teachers with 30 years of contributory and non-contributory periods, including 20 years of work as teachers; persons made redundant pursuant to group lay-offs with 40 (male) or 35 (female) years of contributory and non-contributory periods; persons taking care of children requiring permanent care with 20 (female) or 25 (male) years of contributory and non-contributory periods.

16 If a pensioner has revenues from work or another activity subject to obligation to insurance coverage, which exceed 120 per cent of the average national wage in the preceding quarter, his/her benefit is suspended. With revenues ranging from 60 per cent to 120 per cent of the average wage the pension is decreased, however, not more than by the amount reflecting the social component of the pension. Revenues below 60 per cent of the average wage do not have any influence on the right to an old-age pension.

17 The increase in the minimum old-age pension from 35 per cent to 39 per cent of the average wage in December 1993 and the widening of the rights of the lignite miners may serve as an example of using the pension system for political purposes. See Wiktorow (1995a).

18 For example: in 1996, Ms X became 60 years old having collected 24 contributory years and ten non-contributory years (for example, period of study and care of a child). Since non-contributory periods may not account for more than a third of the contributory periods, in this case to determine the old-age pension level it is possible to consider only eight (a third out of 24) non-contributory years. For simplicity, let us assume that Ms X earned in the selected seven years in the period of 16 years (1980–95) an average income approximately equal to 93 per cent of the national average wage that corresponds to the base amount index. Her old-age pension will thus be equal to (1) 24 per cent of base amount + (2) 24 * 1.3 per cent + 8 * 0.7 per cent = 31.2 + 5.6 = 36.8 per cent of the base amount, which gives a total of 60.8 per cent of the base amount and her earlier earnings.

19 At present these are as follows: nursing allowances due to belonging to the 1st disability group or becoming 75 years of age; veteran allowance; allowance for underground teaching during the war; allowance for former soldiers who were forced to work in the mines as a substitute for military service.

20 The Constitutional Tribunal decided that this regulation was in breach of the Constitution. The president vetoed parliament's decision to restore the allowances.

21 Act on Insurance Activity of 28 July 1990 (*Journal of Laws*, No. 59, item 344, as amended).

22 And perhaps on a large scale, lax eligibility criteria for disability pensions. It is manifested in a high share of persons collecting disability pensions among all pensioners: in 1996 in non-agricultural schemes it amounted to 37.2 per cent. Since 1992 in non-agricultural

systems the number of new disability pensions has exceeded the number of new old-age pensions: in 1996, 121.5 thousand new old-age pensions were granted, 152.6 thousand disability pensions and 62.3 thousand family pensions. See ZUS (1997).

23 In 1996, 80.4 per cent of men and 81.6 per cent of women retired without reaching the statutory retirement age. See ZUS (1997).

24 The number of pensioners under the farmers' scheme went up from 1,355 thousand (including 950 thousand old-age pensions) in 1989 to 2,049 thousand (including 1,258 thousand old-age pensions) in 1995. See GUS (1996); ZUS (1992).

25 In the first year of transition, that is, in 1990 the average wage dropped by 24.4 per cent in real terms and the non-agricultural old-age pension by 12.6 per cent. See GUS (1996).

26 The average amount of non-agricultural old-age pension granted in 1994 was 10.2 per cent lower than the amount of the average benefit paid to all old-age pensioners in December 1994. See Wiktorow (1996).

27 Non-agricultural old-age pensions granted in 1994 contained, on average, 31.6 per cent of the social component. See Wiktorow (1996).

28 In December 1994, 6 per cent of non-agricultural old-age pensioners received a minimum old-age pension. The percentage of the recipients of minimum disability pension was much higher (28 per cent) and among survivor pensioners it was 23 per cent. A total of 18.2 per cent of pensioners were collecting the lowest benefit. In December 1991, the percentage was 10.2 per cent. The growth was caused by a rise in minimum benefits and their indexation. See Markowska (1995a).

29 Labour costs per unit of output are decreasing, however, because in Poland labour productivity is growing (Wiktorow and Grabowski 1996).

30 For a review of concepts on pension system reform in Poland after 1989 see Golinowska (1995, 1996a), Wiktorow (1995b); Zukowski (1996).

31 Act on Pensionary Provision for Employees and Their Families of 1982 (*Journal of Laws*, No. 40, item 267, as amended).

32 In 1990 the Pensioners' Party was founded and has been active in Poland since then.

33 It is also possible on the one hand, due to regulations on earlier retirement plans in companies undergoing restructuring, and on the other, to lenient disability certification.

REFERENCES

Augustinovics, M. (1996), 'Pension systems and reform. Britain, Hungary, Italy, Poland, Sweden', Phare ACE Project Draft Report, Budapest.

Barr, N. (ed.), (1994a), *Labour Markets and Social Policy in Central and Eastern Europe. The Transition and Beyond*, World Bank in association with the London School of Economics and Political Science, Oxford University Press, New York.

Barr, N. (1994b), 'Income transfers: social insurance', in Barr (ed.), (1994a), 192–225.

Bolkowiak, I. (1996), 'Fiscal policy reform in Poland', IPiSS – Social Policy in 1993–1994, Main Problems in the Transition Period', Occasional Paper No. 6, Warsaw.

Dabrowski, M. (1995), 'Cele polityki makroekonomicznej i liberalizacyjnej w Polsce w okresie transformacji' [Objectives of the macroeconomic and liberalization policy in Poland during transformation], in M. Dabrowski (ed.), *Polityka gospodarcza okresu transformacji*, PWN, Warsaw.

de Fougerolles and Golinowska, S. (eds.) (1995), 'Tworzenie prywatnych funduszy emerytalnych w Polsce' [Setting up of private pension funds in Poland], Institute

for East West Studies, Institute of Labour and Social Studies, Bulletin 1 (401), Warsaw.
Doan, O. (ed.) (1995), 'Ubezpieczenia zyciowe' [Life assurance], Poltext, Warsaw.
Florek, L. (1994), 'Evolution of social security in Poland', in von Maydell and Hohnerlein (eds.) (1994), 35–45.
Golinowska, S. (1995), 'System emerytalno-rentowy w Polsce. Rozwój instytucjonalny i polityka', [Pension system in Poland. Institutional development and politics], in de Fougerolles and Golinowska (1995), 77–90.
Golinowska, S. (1996a), 'Reforma systemu emerytalno-rentowego w Polsce. Kolejny etap projektowania i dyskusji, w: Modele reformy systemu emerytalno-rentowego i sciezki dojscia. Kolejny etap dyskusji' [Reform of the pension system in Poland. Subsequent stage of modelling and discussing, in: Models of reform of the pension system and implementation paths. Another state in discussion], Gospodarka i Przyszloœæ, special edition, Institute of Labour and Social Studies, Nowe Zycie Gospodarcze, Club 500, Warsaw.
Golinowska, S. (1996b), 'Polska bieda' [Polish poverty], Institute of Labour and Social Studies, Warsaw.
Golinowska, S. (1996c), 'State social policy and social expenditure in Central and Eastern Europe', Studies and Analyses CASE, No. 81, Warsaw.
Golinowska, S. (ed.) (1997), 'Reforma systemu emerytalno-rentowego' [Pension System Reform], CASE Reports No. 6, Warsaw.
GUS (1993), *Historia Polski w liczbach* [History of Poland in figures], Warsaw.
GUS (1995; 1996; 1997), *Rocznik Statystyczny* 1995; 1996; 1997 [Statistical Yearbook], Central Statistical Office, Warsaw.
Hausner, J. and Owsiak, S. (1992), 'Kryzys finansowy panstwa w procesie systemowej transformacji na przykladzie Polski' [State finance crisis during systemic transformation. The case of Poland], Friedrich-Ebert-Stiftung, Warsaw.
Holzer, J.Z. (1996), 'Struktura plci i wieku ludnosci starszej w Polsce, dzis i w perspektywie dwudziestu lat' [Structure by sex and age of the elderly population in Poland, today and in twenty years], paper presented at the PTE conference 'Starsi ludzie w okresie przemian ustrojowych', 25 November, Warsaw.
Hrynkiewicz, J. (1995), 'Raport o rozwoju spolecznym Polski 1995. Synteza raportu', [Report on social development in Poland 1995. Report synthesis], in UNDP (1995), 228–52.
ILSS (1995), 'Dyskusja wokól rzadowego programu ubezpieczen spolecznych', [Debate on government social insurance programme], *Ekspertyzy – Informacje* Bulletin 5/95, Institute of Labour and Social Studies, Warsaw.
ISSA (1994), 'Restructuring social security in Central and Eastern Europe. A guide to recent developments, policy issues and options', International Social Security Association, Geneva.
Kalaska, M., Kostrubiec, S. and Witkowski, J. (1996), 'Praca nierejestrowana w Polsce w 1995', [Non-registered labour in Poland in 1995], CSO Studies and Statistical Materials, Warsaw.
Kolodko, G. (1992), 'Economics of transition: from shortageflation to stagflation. The case of Poland', in A. Clesse and R. Tokes (ed.), *Preventing New East-West Divide: The Economic and Social Imperatives of the Future Europe*, Institute for European and International Studies, Luxembourg and Nomos Verlagsgesellschaft, Baden-Baden.
Kolodko, G. (1994), 'Strategia dla Polski' [Strategy for Poland], Poltext, Warsaw.

Ksiezopolski, M. (1993), 'Kryzys systemu socjalistycznych gwarancji w polityce spolecznej' [Crisis of socialistic guarantees system in social policy], in Ksiezopolski and Supinska (eds.) (1993), 7–17.
Ksiezopolski, M. and Supinska, J. (eds.) (1993), 'Zagrozenia i szanse polityki spolecznej w Polsce w okresie transformacji' [Threats and opportunities of social policy in Poland in the transition period], Friedrich Ebert Foundation, Warsaw.
Landau, Z. (1991), 'Podstawowe kierunki rozwoju ubezpieczen spolecznych' [Main directions of development of social insurance], in Rozwoj ubezpieczen spolecznych w Polsce (1991), 21–51.
Majcherek, J.A. (1996), 'Nieoplacalna opieszalosc' [Non-profitable sluggishness], *Rzeczpospolita daily,* No. 187, Warsaw.
Malaka, A. (1994), 'Problemy zadluzen skladkowych' [Problems with overdue payments of social contributions], in Materials for 6th Conference of the Polish Social Insurance Association, ZUS Information Materials No. 8 (152), Social Insurance Institution 1992, Warsaw, 30–39.
Markowska, H. (1995a), 'Najnizsze emerytury i renty' [The lowest old-age and disability pensions], ZUS Information Materials No. 3, 13–17.
Markowska, H. (1995b), 'Emerytury i renty przyznane w 1994' [Old-age and disability pensions granted in 1994], ZUS Information Materials No. 8, 23–9.
Maydell, B. von and Hohnerlein, E.M. (eds.) (1994), *The Transformation of Social Security Systems in Central and Eastern Europe*, Peeters Press, Leuven.
Okólski, M. (1988), 'Reprodukcja ludnoœci a modernizacja spoleczenstwa. Polski syndrom' [Population reproduction versus society modernisation. Polish syndrome], KiW, Warsaw.
Piatkowski, M. (1991), 'Ubezpieczenie emerytalne' [Pension insurance], in Rozwój ubezpieczen spolecznych w Polsce (1991), 123–50.
Pierson, P. (1995), 'The new politics and the welfare state', ZeS-Arbeitspapier No. 3/95, Zentrum fur Sozialpolitik – Universitat Bremen.
Plawucka, H. (1995), 'Swiadczenia emerytalne i rentowe' [Pensionary benefits], in *Social Insurance Development in Poland,* 367–419.
PSUS (1992), 'Problemy emerytur, rent i opieki zdrowotnej' [Problems of old-age and disability pensions and health care], Materials from 4th PSUS Conference, Warsaw-Wroclaw.
RSSG (1995), *Reforma systemu emerytalno-rentowego* [Reform of the pension system], Socio-Economic Strategy Council, Council of Ministers, Report No. 9, Warsaw.
Sajkiewicz, B. (1995), 'Minimum socjalne' [Social minimum], *Social Policy,* No. 7, 28–32.
Topinski, W. and Wisniewski, M. (1995), 'Prywatne programy emerytalne – propozycja reform' [Private pension schemes - draft reforms], in de Fougerolles and Golinowska (1995), 126–47.
UNDP (1995), *Polska '95. Raport o rozwoju spolecznym* [Poland '95. Report on social development], United Nations Development Program, Warsaw.
UNICEF (1994), *Crisis in Mortality, Health and Nutrition,* ICDC Unicef, Florence.
Voirin, M. (1994), 'Social security in Central and Eastern Europe: continuity and change', in ISSA (1994), 155–94.
Wiktorow, A. (1995a), 'Reforma systemu emerytalnego w latach 1991-1993. Stan wyjœciowy, zamierzenia, mozliwoœci realizacyjne', [Pension system reform in 1991–1993. Departing point, plans, implementation possibilities], in RSSG (1995), 111–33.

Wiktorow, A. (1995b), 'Kierunki reformy systemu emerytalnego. Przeglad instniejacych projektow', [Directions of pension system reform. Review of existing draft], in ILSS (1995), 7–21.

Wiktorow, A., (1996), *System emerytalno-rentowy. Przeslanki i mozliwoœci reformowania*, Pension system. Premises and possibilities of reform], Instytut Badañ nad Gospodarka Rynkowa, Gdañsk.

Wiktorow, A. and Grabowski, M.H. (1996), *Koszty pracy w transformacji* [Labour costs in transformation], Instytut Badañ nad Gospodarka Rynkowa, Gdansk.

World Bank (1993), *Poland: Income Support and the Social Safety Net during the Transition*, Washington, DC.

Zacher, H.F. (1991), 'Ziele der Alterssicherung und Formen ihrer Verwirklichung' [Objectives of old-age security and their realisation], in Zacher (ed.), *Altersicherung im Rechtsvergleich*, Studien aus dem Max-Planck-Institut fur ausländisches und internationales Sozialrecht, Nomos, Baden-Baden, 25–113.

Zukowski, M. (1994a), 'Pensions policy in Poland after 1945: Between "Bismarck" and "Beveridge"', in J. Hills, J. Ditch and H. Glennerster (eds.), *Beveridge and Social Security. An International Retrospective*, Oxford University Press, Oxford, 154–70.

Zukowski, M. (1994b), 'Transformation of the economic system and social security in Central and Eastern Europe', in von Maydell and Hohnerlein (1994), 61–9.

Zukowski, M. (1996), 'Das Alterssicherungssystem in Polen – Geschichte, gegenwärtige Lage, Umgestaltung', [The old-age security system in Poland – history, current situation, reconstruction], *Zeitschrift für ausländisches und internationales Arbeits- und Sozialrecht*, No. 2, 97–141.

ZUS (1987), *Rocznik Statystyczny Ubezpieczeñ Spolecznych 1946Ü1985* [Statistical Yearbook of Social Insurance 1946–1985], Social Insurance Institution, Warsaw.

ZUS (1992), *Rocznik Statystyczny Ubezpieczeñ Spolecznych 1985-1990* [Statistical Yearbook of Social Insurance 1985–1990], Social Insurance Institution, Warsaw.

ZUS (1995;1996), *Informacja o swiadczeniach pienieznych z Funduszu Ubezpieczen Spolecznych i Funduszu Alimentacyjnego* [Information on cash benefits paid from Social Insurance Fund and Alimony Fund], 4th quarter 1995, 1996, Social Insurance Institution, Warsaw.

ZUS (1997), *Wazniejsze informacje z zakresu ubezpieczeñ spolecznych (system pozarolniczy) 1996* [Main information on social insurance (non-agricultural system) 1996], Social Insurance Institution, Warsaw.

9. Transformation of old-age security in the Czech Republic

Jiri Král and Martin Mácha

9.1 INTRODUCTION

Economic reforms undertaken in the former Czchechoslovakia and then in the Czech Republic at the beginning of the 1990s were accompanied by fundamental social reforms. The aim of the transformation process was to create a social system which would correspond to the needs of a market economy, motivate individuals and social groups to assume greater responsibility for their own socioeconomic situation and achieve economic independence, that is, in particular to not rely on state transfers. It was also an aim to comply with international conventions and to harmonize national legislation with European social insurance regulations. This report proceeds with a brief description of the pension system until 1989 which is followed by an outline of the economic and demographic background.

9.1.1 The Pension System until 1989

Until 1989, the system of pensions was characterized mainly by paternalism and the utilization of social security for other objectives. The decision-making process in the field of social security as a whole was overwhelmingly determined by centrally administered state directives, individuals were treated as objects of state social politics, although it was possible for a person to have a very marginal influence upon the decision-making process. In many cases the state had assumed certain functions which in a democratic society are taken care of by the family, citizen associations, voluntary organizations or private institutions. The system had many failings. Above all, individuals could not fully meet their old-age security needs. Besides the pension itself or individual savings, no other forms of old-age security, such as complementary pension insurance, were allowed.

Generally speaking, pension security was to provide for income in old age. Since its implementation in 1948 it did indeed serve this objective, but it also served many others. In many cases it was used by the government as a political and economic tool. For example, the so-called 'personal pensions' were de facto a reward for loyalty to the regime. The former regime differentiated three categories of workers. Categories of privileged groups of employees within the unified system (particularly miners) were granted special entitlement and benefit payment levels. In some cases social security benefits had been used as a tool to sanction citizens for deviant conduct which did not conform to state requirements. Prior to 1989 the pension system lacked mechanisms which would allow for a flexible reaction to ever-changing economic and social situations or standards of living. For example, there was no indexation mechanism to maintain the value of pensions. In addition, the model had not been designed to respond to the expected demographic development towards the end of the 20th century. During the transition period, Czech social policy played two basic roles – instrumental and conceptual. The instrumental role was designed to create tools to compensate for the social impact created by the economic transition and to ensure the necessary political support. The conceptual role encompassed efforts to design a social reform representing a new concept of social protection for the population. The reform aims to rework the conceptional framework of social policy and introduce new policy instruments. A significant feature of the reform is the reduction of public dependence on state support. The role of the state has been changed and defined more precisely. These changes will be discussed in more detail in section 9.2.

9.1.2 Economic and Demographic Background

Economic transformation in the Czech Republic in the early years has progressed without serious social conflicts and upheavals, although numerous groups of the population have been seriously affected. This favourable result can surely be credited to a considerable extent to a well-designed social policy. The analysis of basic data on the economic development of the Czech Republic shows that the transformation of the economy and its restructuring has been proceeding without significant breakdowns in the macroeconomic stability. By 1996, 70 per cent of gross domestic product (GDP) was already being produced in the private sector. GDP had continued to grow, but following the economic problems in 1997, the dynamics in economic development have decreased. The Czech Republic was well known as a country with low unemployment rates in the early years of transition. Until 1996, the unemployment rate never rose above 3.5 per cent.

The pension system is particularly sensitive to the demographic development, because it is based on pay-as-you-go (PAYG) financing, whereby the payment of pensions to current pensioners is covered, more or less immediately, by contributions collected from those who are economically active. An increase in the ratio of the number of pensioners to economically active persons can be offset either by raising contributions to maintain the level of pensions or by lowering the amount of pensions while maintaining the contribution levels of active persons.

Figure 9.1 *Percentage of persons over retirement age in the active population, Czech Republic, 1980–2020*

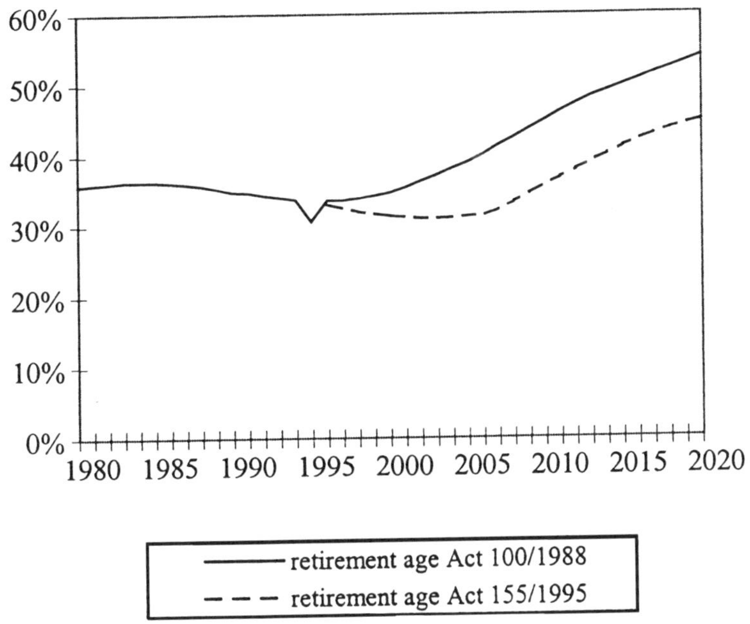

Source: Ministry of Labour and Social Affairs calculation based on Czech Statistical Office (CSU) demographic projections.

An increasing proportion of the general population is approaching retirement age and subsequently applying for a pension or some sort of social assistance. This is an international trend, but compared to other countries the increase in the Czech Republic is relatively modest. Demographic development and forecasts to 2020 indicate that the Czech Republic has made an important policy decision in increasing the retirement age.[1] As a consequence the percentage of persons over retirement age in the active population will be reduced in 2020 from 53.9 per cent (former legal provision) to 44.8 per cent (see Figure 9.1).

9.2 PENSION REFORM SINCE 1989

9.2.1 Overview

One of the first steps of reform were changes in preferential treatment and discrimination in the existing pension system. During the 1990–92 period, all preferential treatment within the system was abolished, including the so-called personal pensions, the amount of which was determined by political decision, and pension privileges ensuing from employment in occupations involving high physical exertion and/or hazardous working conditions. At the same time, discrimination against the self-employed was removed.

In 1993, payment of contributions was separated from the tax system. In connection with the introduction of contributions it was necessary to set up institutions for the collection and management of contributions and thus change the organization of the social security system. The periods of payment of contributions and the amount of the assessment base in respect of contributions have became relevant for the award of pension benefits. However, income from contributions is still state budget revenue, and pensions as well as administrative costs of the pension system are paid out of the state budget.

In 1994, a voluntary system of supplementary pension insurance with state financial support was set up. During the 1990–95 period, pensions were increased on ten occasions. The aim of pension increases consisted not only in alleviating the impact of economic transformation which was accompanied by increased inflation rates, but also in redressing unfounded differences among pensions awarded at different times, and thus creating a sound basis for the new pension insurance act. Price increases during the first years of economic transition, in particular in 1991, had a big impact on the value of pensions in real terms which has not yet been offset, in spite of the fact that the real value of pensions has gradually increased. The proportion of average old-age pension to average wage since 1989 is illustrated in Table 9.1.

The table shows that the relative value of pensions was gradually declining over the period, despite pension increases. There were a number of restrictions consisting, among others, in limits for earnings which were relevant for calculation of benefits, as a consequence of which the amount of pension could not rise in relation to earnings. Pensions awarded in the past were always lower than newly awarded ones since they were based on lower nominal earnings. Thus the problem of the so-called 'old pensioners' was constantly present.

Table 9.1 *Share of average old-age pension in average wage, Czech Republic, 1989–96*

Year	Wage (CZK/month)	Pensions (CZK/month)	Wage to pension (%)
1989	3,170	1,598	50.4
1990	3,286	1,731	52.7
1991	3,792	2,176	57.4
1992	4,644	2,413	52.0
1993	5,817	2,734	47.0
1994	6,896	3,059	44.4
1995	8,172	3,578	43.8
1996	9,676	4,213	43.5

Source: Czech Social Security Administration.

The new pension insurance bill became, particularly during 1994–95, subject to heated political debates triggered by the proposed raising of the retirement age. Legislation, in force from 1 January 1996, regulates the system of benefits in such a way that, in spite of unfavourable demographic trends, it will not be necessary to increase the burden placed on active persons or raise the share of social expenditure in GDP, while it will be possible to link pensions more closely to wage and price variations. Among the most important changes introduced by the new law were a gradual increase in the retirement age, calculation of the amount of pensions on the basis of two tiers (flat rate and earnings related) and a new system of pension adjustments that made it possible for the government to respond flexibly to developments in prices and wages by taking the economic situation into account.

Simultaneously with the adoption of the Pension Insurance Act a separate pension insurance account was established which is an integral part of state financial assets. Both income and expenditure of pension insurance continue to be part of revenue and expenditure of the state budget, but a separate pension insurance account has been created to monitor income from pension insurance contributions, expenditure with respect to benefits and the administration of the scheme. The balance of this account can be used only for the purpose of financing a possible increase in benefits or of covering deficits incurred in previous periods. The reformed pension system is based on two pillars: (a) a general compulsory pension insurance scheme and (b) a voluntary supplementary pension insurance with state contribution.

9.2.2 The First Pillar

The first pillar of the pension system covers all persons dependent on gainful employment, salaried members of co-operatives and the self-employed. Principally it aims at solidarity among social groups and to redistribute high income to middle and lower incomes. The proportion of pension to earnings, the replacement rate, falls from 83 per cent with the lowest wage to 37 per cent with double the average wage.

Pensions in the first pillar are financed by the PAYG system; participation is compulsory and conditions are uniform for all economically active persons. Benefits replace income in old age or in case of invalidity or death. The state guarantees the operation of the scheme in both financial and legal terms. The system is administered by a state institution and its revenues and expenditures are part of the state budget.

Insurance records

Insurance records are periods of employment.[2] Certain changes were introduced regarding the definition and scope of periods which are accepted as periods of participation in insurance, although a premium was not paid for them (so-called 'substitute' periods).

A claim to a substitute period of insurance is valid for a period of participation in pension insurance by the partially disabled, registered as unemployed and actively seeking work; persons in military service; soldiers in additional service; persons performing a civil service; persons taking care of a child under the age of three or of 18 if the child is severely long-term handicapped and requires special care; and persons taking care of incapacitated relatives. Substitute periods are also recorded for beneficiaries of full disability pensions and persons receiving benefits from sickness insurance.

For claims received after 31 December 1995, regulations include times spent in high school and college as a period of insurance. For persons over 18 during this period, it is limited to six years. The insurance record also includes a period of unemployment, in which the jobless are registered at the unemployment office and entitled to unemployment benefits. In such a case a period of up to three years after the unemployed are no longer entitled to unemployment benefits can be calculated. Furthermore, the period of child care calculated was extended from three to four years and the group of entitled persons now includes men, but the period of care for a child may not be calculated for more than one person.

Voluntary insurance

Within the basic system of pension insurance, 'voluntary insurance' was introduced. The voluntary participation in pension insurance is available for persons over 18. This pertains to unemployed persons and students and persons employed abroad. Voluntary insurance is available for unemployed persons no longer entitled to unemployment benefits (during the time of entitlement or when this expires three years prior to entitlement to pension, the participants are still insured under law). The same procedure can be applied to secondary or high school students (with the exception of the first six years of schooling after 18 years of age when participants are already insured by law).

The unemployed and students may pay the premium any time in the future up to the date of the pension application. For employment abroad, premiums may be paid prorated two years from the date of submission of an application for insurance. Also persons over 18 with at least one year of obligatory insurance can participate in voluntary pension insurance. This group's participation is however limited to ten years of voluntary insurance. Premiums may be paid only one year prorated after the submission of an application for this insurance.

Pension claims not taken over by the new system are invalidated. They are transferred to benefit claims under the new system, but are not considered as new applications. Pensions for length of employment in the new system are considered as partial disability pensions or old-age pensions. The pension for a wife and social pensions are considered as full disability pensions or old-age pensions.

For the old-age pension, a gradual increase in the retirement age was introduced: two months for men and four months for women per year until 2007, at which time retirement age will be 62 for men, and between 57 and 61 for women, depending on the number of children.

Benefits

Benefits in the new system are characterized by length of insurance record and achieved income. This applies to old-age, disability and survivors' pensions. Opportunities for early retirement have been extended. A widowers' pension has been introduced. These benefits can be supplemented by the voluntary insurance discussed above. Table 9.2 illustrates the diverse benefits provided by the pension system and its development since 1990.

If a person has a claim to more than one pension – old-age, full disability or partial disability, widows' or widowers' or orphans' – the highest one is paid out in full; other pensions are paid out at the rate of 0.5 of the percentage assessment.

Table 9.2 *Number of pensions and pensioners, Czech Republic, 1990–96 (1000)*

	1990	1991	1992	1993	1994	1995	1996
Number of all pensions	2,951	2,997	3,033	3,052	3,051	3,057	3,006
Old-age	1,736	1,777	1,804	1,815	1,811	1,811	1,775
Disability	353	367	382	398	410	420	402
Partial disability	130	127	123	119	117	117	120
Widows'	635	635	633	630	626	623	621
Widowers'	0	0	4	5	5	5	31
Orphans'	66	63	60	60	60	62	57
Others[a]	31	28	27	25	22	19	0
Number of Pensioners	2,473	2,479	2,509	2,522	2,519	2,523	2,478

Note: [a] Others pertain to social pensions, service retirement pensions, wives' pensions, etc.
Source: Czech Social Security Administration.

Flexible retirement age

The original legal provision (Act No. 39/1994 Coll.), allowed people to retire two years earlier. Retirement eligibility stipulates 25 years of accumulated insurance, and at least 180 days of having been registered at the unemployment office as a job seeker. The pension is then reduced by one per cent of the calculation basis for every 90 days of pension taken prior to the official retirement age. After reaching the retirement age, it was converted to a regular pension without the percentage reduction of tariff.

The reform introduced the opportunity for early retirement three years prior to retirement age. In contrast to the previous early retirement plan, this one is not conditional upon being registered at the unemployment office as a job seeker. The date of retirement is left to the discretion of the applicant. The only conditions are 25 years of insurance, and that the applicant should reach retirement age within three years, as of 1 January 2001, four years, and after 31 December 2006, five years. In the early retirement scheme, the reduction in pension benefit level for a non-working period is lower and permanent even after retirement age is reached. It represents 0.6 per cent of the calculation basis for every, even incomplete, 90 days.

Unlimited accumulation of old-age pension with earnings is allowed only after two years of pension payment. Within these two years, continuation of payment of the old-age pension is granted only when earnings do not exceed twice the amount of the cost-of-living minimum.[3]

From the original legal provision, it is possible to increase an old-age pension benefit level provided that a 'productive' activity is performed after the granting of a title to the pension and that the pension is not paid out at that time. For every 90 days of economic activity that a pension is not being received, an increase by one per cent of the calculation basis is attainable.

Pension formula

The most extensive changes in pension benefits concerned pension calculation: most importantly, the rules for deciding which earnings would be decisive for pension calculation were changed.

Earnings used for the basis of pension calculation will at the beginning be the average earnings during the ten-year span before retirement, and every other year the law remains in effect. The length of the period prior to retirement used to calculate average earnings will be extended by one year every year, until it covers (after 20 years) the period of 30 calendar years.

All earnings within the given period will thus be incorporated into the calculation. The highest earnings for certain periods will no longer be singled out. These earnings, however, will be reassessed so that their levels are maintained in relation to the average wage of the period in which they were reached. This will result in a so-called 'indexation' of earnings, that is, in a multiplying by coefficients that express development of an average wage.

The method of determining the calculation base from indexed earnings while excluding certain active periods remains unchanged compared to pre-reform calculations of average monthly earnings. Only the reduction amount is changed; the personal assessment base (earlier non-reduced average monthly earnings) is fully incorporated into the amount of CZK 5,600. From CZK 5,600 to CZK 11,200, 30 per cent is incorporated (not the original one-third), and from an income of more than CZK 11,200, 10 per cent is considered. These limitations, set by law, will be adjusted regularly so that the relationship between paid-out and newly granted pensions and between pensions and earnings is maintained.[4]

There is a two-tier construction for the setting of the pension benefit level. Every pension consists of (a) a flat-rate basic amount and (b) an earnings-related amount. The flat-rate basic amount is equal for all pensions. It is set and adjusted regularly according to strict legal guidelines.[5] The government is authorized under the law to increase this amount. The basic assessment element is granted only once in conjunction with two or more pensions, and it is not incorporated into the area from which a survivors' pension is calculated.

The earnings-related proportion is calculated from the calculation base. The calculation differs according to the type of pension. For old-age and full disability pensions, 1.5 per cent from the calculation base is given for each year of insurance; for partial disability pensions, 0.75 per cent of the calculation base is given and for survivors' pensions, the basis is the percentage amount of the pension received by the deceased person or to what he/she would be entitled at the time of death. In the last case, rates are 50 per cent for a widows' or a widowers' pension and 40 per cent for an orphans' pension. Pensions at and above CZK 120,000 a year, that is, CZK 10,000 a month, are subject to income tax. The amount of pension will no longer be restricted by a 'pension maximum limit'. Table 9.3 describes the development of the average payment of different pension benefits.

Table 9.3 Average payment of pensions, Czech Republic, 1990–96 (CZK/month)

	1990	1991	1992	1993	1994	1995	1996
Old-age	1,882	2,527	2,706	3,246	3,373	3,782	4,610
Disability	1,736	2,162	2,332	2,897	3,222	3,614	4,456
Partial disability	1,114	1,356	1,425	1,694	1,967	2,311	2,933
Widows'	1,334	1,687	1,838	2,169	2,471	2,806	3,495
Widowers'	0	0	870	1,149	1,419	1,780	2,388
Orphans'	740	914	951	1,108	1,338	1,636	2,181

Source: Czech Social Security Administration.

Adjustment of pensions

The pension insurance law specifies pension adjustments. The most important change in policy is a decrease in the growth of the overall retail price index (from 10 per cent to 5 per cent) which requires that an adjustment or increase of pension, respectively, be made.

Criteria used to adjust pensions now include the development of salaries. Should the index of real wage growth per year exceed one in two successive calendar years before the year in which pensions are increased 'according to prices', the paid-out pensions will also be increased.

Table 9.4 Development of real values of full old-age pensions and average wages, Czech Republic, 1989–96

Year	Old-age pension		Average wage	
	1989=100%	1993=100%	1989=100%	1993=100%
1989	100.0		100.0	
1990	98.4		96.6	
1991	81.5		72.2	
1992	79.8		76.8	
1993	75.6	100.0	79.6	100.0
1994	76.3	100.9	85.8	107.8
1995	80.9	107.0	93.1	117.0
1996	87.0	115.1	101.3	127.4

Source: Ministry of Labour and Social Affairs (MLSA).

The law allows for an increase in pensions according to the principles provided by government decree. The legislative process is consequently accelerated, and the amount of pension continually reflects the price and salary development.

Since 1989, a problem remains that the development of the real value of pensions is very uneven, in particular compared with the development of real wages. The figures representing the real value of the average full old-age pension and those representing the real value of gross wages in the national economy are presented in Table 9.4, taking 1989 and 1993 as base years. The results show a certain decline in the value of pensions since 1989 but a relative increase since 1993. Compared to the development of real wages, pensions performed better at the beginning of the period, whereas since 1993 the growth of the real value of wages has been higher.

Transitory provisions

A ten-year protection period was introduced to maintain minimum pension levels in line with the original regulations. According to this new law as of 31 December 1995, the amount of a direct pension granted before 31 December 2005 cannot be reduced. Pensions will automatically be calculated for the beneficiary in the post-reform period, according to some former and the new legal provisions. Pension payments will be more advantageous to the pensioner. These regulations also affect the survivors' pension calculation. In particular, percentage assessment elements of the survivors' pension are only calculated according to the new pension insurance law.

Organization

The pension system is incorporated into state administration. A subject of the present discussion is the transformation of this system into an independent public legal institution with its own budget. Ever since 1990, political and public debates in the general area of social policy have increasingly addressed this issue.[6] The government coalition of conservative parties has, however, refused to institute a public legal format. There are possible explanations for this: negative experiences with public legal institutions in the system of health care and loss of control over a substantial portion of the state budget. The central executive body is the Czech Social Security Administration (CSSA).[7] It collects and checks the payments of insurance contributions from the insured for pension, sickness and unemployment insurance. It is a budgetary organization which is directly subordinated to the legislative and service supervision of the Ministry of Labour and Social Affairs (MLSA) of the Czech Republic. The CSSA is divided into the Central Administration (CSSA, with offices in Prague) and the District Social Security Administration (DSSA, 76 administrative units), and is associated to the Prague Social Security Administration (PSSA). Between the central and the district offices are remote branches of the CSSA at the level of the former regions (seven administrations). Table 9.5 documents CSSA administration costs between 1993 and 1996.

Table 9.5 Social security administration costs, Czech Republic, 1993–96

	1993	1994	1995	1996
Costs total (CZK):	1,836	2,358	2,697	3,182
Administration	1,550	1,845	2,151	2,372
Investments	286	513	546	810
Costs as percentage of total expenditures	1.5	1.7	1.7	2.0
Number of employees	6,269	7,115	7,452	7,640

Source: Czech Social Security Administration.

Responsibilities concerning the collection of insurance contributions and the keeping of records are divided among the individual levels of administration. The self-employed must apply to the DSSA immediately after beginning economic activity. The DSSA collects insurance contributions, pays out sickness insurance benefits and records important personal data concerning the course of insurance. For the purposes of pension insurance, the DSSA keeps so-called 'registration papers' of pension assurance which contain basic information about earnings in the individual years of gainful employment. Employees in 'small organizations' with less than 25 employees must also be registered for social insurance with the DSSA immediately after beginning employment. Contributions for employees are deducted by the employer and payable to the DSSA. A pension assurance card is established for each employee and kept by the employer. Only after an employee has left a firm is the pension assurance card send to the DSSA. Each new job in a different firm will require a new pension assurance card. Small organizations are legally obliged to inform the DSSA monthly of the number and names of employees, their wages and their absence from work through sickness or other reasons such as maternity leave. In 'large organizations' (25 and more employees) the allocation of tasks and information paths regarding social security coverage is arranged otherwise. Large organizations are obliged to give only monthly reports of the number of employees, the total volume of wages, the overall time worked and also the social security benefits they have paid out (for example, sickness benefits). Such information is provided directly to the regional offices of the CSSA. The amount of benefits paid out is subtracted from the total monthly amount of contributions due so that what is actually transferred monthly to the district office is the net contribution for all employees. The regional offices of CSSA pass on information to the appropriate district administrations which are entitled to carry out checks in large enterprises at regular intervals. Pension assurance cards are established in the enterprises and remain there until the departure of the employee. Only then are they handed in to the CSSA and subsequently sent to the central records in the PSSA. The success of the collection of insurance contributions and the confidence of the insured or their employers in making these payments can be seen in Table 9.6.

Table 9.6 Collection of insurance contributions, Czech Republic, 1993–96

	1993	1994	1995	1996
Outstanding debt in % (total premiums collected to total premiums prescribed)	2.6	2.6	3.9	4.7

Source: Czech Social Security Administration.

The basic ideas of the CSSA concerning organizational changes entail (a) a change in procedures in collection and recording of data, (b) recording additional information on employees of large enterprises, (c) improved recorded identification of the insured, and (d) annual control reports and a more general report on the number of the socially insured and gainfully employed and the record keeping of insurance histories.

Ways of improving the information base on all insured persons are being thoroughly examined. An overview of who and how many are insured has been difficult or impossible to obtain. In particular, information available on employees of large businesses is scarce. Basic aims are to transfer the processing of all insurance cards from businesses to local pension insurance bodies, to submit reports regularly on increases and decreases and annual changes, and to store these reports in the form of insurance accounts kept with the aid of computer technology; in time, existing insurance cards would also be computerized.

Financing

Apart from administration, the second obvious and much discussed problem continues to be how the basic pension scheme will be financed. Pension expenditures, as shown in Table 9.7, represent an important economic part of the GDP, state budget and social expenditures.

The most costly parts of social security expenditures are the subsystems of pensions and health care. Health care expenditures have expanded from 1990 at the expense of other social security programmes. This is presumably an indicator of faulty health care reform. It is constructive to take a brief yet more detailed look at the different branches of social security (see Table 9.8).

Table 9.7 *Social security expenditures, Czech Republic, 1990–96*

	1990	1991	1992	1993	1994	1995	1996
As % of social budget	41.4	28.1	40.1	37.6	37.2	41.1	42.6
As % of state budget	19.1	21.6	21.5	20.8	22.6	25.4	25.6
As % of GDP	7.8	7.6	7.8	7.9	8.0	8.8	8.8

Source: Czech Social Security Administration.

Table 9.8 *Social expenditures structure, Czech Republic, 1990–1996 (branches as % of social budget)*

	1990	1991	1992	1993	1994	1995	1996
Pension security	41.1	38.1	40.1	37.6	37.2	41.1	42.6
Sickness and maternity benefits	8.1	6.3	6.4	6.1	7.0	6.8	7.0
Unemployment benefits and employment policy	0.0	1.7	2.0	1.1	1.1	0.9	0.9
Family allowances	10.8	9.1	8.7	7.4	7.9	7.2	7.0
Health care	27.1	26.0	27.4	35.0	35.2	34.6	33.3
Administration costs	0.4	1.5	1.3	1.8	2.0	2.2	2.1
Social assistance benefits	4.8	3.3	4.4	4.6	5.0	4.9	4.4
Others	7.7	14.1	9.7	6.6	4.6	2.3	2.7

Source: MLSA.

Because of a higher wage growth in relation to the average growth of pensions and also due to a relatively low rate of unemployment (3 per cent) the revenue from insurance contributions during 1993–95 was higher than the total expenditure in benefit payments, in spite of rising numbers of pensioners. As a consequence, from 1 January 1996 it was possible to reduce the rate of contributions from 27.2 to 26.0 per cent. Employee contributions amount to 6.5 per cent of gross wages whereas employers pay 19.5 per cent of the total pay-roll; self-employed persons pay 26 per cent of at least 35 per cent of the difference between their revenues and expenses before tax. Overviews of the development of CSSA revenues and expenditures are presented in Table 9.9 and 9.10, respectively.

Table 9.9 Collected insurance contributions and fines, Czech Republic, 1993–96 (million CZK)

	1993	1994	1995	1996
Insurance contributions	108,404	129,463	146,076	165,228
Penalties	423	2,724	3,362	3,624
Fines	25	42	33	30
Surcharges	6	7	6	5
Others	2	4	2	
Total	108,860	132,240	149,479	168,887

Source: Czech Social Security Administration.

Table 9.10 Pension expenditures, Czech Republic, 1990–96 (million CZK)

	1990	1991	1992	1993	1994	1995	1996
Total[a]	45,531	56,052	63,699	73,638	83,630	103,691	122,365
Old age	31,483	38,803	44,188	50,864	57,759	72,035	85,064
Disability	6,556	8,222	9,525	11,505	13,507	17,037	19,887
Partial disability	1,580	1,764	1,821	1,942	2,122	2,966	3,967
Widows'	5,161	6,528	7,379	8,467	9,274	10,119	11,681
Widowers'		14	40	48	62	106	330
Orphans'	507	549	578	634	724	1,150	1,432
Other[b]	244	172	168	178	182	278	4
State compensatory contribution	1,547	3,665	4,918	6,158	5,595	0	0

Note: [a] This figure excludes state compensatory contributions. [b] Social pensions, service retirement pensions, wives' pensions etc.
Source: Czech Social Security Administration.

There are still certain questions remaining which are related to issues of funding the basic insurance scheme and are the subject of both expert and political discussions. Agreement in principle has been reached that the PAYG scheme should be maintained. It has also been suggested that within the framework of this main financing system, a certain fund could be gradually established, the assets of which could be invested and the returns subsequently used for the benefit of the insured. However, calculations based on projected demographic development have shown that the current contribution rate will not suffice in the near future to cover pensions at their present level (in real terms). It has been estimated that even under more restrictive entitlement conditions it will be necessary to increase contribution rates gradually from the present 26 per cent up to 37 per cent by the year 2020.

A decision is yet to be made on the issue to what extent such a pension insurance fund should be independent from the state budget. The latest step of the reform, the introduction of a specific pension insurance account, represents a significant shift in the present system of financing pension insurance expenditure exclusively from the state budget. This change reflects a certain shift of opinion with respect to financing pension insurance. In the liberal economists' view, such a step meets only a minimum requirement to reduce state intervention. However, considering the potential political impact of a pure liberally-oriented policy in pension insurance, this step represents the maximum that can be achieved under present circumstances. Experiences with relatively drastic reductions of state support or intervention in other areas has been overwhelmingly negative. Two examples are the serious financial problems in the public health and cultural sectors, due to the withdrawal of state funding. If such reforms are to be implemented, then implementation will have to proceed carefully and gradually.

9.2.3 Supplementary Pension Insurance

The supplementary pension insurance introduced in 1994 is based on the principle of a defined relationship between contributions made by participants and their future pension rights. Therefore, in contrast to the first pillar, the application of solidarity and repatriation principles is restricted. The scheme is characterized by voluntary participation and is run by private institutions (pension funds) which are essentially profit based and operate in a competitive environment. Pension plans are fully funded, there must be full coverage of the acquired rights by the fund's assets and the pension plans are defined contribution plans.

The State Contributory Supplementary Pension Insurance Act constitutes the legal framework for the whole system. The law provides for transferability of participants' pension rights, stipulates maximum qualification periods for payment of pensions, defines the types of benefits and defines also the power and authority of state supervision which is implemented by the Ministry of Finance. The ministry approves the appointment of members of pension fund boards, their custody bank, statutes and pension plans.

There are also certain state-regulated social elements in the scheme. Regulations limit distribution of profit – only 10 per cent of earned profit can be distributed among shareholders; at least 90 per cent must go to the benefit of insured persons. A specific type of state support has been introduced: a direct financial contribution is provided from the state budget in relation to the amount of contribution made by the participant. This method has been substituted for favourable tax treatment of contributions; privileged tax treatment is, however, still available for payment of benefit and in connection with pension fund investment. The state subsidy to the supplementary pension insurance has been reduced and is no longer increased if the participant's contributions have exceeded 5 per cent of the average wage. The amount of state contribution is shown in Table 9.11.

Table 9.11 *State contribution to supplementary pension insurance, Czech Republic (CZK)*

Amount contributed by participant	Amount of state contribution[a]
100 to 199	CZK 40 + 32% of the amount above CZK 100
200 to 299	CZK 72 + 24% of the amount above CZK 200
300 to 399	CZK 96 + 16% of the amount above CZK 300
400 to 499	CZK 112 + 8% of the amount above CZK 400
500 and over	CZK 120

Note: [a] In the first two years of participation the state contribution is raised by 25 per cent.

Citizens can choose among several pension plans. However, it is not easy to know which plan may suit the individual best. Much depends on individual situations, means available, and expectations. Each fund can structure the proposed package to meet the needs perceived by different income, age, professional, regional and other groups. Contributions made by participants are paid from their after-tax income (the same applies to cases where the employer might wish to supplement his/her employees' contributions). However, as far as individuals are concerned, this taxation is compensated by the state contribution.

Benefits paid by the supplementary provision are taxed only when the corresponding part of the benefit has been created by financial operations of the fund. The parts corresponding to participant and state contributions are tax free. The taxable part of benefits is subject to a privileged tax rate that is also applicable to interest on savings of the population or benefits paid by private insurance companies in respect of private insurance plans. In addition to the privileged rate, a further advantage is that the payment of tax from interest and dividends is deferred until the period when pensions are paid and thus the full amount of interest and dividends is capitalized and contributes towards the final amount of the participant's benefit.

Pension funds also have a privileged income tax rate (25 per cent as of 1 January 1996), distinct from other companies (39 per cent as of 1 January 1996), and their income from interest and dividends is tax free. Qualified pension funds must be approved by a state authority which supervises the fund's operations and activities.

First permits for the establishment of pension funds were granted in September 1994. However, a meaningful impact of the state contributory supplementary pension insurance scheme on the overall level of citizens' income from pension insurance cannot be expected before 2005.

In June 1995 there were 41 pension funds with approximately 1,500,000 participants, covering more than one-quarter of the entire active population. According to preliminary estimates, the state subsidy paid to all participants in 1996 will amount to roughly CZK 1.78 billion which corresponds to less than 0.5 per cent of the state budget. The sum of pension funds' total assets equals approximately CZK 11 billion, or roughly 0.8 per cent of GDP in 1996.

9.3 INFLUENCING FACTORS AND FUTURE PLANS

9.3.1 Influencing Factors

In the development of main principles defining pension security concepts in relation to the transformation period, two important phases of the reform strategy can be differentiated which have been a base for further decision making and implementation procedures.

The first stage, reflected in document analyses, political programmes and related opinions, can be called the development of a 'federalist concept'. From 1989, its relevance and applicability to the division of the federation grew. Inspired by the 'Bismarck model', the reform ideas derive mainly from models of a classical system of legal public (social) insurance though they are combined with other approaches. Other conceptual elements developed particularly in that period were corporation and the idea of creating a pension security fund within the privatization of state enterprises.

The second stage in the discussion can be placed starting from the split of the federation until 1996. This stage is characterized by the orientation towards a more 'liberal model' of basic pension security and by an attempt to transfer the earnings-related component of pensions to supplementary systems. In addition, the consistent maintenance of the principles of citizenship and citizen equality are noteworthy. Lastly, more attempts to enforce radical reforms of pension system are evident in this period.

The year 1996 heralded elections in the Czech Republic; in other words it was a year when social policy logically became even more sensitive to political influences than it had been earlier. The trends of political discussions and exchange of opinions can be illustrated most clearly by an analysis of the individual electoral programmes (for the 1996 elections) of the strongest political parties. Here basic ideas of the concept of social policy, including pension insurance are discussed. The programmatic social policy approaches of the main parties are briefly outlined below in order to elucidate the political arena in which future pension policy making will take place.

The *Civic Democratic Party (ODS)* emphasizes that the new system of pension insurance has to take into account the expected change in the age structure of the population. The raising of the retirement age is thus considered as inevitable. This is seen as the only measure that will not make it necessary to raise insurance contributions. The ODS does not support a policy of separation of the pension financing system from the state budget. Rather, they advocate that the state should guarantee basic pensions while promoting the idea that the younger generation should develop a certain degree of independence from state pensions through additional private insurance.

The *Civic Democratic Alliance (ODA)* is also aware of the need to raise the retirement age. In contrast to the ODS it supports the idea of separating the system for financing pensions from the state budget and changing it into a funded system which will enable capital valorization of the means acquired by the collection of insurance contributions. It supports the creation of a system which will raise the motivation and the personal share of the individual in the provision of old-age security. The ODA is aware that an exemption should be made for those who no longer have time to save for their pensions.

The *Christian Democratic Union/Czech People's Party (KDU–CSL)* coalition support a different strategy for raising the retirement age. They do not consider implementing such a measure before 2005. The coalition actively rejects current reform proposals on the grounds that it considers such a policy to be a move towards a gradual reduction in the proportion of a pension insurance based on solidarity and its replacement by individual additional insurance. They are working towards the maintenance of an average level of pensions amounting to approximately half of the average gross wage. The KDU–CSL is strongly in favour of the separation of pension insurance from the state budget.

The *Czech Social-Democratic Party* (*CSSD)* promised in their programme to ensure the revision of the Law on Pension Insurance and abolish the raising of the retirement age. They point out the favourable influence of the original retirement age on reducing the amount of unemployment. According to the CSSA, additional insurance should be the result of a voluntary decision, not economic pressure. For this reason the social democrats intend to work for a basic pension which will guarantee a dignified old age. They propose the establishment of an independent Social Insurance Company, administered by representatives of insured persons and employers and guaranteed by the state.

The *Communist Party of Bohemia and Moravia* (*KSCM)* wants to ensure pensioners political and ethical conditions for a contented life and active participation in social events. They promote the passing of the Law on Pension Insurance. They want to raise the real value of old-age pensions to the level of 1989 and demand automatic and prompt valorization of pensions, not only in connection with inflation, but also with the growth of wages. They propose a return to the lower retirement age, and they want to eliminate the alleged discrimination against working pensioners and introduce protection against the misuse of pension insurance funds for other purposes.

The post-election distribution of the political forces of these opinion groups in 1996 is very interesting for the perspective of further development in pension security. The ODS, the ODA and the KDU–CSL are in governmental coalition (although we can see quite broad differences in their pension security concepts), but they do not represent a majority in the Czech Parliament (the coalition has 100 votes; the opposition also has 100 votes).

But political parties are not the only relevant actors. Trade unions are also interested in pension security development and they are able to put pressure on the government through their close relations with the social democrats or by organizing demonstrations or strikes (as they proved in 1995 when they organized the biggest demonstration since 1989 as a protest against the Basic Pension Insurance Act No. 155).

On the other hand, the reformers in the political arena who are a part of the state's policy-making apparatus are well placed to formulate, organize and push through policy preferences. They have access to a very experienced and well-informed staff of experts in the MLSA. Therefore they already have – together with the private liberal economists and capital market specialists – a favourable environment in which to develop reforms, especially on the technical side.

In 1995 the Institute for Research into Public Opinion conducted a survey of the public's views on the basic pension insurance. The findings show that the majority of the respondents do not favour the raising of the retirement age, or welcome the prospect of early retirement, and think that the funding system should be independent of the state budget.

Transformation of the Czech pension system and the results achieved are in conformity with the recommendations made by the Organization for Economic Co-operation and Development (OECD) which was the only international organization to have a significant impact on Czech pension reform until the end of 1996.

According to the OECD experts,[8] the growing costs of pension insurance and the ensuing financial burden placed on active persons is, at present, the main single problem. Therefore, it has been suggested that a pension system should be designed which would be acceptable to all generations, such as the following:

1. One in which the retirement age is gradually increased and early retirement with the corresponding (actuarial) reduction of benefit, as well as deferred retirement with the corresponding increase in benefit, is possible. This approach is fully compatible with the new Czech scheme (in force since 1 January 1996).
2. One in which more stringent eligibility requirements exist by extending the insurance period to qualify for entitlement (for example, by extending the minimum waiting period to qualify for a reduced old-age benefit).
3. One in which the level of benefits is reduced by:
   - reducing the replacement rate (which had been declining during the first years of transition but, more recently, has remained constant and its present level should not decrease further, at least during the next two or three years);
   - restricting the volume of increases in current pensions (the new regulations enable the government to reduce the percentage of revaluation significantly);
   - extending the period from which earnings will be taken into account for the determination of the amount of pension (the period will be gradually extended from 10 to 30 years);
   - taxing all pensions (the regulations introduced on 1 January 1996 will have a more significant impact in the years to come);
   - reducing earned income (the present ceilings for reduction of earned income are CZK 5,600 and CZK 11,200, respectively); and simultaneously:
   - introducing a (higher) ceiling for the payment of contributions (no ceiling exists at present);
   - abolishing preferential tax treatment (all privileged tax treatment within the benefit system has already been abolished);
   - not relying exclusively on the system of defined benefits, or on the state scheme (since 1994 there have been two independent systems which are based on contradictory principles).

9.3.2 Political Discussion about Future Plans

Main criticisms of the current system

One of the main controversial issues is the organization of pension security. Critics of a state-run system pointed out the lack of democratic (self-governing) control, because money is collected by the state and goes to the state budget. This kind of criticism comes especially from social democrats and trade unions.

Among the general public a point of criticism is that no serious attempt has been made to reform pension insurance for current pensioners and that recommendations to reform the present pension system are directed above all to dual and combined systems which only affect future generations.

It is also believed that there is reason for concern about the new voluntary insurance system. Such a model, with state contribution, is yet to be tested and thus many people are justifiably cautious. There are also some inaccuracies in the current law on voluntary insurance, but above all, there are doubts about whether it is prudent to make such changes in fundamental principles (for example, unification of the system of savings and insurance). Those arguments are broadly used by different actors regardless of their political background.

Of course the living standard of pensioners is generally criticized, mainly on the ground that after seven years of reform pensions have not sustained at least their real value of 1989. This was the main platform of the increasingly powerful 'pensioners' party.

Finally, an overall criticism on current reform coming again from the central left of the political spectrum is the unilateral consideration of economic aspects and the neglect of social, historical and cultural factors that are inherent in social security traditions in the Czech Republic.

Future financing of the system

With regard to the future financing of pension security, two basic concepts have been discussed. The first one was represented by the Czech government in 1997, in which the ODS had a majority. This concept is based partly on current financing and partly on capital-financed obligatory savings.

The second concept is mainly represented by the social democrats, who want to preserve the system of current financing in which allowances are paid out immediately from collected contributions and to seek a solution to the problem of increasing expenditures on pension insurance within the framework of this system.

A system of current financing, as conceived under the first concept, is very sensitive to demographic development, whereas the capital-financed system component is more sensitive to economic development. Since the aim of pension insurance is to ensure an adequate income in old age, disablement and death which is commensurate with that earned during the period of economic activity, and which has the lowest possible tax burden (through the payment either of insurance contributions or taxes), the optimal solution seems to be the 'diversification of pension savings' consisting of an obligatory system with PAYG-financed benefits in combination with capital savings and an additional voluntary insurance. For such a policy to be implemented successfully, however, a public consensus on several issues is needed. For instance, it is necessary to determine the proportions of the PAYG-financed and the capital-funded part in the level of allowances. This involves such choices as uniform minimum pensions, eventually supplemented with a merit component from the currently financed system, and as a pension derived exclusively from the amount of contribution paid (actually from savings). If more significant social redistribution is desired, the current system could also be financed from indirect taxes and it would thus be possible to include the 'grey and black economy'. Just another example of a problem to be dealt with is the possibility of covering expenditures during the transformation period from the PAYG-financed system to a new arrangement.

For the full transformation from the PAYG system to a capital-funded system it would be necessary to ensure financial means to cover all pensions paid out by the present system up to its termination and – at the same time – to cover all future liabilities emerging from the contributions paid by currently economically active persons (this means a financial volume of around 2.5 times the GDP). This option is quite unrealistic and therefore it has been recommended that only a partial replacement of the current system should be considered. The financial means essential for the transformation would be less, in keeping with the measure of preservation of the current system. Sufficient means can be acquired more readily partly by continued but reduced contributions for the PAYG system and partly by external sources, for instance, by the issue of state bonds. The time horizon of the transformation of the present financed system to a new combined system influences the 'double' burdening of the middle generation. An important question is thus whether it is better to have a long-term transformation or the maximum possible shortening of this process.

One of the prerequisites of the reform is the ability of the administrative system (the CSSA) to establish individual accounts for all the insured and calculate the entitlements to date.

If in fact smaller reform amendments are required, it would be possible as a first step, within the system of current financing, to separate the financing of pension insurance from that of other social benefit provision. This would most likely lead to a more efficient and transparent system of financing. In order to improve the financial situation the idea of establishing a capital reserve within the system has also been discussed. There are several ways of implementing this. While preserving the present legal arrangements and also the present replacement rate (44 per cent), certain small surpluses could be expected after a few years. Even with their capitalization, however, in the long run the fund would have a deficit from the year 2008. If the raising of the retirement age is continued even after the year 2007 this deficit would not be eliminated, merely reduced.

Reform measures have to be gradual for socio-political reasons as well. It would not be prudent to reduce allowances in the next ten years since given the short period that the system has been in existence, the allowances from voluntary additional pension insurance are still minimal. Without compensation, the reduction of the level of allowances from the basic system would mean a reduction in the standard of living of pensioners. Also the conditions of entitlement cannot be made stricter in a financially significant manner (for example, speeding up the raising of the retirement age, evaluation of disablement).[9] With regard to possible external sources of financing, there has been discussion about income from privatization. Realistically it could be expected that the National Property Fund at the beginning of 1998 would have shares amounting to a value of CZK 150 billion. Even if the total amount was invested all at once, the positive balance of the pension fund would last only until 2014.[10] For the pension fund to have a positive balance up to the year 2020, it would be necessary either to invest CZK 400 billion in it at once or subsidize it annually with a sum corresponding to 3 per cent of the volume of the measurement basis.

In conclusion, the acquisition of the necessary means for the maintenance of the financial balance of the current system from internal resources is at an impasse from the socio-political viewpoint and external sources are insufficient. It will therefore be necessary to consider the second concept of financing, because the preservation of the PAYG system will sooner or later need either to increase the contribution rate or to have support from the state budget or both to cover expenses. Under such circumstances it would be prudent to invest in a gradual transformation.

Economists promise themselves that the development of obligatory pension savings will stimulate the capital market and the economy by increasing the volume of savings of the population, even at the cost of putting the State temporarily in debt, for instance through a system of state obligations. According to international experience, however, this result is not unequivocal. From the point of view of the MLSA, the social consequences of the transformation take priority. The present state of reform preparation is a developed concept of the financing of pension insurance concentrated mainly on analyses of various possibilities of the solution and preliminary model calculations. The results indicate that further decision making should involve a compromise between the two above-mentioned directions, that is, the preservation of the PAYG-financed obligatory basic system of pension insurance and obligatory savings.

The target structure of the future whole pension income could be as follows: the overall relation of pension to gross wage will amount to roughly 65–70 per cent, of which 55–60 per cent would be ensured by the obligatory system and 10 per cent is projected to be provided through voluntary additional pension insurance with state contribution. With the combination of the currently financed system and obligatory savings the ratio could, for instance, be as follows: 15 per cent uniform pension from the currently financed system, 25 per cent merit pension (derived from earnings and length of period insured) from the same system and 15–20 per cent pension from obligatory pension savings.

The basic decision on further procedure will, however, also require the preparation of much basic information material and model calculations. In making a decision it will also be necessary to consider the organizational–administrative possibilities of eventual transformation and, last but not least, its social consequences.

NOTES

1 This was envisaged by the provisions of Act No.155/1995.

2 Unless specified otherwise by the particular international convention, a period of employment abroad is considered for Czech pension insurance if the premium is paid voluntarily to the Czech insurance body. A period of employment for a non-resident is considered for Czech pension insurance, if the period results in participation in insurance.

3 The government is authorized to increase the amount defined as the cost-of-living minimum by a decree. This followed an increase of prices by 5 per cent. From 1 October 1996, for an individual the amount of CZK 5,780 monthly is necessary to maintain a basic standard of living.

4 These sums were increased in 1997 by governmental decree. Before 1 January 1997, the limits were CZK 5,000 and CZK 10,000.

5 The basic amount represented CZK 680 monthly as at 1 January 1996, from 1 April 1996 it was increased to CZK 920, and from 1 October 1996 its increase to CZK 1,060 was approved.

6 In connection with a preparation of the Concept of Social Politics, but also later on, for example as in the election programmes of political parties in both elections in 1992 and 1996 or a wide discussion about a compulsory pension security in 1995.

7 Its functions and authority are regulated by Law No. 582/1991 Sb. of 1 January 1992.

8 Report on ageing, published in the first half of 1996.

9 Perhaps, one possibility may be the gradual restriction of substitute periods: at present, if all substitute periods were abolished it would be possible to reduce the contribution rate by roughly a third; in the case of their partial reduction, to around half, while preserving the present contribution rate, certain capital could be created which, through investment, would ensure the positive balance of the pension fund even after the year 2020, provided that there was also a continuation of raising the age limit after 2007.

10 For comparison, expenditure on pension insurance in 1997 is budgeted at CZK 153 billion.

REFERENCES

Burcin, B. and Kuera, T. (1995), 'Actual state and perspectives of population development in the Czech Republic until 2020', *Katedra demografie PF UK*, Prague.

Czech Administration of Social Security, Ministry of Labour and Social Affairs, 'Complete Outline of Social Benefits according to the State on 1 June 1993', Prague.

Federal Ministry of Labour and Social Affairs/Ministry of Labour and Social Affairs of the Czech Republic/Ministry of Labour and Social Affairs of the Slovak Republic, (1992), 'National Basic Indices from the Sphere of Social Security 1957–91', Prague.

Horálek, M. (1996), 'Development of the Czech economy 1990–1996', Working Paper (Japanese university lectures).

Mácha, M. (1996), 'Social Protection System in the Czech Republic', Research Institute of Labour and Social Affairs, Prague.

Mácha, M., Horálek, M. and Kux, J. (1996), 'Main Economic and Social Indicators of the Czech Republic', Research Institute of Labour and Social Affairs, Prague.

Mácha, M., Papeš, Z., Moyzesová, D. and Bruthansová, D. (1993), 'Suggestions for the Development of the Social Insurance Scheme from the Point of View of Global Trends and Foreign Experiences', Research Institute of Labour and Social Affairs, Prague.

Ministry of Labour and Social Affairs of the Czech Republic (1996), 'Draft of the Act on Social Assistance', Prague.

Ministry of Labour and Social Affairs of the Czech Republic, *Statistical Yearbook from the Sphere of Labour and Social Affairs*, 1993–96, Prague.

10. Transformation of old-age security in the Slovak Republic

Margita Hurcíková and Karol Pekník

10.1 INTRODUCTION

This chapter summarizes basic changes in the pension system during transformation in the Slovak Republic. In the first section, basic data on economic developments and demographic changes in the population are presented. It is within this basic context that the process of transformation takes place. The second section focuses on the transformation of the pension system, followed by a third section dedicated solely to the draft of the New Basic Pension Act which is unlikely to come into force before 1998. The chapter concludes with an overview of the pension reform debate and the focus shaping the debate as well as some policy recommendations.

10.1.1 Economic Background

One has to remember that in 1989 when transformation began, the Slovak Republic was still a member of the Czechoslovak Federation. This meant that the same economic measures were implemented federation-wide. This proved to be less suitable for the economy of the region designated today as the Slovak Republic, than for the region currently called the Czech Republic. The devaluation of the Czechoslovakian currency in 1990, for example, generated much more tension in the area of today's Slovak Republic than in that of the Czech Republic.

The Slovak economy did, of course, have the weaker starting position of the two regions, indicated by the lower per capita GDP and labour productivity. Slovakia started with a much higher unemployment rate and the absorption of workers that had been released by the state-owned enterprises into the expanding private sector was also much lower than in the Czech Republic. Moreover, the Slovak Republic inherited an underdeveloped industrial structure which was less flexible in terms of essential changes and oriented mostly towards heavy industry and conventional heavy arms production, such as tanks. This was a consequence of strategic political decisions taken mostly under the influence of the Soviet Union and in compliance with the Warsaw Pact.

While in 1989 the Slovak Republic reached a gross domestic product per capita in stable prices equal to 87 per cent of the Czech Republic, this figure fell to 77 per cent by 1992. This was caused by the decline of GDP per capita by 26 per cent in the Slovak Republic within these three years. The extremely rapid deterioration of the economic system led to problems in the whole financial sector. A major problem was the insolvency of many state-owned enterprises. Many of them took part in the voucher privatization scheme which came with high credit insolvency inherited from the old socialist system. Many joint stock companies created by the voucher privatization scheme have not yet been able to solve the problem of insolvency and have to pay debts which they did not incur.

In 1994–95, despite a low level of foreign investment, continuing problems resulting from privatization and a permanently tense political atmosphere, the economic situation in the Slovak Republic improved: whereas in 1993 the GDP in stable prices decreased by 4 per cent – and this decline can be explained mainly by the split into the Czech and Slovak republics – in 1994 the growth rate was 4.9 per cent and in 1995, 7.4 per cent. The deficit of the state budget decreased from 23 billion crowns in 1993 to eight billion crowns in 1995. Inflation was reduced from 23.2 per cent in 1993 to 10 per cent in 1995. It is questionable to what extent these favourable results were due to the gradual transformation pushed forward by the state's restructuring and modernization of the economy, or to the economic initiatives in the private sector in connection with generally improved economic circumstances.

But in 1996 the economic situation started to deteriorate. Despite the fact that GDP continued to increase and inflation was still very low, some economic indicators pointed to shrinking productivity. Among the common main problems were a high tax burden on enterprises; a slowdown in exports compared to imports; regional concentration of economic growth; and permanent problems of state budget financing.

The deficit in the state budget increased in 1996 to almost 30 billion crowns. Signs relating to the development of state finances do not point to optimistic trends for the near future. It is expected that the state budget deficit for 1997, provided that the most essential items of it are approved, will reach about 35 billion crowns.[1] The social sector will be the most likely casualty of the shortfall.

In the Slovak Republic, the transformation also led to permanent unemployment problems; in several regions unemployment reached about 25 per cent and the average unemployment rate (around 13 per cent) would be even higher if some ten thousand persons with Slovak citizenship did not work in the Czech Republic. Although there are various programmes and incentives to stimulate job creation, the results are not satisfactory for a number of reasons. At the end of 1996, the National Labour Office was established to cope with the problem of unemployment.

10.1.2 Demographic Background

Apart from the economic problems, the demographic development has to be considered when reforming the pension system. Life expectancy in the Slovak Republic is much lower than in advanced market economies. Life expectancy at birth is approximately 68 years for men and 78 for women, and at retirement age it is 14 and 22, respectively.

Despite the current age structure it has been predicted that the ratio of the working-age to the old-age population will decrease. Table 10.1 shows projections for future developments of the old-age dependency ratio.

Table 10.1 Development of the old-age dependency ratio, Slovak Republic, 1995–2015

	1995	2000	2005	2010	2015
Total population (1,000)	5,365	5,474	5,590	5,670	5,710
Population of working age (1,000)	3,220	3,364	3,426	3,395	3,373
Population of pension age (1,000)	930	947	996	1,094	1,194
Dependency ratio	3.46	3.55	3.44	3.10	2.82

Note: Working age is from 15 until pension age is reached; for men 60 and for women 55.
Source: Slovak Statistical Office (1993).

The demographic projections of the table illustrate that the dependency ratio will decrease within the next 20 years from 3.46 to 2.82. This means that in the year 2015 one pension has to be financed by 2.82 persons of working age.

10.2 PENSION REFORM, 1989–97

In the following, the former pension system in the Czechoslovakian Republic is outlined as the starting-point. After an overview of the pension system under the influence of the transformation process, the changes in legislation since 1989 will be described in detail.

10.2.1 Pensions in the Czechoslovakian Republic

To be able to understand the current problems and circumstances of pension reform in the Slovak Republic, we have to be aware of the former system in the Czechoslovakian Republic. The main regulations of the old system are still in force and hindering generally fundamental changes.

Until the end of 1992, there was a uniform state system of social security in the former Czechoslovak Republic.[2] Social security was guaranteed for all persons with benefits and services provided exclusively by the state and fully financed by the federal budget. The old pension system was characterized by:

- extended coverage,
- various types of benefits and a multitude of politically motivated privileges,
- a highly redistributive pension formula,
- pay-as-you-go (PAYG) financing and
- a state guarantee for the solvency of the system.

The public pension system was universal, covering nearly the whole population.[3] Benefits provided by pension insurance were old-age pensions, invalidity and partial invalidity pensions, widows' and orphans' pensions, social and personal pensions. The general retirement age was 60 for men and 53–57 for women (depending on the number of children brought up) but there were many exceptions.

The amount of pension payment depended on the length of service,[4] the wage level and the working category.[5] The general condition of entitlement for an old-age pension was 25 years of employment. This service record was required for entitlement to the basic sum, whose amount depended on the occupational category. A longer service time in the Slovak Republic increased the pension amount by a certain percentage for each year.[6] The individual wage was based on five years of the highest salary during the last ten years of employment, but in a degressive form.[7] The model described thus far is still operative in the existing pension system in the Slovak Republic. In general, the higher the wages are, the lower the replacement rate of the old-age pension. Table 10.2 shows the spectrum of differences within the compensation scheme.

The average gross monthly wage in 1989 was 3,100 crowns and in 1995, 7,200 crowns. Therefore the limit of maximum insurable earnings affected a greater number of pensioners each year.[8]

Table 10.2 Replacement rate of the old-age pension,[a] Slovak Republic

	Replacement rate in per cent			
	after 25 years of employment		after 35 years of employment	
Average monthly wages in crowns	by gross wages	by net wages	by gross wages	by net wages
2,500	50	67	60	80
4,000	38	50	45	60
6,000	31	41	37	49
8,000	24	32	29	39
10,000	20	27	24	33
15,000	14	18	16	22
20,000	10	14	12	16

Note: [a] replacement rate for the third working category (see Notes 6 and 7).
Source: Lubyová (1996).

Various other aspects were taken into account when calculating the pension, for example, the special merit of employees working in the sciences, state administration and public services, including political commitments (the so-called personal pensions) or during times of antifascist resistance (1939–45). Simultaneously, social circumstances were considered, mainly in the case of the loss of the breadwinner, for handicapped and disabled citizens and for old-age pensioners whose pensions were below the minimum subsistence level.

Self-employed persons were generally discriminated against with regard to claims and pension level. With this policy the totalitarian regime tried to set negative incentives for anybody who was not willing to be part of the system or who tried to avoid employment in the planned socialist economy.

All in all the pension system at the outset of the transformation process in 1989 was characterized by extraordinarily strong elements of paternalism. It was based on the idea that the public pension was sufficient and that there was no need for supplementary pension schemes or private provision. Furthermore the state was more or less a monopolist in all areas of social policy, for example, there were rarely any non-governmental welfare organizations in the Czechoslovakian Republic.

Until 1992, the finances for pension insurance were supplied by the Czechoslovakian state budget. There were no insurance premium rates. According to the set criteria of the state plan, enterprises and employed persons paid various taxes into the state budget.[9] The financing system of old-age security was not transparent. Neither employees nor employers knew what part of their taxes was used for social expenditures, including pensions. In principle, there was no limit to the ways in which the state could disburse its funds. State revenue served as a single complex collection fund up to 1993. Until that year, the state used its discretionary power to fix pension expenditures annually.

Finally, it should be noted that supplementary pension provision did not exist and private insurance was also quite rare in the former Czechoslovakian Republic. There was one single life insurance institution which was administered by the state authorities, namely the Czechoslovakian State Insurance Company with its branch in Bratislava. Neither the state nor state enterprises offered this form of supplementary provision because there was no incentive to participate; the population was in principle not interested in additional savings for the future.

10.2.2 The Concept of Systemic Transformation of the Pension System

It was not possible to adapt the existing pension system all at once to the rapid political, economic, ownership and institutional changes that started immediately after November 1989. It was realized that the so-called 'shock therapy' connected with experimentation and unclear results could not be applied to the social sphere. This was not considered the best solution. Therefore a gradual method was chosen. For the pension system this meant reducing state involvement step by step and changing over to a system of higher personal responsibility for old-age security.

The starting basis for the systemic transformation of the pension system was approved in the Czechoslovakian federal parliament in 1990. It then took until 1992 for these ideas to be translated into concrete plans and measures. Czech and Slovakian social and pension experts collaborated on this plan. Naturally the experts had different ideas about the future development of the pension system. With the dissolution of the former Czechoslovakian Federation at the beginning of 1993, this mutual co-operation more or less ended and the preceding conceptual ideas on pension issues and different developments in both republics have been interpreted in accordance with their different political structure. Thus despite the fact that the countries began the transformation of the pension system together with the development of similar conceptual approaches, these approaches are being developed differently.

Following the legal succession of the former Czechoslovakian Federation the Slovak Republic maintained all generally binding regulations including international agreements in the field of pension security. However, despite differences in conceptual development, the implementation of several pension measures was the same because the former Social Security Act of 1988 was generally in force until the end of 1995 in both republics. Further development in pension security has been concentrated particularly on changes in the organizational structure of institutions and not on the benefit side. For instance, the complex tax reform, with the introduction of value added taxes, started on 1 January 1993, more or less introduced a new system of financing. The 1993 state budget of the Slovak Republic no longer included pension benefits, sickness insurance and health-care expenditures. The financing of these benefits was from that point on covered by collected contributions, separate from the state budget.

A last example is an act passed in January 1993 in the Slovak National Council establishing the National Insurance Institution as a public service institution to administer sickness, health and pension insurance. The work defining the new state pension system and supplementary pension schemes was ongoing. By 1996 the legislation for all these issues was largely formulated, and was due to be implemented during 1998.

10.2.3 Development of Legislation, 1989–97

Preferences and privileges

The old pension system was characterized by numerous special regulations and privileges. These were either related to 'occupational categories' or due to special political commitments. Higher benefits were also provided for professional soldiers and members of the National Security Corps (police), prison wardens and workers of special merit in the fields of the economy, sciences, education, culture, defence and state security administration, and, last but not least, on the political scene. The most privileged class of beneficiaries consisted of persons with an active political commitment. Discretion regarding the award of these 'personal' pensions was used on a case-by-case basis by the federal government. In principle each ministry disposed of a certain quota of personal pensions, though the selected persons also had to be approved by the trade union committee and the committee of communist organization.

As mentioned above, the self-employed were discriminated against in the old system. In 1990, the first reform measures were installed to include the self-employed[10] and to gradually abolish 'personal' pensions.[11] In a further step, in 1991 some groups of beneficiaries were excluded from the pension system, namely members of the People's Militia and voluntary auxiliary members of the police.

The differentiation of pension payments by occupational category was also one of the first problems to be dealt with. In 1992, former occupational categories were invalidated by law. This is considered as one of the first fundamental steps towards a system without preferences. Claims acquired while in employment up until 31 December 1992, however, remain valid until 31 December 2016. This means that if a person has worked for two-thirds of the time required in a job classified in the occupational categories I and II by 31 December 1992, he/she would be entitled to a pension at an earlier age according to the respective category and a more advantageous calculation of the pension.

Although these changes were stipulated by law, implementation was postponed again and again in the following years. From 1993–96 the differentiation of working categories was prolonged every year for one more year.[12] The delay in implementation has been justified by the lack of supplementary pension insurance to secure income positions of pensioners who would lose some of their privileges. This argument has been accepted by all parties involved, namely by the confederation of trade unions and the association of employees. The situation in 1997 has not yet changed and it is expected that this justification will continue to be used until new legislation provides another solution.

Pension formula and indexation

Until the end of 1996, there were no substantial changes concerning the pension formula. There were only slight amendments stipulating pension benefits for those working during retirement, creating additional child allowances and introducing the entitlements for a social pension.

The most important changes on the benefit side were new regulations for the indexation of pensions, which became necessary due to rising inflation in the transition to a market economy. This was started in 1991. As a general rule, pensions should be raised as soon as wages have increased by at least 5 per cent since the last pension indexation or as soon as the cost of living has increased by at least 10 per cent. Periodic adjustments should take place at least every three months. This might be done in two different ways:

- by a fixed sum, if pensions are adjusted because of an increase in the cost of living, or
- by a certain percentage, if pensions are adjusted because of an increase in average wages.

By the end of November 1996, indexation of pensions had taken place ten times: four under the former Czech and Slovak Federal Republic and six since 1993. The above-mentioned mechanisms combine elements of an automated index with administrative discretionary elements because the fixed sums and the percentage increases for different types of pensions have been stipulated ad hoc each time on a case-by-case basis by the Slovak National Council. It was more or less a matter of bargaining within the framework of the approved regulations.

However, regardless of regulations, indexation did not always take place, especially since 1993. As a typical example, in 1995, indexation was postponed for some months. One of the main problems was that the indexation criteria were worded in such a way that they were open to different interpretations by the government, the Trade Union Confederation and the public, respectively. The government has consistently tried to hinder adjustments owing to the state budget's deficit. When pension reform is discussed in the Slovak National Council the parties focus mainly on how, how much, and when indexation should occur.

Table 10.3 *Development of maximum, average and minimum amounts of pension by indexation, Slovak Republic, 1989–96 (crowns/month)*

	Nov. 1989	Jan. 1991	March 1993	Sept. 1994	June 1995	July 1996	Index 96/89
Highest pension limit	3,800	3,800	4,100	4,350	5,040	5,650	149
Limit for the third category	2,800	2,800	3,300	3,640	3,940	4,290	153
Average old-age pension	1,465	1,918	2,401	2,882	3,320	3,720	254
Sum when pension is sole income							
single household	1,000	1,400	1,980	1,980	1,980	2,507	251
couple household	1,700	2,400	3,360	3,360	3,510	4,428	260
Sum of social pension							
individual	1,000	1,400	1,980	1,980	1,980	1,980	198
another dependent	1,700	2,400	3,360	3,360	3,510	3,510	206
Minimum limit of							
widows' pension	450	490	870	870	1,190	1,190	264
widowers' pension	400	400	870	1,100	1,190	1,330	333
orphans' pension	400	430	610	610	660	750	188

Experience has shown that indexation of pension benefits has allowed for provision of old-age security to be adapted to the financial capabilities of the state during transformation. It was, moreover, an instrument which contributed to the gradual abolition of the old pension system privileges, since pension indexations practically eliminated the differences in the pension amount due to privileged status. The results of indexation and the changes in relations between the main types of affected pensions is presented in Table 10.3.

Pensioners' income situation

Despite pension indexation the living standard of pensioners is still much lower than it was at the beginning of transformation. However, the decline until 1995 was not as great as in households of workers and farmers. In 1996 the situation improved for all social groups by 3–5 per cent on average, except for the self-employed, where it was higher (see Table 10.4).

Table 10.4 *Index of real net financial income per household member, Slovak Republic*

	Breadwinner of the household is:				
	self-employed	white-collar worker	blue-collar worker	farmer	pensioner
1994 (1989–100)	89	77	67	65	71
1995 (1998=100)	87	80	68	66	73
1995 (1994=100)	98	104	101	101	103

Source: Slovak Statistical Office (sample survey on family budget) and own calculations.

In 1995, when macroeconomic development was very positive compared to the previous years, the real increase in the standard of living was by contrast almost negligible in most social groups. Compared in absolute figures, in 1995 a pensioner's income was lower than that of white-collar workers and the self-employed but higher than blue-collar workers income. This and income structure are shown in Table 10.5.

Table 10.5 *Income situation of breadwinner, Slovak Republic, 1995*

	Net income/breadwinner of the household is:				
	white-collar worker	self-employed	blue-collar worker	farmer	pensioner
White-collar worker =100	100	98	91	93	93
in money	94	94	93	88	92
in kind	6	6	7	12	8

Source: Slovak Statistical Office (sample survey on family budget) and own calculations.

The real net financial income per member of a pensioner's household did not decrease more dramatically mainly owing to indexation, which also helped at least partly to compensate for the exclusion of pensioners from the labour market. In 1987, 33 per cent of old-age pensioners were economically active, falling to 8 per cent in 1992 and 5.6 per cent in 1996.

The living standard decrease in pensioner households was also mitigated by other financial resources: in a typical pensioner's household with no other economically active family members, income from pension insurance fell from 95 per cent to 90 per cent of total household income. This was mainly due to higher drawings on savings of these households which helped maintain certain living standards.

All in all, pension development in the Slovak Republic has more or less corresponded to the state of the economy. But it is less satisfactory when compared with the development in the Czech Republic.

Until 1992 the purchasing power of pensions was similar in both republics. But at the end of 1996 the pensions in the Czech Republic in nominal terms were approximately 10 per cent higher, while the real purchasing power for Slovakian pensioners fell at the beginning of 1997 to a level 25 per cent lower than in the Czech Republic. By the end of May 1997, this difference in real purchasing power levelled off to 10 per cent because of the unexpected devaluation of the Czech crown. The remaining differences are attributable to various factors. The main one is the relatively low efficiency of the economy and permanent financial problems of the state.

Organization

Under the Czechoslovak Republic only formally independent organizational institutions for social security existed. Social security was fully financed through the state budget. The institutions administering social security were not financially independent.

In 1990–92, prior to the separation of the Federation, there had already been extensive discussions on the future organization of sickness, pension and health insurance. There was a consensus among pension security and sickness insurance experts that an independent so-called Social Insurance Institution should be established for pensions, separate from the existing Slovak Social Security Administration, and that another independent institution, the so-called Health Insurance Office, should be created. Discussion on creating separate and independent institutions was triggered by the tax system reform which became effective on 1 January 1993. Consequently, for the first time pension benefits, sickness insurance benefits, and health care all had to be financed from insurance contributions, and not from the state budget. Independent institutions were intended to guarantee financial independence.

A political decision to the contrary was made, however. The lack of pre-existing organizational and institutional arrangements to collect separate contributions for health insurance was the main reason why, at the end of 1992, it was decided to establish one single institution to provide all three forms of social security: sickness, pension and health insurance. This postponed the discussion on social policy objectives and the transformation of the social security system as a whole.

This single administrative organization was called the National Insurance Institution and was established on 1 January 1993. It became responsible for the basic state pension insurance, sickness insurance and health insurance. Each form of insurance had an individual fund and separate finances. The law stipulated explicitly that the means of the Pension Fund Administration could be used solely to finance pensions. Power to make decisions on the principal issues of the activities of the National Insurance Institution were vested in its self-governing bodies, namely the Assembly of Representatives, the Governing Board and the Board of Supervision. The Assembly of Representatives was the principal body. It approved the budget of the National Insurance Institution, the accounting balance, and further internal management. It consisted of nine representatives of the insured, who were appointed by the Trade Union Confederation, of nine more state representatives appointed by the government, and a further nine representatives appointed by employers' unions and associations. All representatives were approved by vote in the Slovak National Council. The Governing Board made decisions on all important issues connected with the activities of the National Insurance Institution not reserved for the Assembly of Representatives. The highest executive body of the National Insurance Institution was the Directorate, headed by a director-general who had a statutory mandate. His power included appointing and recalling directors of individual fund administrations and heads of regional administrations and funds.

By the end of 1993, the law which established the National Insurance Institution was amended. The authority of the Assembly of Representatives was weakened and it was stipulated that the budget and accounting balance shall be approved by the Slovak National Council, and the articles of the National Insurance Institution by the government of the Slovak Republic. The amendment's aim was to modify the unclarified delegation of authority between self-governing and executive bodies. In addition to solving problems of authority in administration, there were problems concerning financing. Collected contributions did not suffice to cover the pension benefits. The state did not meet its obligations to pay contributions for a set group of the population. It took several months to remit contributions to cover earmarked state subsidies.

Despite some legislative amendments the institutional arrangement did not meet expectations: it was ineffectual and became an organizational mess; a situation that was perpetuated as a result of an unclear division of responsibilities. A year after its establishment, in the certainty that it would never function appropriately, the institution was abolished.

In 1994, the Social Insurance Institution succeeded the National Insurance Institution and still exists. It has self-governing organs (Governing Board and Supervision Board) and executive organs (the Directorate and district offices). Countrywide supervision of the implementation of pension and sickness insurance is done by the Ministry of Labour, Social Affairs and Family and the Ministry of Finance. Its establishment can be considered as a success, especially with respect to the financing of the pension benefits from separate contributions and the relative institutional independence. Given that pensions are fully guaranteed by the state, absolute independence is not feasible. The period from 1993 to 1996 was one of crystallization of the new institutional arrangement, in particular the acceptance of the decentralization of responsibilities. Despite improvements and consolidation, the division of responsibilities still needs to be clarified, especially with regard to the supervision of the whole system.

Financing and problems of contribution collection

As described above, until 1993 there was no independent financial contribution scheme for social security. All social expenditures were financed by the state budget. In 1993, a PAYG system was introduced for pension, sickness and health insurance schemes and the Employment Fund. Contributions have to be paid by employers, employees and also by the state. Thus one of the main goals for the transformation in the sphere of social security set in 1990 at the time of the Czech and Slovak Federal Republic was realized.

In the Slovak Republic the newly established National Insurance Institution became financially independent and in this way was formally functioning apart from the state budget. Contributions for pension insurance were to be used exclusively for pension expenditures and not for other purposes, such as covering the state budget deficit as had been the practice in the past. Financial independence was difficult to achieve. In particular, the Ministry of Finance was not willing to accept the loss of authority to the National Insurance Institution. Gradually the situation has improved and at present the system generally works.

According to legislation, by 30 June 1993, at the latest, collected contributions to pension security and sickness insurance were be transferred to a special account of the state budget and were thereby earmarked for pension expenditures.[13] This, however, did not keep the state from again using insurance funds to alleviate the state budget deficit in 1994.

In order to resolve continuing problems it was decided that this could only be done by replacing the system entirely. Consequently, 1994 was the second and last year of existence of the National Insurance Institution. The so-called Social Insurance Institution was established to take care of pension and sickness insurance.

Each of these two different insurance schemes has separate accounting. With regard to pension insurance its basic revenues are contributions, payment of sanctions from contributors and income from property and state transfers. Basic expenditures are pension and sickness benefit payments and administrative expenditures for self-governing and executive organs.

The new system for pension and sickness insurance became more independent of the state budget than the previous one. Some financial links between the state and the social security budget exist, however. For example, the state guarantees payment of insurance benefits; that is, it draws upon general funds for a repayable loan. In 1995 this was not necessary because social insurance revenues reported a surplus of 4 billion crowns. There was a surplus again in 1996, despite financial problems and disputes with the Ministry of Finance during that year. By the end of 1996, according to preliminary data, the insurance budget was reported to have accumulated a surplus of between 5 and 6 billion crowns, which was mainly attributed to savings in sickness benefits.

In 1997 the surplus of the social insurance budget again led to financial disputes between the state and the Social Insurance Institution. The state reduced the monthly contribution for pension security for policy-holders (students, soldiers in national service and other groups) from the hitherto 384 crowns to 70 crowns monthly, arguing that accumulated reserve funds, even in the case of a contribution decrease, were large enough to cover two pension increases in that year.

The management of the Social Insurance Institution vehemently opposed this decision, made by the Ministry of Finance. First, the social insurance budget required more than three billion crowns from the state. Furthermore, according to the Institution, undisturbed running of the system required building a reserve fund of at least 15 billion crowns (to cover pension payments for three months). Without reserves, a negative long-term tendency in the financing of the system will develop. Both the Trade Union Confederation and the Employers' Association agreed and supported social insurance management on this issue. The Ministry of Finance was nevertheless not willing to accept the above-mentioned argumentation of the Social Insurance Institution. The ministry argued that state revenues should have priority; in particular under the current severe financial circumstances, pension reserves should be used for benefit increases until the reserves have been exhausted. It is estimated that reserves would then last until the budget year 1998–99.

To shed light on the structure of revenues and expenditures of the Social Insurance Institution budget and its macroeconomic relevance, the basic data

Table 10.6 *Revenue structure of the Social Insurance Institution's budget, Slovak Republic, 1995–97 (bn crowns)*

Contributor	Pension insurance			Sickness insurance		
	1995	1996	1997	1995	1996	1997
Employers	29.6	34.9	36.7	5.2	4.3	6.2
Employees	8.2	9.2	10.0	2.1	2.5	2.7
Self-employed	1.6	1.9	2.2	0.3	0.3	0.4
Employment Fund[a]	0.4	0.7	0.7	0.0	0.0	0.1
State[a]	4.7	3.3	0.5	0.0	0.0	0.0
Other (penalties etc.)	–	0.9	1.4	–	0.2	0.0
Total	44.5	50.9	51.5	7.6	7.3	9.5

Notes: 0.0 means less than 100 million crowns and therefore no revenues.
[a] Employment Fund pays for job seekers; the state pays for those not gainfully employed, such as students in secondary schools and universities, soldiers in basic military service.
Sources: Národná obroda, 25 September 1996, and internal materials of the SII.

Table 10.7 *Social expenditures and their share of GDP, Slovak Republic, 1989–96*

	1989	1990	1991	1992	1993	1994	1995	1996
In billion crowns:								
1. Pensions:	18.0	19.1	24.0	28.0	32.7	37.1	42.9	47.4
old-age pensions	10.8	11.6	14.9	17.5	20.2	23.0	26.9	30.0
other pensions	7.2	7.5	9.1	12.5	12.5	14.1	16.0	17.4
2. Sickness insurance	4.1	4.3	4.5	4.9	5.1	5.7	5.7	7.4
3. State social payments	7.1	7.5	8.3	8.8	8.5	10.3	13.5	13.9
4. Social assistance	1.5	1.7	2.0	3.8	4.7	6.7	7.6	7.9
5. Financial contribution to registered job seekers	0.1	2.7	1.7	1.9	1.7	1.6	1.5	1.5
In per cent:								
6. Pensions to all social benefits incl. item 5	58.6	58.2	57.8	60.3	61.8	60.3	60.2	60.7
7. Items 1–5 to GDP	12.4	12.7	14.0	15.1	15.6	15.4	15.2	13.4
8. Pensions to GDP	7.3	7.4	8.1	9.1	9.6	9.3	9.1	8.0

Note: Item 5 was included in social benefits despite the fact that legally this insurance system is outside the social security system.
Source: Statistical Yearbooks of the Slovak Republic.

are presented Tables 10.6 and 10.7.[14] Table 10.6 shows that insurance contributions are paid by employees, employers, the self-employed, the state and the Employment Fund.[15] Insurance rates for individual areas of social insurance are closely linked. It is a system of 'communicating vessels'. With regard to the contribution revenue, competition existed among particular social insurance sectors and still exists.

For example, in 1995, the health authorities started a campaign to transfer sickness insurance benefit provision from the Social Insurance Institution to their authority, arguing that health and sickness insurance have much more in common than pension and sickness insurance. However, the ulterior motive behind this campaign was to benefit from sickness insurance savings. Since the total health insurance contribution revenue often exceeded total sickness payments (due to the fact that the daily payment for those with higher wages is relatively low) such an arrangement would have strengthened the financial base in the area of health services. This proposed change was later rejected by the government. The development of contribution rates is presented in Table 10.8.

Table 10.8 Development of contribution rates, Slovak Republic, 1993–96

	1993	1994	1995	1996
Employees, total	12.0	12.0	12.0	12.0
pension insurance	5.9	5.9	5.9	5.9
sickness insurance	1.4	1.4	1.4	1.4
health insurance	3.7	3.7	3.7	3.7
Employment Fund	1.0	1.0	1.0	1.0
Employers, total	38.0	38.0	38.0	38.0
pension insurance	20.6	20.6	21.6	22.6
sickness insurance	4.4	4.4	3.4	2.4
health insurance	10.0	10.0	10.0	10.0
Employment Fund	3.0	3.0	3.0	3.0
Self-employed/co-operative workers	50.0	50.0	48.0	50.0
pension insurance	26.5	26.5	26.5	28.5
sickness insurance	5.8	5.8	3.8	3.8
health insurance	13.7	13.7	13.7	13.7
Employment Fund	4.0	4.0	4.0	4.0
State total	46.0	46.0	45.0	44.0
pension insurance	26.5	26.5	26.5	26.5
sickness insurance	5.8	5.8	4.8	3.8
health insurance	13.7	13.7	13.7	13.7

Insurance contributions are a heavy burden especially for the self-employed, but also for employers. The state, however, pays according to a considerably lower calculation basis.[16]

There are no reliable data available which furnish information on the extent of losses caused by the shadow economy. However, it is plausible that high contribution rates might have led to the avoiding of contribution payments. The figures in Table 10.8 also show that there were less substantial changes in contribution rates.[17] More substantial changes have taken place in the insurance calculation basis, particularly on the side of the state. Within the system of contribution collection, the administrative section and its organization are reasonably consolidated. Penalty rules are applied when contribution payments are not made. The administration completes the registration and de-registration of all attached legal entities with regard to the number of people employed and reports them directly to the relevant branch of the Social Insurance Institution. Failure to register properly carries a penalty of 100 crowns for each employee for each calendar day of violation. Penalties and fines are also foreseen for late payment of contributions.

Individual pension assurance cards were introduced for each employee. The Social Insurance Institution is authorized to verify the accuracy of the documented data concerning pension and sickness matters. Despite this control system, for different reasons (mainly financial insolvency, but also technical problems and speculative behaviour), approximately 5 per cent of contribution revenues are missing.

Sometimes there are illegal procedures to avoid paying contributions. A likely case is one in which owners of a limited liability company or joint-stock company are in financial trouble or unwilling to pay contributions, and thereupon establish a new limited liability company with identical content. The financial means are transferred to the new firm and the old one retains the debts. So far there has been no way to prevent such a transaction. The greatest debtors to the Social Insurance Institution have been privatized state enterprises, agricultural co-operatives and health institutions.

In the future, financing social security will remain an important topic in pension reform debate. In the long term, according to predictions made by the Ministry of Labour, Social Affairs and Family, if the retirement age is not increased, a considerable deterioration in the old-age pension ratio (together with all other types of pensions) to the average wages can be expected. One of the estimates is based on a calculation in which the retirement age is gradually increased by two years for men and by five years for women until 2015–20. However, such a measure was not proposed in the new draft of the Act on State Social Insurance. With regard to future Social Insurance Institution revenues, there are three main scenarios with respect to long-term developments of the pension system: basic, optimistic and pessimistic (with different inputs of GDP growth, unemployment rates, wage dynamics, rates of contribution collection, different contribution rates, etc.). The basic scenario shows that if the retirement age is not increased and the contribution rate is unchanged, then a decline in the average old-age pension ratio to average gross wages from 43.5 per cent in 1995 to 36 per cent by 2005 can be expected. Even worse, prognoses of reputed financial institutions have suggested that provided that the economic prognoses are correct, the pessimistic scenario is the most realistic.

10.3 THE NEW PENSION CONCEPT

10.3.1 The Draft of the New Basic Pension Act

Agreement regarding orientation and design of the new pension system has been more or less reached by all parties and approved on three levels of government. In 1996 the paragraph wording of the draft law was formulated. Afterwards it was submitted to the government and later to the Slovak National Council for approval, which was planned for the end of the first half of 1997, but has since been continually postponed. It is unlikely that many changes or supplements will be added since the same political power relations exist in the Slovak National Council as in the government. But at present, it is still uncertain when the law will become effective. The main features of the new Pension Draft Law are the following:

- it is obligatory;
- it is a universal insurance system covering all economically active persons regardless of the type and form of their labour activity;
- benefits are financed in an independent PAYG system separated from the state budget;
- benefits are automatically adjusted to living costs and average wage increases.

The pension insurance provides allowances for loss of income during old age, invalidity and in the event of the loss of the breadwinner. In the draft law, equal claims under equal conditions to all persons participating in the system are guaranteed. This represents a change from the present pension system in which there was preferential treatment for some groups or individuals. There will be a stricter link to previous economic activities and income under the new system.

Men will be entitled to a pension at the age of 60, women at 53 to 57 depending on the number of children raised. Both sexes must have at least a 25-year insurance record to be eligible for a pension. However, the possibility of increasing this to 30 years by 2003 is under discussion. The retirement age for pension entitlement remains the same. People who are insured for at least 15 years are entitled to an old-age pension at the age of 65. The draft law also stipulates the conditions for early retirement. People are entitled to this type of pension if they have been insured for at least 25 years and have at least three years before they reach pension age, are not gainfully employed and do not receive unemployment benefits. The draft law regulates the pension payment in the event of continuing employment of a pensioner; in that case it is possible, after fulfilling the years of compulsory pension insurance, to continue participation in the pension system voluntarily.

In contrast to present regulations the widowers' pension will be granted under the same conditions as a widows' pension. Financing will continue to be done on a PAYG basis. New regulations also stipulate the organization and management of the Social Insurance Institution.

In summary, in comparison with the existing basic state pension insurance there are no changes with respect to the PAYG method, the retirement age, the mandatory approach, the pension taxation and the basic administrative structure.

Nevertheless, the proposed new pension formula is quite different.[18] According to the draft, the pension will be calculated only on the basis of income from which premiums had been paid into the pension insurance. The so-called 'personal income point' will be derived from the ratio of the personal calculation basis (that is, the income from which the premium is paid) to the general calculation basis (average monthly wages).[19]

Thus, the formula in its initial stage was proposed in the following form:

$$Y = R * D * A$$

where

Y = old-age pension,
R = personal income points,
D = period of insurance, and
A = valorization coefficient.

The personal income points R express the ratio between the individual average income and the average income of the total economically active population. For example, if the individual average wage of an insured person in 1998 is 10,000 crowns monthly and the national average is 8,000 crowns, the ratio R is 1.25. An average income point is calculated for the whole insurance record. In a second step this individual average income point will be reduced. This will be done as follows:

- up to a value of 0.5, no reduction,
- in the interval 0.5 to 1.2, only one-third of achieved value is considered,
- in the interval 1.2 to 2.0, one tenth of achieved value is considered and
- in the interval above 2.0, complete reduction.

For example: an insured person who achieves in his/her working career an average personal income points value of 1.3 will have a reduced 'personal income point' *R* of:

$$0.5 + (1.2–0.5) * (1/3) + (1.3–1.2) * (1/10) = 0.74333.$$

The valorization coefficient *A* is the most controversial factor in thc discussion. On the one hand it is proposed that *A* should be adjusted to the financial situation of the Social Insurance Institution. On the other hand, it is argued that this could disadvantage the pensioners. It would be much better to have an automatic adjustment of *A* to the level of the growth in the cost of living and the growth in average wages. For 1996, coefficient *A* was set at 142 crowns. Taking the adjustment of *A* for every successive year into account it is necessary to multiply the set amount by 1.12.[20]

Providing that the starting level of the coefficient and its valorization is applied and if an insured person with an *R* of 0.7433 is insured for 39 years, his or her pension in the first year of implementation of the new law (that is, in 1999) would be:

$$Y = 0.7433 * 39 * 142 \text{ crowns} * 1.12 * 1.12 * 1.12 = 5784 \text{ crowns}.$$

The existing pension distribution is expected to change. Some pensioners will gain, some will lose, but the individual pension levels will generally not vary greatly. The average old-age pension in relation to average wages will probably decline.

According to the draft law, for the transition period, total personal income points will be determined based on a ten-year period prior to entitlement. This reference period will later be gradually extended to cover the whole working period of the insured. This method of calculating the benefit level will also serve as the basis for determining the widows', widowers', orphans' and invalidity pensions.

10.3.2 Supplementary Pension Insurance

The Supplementary Insurance Act was approved by the Slovak National Council at the beginning of 1996 and was originally scheduled to become effective on 1 July 1996. However, for legislative, administrative, organizational and technical reasons it was postponed several times and did not succeed until the second quarter of 1997, albeit in a limited way. Supplementary pension funds can be set up by a single employer, a group of employers, a trade union organization, a group of trade union organizations, or by a confederation of both types of organizations, under the condition that the fund covers at least 100,000 employees and is secured by a bank deposit of at least 30 million crowns (less than one million US dollars).

By the end of 1996, four groups/organizations fulfilled the requirements and their applications were submitted by the Ministry of Social Affairs, Labour and Family to the government for approval. At the beginning of 1997 only one of the applications had been approved.

The supplementary pension scheme is based on the principle of voluntary participation. It is stated by law that the precondition for an employee's participation is the participation of the employer, which is clarified in the form of a written contract. In other words the employer is not obliged by law to offer supplementary insurance. As enterprises which are fully or partly financed by the state are not allowed to establish a supplementary pension scheme, civil servants are excluded from pension insurance.[21]

The contracts for the supplementary pension insurance must be settled between the insurance institution and the employer, between the insurance institution and the employee and also between the employer and the employee. All three types of contracts have respective requirements specified by law.

Contributions are paid by the employer. The amount of both the employer's and the policy-holder's contribution is stipulated in the relevant contracts. Employers' contributions up to a maximum of 3 per cent of wages are considered as costs of the enterprises and employees' contributions decrease their taxable income. Eligibility starts at the age of 50 and after at least five years of contribution payments. The highest administrative authority of the supplementary pension insurance is the Ministry of Labour, Social Affairs and Family in co-operation with the Ministry of Finance.

10.3.3 Private Insurance

Additional private provision such as life insurance is not widespread in the Slovak Republic, although there are expectations that this will change in the future.[22] A reason for the still low distribution of private life insurance might be that there are no incentives (for example, state subsidies, tax deductions) to promote additional private provision.

10.4 PENSION REFORM DEBATE

10.4.1 Some Characteristics of the Reform Issues in the Domestic Scene

In order to understand the pension reform debate in the Slovak Republic it is important to understand the attitudes of the Slovak population towards social policy. The pension system inherited from the Socialist era had been functioning for more than 40 years without serious problems and became an undisputed tradition that was taken for granted. Moreover, a majority of the population are of pensionable or pre-pensionable age, and are rather conservative in this matter: the majority do not see the need for radical and rapid systemic changes. Therefore pension reform became a very sensitive issue, particularly in the political scene where each vote is being fought for. Of central concern is maintenance of the living standard of the present pensioners and those of pre-pensionable age.

Furthermore, there have been reservations about the imposition of foreign models. Considering the circumstances in Slovakia, some measures used abroad could prove to be imprudent or unrealistic. The PAYG method was, for example, the best solution to secure financing. Certain suggestions for securing financing through privatization schemes by the state were unrealistic. Also the idea to shift the basic pension system to the private sector, an approach applied in some Latin American countries, was unrealistic under Slovakian conditions because the banking sector is neither financially nor institutionally consolidated.

As described above, elements of the new pension system are constructed in many aspects on the basis of the old one. This has been criticized by economists and social policy experts, who argue that the new pension concept in many ways is only a modification of the old system and that the historical occasion for shedding the outdated system and to replace it with a modern one has been lost.

With regard to mass media influence, there is a professional periodical *Práca a Sociálna Politika* (*Labour and Social Policy*) in which various articles on pension issues have been published regularly. From time to time articles and interviews dealing with these problems can also be found in daily newspapers, so the population is theoretically informed about new developments; however, in TV or radio broadcasting there is little coverage of pension issues.

The economic periodical *TREND* frequently gives space to authors whose contributions contain statistics and comparative systemic analyses as well as those presenting information on new developments in the field of social policy. Finally, the Association of Pensioners is influential in its active role of educating the public through everyday activities and through permanent lobbying of parliamentary deputies.

10.4.2 Foreign Assistance

Various conceptual ideas which crystallized in the pension reform debate and their subsequent translation into technical and legislative regulations have largely been considered to be the result of foreign assistance. Experiences of applying foreign expertise in the pension insurance transformation process have been very diverse and sometimes very limited. A major criticism is that in some instances general analyses of conditions were made without a knowledge of specific problems of the country. In other cases there were tangible positive outputs, especially in helping to prepare the draft law on social security and a draft law on supplementary pension insurance. There is continuing co-operation with the International Social Security Organization. Technical aid has been provided according to the Framework Agreement between the Slovak Republic and the European Commission within the PHARE programme. Between 1993 and 1996, EU experts were working at the Ministry of Labour, Social Affairs and Family of the Slovak Republic, helping to develop new approaches and conceptual orientation. EU foreign aid, including the PHARE programme, has been utilized by the Social Insurance Institution to modernize its filing system, to build up a central register of beneficiaries and to improve contribution collection. Co-operation with the Organization for Economic Co-operation and Development (OECD) has been focused on building up an information database. Help was provided by the French Institute for International Social Co-operation (ICOSI – Institut de Coopération Sociale Internationale) in developing the draft on supplementary pension insurance. There has been mutual co-operation and consultations with the partner ministry in the Federal Republic of Germany in preparation of the draft law on social security. Other sources of assistance chiefly influenced debate rather than provided concrete plans or laws. Experts from the ILO (in 1994), the World Bank (in 1994) and the OECD (in 1995), each provided, for example, an analysis of the pension system.

The main conclusions of the ILO report are that pensions are too low and the coverage of the system is too broad. It was recommended that an indexation of maximum insurable earnings linked to the dynamics of average wages should be developed. Moreover, the government's plan to implement early retirement with reduced old-age pensions was supported. It was stated that ILO Convention No. 102 on minimal standards of social security, which requires that after 30 years of employment a pension be equal to at least 40 per cent compensation of past earnings, was not met.

The World Bank experts judged the pension system in international comparison to be relatively extensive since it is part of the general system of social support. It criticized the relatively short period which is the basis for the pension benefit calculation and recommended an increase in the retirement age and a reduction in the number of supplementary old-age pensions.[23]

The OECD report evaluated the social security system from a macroeconomic perspective and analysed the pension system only marginally. It criticized the insufficient pension indexation compared to the price dynamics. With regard to the retirement age, the report noted that 'in the future the retirement age, which is in comparison to international standards extremely low, should be increased'. The finding showed that about 50 per cent of all pensioner households without economically active members live below the poverty line, when defined by the minimum wage. Co-operation with foreign institutions and experts continues; it has tended to be of an advisory nature without any obligation on the part of the Slovak participants.

10.4.3 Recommendations for the Near Future

There is still room for improvement in the basic pension insurance system. A priority should be the introduction of legislative, organizational and regulatory measures to enforce contribution collection, to cancel the existing model of maximum insurable earnings (the upper pension limit) to link the latter to wage dynamics and lastly to conceive of a mechanism which ensures that the ratio of the average old-age pension to the average gross wage at least remains at its existing level.

In addition, such a valorization mechanism should be improved and become more transparent, defining more clearly the rules on when to increase by a fixed sum and when to increase by a certain percentage linked to wage and price increases.

Beyond this a main task for the future will be the raising of the retirement age which has so far been neglected in legislation. In view of the fact that the Slovak Republic is dealing with an ageing population, legal conditions for the rising early retirement would be prudent. Another measure for dealing with this problem could be to promote gradual retirement.

Lastly, the continuing financial problems between the state budget and the social security budget are critically in need of a solution. One step in this direction might be to establish clear legally defined relations between the state and the Social Insurance Institution. With regard to supplementary provision, the state is required to improve the legislative, organizational and financial conditions which will create the conditions for everybody to be able to join this type of insurance. Measures like this also support the development of individual private provision (the third pillar). Here it is necessary to build a legislative framework to allow for better state control of private insurance funds.

NOTES

1 From a macroeconomic point of view this is not such a serious problem. Although the deficit would amount to 5.5 per cent of GDP, according to the measuring methods of the IMF, which compensates the receipt and payment of credits, it amounts to only 1.5 per cent of GDP.

2 Thc last basis status of the social security system before 1989, including pension security, was defined by the Federation in the Social Security Act No. 100 of 16 June 1988.

3 Covered were: employees in active employment, members of cooperatives, deputies of various levels of representative bodies, professional judges, artists, students, persons supplying various services to the public based on permission of regional national committees, local government bodies, professional soldiers and members of the police, court and prison wardens, private farmers and other self-employed if they paid contributions, civilians serving in the armed forces, members of the Peoples' Militia, participants of civil defence, voluntary firemen, blood donors, voluntary health workers of the Czechoslovakian Red Cross and other groups.

4 There were additional 'substitute periods', for example, education, National Service, child care up to the age of three, unemployment and so on.

5 There are three different work categories. The first work category led to the highest pensions. It included those who worked permanently underground, in deep mines, and those who worked in a chemical, carcinogenic environment and other hazardous working conditions. The second work category included very tiring occupations as well as those involving an increased danger of injury or occupational disease. The third work category contained all other occupations.

6 The amount of old-age pensions according to basic calculation methods was 50 per cent in the third work category for 25 years. Starting with 26 years of employment, the basic sum was increased by 1 per cent for each year of employment (to a maximum of 75 per cent); in the second work category, 55 per cent for 20 years of employment and for each subsequent year an increase by 1.5 per cent (to a maximum of 80 per cent); and in the first work category, 60 per cent for 15 to 20 years of employment, with an increase of 2 per cent (to a maximum of 90 per cent). In addition there are absolute limits to the pension payment level.

7 An average monthly wage up to a maximum of 2,500 crowns was fully included. Further, one-third of the difference between 2,500 and 6,000 crowns as well as one-tenth of the difference between 6,000 and 10,000 crowns were included. Income exceeding 10,000 crowns was not considered. This clearly shows the higher the wages, the relatively lower the pension advantage. This principle existed for many years before 1989 despite the continuous increase of wages and is in principle applied at present as well, although after 1989 there were some corrections in the framework of pension indexation.

8 This contradicts ILO convention no. 102, which requires at least a replacement rate of 40 per cent after 30 years of employment.

9 Enterprise gross profits were taxed by a very differentiated system according to the sectors and branches. Economically active persons were taxed by a progressive payroll tax which decreased with the number of children.

10 Since May 1990, the pension system has covered the self-employed: businesspeople, private farmers, artists, professional sportsmen and women, including co-operative workers among others. The self-employed pay a contribution of 25 per cent of a voluntarily set income in a range between 2,000 and 10,000 crowns.

11 An amendment of the Social Security Act of 1988 has abolished personal pensions. In the first stage these pensions were set at a uniform level of 2,200 crowns a month. In 1991 all

personal pensions were recalculated into relevant pension types. With this second and final stage the issue of personal pensions was definitely solved.

12 With the consequence that existing entitlements are now protected until 2020.

13 In principle they were earmarked though there was often a delay in transfer to the National Insurance Institution because of the state budget deficit. This led to considerable liquidity problems for the National Insurance Institution.

14 Throughout this chapter, 'crowns' denotes Czechoslovak crown up to December 1992. All references made to data from January 1993 are made in Slovak crowns.

15 The employment fund was established to finance the active as well as the passive employment policy.

16 In 1996 the calculation basis was the gross wage for employees; the payroll for employers; for the self-employed it was derived from their income tax; whereas for the state it was less than the minimum wage.

17 The decline in sickness insurance rates in 1996 compared to 1995 reflects the difference between total sickness insurance contribution and total sickness benefits. Contributions increased because of constant substantial wage increases. The daily absolute maximum of these benefits is only 250 crowns which is much lower than the earned net daily wages.

18 It must be noted that the final details of the formula are not yet definite. Therefore we are not referring to the final version here.

19 The general calculation basis for a calendar year is 12 times the average monthly wage. The maximum number of personal income points in a calendar year corresponds to the maximum calculation basis used for determining premiums for pension insurance.

20 Both level and valorization are estimated and calculated according to the existing situation.

21 This means that approximately a quarter of all economically active persons are excluded from this insurance.

22 Slovakia expects a boom in life insurance, *TREND*, 16 October 1996.

23 For a description of the ILO and World Bank reports, see Lubyova (1996).

REFERENCES

Bálintová, R. (1994), 'Doplnkové penzijné poistenie-druhý stupen penzijného zabezpeèenia' [Complementary pension insurance – second grade of pension security], *Práca a Sociálna politika*, December, 11–13.

Blajsko, A. (1995), 'Sociálna pomoc v transformujúcom sa sociálnom systéme' [Social assistance in the transforming social system], *Práca a Sociálna politika*, Ministerstvo práce, sociálnych vecí a rodiny, 1993–96, October, 2–3.

Hanker, J. (1994), 'Výskum sociálnej sféry v období transformácie' [Social sphere research in the period of the transformation], *Práca a Sociálna politika*, March, 2–5.

Jurina, L. (1995a), 'Termín sociálne reformy sa pravdepodobne nedodrzí' [The date of social reform is unlikely to be met], *TREND,* 1 February.

Jurina, L. (1995b), 'Neefektívne socialistické sociálne zabezpeèenie by sa malo do roku 1999 pretvorit na moderný sociálny systém' [Ineffective socialist social security should by 1999 be transformed into a modern social system], *TREND,* 21 June.

Jurina, L. (1996), 'Poistné sa v najblizších rokoch udrzí na súèasnej úrovni' [The contribution rates in the next years will not be changed], *TREND,* 25 September.

Kárász, P. and Renèko, J. (1997), 'Základné makroekonomické proporcie vývoja ekonomiky Slovenska v roku 1997' [The main characteristic macroeconomic structure of economic development in Slovakia in 1997], *Národná obroda*, 12 February.

Kunicová, J. (1995), 'Sociálnej politike chýba jasne definovaný rozmer' [Social policy lacks a clearly defined approach], *TREND*, 20 September.

Lubyová, M. (1996), 'Systém dôchodkového zabezpeèenia v Slovenskej republike' [The system of pension security in the Slovak Republic], *TREND*, 30 September.

Mikloš, I. (1995), 'Slovenské skúsenosti ukazujú, ze nemozno transformovat ekonomiku a súèasne budovat štát blahobytu' [The Slovak experience shows that it is not possible to transform the economy and at the same time to build up a welfare state], *TREND*, 12 April.

Ministry of Labour, Social Affairs and Family (1995), 'A booklet on Social Policy', Bratislava.

Pekník, K. (1988), 'K základným vztahom medzi príjmom na obyvatela a štruktúrou rozlozenia príjmov podla domácností v CSFR a na Slovensku za obdobie 1956-1988' [Basic links between per head income and income distribution by household in the Federation and the Slovak Republic in the period 1956–1988], mimeo, Federal Institute of Economic Research, Bratislava.

Pekník, K. (1995a), 'Structural changes in income in the Slovak Republic during the period of transition', mimeo, paper prepared for IWM SOCO Project 'Social Costs of Economic Transformation in Central Europe', Bratislava.

Pekník, K. (1995b), 'The Evolution of the Banking Sector in the Slovak Republic during the Transformation', Instituto di studi e documentazione, Trieste.

Rusinák, P. (1995), 'Transformácia systému sociálneho zabezpeèenia' [Transformation of the social security system], *Práca a Sociálna politika*, July–August, 2–3.

Stanek, V. (1994), 'Zámery sociálnej reformy na Slovensku' [The aim of social reform in the Slovak Republic], *TREND*, 19 January.

Suda, P. (1996), 'Návrh zásad zákona o sociálnom poistení prešiel pripomienkovým konaním' [Discussions concerning the proposal of the principles on social insurance], *TREND*, 31 July.

Tkáè, V. (1993), 'K transformácii sociálneho systému' [The transformation of the social system], *Práca a Sociálna politika*, 2–3, September 1993.

TREND, 'Doplnkové dôchodkové poistenie prispieva k sociálnemu zmieru' [Supplementary pension insurance contributes to social conciliation], 6 March 1996.

TREND, 'Koncepcia transformácie sociálnej sféry' [The transformation concept of the social sphere], 28 June 1995.

TREND, 'Nový model základného dôchodkového zabezpeèenia je len modifikáciou starého systému' [The new model of basic pension security is merely a modification of the old one], 15 May 1996.

TREND, 'Nádej na skutoènú reformu sociálnej sféry je takmer mizivá' [The hope for real reform of the social sphere is dwindling], 11 September 1996.

TREND, 'Reforma systému dôchodkového zabezpeèenia pripomína perestrojku' [The reform of the pension system resembles 'perestroika'], 11 September 1996.

Velecký, M. (1996), 'Koncepciu transformácie sociálnej sféry kritizovala l'avica i pravica' [The transformation concept of the social sphere criticized by both the right and the left], *TREND*, 14 February.

Vladárová, M. (1995), 'Tvorcovia koncepcie sociálnej politiky sa uchýlili ku skrytým manévrom voèi odborom' [Creators of the social policy concept turn to secret manoeuvring against the trade unions], *TREND*, 19 July.

Woleková, H. (1995), 'Tvorcovia koncepcie sociálnej reformy neposkytli priestor súkromnému sektoru' [Creators of the social policy concept did not allow for the private sector], *TREND,* 9 August.
Zbudila, M. (1995), 'Penzijné fondy sú vo svete bezné, Slovensko na ne iba èaká' [Pension funds in the world are the norm, Slovakia has to wait for them], *TREND,* 6 December.

11. Transformation of old-age security in Hungary

Ottó Czúcz and Mária Pintér

11.1 INTRODUCTION

Since 1989 the Hungarian pension system has become rather complex. The political, social and economic context has undergone a significant process of transformation. However, the pension system did not adapt sufficiently or adequately to these changes. The resulting problems have become focal points of debate. Reform plans to transform the system and the recurrent debates have led to widespread uncertainty among the population, who are worried about whether they can continue with a system that had been reliable for many decades. This chapter will outline the challenges faced by the pension system resulting from the rapid social and economic transformation and the possible ways out of this situation in Hungary.

This task is far from simple. The old-age pension system in Hungary in itself is a complex structure. The different sub sectors of this structure are not separated, which makes it difficult to establish transparency. As well as old-age benefits, disability, dependants' and even accident benefits are paid from the same Pension Fund. The various changes in society have had a variety of effects on these benefit subgroups. For instance, increased unemployment and the fear of becoming unemployed make the option of escaping to early retirement more attractive, even if it means living on a disability pension. In addition, the growth in the number of fatal work accidents – a phenomenon verifiable in new enterprises operating on a lower technical level and on a shorter time scale – has a perceivably unfavourable effect on the number of dependants' pensions being claimed. On the other hand, due to the decrease in the number of contribution payers the problems of financing are growing enormously.

Finally, statistical observation and analysis of the developments in the field of pension security are difficult, because the statistical data given below do not provide information solely on pension insurance: they also include data on the above-mentioned subsectors.

11.1.1 Main Economic Changes

Among the changes affecting the pension system, the most significant ones are related to the economy. GDP started to decrease each year after 1989. Table 11.1 shows that the nadir was reached in 1993, when GDP was 18 per cent less than the 1989 figure. The recession period was followed by a short recovery period: GDP grew by 2.9 per cent and 1.5 per cent in 1994 and 1995, respectively. This growth, however, took place under unstable circumstances: equilibrium deteriorated rapidly and had painful long-term economic consequences. The current account deficit as a percentage of GDP was 9.4 per cent in 1994, which is nearly twice as much as the very high level in 1989. The state budget deficit, which characterizes the lack of internal financial balance, amounted to 8.4 per cent. In order to check the deterioration in the current account equilibrium, the new Minister of Finance devised a package comprising a one-off devaluation, the introduction of a supplementary custom levy and other measures restricting demand. This so-called 'Bokros package' succeeded in slowing down the deterioration in the equilibrium, but at the same time economic growth declined again. Moreover, there were also other important areas in the economy where decreases became evident while inflation accelerated. In 1996 these tendencies changed slightly: GDP increased, while the external and internal balance started to improve significantly. The 1996 statistical data indicate that many of the important economic sectors were no longer in recession. Nevertheless, in 1996 GDP was still 14 per cent lower than in 1989.

Table 11.1 Main characteristics of economic development and the change in the financial balance, Hungary, 1989–97

year	GDP (previous year = 100)	GDP (1989=100)	Balance of current account as % of GDP	Balance of public finance[a] as % of GDP
1989	100.7	100.0	–4.9	–2.7
1990	96.5	95.9	0.4	0.3
1991	88.1	84.9	0.8	–3.0
1992	96.9	82.3	0.9	–7.0
1993	99.4	81.8	–9.0	–6,5
1994	102.9	84.1	–9.5	–8.4
1995	101.5	85.4	–5.3	–6.6
1996	101.3	86.5	–3.7	–3.1
1997[b]	104.6	86.6	–2.1	–4.5

Notes: [a] Without the privatization revenue [b] Preliminary figures.
Source: Ministry of Finance (1998).

Both employment relations and the structure of the economy changed. The state and the co-operative sectors of the economy – having played a significant role – were gradually displaced. This was primarily a consequence of gradually implemented privatization, but the economic crisis also contributed. Between 1989 and 1994, the number of state-owned companies was reduced to a third of the previous amount. Concomitantly the number of self-employed persons and individual entrepreneurs grew.[1] This far-reaching restructuring, however, caused significant changes in the status of social insurance. In the preceding period, collection of the contributions had been relatively easy, since they could be collected almost automatically from state-owned large companies, which accounted for most businesses. Following fragmentation of the enterprises, the social insurance administration organizations have had to liaise with many more businesses. Many of the newly established ones proved unable to survive. They terminated their undertakings and frequently left significant debts behind. All these factors contributed to making the collection of social insurance contributions very difficult.

The pension system was also sensitive to changes in the labour market. Systems based on the pay-as-you-go (PAYG) method are particularly sensitive to demographic changes. Therefore when, at the beginning of the period under review, the number of active employees markedly decreased and, parallel to this, the number and rate of the unemployed started to increase, significant problems were expected to ensue. The development is

Table 11.2 Economically active population, Hungary, 1989–97

Year	Economically active population (1000) [a]	Unemployment rate (%) [b]	[c]	Ratio of employed within the population	Activity rate [c]
1989	5,519	0.3	–	52.8	–
1990	5,496	0.4	–	52.7	–
1991	5,404	1.9	–	51.2	–
1992	5,202	7.8	9.8	46.4	58.6
1993	5,015	13.2	11.9	42.2	56.0
1994	4,769	13.3	10.7	40.2	54.0
1995	4,565	11.4	10.2	39.5	52.5
1996	4,470	11.1	9.9	38.9	51.8
1997	4,453	10.7	8.7	39.1	51.1

Notes: [a] Data of the labour balance of the national economy [b] Ratio of registered unemployed to economically active population [c] ILO standard.
Source: CSO, *Statistical Yearbook of Hungary* (1996).

illustrated in Table 11.2, where the data clearly show the recent dramatic decrease in the proportion of the employed. Between 1989 and 1996, more than one million jobs ceased to exist. All these data seem to justify the statements made by economists and sociologists in the early 1980s that the so-called 'unemployment within the factory gate' would reach 25 to 30 per cent of the total employment. None the less, the greatest direct effect on the dramatic decrease in the number of the employed was the collapse of the former Eastern European markets and of COMECON. Parallel to this we can observe that the registered number and rate of the unemployed increased significantly.

Throughout the period, inflation became a heavy burden.

Table 11.3 Development of consumer price index (CPI), real wage and real income, Hungary, 1989–1996

Year	CPI (previous year=100)	Real wage (previous year=100)	Real income (previous year=100)
1989	117.2	100.9	103.4
1990	128.9	96.3	98.2
1991	135.0	93.0	98.3
1992	123.0	98.6	96.5
1993	122.5	96.1	95.3
1994	118.8	107.2	102.7
1995	128.2	87.8	94.7
1996	123.6	95.0	99.9

Source: CSO, *Statistical Yearbook of Hungary* (1996).

The figures in Table 11.3 show that the real value of pension benefits decreased throughout almost the entire period, but they also show that real wage development was affected in nearly the same way.

11.1.2 Demographic Development

Demographic development also affects the future of the pension system. In Hungary this is, compared to other Eastern European countries, a much more severe problem. This is apparent if we look at the old-age dependency ratio and at the change in average life expectancy.

Figure 11.1 Old-age dependency ratio, Hungary, 1990–2020

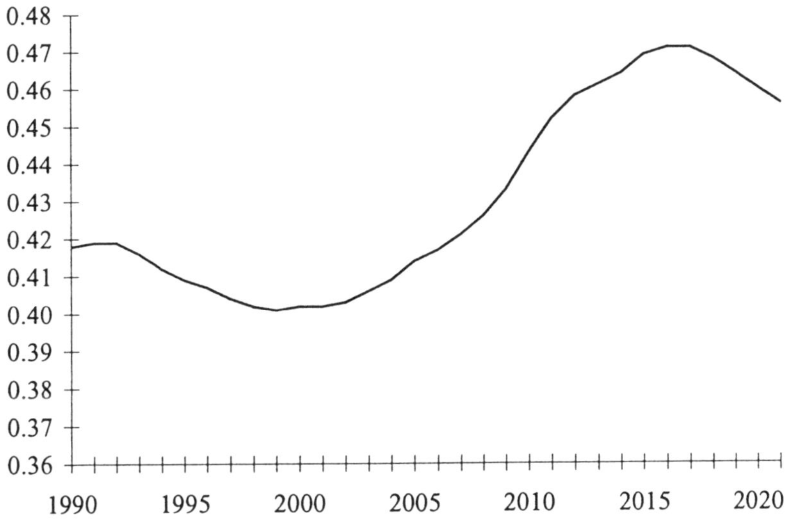

Source: Ministry of Finance, Ministry of Welfare Pension Task Force (1997).

Figure 11.1 illustrates the development of the old-age dependency ratio based on demographic forecasts to 2020. Although the development shows a slight decrease in the old-age dependency ratio until 2000, afterwards the ratio will, according to the forecasts, increase up to 0.47 in 2016. This means that for every one person above working age there are two people of working age. Table 11.4 shows the average life expectancy of men and women at different ages.

Table 11.4 Average life expectancy at different ages, Hungary, 1970 and 1991

	1970		1991	
Age	Men	Women	Men	Women
0	66.3	72.1	65.0	73.8
50	22.9	26.7	21.1	27.3
60	15.2	18.2	14.7	19.2
70	9.2	10.9	9.5	12.0

Source: Central Statistical Office.

On the basis of the above, the logical conclusion would be that the pension system should be adjusted to its changing environment. The post-1989 development of the pension system can essentially be divided into three phases.

The phases are, however, not sharply distinct and often overlap. Following the changes, in the first phase of economic transformation the pension system absorbed part of the social tensions generated by the transformation processes. This characterizes the system in the period from 1990 to 1993. The second phase, from 1992 to 1995, was characterized by the changes effected within the system in order to reinstate and consolidate the pension system's financial situation. Finally, 1995 to 1997 can be characterized as a third preparatory phase of fundamental changes and reform of the pension system, an important part of which was the approval of proposed measures.

11.1.3 Starting-point of the Pension System

By 1989, the Hungarian pension system had become one of the most important components of the institutional structure of the social security system. For several years, 9–10 per cent of GDP had been spent on pensions. In 1989, 23.4 per cent of the inhabitants were pensioners, that is, approximately one-third of the total number of voting citizens were dependent on a pension as the basic source for living.

The pension system in Hungary dates back to 1928. At first it covered only the employees of industry and trade. The pension age was 65 years for both men and women and was reduced to 60 in 1944. Until the 1950s the benefit level was rather low. At first, funded financing of the system was planned. Once applied it resulted in dynamic capital accumulation. In the first four years, the institutions had only revenues. These were invested and saved under good interest rate terms. From 1933 on, the disability and surviving family members' benefit payment was introduced, followed by the first old-age benefit payment in 1937. In its original form, the system operated for approximately 15 years. During this period, its revenues grew significantly. As in other countries, the economic crisis in the 1920s, in addition to the Second World War, had a strong impact on the pension system, especially on its financial reserves. By 1945, the whole system collapsed. In this situation, the decision was made to move from the funded to the PAYG system. The level of the pension payment was no longer dependent on the paid contribution, but on the wage before retirement. Between 1950 and 1958 the system was modified significantly three times. One of the first major steps in this direction was a 1951 piece of regulation establishing general eligibility criteria, calculation of pension benefit and the employer's and employee's shares of the contribution. It stipulated, for example, that a minimum ten-year insurance period was necessary and that men were required to be at least 60 years of age when they first made a claim but not older than 65, while for a woman the age requirements were 55 and 60, respectively. The pension was henceforth designed to consist of a main pension and a pension supplement. The main pension was 15 per cent of average wages of the period preceding retirement, if the person retired at the earliest age of his/her category. At the upper age limit, the main pension could reach 30 per cent of the preceding average wages. Employers' contributions, formerly 3 per cent, were raised to 4 per cent. Employees were exempt from paying contributions. According to the system modified in 1954, employers paid 4 per cent and employees 3 per cent. In addition, the flexible retirement scheme was abandoned and eligibility criteria set the age for men at 60 years and for women at 55. The basic pension level was increased to 50 per cent. Further structural changes in the pension system took place in 1958 after the revolution of 1956. Entitlement to the full pension was tied to 25 years of service. From 1970, those who had less than 25 but more than 10 years of service could receive prorated pensions.

The pension system in 1989 was based on regulations stipulated in Act II of 1975. In order to balance increasing expenditures, the amount of contributions to be paid was raised to 17 per cent. Subsequently employers contributed a uniform amount – except in the public sector and a few insignificant categories of employers where the employer had a 10 per cent rate. The 1989 pension system covered a large part of the population: pensioners themselves as well as related claimants. It covered more than 80 per cent of the active population.

Citizens not eligible for a pension by the time they reached old age and who had no other sources of income, could obtain a modest social allowance within the framework of Hungarian social assistance. The latter is operated independently of the pension system, both with respect to funding and organization. Social assistance benefits are provided by local self-governments and are means tested, but this type of assistance will not be discussed in further detail.

Table 11.5 System dependency ratio and pension level, Hungary, 1950–95

Year	Insured in ,000	Pensioners in ,000	Average wage HUF/month	Average pension HUF/ month	Depend. ratio	Pension level
1950	1,867	526.6	613	147	0.28	0.215
1955	2,594	567.6	1,141	284	0.22	0.249
1960	2,985	722.9	1,575	510	0.24	0.324
1965	3,417	1,128.0	1,764	570	0.33	0.323
1970	3,949	1,416.5	2,139	764	0.30	0.357
1975	4,219	1,774.8	2,881	1,347	0.36	0.468
1980	4,230	2,050.0	4,014	2,205	0.43	0.549
1985	4,164	2,280.0	5,866	3,353	0.50	0.572
1990	3,906	2,520.2	10,108	6,683	0.61	0.661
1995	3,160	3,026.6	25,891	16,030	0.96	0.619

Sources: Bod (1995), p. 11; Pension Insurance Administration (1995), p. 26.

As mentioned earlier, after the Second World War the Hungarian system was transformed into a PAYG system. Table 11.5 shows the dependency ratios and the pension rates.

The data suggest that some groups below pension age also receive pension benefits: for example, disability or survivors' benefits. Two conclusions can clearly be drawn from the above. On the one hand, the legislation has widened the scope of persons covered, on the other, there has been a significant increase in the number of employed persons. Beyond this the system's expenditures have risen considerably. The system constitutes a large uniform state programme.[2] Old-age benefits are based on individual entitlements and are mainly dependent on two factors. Benefit level calculations are based on the five years preceding retirement, from which are taken the average earnings of the most favourable three years and, second, on the number of years in service. Figure 11.2 illustrates the scale that is used.

*Figure 11.2 Replacement rate (%) depending on years in service, Hungary**

Note: * After the forty-second year each year is weighted by 0.5 per cent.

The figure clearly shows that the individual years in service are appreciated by raising the pensions by varying rates. The replacement rate foresees higher rates for each individual year for those with shorter service periods compared to those with longer service periods. At the time this system was designed there was a large number of beneficiaries for whom only in later periods of their lives would it become possible to find employment conditions which included insurance coverage. For example, those who had been self-employed farmers in agriculture, and who joined the co-operatives at the end of the 1950s and the beginning of the 1960s. Thus this marked the earliest time for beginning an insurance period. For them a linear scale would have been disadvantageous and they could not be blamed for not being able to acquire a service period earlier. Therefore the system has an important redistributive feature. The other factor influencing the pension amount is the individual wage. However, the given wage is only partially taken into consideration in the process of pension determination. In order to eliminate the spread of pensions, the contemporary system considered the earlier wage over a certain level (HUF 10,000 per month at that time) at a decreased rate.[3] This also has sizeable redistributive effects.

In addition, the Hungarian system provides for a minimum pension, that is, pensions calculated using the relevant pension formula but falling below the legal minimum are supplemented with an allowance to meet the legal minimum. The costs of the supplementary benefits are borne by the general income of the fund. This is one further example of the strong redistributive character of the system. Finally, in accordance with Hungarian law, pensions are exempt from tax. This is because in pension determination, incomes net of tax are taken into consideration.

In 1989 the retirement age for men was 60, and for women 55, provided that they had acquired a service period of at least ten years. Conditions for retirement following hard or extremely dangerous work, were more favourable.[4]

Although the inflation of the 1980s compared to the later period of transformation was relatively low, pensions were already being increased regularly by 2 (and later 5) per cent per annum. These increases occurred within predetermined minimum and maximum pension payment levels. As a result of such policy, those on a low pension were awarded a higher-than-inflation increase, while the increase in higher-level pensions was lower than inflation. Consequently after a few years of retirement a degree of levelling out of pensions resulted, generating a significant debate over the fairness of the pension system.

In 1989, employers paid a uniform social insurance contribution at a rate of 43 per cent to cover all social insurance benefits (that is, sickness and maternity allowances, family support and accident benefits, in addition to pension benefits). There was no upper limit determined for the contribution payable by employers. Employees paid a contribution at a rate of 10 per cent. This employee obligation, however, was restricted to a certain income limit, that is, of HUF 240,000 per annum in 1989, or HUF 20,000 per month, respectively. Any income in excess of this was exempted from the employee's obligation of contribution payment. Contributions have to be paid on any income of any work performed. For instance, in addition to wages, contribution is payable after profit sharing at year end, on different bonuses, rewards, as well as benefits in kind, and any income paid on the basis of legal employment status.[5]

Prior to 1989,[6] the social insurance system operated essentially as an institution under the control of the state and as a part of the central budget. Its status was basically determined by the actual status of the state budget, as well as the relationship between the actual economic policy and the prevailing philosophy regarding state care. Consequently, social insurance contributions were not only part of the state's finances but also functioned as an income regulation tool affecting the cost of labour.

In summary, by the end of the 1980s the Hungarian pension system had matured and significant internal debts had accumulated. This situation was aggravated by the aforementioned manifold problems, as well as other factors brought about by demographic and financing problems, and it developed such that it became necessary to rethink its future development. This was a time, however, when a new social and political situation had developed in consequence of the collapse of the Eastern European bloc and COMECON, providing the existing problems with new dimensions.

11.2 CHANGES IN THE PENSION SYSTEM: 1989–97

11.2.1 Pension Reforms: 1989–92

In the first period immediately following the introduction of the new political system, certain restrictions were placed on social insurance systems such as the pension system. The impact of changes in the economic system became apparent. Many companies experienced severe difficulties. They had to reorganize while being exposed to the market effects, and with scarcely any recourse to state resources. Unemployment and social tension grew. Despite a general recognition of the necessity of reforms in social policy, the new political forces empowered by the elections which had been held in the spring of 1990 were very cautious about introducing fundamental reforms in the first phase. Such decisions might be partially explained as a measure to promote the political stability thought to be necessary for the blossoming market economy to curtail growing social tensions. Nevertheless some important reform measures were started.

As a part of this reform effort in 1989, in order to reduce the direct control exercised by the state – and in line with that, the direct liability of the state – the so-called Social Insurance Fund was established with a certain scope of independence. This was part of a more general effort to increase the independence of social insurance and that of a self-financing principle, as well as to increase revenues and consolidate reserves. In line with the fund system, social insurance, to a certain extent, was separate from the state budget. The related administrative tasks were performed by the National Social Insurance Administration. Much of the decision-making power remained in previous hands, however. Considerable control over the fund continued to be exercised by the Ministry of Social Affairs and Health. Decisions, bills and other laws related to policy development were prepared in the ministry. The social insurance administrative staff were essentially involved only in the technical tasks related to the delivery of the benefits.

The possibility of exemption from age requirements for retirement was introduced. This was to reduce tensions in the labour market.[7] Application of this rule is subject to agreement between employer and employee, provided that the latter has less than five years left until retirement age and would otherwise be made redundant. In cases of early retirement, the employer pays the amount of pension due to the prospective retiree every six months until he/she reaches the retirement age. This measure caused plenty of problems later. Many employers became bankrupt and there was no one left to comply with such payment obligations. In 1991, in order to mitigate these tensions, pre-retirement was introduced. This was available to the unemployed who had less than three years left until reaching retirement age and who could not rely on finding a new job. Pre-retirement pension payments are financed by the Solidarity Fund which also finances unemployment benefits.

The head of the social insurance administration has been authorized to provide and determine payment levels of an exceptional pension benefit up to a maximum determined in the social insurance budget.[8] This was also obviously aimed at subsidizing those who were encountering difficulties during the transition period.

In the first phase of being in office, the new government passed a resolution concerning the establishment of the Unlawful Advantages Investigation Committee, which was responsible for investigating the measures implemented in the preceding period concerning more favourable benefit levels and for making recommendations on appropriate methods for abolishing those benefits.[9]

Some pensioners were compensated[10] by a sum of between HUF 2,400 and HUF 4,000, depending on the amount of the pension. After this one-off compensation, in order to counterbalance the continuing effects of inflation, an automatic compensation system was introduced as of 1991. The valorization was bound to the wage increase expected for the given year and, as from 1995, to the actual wage increase of the previous year. This solution resulted in a spectacular annual increase in the nominal amount of pension expenses, although the real value of the benefits could not be maintained.

The fall in the real value of pension benefits was a source of increasing unease among pensioners.

Even though the minimum service period requirement was increased in 1980 from ten to 20 years, this measure did not become effective until 1990. This time, however, it became clear that although there was a preparatory period of ten years, many people would encounter difficulties in fulfilling the criteria since they had not acquired a sufficient number of service years. For this reason, further application of the old regulation was made possible by reintroducing the so-called partial pension.[11]

The income ceiling to be considered in the degressive calculation of the average wage forming the basis of a pension was adapted,[12] and on 1 January 1991[13] and later in the middle of the year,[14] decisions were made regarding supplementing pensions under certain circumstances.

All these measures – mostly extensions of rights and eligibility and retribution for earlier violations – could be taken in the period in which the 1989 social insurance budget showed a significant surplus.[15] The newly empowered political forces, however, soon had to learn that the factors leading to such a surplus were temporary. By 1991 the social insurance budget situation worsened unexpectedly. Significant tensions within the system became transparent, which called for a rethinking of the system. Against this background the first draft of a pension reform proposal was developed.[16] The National Assembly reported that the system was characterized by financial instability and the absence of reserves, own assets and the actuarial basis of the benefits. A resolution was thus declared, announcing the commitment of the political parties to the most comprehensive institution of the social security: it was to continue – in the future as well – to be a compulsory social insurance covering the widest possible range of people and granted by the state. At the same time, however, the scheme needed to be designed more accurately. One important change in this design was that the organizations of health insurance and pension insurance should be separate. Reform of the pension system called for a 'three level' pension structure.

- The first level, the so-called 'basic' pension level, entailed a national basic pension. But the Resolution of the National Assembly stated that in the current economic situation a national basic pension could not be introduced. Until its implementation, those affected would be provided with subsidy-like allowances ensuring a minimum standard of living.
- The second tier is a pension payment structure adjusted to the contributions paid, financed by a PAYG system. To this end a modified version of the existing centrally organized and unified system was more easily implementable and politically acceptable. A model differentiated and decentralized per branch and/or per profession was also feasible.

- The third level consisted of a benefit acquired through voluntary and supplementary insurance.

A period of ten to 15 years was estimated to be needed to implement the plans. The resolution prescribes the amendment of several components of the pension system, detailed hereunder.

11.2.2 Amendments made between 1992 and 1995

The organizational separation of pension and health insurance and the instituting of self-government commenced as of 1992.[17] Self-government makes them independent of the actual status of the central budget. The division of the branches of insurance, however, required the division of the contributions between the branches. The rate of the employer's contribution was increased by one percentage point to 44 per cent, of which 19.5 per cent is paid to the health insurance fund and 24.5 per cent to the pension fund. The employer's contribution, at a uniform rate of 10 per cent, was also divided so that 4 per cent was remitted to the health insurance fund and 6 per cent to pension insurance. The ceiling of employee contributions was increased significantly, reaching HUF 900,000,[18] and the range of incomes liable for contribution was widened slightly.

The two branches, however, waited in vain for their reserves to fill up. In particular, the state was not able to adhere to its commitments. The non-reimbursable conveyance of state assets from the central budget (as promised in the Resolution of the National Assembly no. 90/1991), valued at HUF 300 billion, to facilitate the independent operation as well as to mitigate, at least partly, the intergenerational disproportionalities, was thus partly affected. The two branches were provided with assets valued at scarcely more than HUF 60 billion, the majority of which consisted of buildings and shares.

A decision was made to gradually extend the period for which the average wage was to be considered for pension calculation.[19] As a first step, the period for which the average wage was computed was increased to four years (instead of three). Later all incomes liable for insurance contribution and received after 1 January 1988 were subject to these new conditions.[20] By binding the calculation mechanism to a fixed date, in the coming period the average wage of a longer period of the active life cycle would be taken into consideration when determining the pension. Such a mechanism for calculating the benefit is based on data that represent more accurately the actual life-income. This, of course, gives rise to another problem. During an inflationary period the value of the nominal average wage will be significantly undermined. In order to counterbalance this problem a partial valorization system was introduced. According to the existing regulation this aims to maintain the real value relations, with a time lag of almost three years.

A gradual increase in the female retirement age is prescribed.[21] This is especially justified because Hungarian regulations – compared with those internationally – foresee a rather low retirement age. A sample analysis performed in 1993 showed that the actual retirement age is much lower than the statutory retirement age (see Table 11.6).

Table 11.6 Actual retirement age, Hungary, 1993

	Male	Female	Total
Old-age pension	58.6	55.1	56.7
Disability pension	47.9	46.4	47.3
Total	54.0	52.7	53.3

It has already been mentioned that in 1991 the National Assembly passed a resolution on the gradual increase of the retirement age. The idea was that as a first step, female retirement age should gradually approach that of the males, and after this levelling in 2003, the uniform retirement age should be increased to 62 or to 65. At the end of 1993 the National Assembly approved the relevant legislation. According to the ideas prevailing at that time, female retirement age could be increased as of 1 January 1995 every two years by one year so that by the year 2003 women could retire after reaching the age of 60. With one of the first amendments approved by the National Assembly elected in 1994, this resolution was passed. However, it outlined the elements of the so-called flexible retirement scheme too vaguely so that the increase in the retirement age will largely be ineffective. This means that women can retire after reaching the age of 55. However, should the woman's employer wish to terminate her employment, he may do so only after the woman has reached the specified increased retirement age.

In addition, the possibility of voluntary insurance was introduced. Stricter rules were determined with respect to jobs entitling age exemption,[22] which reduced the length of the service period recognized without contribution payment,[23] and increased the minimum number of years in service which give entitlement to a partial pension from ten to 15 years.[24]

On 16 November 1993, the National Assembly approved the Act on Voluntary Mutual Insurance Funds,[25] which provides for supplementary pension funds to be established. Some private insurance companies tried to expand life insurance products offering the opportunity to make a savings provision for old age, but they did not become popular.[26]

For the time being no changes were effected concerning the previously developed practice of pension indexation: the so-called wage-tied automatic compensation system was applied. In particular, this pension system increases payments by the rate of the wage increase expected for the given year. This solution has always been subject to fierce debates. The major points of criticism are that effects are carried forward, or that the expected rate of the annual wage increase was underestimated and therefore had to be corrected in the succeeding year.

In 1995 the system was modified. Pensions were adapted to the average wage increase of the previous year (based on the figures disclosed by the Central Statistical Office). The adjustment of the benefit level took place twice a year: in January and in July. However, the higher payments were always made a few months later since the calculations and remittances also took some time. The maintenance of real value was not successful, as shown by the figures in Table 11.7.

Table 11.7 Real development of pensions and wages, Hungary, 1990–97

	1990	1991	1992	1993	1994	1995	1996[b]	1997[c]
Pension increase[a]	22.0	25.6	20.0	18.0	24.8	15.4	12.6	19.5
Net average wage increase	21.6	25.5	21.3	17.7	27.3	12.6	16.9	21.5
Consumer price index	28.9	35.0	23.0	22.5	18.8	28.2	23.6	18.0
Change in the real value of pensions	–5.4	–7.0	–2.4	–3.7	5.1	–10.0	–8.9	1.3
Change in the real value of wages	–5.7	–7.0	–1.4	–3.9	7.2	–12.2	–5.4	3.0

Notes: [a] Index determined on the basis of the increase in pension expenditure; [b] Preliminary actual data. The rate of pension increase does not include the one-off HUF 3,000 benefit; [c] Planned figures.
Source: Pension Insurance Self-Government Administration.

11.2.3 Organizational Structure

The organization and management of pension insurance was also transformed considerably. In accordance with a law adopted in 1991 providing for management by self-government, social insurance representatives were elected in May 1993 and the two autonomous bodies, the two general assemblies, to manage the two insurance branches were established that June.

Separation of the two insurance branches was, however, not completed until 1994. By then the rationalization procedures were almost complete and the financing of benefits covered jointly by the two funds on a temporary basis, in proportion with revenues, ceased.

The highest decision-making authorities are the two respective general assemblies. Representatives of the insurees were elected to the assemblies in 1993 in the course of national elections. At the election, votes could be cast on candidate lists compiled by the seven trade unions using national networks (Trade Union Confederation). The number of representatives to be elected from the various lists was proportional to the votes cast. The trade unions thus obtained considerable influence in the new social insurance management structure and in decisions related to social insurance. Representatives of employers could be delegated by nine national employers' associations. Interestingly, representatives of the public administration staff, that is, government bodies, did not take part in the general assemblies as elected members or delegates; their function was to observe the development of the two self-governments and to act in an advisory capacity. This solution was also intended as a safeguard against government influence.

The composition of the two assemblies differed in some respects. The Health Insurance General Assembly provides parity: insurees were represented by 30 elected members and employers by 30 delegated members. In the Pension Insurance General Assembly, insurees were represented by 36 elected representatives: four of them were delegated by the bodies representing the rights of pensioners and 24 represented employers' interests.

The legal framework of self-government also ensured that there was regular supervision by the government and the State Audit Office. Should they detect any serious breach of law in operations, it would be possible for either of them to prevail upon parliament to annul the decisions of the particular assembly or ultimately to suspend its activity.

The budgets of the two social insurance funds are approved by parliament: initially in the form of a bill prepared by each assembly and then submitted by the government. However, serious debates over the various items of the budget took place between the government and the assemblies. These debates slowed down the finalization and adoption of the state budget considerably. With regard to this, at the end of 1995 the government persuaded parliament to adopt a provision of law which amended the previous order of preparation and submission somewhat. According to the new rules, every year the two social insurance organizations must prepare by 31 July the draft budget for the following year. If it is not completed by this deadline or the government does not agree with essential points set forth therein, the government may submit its own amended version to parliament. Parliament may then determine budget projections for the insurance funds for the following year on the basis of that proposal. It is perceivable that this solution may considerably infringe the principle of independent decision making.

The main goal of the measures taken between 1993 and 1995 was to attempt to restore the financial balance of the pension system. It became gradually clear, however, that management of the accumulating problems would require more far-reaching interventions. More and more experts considered a comprehensive reform unavoidable. Views diverged strongly, however, with respect to the urgency of reform and the direction that the measures should take.

11.3 MAIN FINANCING PROBLEMS OF THE CURRENT PENSION SYSTEM

Almost throughout the period in question there was an ever-increasing financial deficit. In 1989, the first year of independence for the Social Insurance Fund, there was temporarily a surplus revenue of almost HUF 27 billion. This had disappeared by 1990 and the budget broke even that year. In 1991, the fund closed the year with a deficit of HUF 22 billion, in 1992 with 31 billion, and in 1993 with 33 billion. By 1994 the amount of the deficit exceeded HUF 42 billion. Pension Insurance Fund data are available only for the years following the separation of the two insurance branches. Table 11.8 shows actual and real deficit of the Pension Insurance Fund from 1992 on.

Table 11.8 *Actual and real deficit of the Pension Insurance Fund, Hungary, 1992–96 (billion HUF)*

	1992	1993	1994	1995	1996
Actual balance *of which:*	–9.6	–7.4	–22.8	–18.2	–25.1
Settlement of the 1991 deficit[a]	2.9	1.4	3.6	–	–
Reserving the return on own assets[b]	6.5	–	–	–	–
Deficit covered by sales of assets	–	–	–	–5.3	–1.2
Expenses covered on a temporary basis[c]	21.8	25.8	5.3	–	–
One-off reallocation to the Health Insurance Fund	–	–	6.1	–1.0	1.4
Real balance	+21.6	+19.8	–7.8	–24.5	–24.9

Notes: [a] Replenishment of liquidity reserve; [b] Provided by law; [c] Benefits to undergo rationalization.
Source: Data of the Self-Government.

It can be seen from the data that if, for the calculation of the balance, we deduct the expenses paid on behalf of the state budget from the total balances, then the 'real balance' was negative only from 1994. Nevertheless, it is probable that in the future, should current trends continue in the area of pension insurance, we shall have to reckon with a gradually and constantly deteriorating financial situation.

One of the main factors causing financial difficulties was that pension expenditures continued to increase dynamically compared to the previous period. This can be traced back primarily to the inflationary trends of the entire economy. While in the previous decades expenditures doubled every five years, in the period from 1990–94 they increased by 25 per cent per annum on average. Thus the 1994 expenditure figure amounted to 2.5 times the 1990 figure, and 3.2 times the 1989 figure. This can be seen in Table 11.9.

Table 11.9 Expenditures of pensions and pension-like benefits, Hungary 1970–94 (billion HUF and per cent)

year	Pension expenditures (billion HUF)	Pension expenditures (% of GDP[a])	Average annual increase (%)
1970	13.0	3.5	11.0
1975	27.1	5.1	15.9
1980	56.0	7.1	15.6
1985	91.7	8.1	10.4
1990	202.1	9.0	17.1
1991	262.8	10.6	30.1
1992	321.9	11.2	22.5
1993	394.9	11.3	22.7
1994	498.4	11.5	26.2
1995	511.9	9.1	2.7
1996	584.8	8.5	14.2
Permanent pensions tasks (following rationalization)			
1992	288.7	10.0	
1993	344.4	9.8	19.3
1994	436.9	10.1	26.9

Note: [a] The data of the GDP time series 'linked' for the years were quantified in two ways. This reduces the quotient of the year 1970 by 0.5 per cent.
Source: Data of the Self-Government.

However, if we eliminate the effects of the inflationary changes of the economy from these aggregate data, then, paradoxically, the dynamics of the increase in pension expenditures is lower today than in the 1970s and 1980s. The amount of social policy expenditures expressed as a proportion of GDP increased abruptly during the 1980s and 1990s, thereafter stabilizing. If we characterize the 1970s as the period of extending rights and the 1980s as the period of maturation and saturation, the 1990s will be seen as the period in which adapting to changed economic conditions, rationalization and the striving for the preservation of benefit values became important.

Parallel to this, contribution payment discipline in the course of the changing economy deteriorated dramatically. Prior to this time, payment contribution delinquency was practically unknown. Collections were made almost automatically from the state-owned companies, which then dominated economic life.

However, the situation changed considerably after 1989. On the one hand, as a consequence of the transformation of the economic system, privatization, and the bankruptcy or liquidation of most enterprises, social insurance payments increased dramatically. By the beginning of 1996, these had increased to HUF 225 billion (for the two branches aggregate), amounting to more than 20 per cent of their combined total annual expenditures. According to the World Bank, in 1990 the increase in pension expenditures was caused by several factors. The calculations in Table 11.8, based on World Bank estimates, express the relative importance of various factors in five-year periods.

Table 11.10 Factors explaining the increase in pension expenditure, Hungary, 1970–94 (on a logarithm scale, in %)

	Pension expenditure/GDP	Eligibility saturation	Dependence	Pension level	Employment	Productivity
period	increase	increase is an expenditure increasing factor			increase is an expenditure reducing factor	
75/70	100	56.7	−10.3	52.2	10.4	−9.0
80/75	100	38.4	7.1	57.8	1.7	−4.9
85/80	100	54.5	42.7	83.6	3.4	−84.3
90/85	100	87.2	31.9	72.9	5.5	−97.4
94/90	100	56.1	−7.2	−23.3	114.4	−40.0
94/70	100	54.1	5.0	43.6	28.2	−31.0

Source: World Bank.

If we (a) examine these factors by combining them and arranging them in three groups, (b) handle eligibility and the pension level factors jointly as 'the condition of the pension system', and (c) separate the dependence factor as the 'demographic condition' of the changes and the combined value of employment and productivity as the 'group of economic conditions', then their aggregate effect shows the following picture: the relative increase in pension expenditure to GDP in the past quarter of a century took place almost autonomously, as a direct result of the pension system. The eligibility and pension level factors determined almost 98 per cent of the increase in expenditures. Barely 5 per cent of the increase in expenditures can be explained by demographic changes. On the contrary, economic conditions reduced the increase in pension expenditure in relation to GDP by almost 3 per cent.

11.4 REFORM DISCUSSION AND PENSION REFORM 1997

Since the beginning of 1995 there have been a series of measures aimed primarily at steadying the financial balance: for example, an old-age pension cannot exceed the amount of the earlier average wage even if it is lower than the legal minimum[27] and the contribution obligation was extended to affect such income as services in kind.[28] However, the main emphasis of reform has shifted increasingly towards the introduction of a new pension system. In connection with the latter there are three competing concepts which are important. First, the Ministry of Welfare and the Pension Insurance Self-Government put forward a proposal which chiefly follows the principles of the parliamentary resolution adopted in 1991. The pension system sketched out here consists of three tiers:

- the first level consists of a basic benefit to be received by all insured persons (or as a civil right if the difference is financed by the state budget);
- the second layer is made up of a PAYG system following stricter actuarial principles than in the existing system. Pension benefits are based on the previous average income and the number of years of service acquired. This insurance coverage along with the basic benefit could achieve a replacement rate of approximately 60 per cent (20 and 40 per cent, respectively);
- the third level of insurance would be the voluntary personal supplementary insurance provided by various insurance companies.

A second reform concept was completed by the Welfare Subcommittee of the Public Finance Adjustment Committee in August 1995. This concept was based on the notion that the transformation of the pension system became necessary since there were fundamental changes in social and economic conditions. The concept addresses problems which arose from:

- considerable changes in the structure of insurees;
- dysfunctions in the previous pension system related to solidarity and social and insurance functions;
- a considerable loss of real value of the pension payment; and
- the question of a system permanently able to finance itself and to adapt to economic and demographic processes and which imposes an acceptable contribution burden on the active groups.

Thus their reform proposal entailed a uniform system which:

- ensures a replacement rate of 60 to 65 per cent on average (or 65 to 70 per cent under more favourable economic circumstances);
- creates incentives and sanctions which increase the probability that most retirement occurs between the ages of 62 and 64;
- is supported by actuarial calculations;
- ensures a minimum pension level for elderly persons not obtaining benefits that would secure an adequate standard of living through the work pension scheme or based on an individual assessment of needs; an additional allowance or a standard basic pension, or a minimum pension incorporated in the pension scheme would be granted. For all three options the state budget would provide the resources;
- finances the mandatory work pension scheme on a PAYG system; and lastly
- provides for a component of individual choice regarding supplementary insurance by accumulating savings in the voluntary supplementary private pension schemes.

By the time these plans were developed, there had been agreement within the government to implement even more radical solutions. An important component in the stabilization programme of the new Minister of Finance adopted in March 1995 was the acceleration of public finance reforms (within that of pension reform). With the involvement of a number of foreign consultants (most of them from the World Bank), new preparatory works have begun under the control of the Ministry of Finance. The first drafts and feasibility calculations were prepared in late 1995 or early 1996. The direction of this work was endorsed by a government resolution in May 1996. The new concept was again submitted to the government in December 1996 (at that time as a joint proposal of the ministers of finance and welfare). This concept emphasized that the system should strengthen the interest of the insurees in participating in social insurance policy making, simplify the determination of pensions, and, in order to make the tax and income policies consistent, shift to determining gross pensions after the year 2009.

Such a system would have two mandatory pension components supplementing each other: the social insurance pension (planned to cover about two-thirds of the old-age benefit); and the mandatory private pension that is generated from the payments to the individual account of the insuree. These savings, increased by interest, are exchanged for pension benefits; if the insuree dies before reaching retirement age, the savings could be inherited by the family of the deceased. Supplementary voluntary pension insurance schemes could increase old-age revenues. Such a policy could be promoted by significant tax breaks. A guaranteed minimum standard of living for pensioners would be provided for by an old-age allowance, which would be means-tested. The shift to the new structure was proposed by the experts from the Ministry of Finance.[29] It is argued that such a system would encourage more participation in the pension system by individuals and employers alike. The sharing of the contribution between insuree and employer as well as the duration of contribution payments should make participation in the legal economy and also paying social insurance liability charges more attractive. Great hope is attached to the incentives provided by the ability to inherit savings paid into private funds. Long-term public savings could increase the credit available to the economy, ensuring additional development sources for the economy, consequently reducing inflation and interest rates and thereby the interest burden on public finances. In the interim, however, deficits would be incurred in the PAYG subsystem, but this again would be offset by the concurrent increase in long-term public savings.

This pension reform is also expected to be instrumental in managing the extra expenditures, which will rise dramatically after 2010 due to the ageing of the population. This also addresses the normative issue that providing for the pensions of parents should not constitute an unbearable burden for the younger generations. A strong argument in favour of this pension scheme is that it would improve economic competitiveness, which depends to a large extent on how the burden on active labour can be reduced. It could also constitute a step forward in that by improving the contribution compliance rate the social insurance burden falling on entrepreneurs can be mitigated, and that thereby the competitiveness of goods produced in Hungary and the efficiency of employment can be improved. And finally, according to the authors of the draft, the model calculations demonstrate that the planned pension reform is financially viable. The budget deficit due to the creation of the funded tier is expected to be kept under one per cent of GDP. The public finance deficit to GDP can thus remain under 3.5 per cent, and the state debt to GDP ratio can stabilize at 55 to 60 per cent. Simultaneously, by 2010 the savings to be generated in the funded tier will reach 2 per cent of GDP, and in subsequent years 3–4 per cent. In the long term, all this may double the options to take domestic loans by enterprises, and so give an additional momentum to boosting economic growth.

This proposal has also been subject to a wide range of criticism by independent consultants and the Pension Insurance Assembly. Most importantly, it was argued that in the wake of the new pension system, the replacement rate would go down from the current 60 to 62 per cent to 42 per cent for those who cannot or do not want to join the new system (for those entering the mixed system the replacement rate would fall to an overall 54 per cent by 2050). The concept promises an acceptable level of pension benefits only for the current career starters and for men with high earnings and stable jobs throughout their active career, and for all other groups a lower than current level of benefits should be expected. This gradual breakdown of the benefits level would reduce the attractiveness of the system. In addition, it has been argued that the model calculations were based on an optimistic scenario of economic development and do not consider potential economic difficulties. This questions the reliability of the calculations.

The shift to the new system is expected to result in a huge deficit in public finance possibly causing unfavourable economic consequences such as higher inflation and so on. According to calculations made by the Pension Insurance Assembly, in the year when the funded tier is started a HUF 90 billion deficit may be reached in the PAYG system, a figure almost three times higher than that expected by the Ministry of Finance. In addition, the operating costs of the new system are estimated by some experts to amount to three times the current costs. Finally, a number of constitutional doubts have also arisen in connection with the new system. One reason was that originally, determination of pension rates was to be made using separate calculations on the basis of separate mortality tables for men and women. Moreover, it was foreseen that it should be possible to enforce payment of contributions in the funded tier directly through the state, although benefits would not be warranted by state guarantee. It was therefore suggested by the Pension Insurance Assembly even before the adoption of the parliamentary draft that the system be modernized on the basis of the proposals formulated earlier with the Ministry of Welfare (or perhaps a later version).

On 15 July 1997, parliament decided essentially to adopt the acts containing the concept elaborated by the Ministry of Finance.[30] So from 1 January 1998 there was to be a gradual shift from the recent uniform structure. As a main feature of this new plan in the forthcoming period citizens can acquire old-age protection in the framework of two pension systems operating side by side. One option is to have recourse to the (somewhat modified) recent system (hereinafter called the social insurance pension system); the other is the so-called 'mixed pension system'. Two groups of insurees will be part of the 'mixed system':

- those insured through compulsory membership; this applies to those who started their career or entered employment for the first time after 1 July 1998 (but before the age of 42), and
- those insured on a voluntary basis; this option is available to persons insured in the former system who choose this system since it may provide more favourable benefits. It is required, however, that the insuree be younger than 47 and thus until the retirement age of 62 reserves in the private fund can be accumulated for at least 15 years.

All other insurees are covered by the social insurance pension system.

The pension reform brought about changes in the contribution payment. The aggregate rate of contributions payable by employers and insurees for those belonging to the social insurance system would not change, but their proportions would vary. As of 1 January 1998 the employers' pension contribution rate would be 24 per cent, as of 1 January 1999, 23 per cent and as of 1 January 2000, 22 per cent. As of 1 January 1998 the rate payable by insurees would be 7 per cent, raised twice by one percentage point in the following years. For those belonging to the mixed system, employers would pay into the social insurance fund the contributions mentioned above (that is, 24, 23 and 22 per cent), while insurees would pay one per cent of their income into this fund. In addition, insurees would be obliged to pay a membership fee into the private pension fund on the basis of their income subject to pension contribution: as of 1 January 1998, 6 per cent, as of 1 January 1999, 7 per cent and as of 1 January 2000, 8 per cent.

The rules concerning benefit rates payable in the new first pillar also changed. The principle of the calculation does not change; the rate of pension continues to depend on the recognized service period and average monthly earnings. However, according to the plans following the year 2012, contrary to the current practice the rate of pensions will be calculated on the basis of average gross earnings, and from then on pensions will become taxable income. The rate of old-age pension for a person eligible only for a social insurance pension will be calculated after the acquisition of a service period of 20 years at a rate of 33 per cent. This base rate will be increased by 1.65 percentage points for each further year of service. With a service period of 40 years, 66 per cent of the average earnings can be achieved. However, if a person is also a member of a private pension fund with a service period of 20 years, he or she can receive only 24.4 per cent of gross earnings as a benefit (under the social insurance pension system), and each further year the rate will be increased by 1.22 percentage points. Thus after acquiring the 40th year of service period he/she can receive 48.8 per cent of his/her average gross earnings. Of course, supplementary payments under the private pension system are made separately. Their rate depends on the amount of savings and return on investments. Old rules apply on a temporary basis for people retiring between 1998 and 2012. In accordance with earlier regulations the retirement age increases gradually to 62 years both for women and men. The new rules allow retirement before reaching retirement age at the request of the insuree. However, this results in a proportionate reduction in the pension.

The mechanism serving to preserve the value of benefits also changes. Instead of the rate of increase of average net earnings in the previous year, in the year 2000 the nominal value of benefits will be increased by the mean of the consumer price index and the increase of average net earnings with weights of 30 and 70 per cent, and 50 and 50 per cent, respectively, from 2001.

A separate law[31] regulates the detailed conditions of the establishment, operation and supervision of private pension funds.

In addition to the pension benefits already discussed, a supplementary benefit, the so-called 'old age allowance',[32] can be awarded to old persons (over 62) by the local authority. Entitlement is based on monthly income or per capita income of the person and cohabiting spouse (life partner) which may not exceed 80 per cent of the actual lowest monthly amount of old-age pension (95 per cent in case of a single person). The monthly allowance amounts to 80 per cent of the actual lowest old-age pension payment for couples and 90 per cent for singles. Thirty per cent of this allowance is to be covered by the budget of the local authority, while 70 per cent (the total amount of the allowance paid to recipients living in residential institutions and to homeless people) is reimbursed from the state budget.

The provisions concerning the amended pension system went into effect on 1 January 1998. We are not able to evaluate the system until it has been in operation for a few years. Until then we hope that the new system will indeed promote favourable economic and social development as was intended by those who were instrumental in launching the reforms.

NOTES

1 In 1993, more than half of GDP was produced by small and private enterprises, while in 1989 this share was only 14 per cent.

2 Special regulations apply only to professional soldiers of the armed forces and individuals holding a ministerial post or a position higher than that. Their numbers are negligible.

3 Ninety per cent, 80 per cent, 70 per cent and 60 per cent of the wages, HUF 10–12,000, 12–14,000, 14–16,000 and above, respectively, can be taken into consideration. § 100 of the Decree of the Council of Ministers no. 89/1990 (VI.1.).

4 After ten or eight years (men and women, respectively) at an extremely dangerous workplace, two years' exemption was granted, and after each further service period of five years an additional exemption of one year was possible. People working under conditions of high atmospheric pressure had even more favourable terms: they were granted two years' exemption after six service years, and an additional year for each further three-year period.

5 In respect of persons covered by insurance obligations emanating from contracts governed by the Civil Code: that is, prior to 1995 those who made their living on remuneration obtained as commission or through entrepreneurial contracts were subject to the application of such a practice. Persons with a low income, that is, income under 60 per cent of the amount of the actual minimum wage, were not included under the scope of the insurance law. They were therefore not burdened with contribution payment obligations. Such periods were thus not taken into consideration when calculating the eligible service period.

6 Since 1984, direct state control of this institution was prescribed by Resolution 5 of 1984 of the government. Prior to this, social insurance was controlled – at least nominally – by the trade unions.

7 Decree of the Council of Ministers 5/1990 Mt.

8 Article 3 of the Decree of the Council of Ministers 147/1989 (XII.27.) Mt.

9 One decree aimed at offsetting disadvantages for persons sentenced in a manner violating the law (for example, in the area of eligibility to pension) between 1945 and 1963. This was followed later by laws settling the social insurance conditions of those who had suffered disadvantages due to racial, ethnic or other reasons between 1938 and 1945, and on the compensation of persons disadvantaged by legal pension aspects in the period prior to 1952. A portion of the compensation bonds issued for these persons could be swapped for a supplementary pension at the pension insurance organization.
10 Government Decree 81/1990.
11 Article 1 of Act II of 1991.
12 From this date on, wages less than HUF 12,000 were fully, wages above this ceiling were degressively, considered in pension determination.
13 Resolution of the National Assembly 1/1991 (I.18.).
14 Resolution of the National Assembly 42/1991 (VII.25.) and Government Decree 99/1991 (VII.25.).
15 In the first year of its independence, the Social Insurance Fund saw a temporary income surplus of HUF 27 billion. This could be derived from two facts which unfortunately had a temporary effect: the contribution rates were increased in the previous year and, due to the cessation of central regulation, the increase in the average wage exceeded the plans significantly. (Average wages increased by 18.5 per cent instead of the planned 7 per cent.) This surplus, however, was a one-off phenomenon. Serious problems arose in relation to social insurance.
16 Resolution of the National Assembly 60/1991(X.21).
17 The self-governing management is regulated by Act LXXXIV of 1991.
18 Paragraph 21 of Act IX of 1992.
19 Article 7 of Act IX of 1992.
20 As of 1 March 1993, based on Article 39 of Act VIII of 1993.
21 Article 11 of Act VIII of 1993.
22 Article 20 of Government Decree 48/1992 (III.13.).
23 Article 26 of Government Decree 48/1992 (III.13.).
24 Article 11 of Act VIII of 1993.
25 Act XCIV of 1993.
26 Since then almost 200 voluntary pension funds have been established, mostly with companies, organized by trade unions and other interested bodies and financial institutions. The total number of members of such funds is about 200,000, and the size of the assets managed by them is estimated at HUF 6 billion.
27 Article 4 of Act XII of 1995.
28 Article 8 of Act XII of 1995.
29 Ministry of Finance (1996), pp. 9–12
30 These issues are regulated by the provisions of Act LXXX of 1997 on eligibility to social insurance benefits and private pension and the coverage of these services, Act LXXXI of 1997 on the social insurance pension benefit, as well as Act LXXXII of 1997 on private pension and private pension funds.
31 Act LXXXII of 1997 on private pension and private pension funds.
32 The relevant rules are encapsulated in the newly enacted articles 32/A to 32/E of Act III of 1993 on social administration and social benefits.

REFERENCES

Antal, K., Réti, J., Rézmovics, Á. and Toldi, M. (1995), 'The development of pension expenditures and the changes of the pension system in the nineties', Research Institute of World Economics of the Hungarian Academy of Sciences: Pension System and Pension Reform, 38–66, Budapest.

Augustinovics, M. (1993), 'A reasonable pension system. A draft concept', *Economic Review* 5, 415–31.

Augustinovics, M. (1995), 'The long term balance of the pension fund – Macro simulation', Research Institute of World Economics of the Hungarian Academy of Sciences: Pension System and Pension Reform, 67–95, Budapest.

Augustinovics, M. and Johnson, P. (1997), 'Concluding remarks: system and reform design', in M. Augustinovics (ed.), *Pension System and Reforms – Britain, Hungary, Italy, Poland, Sweden*, PHARE ACE Project Draft Report, Budapest.

Augustinovics, M. and Martos, B. (1995), 'Calculations and conclusions concerning pension reform', *Economic Review*, 11, 993–1023.

Bod, P. (1995), 'The establishment of the Hungarian social insurance pension system', Research Institute of World Economics of the Hungarian Academy of Sciences: Pension System and Pension Reform, Budapest.

CSO (Central Statistical Office), *Statistical Yearbook of Hungary*, various editions.

CSO (1996), 'Main social and economic processes'.

CSO (1997a), 'Social incomes, social situation of households (1996)', Pension Work Group of MoF and MoW: Background information on pension reform, Budapest.

CSO (1997b), 'The situation of pensioners (1997)', Pension Work Group of MoF and MoW: Background information on pension reform, Budapest.

Czúcz, O. (1993a), 'Das Rentensystem in Ungarn – Leistungsarten, Voraussetzung ihrer Liquidierung und Hauptgründe der notwendigen Umgestaltung des Systems', *Deutsche Rentenversicherung*, 11, 737–50.

Czúcz, O. (1993b), 'The social insurance self-government and the state control – Some disputed questions of the pension insurance control', *Review of Legal Sciences*, 8–9, 299–308.

Czúcz, O. (1994), 'Közgazdasági és Jogi Könyvkiadó' [Old age pension systems], Budapest.

Hablicsek, L. (1995), 'Long term scripts of the population – Hungary – 1995–2050. A study', Prepared for the Pension Work Group of the MoF, Budapest.

Kornai, J. (1989), 'Impetuous pamphlet on economic transition', Budapest.

Kornai, J. (1995), 'Principles to the reform of the welfare system', *Magyar Hírlap*, 15.

Kornai, J. (1996), 'The citizen and the state: the reform of the welfare system', *Mozgó Világ* 2.

Kovács, C. (1997), 'Historical review of the changes in the old age pension age (1912–1975)', Pension Work Group of MoF and MoW: Background information on pension reform, Budapest.

Martos, B. (1995), 'The start and operation of the scoring system of individual pensions', Research Institute of World Economics of the Hungarian Academy of Sciences: Pension System and Pension Reform, 96–112, Budapest.

Ministry of Finance (1996), 'The proposal of the government for the new pension system (3382/1996)', Budapest.

Ministry of Finance (1998), 'Economic transformation in figures', Budapest.

Ministry of Finance, Ministry of Welfare Pension Task Force (1997), *Background Information to the Pension Reform*, Budapest.

Pension Insurance Administration (1995), *Statistical Yearbook 1995*, Budapest.

Simonovits, A. (1997), 'The case of Hungary. Pension system and reforms – Britain, Hungary, Italy, Poland, Sweden', in M. Augustinovics (ed.), *Pension System and Reforms – Britain, Hungary, Italy, Poland, Sweden*, PHARE ACE Project Draft Report, Budapest, 51–77.

Voirin, M. (1992), 'La securité sociale dans les pays d'Europe centrale et orientale: Reformes et continuité', *Revue Internationale de Securité Sociale*, 4, 1–42.
Welfare Sub-committee of the Public Sector Adjustment Committee (1995), 'The main directions and the starting tasks of the long term reform of the pension system (version 2, draft)', Budapest.
World Bank (1995), *Hungary: Structural Reforms for Sustainable Growth*, Washington, DC: World Bank.

Index